Small Screens, Big Ideas

For my parents, David and Belinda Lawson,
who bought their first television set in 1959

SMALL SCREENS, BIG IDEAS

TELEVISION IN THE 1950s

Edited by

Janet Thumim

I.B.Tauris *Publishers*
LONDON • NEW YORK

Published in 2002 by I.B.Tauris & Co Ltd
6 Salem Road, London W2 4BU
175 Fifth Avenue, New York NY 10010
www.ibtauris.com

In the United States of America and in Canada distributed by St Martin's Press
175 Fifth Avenue, New York NY10010

ISBN 1 86064 683 2 hardback
ISBN 1 86064 682 4 paperback

A full CIP record for this book is available from the British Library
A full CIP record for this book is available from the Library of Congress

Library of Congress catalog card: available

Project Management by Steve Tribe, London
Printed and bound in Great Britain by MPG Books Ltd, Bodmin, Cornwall

CONTENTS

ILLUSTRATIONS

PREFACE AND ACKNOWLEDGEMENTS

This collection has been some time in the making and I am delighted finally to be able to see it as a whole. Many friends and colleagues have supported me during the various trials and tribulations of the editing process. Amongst these I particularly want to acknowledge, with grateful thanks, Mary Beth Haralovich for her infectious enthusiasm for the project at various critical stages; John Ellis for his support at a particularly crucial moment; and my editor at I.B.Tauris, Philippa Brewster, for the confidence and trust she has shown in me. My daughter, Nancy Thumim, has been an invaluable and rigorous critic and I am not only grateful but also proud to acknowledge her scholarly support during the writing and editing of the volume. Finally I wish to recognize the great patience of the contributors to this volume, their cheerful willingness to revisit, revise and sometimes to rethink their essays, often in the midst of many other pressing deadlines, and to record my great pleasure in working with all of them.

Madeleine MacMurraugh-Kavanagh's essay 'The BBC and the Birth of The Wednesday Play, 1962–66: Institutional containment versus "agitational contemporaneity"' was first published in the *Historical Journal of Radio, Film and Television* vol 17:3, 1997; a version of Lisa Parks's essay 'Cracking Open the Set: Television repair and tinkering with gender 1949–1955' appeared in *Television and New Media* vol 1:3, August 2000; and a version of Susan Murray's essay 'Lessons from Uncle Miltie: Ethnic masculinity and early television's vaudeo star' will appears in *Cinema Journal*, University of Texas Press. Permission to publish the essays here is gratefully acknowledged.

The BBC is acknowledged as the copyright holder of the still from *The Quatermass Experiment*; Canal+ holds the copyright on the three illustrations from ABC's *Tales of Mystery and Imagination*; thanks to both for permitting publication.

INTRODUCTION

SMALL SCREENS, BIG IDEAS

Janet Thumim

Television and history

The essays in this volume all explore aspects of the history of television in the USA and the UK, broadly within the formative period of the 1950s. Their scholarly focus entails the imaginative recall of a lost object, that is to say that though there may in some cases have been access to recordings, to production notes, to reviews, letters or similar items from the discourses which accompanied, or proliferated around, the programme, there can never have been access to the 'structures of feeling', to borrow Raymond Williams' invaluable formulation, within which both production and reception took place. Here is the epistemological problem at the heart of all historical research. The problem is particularly acute in the case of television history, since the object of study appears to offer the historical 'real' in a way that arguably less complex materials either do not propose at all or, better, can acknowledge as an absence. The enormous popularity of 'early' television texts with today's audiences, evidenced in the proliferation of rerun channels such as Nick at Nite and UK Gold, suggests the extent to which such programmes – for viewers and for scholars – may stand in *themselves* as a form of 'knowledge' about life in the 1950s.

The acknowledgement that functional boundaries between the public and the private spheres have been disturbed by the advent of mass broadcasting is now a trope of television studies. The insistent simultaneity of television's heterogeneous imagery may in itself have contributed to the paradigm shift – from modernism to post-modernism – the imperative to ascribe order to the incommensurate flow of meanings resulting in the post-modern evacuation of referent from signifier. In a characteristically acute comment, John Corner points to ways in which television has 'radically altered the scale, speed of circulation, and nature of knowledge in society' noting also that 'The extension of the public knowledge field by television, a process coextensive with television's steady colonization of everyday life . . . has changed the nature both of public life and private life' (1999:118). In a call for precisely the kind of detailed attention offered in the essays that follow, Roger Silverstone insists that 'It is in the dynamics of the particular that we will be able to identify, if not fully comprehend, the forces of structure: the forces both of domination and of resistance' (1994:164). One of the intentions of this volume, then, is to examine just how the circulation of knowledge about society and the individuals comprising it came to be articulated during the formative period of mass broadcasting, and to do this in the light of feminist interventions into cultural theory.

The problems raised by these contributors' intentions to explore the relation between emergent media forms and genres and broader social developments turn on the impossibility of *knowing* an historical audience. Forms, representations and technologies can be discovered and described, but the understandings of these produced by contemporary audiences – on which, of course, the overarching questions about social change must rest – can only ever be a matter for speculation. Thus a central question, both for our predecessors in the 1950s and for the scholars contributing to this volume, is 'what is television?' Just as central, I contend, is E.H. Carr's question 'what is history?' for, as Carr reminds us, the historian always reveals more about his or her own period than about the supposed pretext for the study – the historical object itself (Carr 1964).

More straightforward, perhaps, are explorations of industrial practices in the emergent institution – but these are so thoroughly enmeshed in the social matrix that here too is the risk of over-emphasizing those practices (such as funding, employment, publicity, legislation, housing and so on) for which evidence *is* available. Most interesting of all is the dilemma posed to scholars – all of whom are, in comparison to the Fifties audience, relatively sophisticated or 'skilled' viewers – in *seeing* at all what was 'on television' in the 1950s. Abercrombie and Longhurst suggest that 'the skilled audience is more likely to be an active audience' (1998:32) and while their proposition is in itself uncontentious, it does beg the questions this volume raises about the television audience in the 1950s. This was certainly *un*skilled in relation to today's audiences, but, as these essays suggest, it can by no means be considered inactive.

That television does indeed have a dynamic relation to the processes of daily life – and hence to broad social change – is now widely accepted, and was of course the premise underlying both commercially funded and public service television during the 1950s. However, theoretical conceptions of the audience have been subject to change both as a consequence of developments in the academic landscape, as it were, and of the ever-expanding and now ubiquitous presence of television and its necessary corollary, an increasingly sophisticated and 'knowing' audience. The question arises as to whether changing paradigms intending to account for what audiences do/have done can satisfactorily describe the activity of historical audiences or, bearing in mind Carr's diktat, whether they can merely account for how we *think* (now) about the activity of such earlier audiences.[1]

The shift during the 1950s from a vaudevillian to a realist aesthetic may account for the dominance of sitcoms and soaps with their dependence on contained and/or predictable narratives of the contemporary everyday world. However, though these did propose a contiguity between the experiences of protagonist and viewer, it is also true that in other programme forms an overt 'performativity' remained a central strategy. To what extent, we may ask, does the shift from 'having' to 'appearing', cited by Abercrombie and Longhurst (following Debord) as a feature of late capitalist society,[2] enable further insight into the 'lost' audience of the 1950s and its viewing strategies? In their direct address to camera the 'hosts', 'hostesses' and 'presenters' solicited responses from the viewer in his/her domestic context – not to mention that solicited by the ubiquitous advertisements – and television's continually reiterated representations of domestic interiors could be understood to have offered a mirror, as it were, to domestic audiences, thus encouraging them to consider *themselves* as a spectacle, as performers. This self-consciousness would have been reinforced, too, in the suburban developments with their picture windows and open curtains offering the 'private' domestic interior as a spectacle to the passing 'public'. It is indeed tempting to deploy Abercrombie and Longhurst's performance/spectacle paradigm in analysis of this feature of televisual address and its consequences, but in so doing we surely risk a further elision of the very differences between then (1950s) and now (2000s) which might allow our retrospective understanding of the functional relations between technology, audience and institution. Both history and knowledge are at stake here: in her introduction to *The Persistence of History*, Vivian Sobchak writes that in television 'the event and its representation, immediacy and its mediation, have moved increasingly towards simultaneity' (1996:4). It is not that new technologies and the social processes which they engender *begin* with mass broadcast television in the 1950s – they are already begun with the explosion of audiences for cinema in the early part of the century – but that, in the 1950s, the domestic site of consumption and the self-conscious simultaneity of audiences' television experience makes it part of everyday life, part of mundane experience in ways that fundamentally alter previously crucial structuring boundaries such as those between past and present, here and there, self and other/s. It is precisely such boundaries and structures which allow the individual's formation of knowledge. Hence television's pervasive simultaneity impacts on the very nature of what can be deemed to be knowledge. Sobchak cites promotional material for the History Channel, appearing on cable television in the USA in 1994, which proclaimed 'If you couldn't be there the first time, here's your second chance' and its trademark slogan 'All of History. All in one place' (1996:4) which, in its anti-historical naiveté, recalls the US President Wilson's infamous remark about D.W. Griffith's shockingly racist 1915 film *Birth of a Nation*, that it was like 'seeing history by flashes of lightning'. The feminist philosopher Lorraine Code emphasises the epistemological significance of the very questions which televisual simultaneity seems, mischievously, to dissolve in its ceaseless and homogenising flow: 'These are questions about how credibility is established, about connections between knowledge and power, about the place of knowledge in ethical and aesthetic judgements, and about political agendas and the responsibilities of knowers' (1991:7). And they are precisely the questions, it seems to me, that we need to put to the material of broadcast television – at the level of the institution (who broadcasts?), of schedules (who plans?), of programmes (who speaks?) – and that may be enabled by the detailed exploration of mass broadcasting's 'beginnings' offered in this volume. And in their epistemological focus these questions can only be answered, apropos of television, by considering the audience, for it is here that the consequence of television's hegemonic power – or of its subversive potential – may be discovered. I have drawn attention to the difficulties of 'knowing' the historical audience, but we should also acknowledge similar difficulties in knowing the contemporary audience – despite the late twentieth-century proliferation of audience studies.

Though it is likely that very different imperatives govern audiences' understanding of material defined as 'factual' and that announced as 'fiction', their contiguity in the flow of television and the contribution both make to the formation of knowledge suggest that we should 'stand back' from generic difference in attempting to understand television's effect on epistemology. Working on an early draft of this essay in the Spring of 1999 I was troubled by the seeming impossibility of discerning the 'truth', or even plausible motivations for the conflicting interpretations of truths, in the television coverage of current events in Serbia and Kosovo. On one level the nearly continuous coverage of BBC News 24's cable channel offered an extraordinary and surely unprecedented level of 'information': images of targets as seen from the bombing planes; images of buildings collapsing at the moment of impact, as seen from the ground; images of refugees at the borders, seen from within the crowd at ground level and also from the air; video-linked live interviews not only with 'our' reporters at the scene/s and with local protagonists (victims, medics, aid-workers) but also with Serbian politicians, European and UN officials; the more familiar and, in this context, strangely archaic exhortations of 'our' leaders (the British prime minister, Tony Blair, and the US president, Bill Clinton) aiming to secure 'our' approval for actions taken in 'our' names. Here are polemic, prediction, deduction and inference from as many positions as there are protagonists. Yet this proliferation of incommensurate 'information' in words and images – delivered in forms drawing on the generic conventions of news and war reporting but also of melodrama, epic, testimonial, confession – though compelling, refuses me the very coherence necessary to 'know' what is happening. What is real, except the anxiety I feel? And is my anxiety about the impossibility of (my) knowing, or about the unpredictable and as-yet-unknowable consequences of these events? Responsible knowing – 'knowing well' as Code terms it – in the age of electronically enabled and simultaneous exchanges of such 'information' must entail a more thorough and widespread interrogation of epistemology as it is configured through televisual forms. In the late 1990s we watch television routinely: it is a routine founded on the experience of our parents and grandparents during the 1950s. Considering *what* they watched and *how* they watched – which is what this book attempts – may enable some productive distance from our naturalized routines, though we should never forget that 'even if you can see someone watching a screen' as anthropologist Marilyn Strathern writes in her foreword to *Consuming Technologies* (Silverstone and Hirsch, 1992) 'you do not know what that person is seeing.'

The 1950s

How do we know the 1950s, now? It was the decade before the famously, and controversially, polarized 1960s, a time defined negatively by what it lacked, or forbade. Despite the rosy – or, in many cases, less than rosy – recollections of parents and grandparents and, for some of us, the hazy memories of childhood, the more significant 'information' about the period is gleaned from the images purveyed through popular cultural artefacts of the time re-run, re-screened, re-consumed in our present days. The Fifties movie or TV programme appears to offer veracity untainted by hindsight or nostalgic misrememberings. But there's an inevitably partisan selection at work in these images: not so much the Fifties as they were, rather the Fifties as contemporary programmes proposed them to be. From such material unifying myths emerge, myths suggesting a golden-age explosion of consumer goods and employment opportunities, of the establishment of harmonious two-parent families in leafy suburbs, of the promise and excitement of new technologies, improved facilities in medicine, transport, leisure all democratically available to newly classless societies. And then there are the opposite myths of repressed, anxious citizens struggling to live decent lives in post-war wastelands, of the restricting double standard reapplied to women following their wartime emancipation, of the rise in crime amongst juveniles, of the misery of unwelcome immigrants, of racism, poverty, mental ill-health. Neither of these extremes does justice to the provisional, contradictory and experimental realities. Many apparently 'natural' features of late-twentieth century western life and values have their then-tentative origins in the 1950s. Whether positive or negative it was undoubtedly a time of upheaval in every sphere of existence – in science, technology, arts and philosophy, in democratic politics, in post-colonial relations between the so-called third and first worlds, in familial relations, most of all perhaps in the perceived relation between the individual and the various collectives in which s/he participated.

The polarization of 'East' and 'West' following the second world war required a continual public demonstration of the efficacy of the market place, necessarily defined against the planned and controlled economies of eastern bloc countries, and in its turn this required both an expanding and flexible labour force and a similarly available army of consumers. Social stability – an unarguably desirable goal following the tragic upheavals of the 1930s and 1940s – was conceived in the west as coterminous with a vibrant free-market economy. It was also, rather paradoxically, considered to equate with a national unity: that is to say difference seems to have been disavowed, feared – characterized negatively as something to be avoided, or hidden, at any cost. Hence the continuing attempts in the USA to assimilate the richly diverse ethnic groupings into a mythical 'white' America. Hence also the British inability, or refusal, to recognize or integrate the post-war influx of black colonial subjects despite their centrality to Britain's expanding economy. In both countries too – though the pattern is less equivocal in the USA – the prized model of the (white) nuclear family with domestic mother and breadwinning father is located not in the vibrant inner city but in an idyllic quasi-rural setting: in practice this meant in the suburbs or the soulless 'new towns' so beloved of planners at that time. The anxieties produced by the gap between mythic definitions of social cohesion and the real experience of individual subjects were amplified by the contemporary explosion in communications. Not only increased access to transport and mobility but also to an increasing variety of profit-motivated print media and, of course, to television itself where, daily and nightly, viewers were offered models of consumption *and of behaviour* against which to measure their own achievements or shortcomings.

During the 1950s, then, multi-channel television broadcasting to audiences numbering millions of viewers found its place at the centre of national life in the USA, a position it was to achieve a little later in the UK. What television could be, should be, and was to be were questions accompanying all discussion of programmes, reviews, and debates on various pertinent issues ranging from the jockeying for power of the big corporations to questions of censorship and the proper control of content. While television itself was under construction, so too, in a sense, were the societies – in the USA and the UK – with which it had such a close and reciprocal relation. In Britain this entailed the post-war reconstruction and coming to terms with the loss of colonial power, whereas the post-war, consumption-driven and booming economy of America was intent on maintaining its position as the dominant global economic and political power. In both contexts, as I have suggested, the manufacture of consensus around national identity was a crucial feature of social discourse: pre-war society must be renewed in the brave new post-war world by the acknowledgement of a proud, united, stable and above all an homogenous national community. Many of the essays that follow make reference to this aspect of emergent television's hegemonic 'work'. The expansion of industrial production of small consumer durables required, in the USA as in the UK, an investment in the home, and the drive towards homogeneity resulted in these homes being increasingly located in new suburban developments accessed by new automobiles, fuelled in America by home-produced and cheap gasoline. The preferred model for post-war citizenry was the white, middle-class, home-owning family operating as a devolved unit of the patriarchal state. And this was the model towards which both programming and advertising was addressed. Television's address not only privileged this group but also participated in its formation through its constant flow of broadcast material offering representations – of goods, locations, domestic interiors, behaviours – to which its audiences might be expected to aspire.

Thus in the USA an ideal version of domestic America – 'land of the free' – was called on to buttress American world domination in general and the post-war NATO alliance's cold war opposition to the communist 'bloc' (including the USSR, China and, later, Cuba) in particular. Given the vast size of America, the many newly-juxtaposed ethnic traditions it encompassed, not to mention its own absorbing but relatively short national histories,[3] it is hardly surprising to note differences between the realities of life for most and the ideal purveyed in fictive representations. And here exactly is the stuff of hegemonic struggle in the arena of cultural production and consumption. Primary definitions of gender, ethnicity and class are contested in the detail of performance, address and discourse: together these make up the definitions of national identity circulated in discourse and perpetuated in myth. Though the broadcasting environment in the UK was, at the institutional level, very different from that of the USA, I would nevertheless suggest that the larger picture – the 'working-through'[4] of national and individual identities implied in the concept of hegemony – is similar. It is at the level of the individual – the fictional or documentary representation of character and the discrete viewing subject – after all, that broad propositions are personalized and in this way made legible to audiences. As Abercrombie and Longhurst note 'Performances for diffused audiences are public *and* private. Indeed, they erode the difference between the two' (1998:76). Through empathy, identification or contestation viewing subjects incorporate elements of the propositions contained in performances into their own sense of self, and on the mass scale characteristic of broadcast television's reach these individual acts of viewing and under-standing coalesce to become part of the motor of social change. The close examination of celebrated and, therefore, by definition widely consumed rep-resentations – such as Milton Berle's Uncle Miltie, or George Burns and Gracie Allen – offered in this volume engages with precisely this level of detail. As a consequence they begin to reveal the ambiguities, anomalies and fractures far more characteristic of America in the Fifties than the ideal version encapsu-lated in the iconic sitcom might suggest. In these discussions the polarized and hysterical politics of McCarthy, the escalating violence and heroism of the civil rights movement and the widespread contestations of gender defini-tion that preceded the emergence of the 1960s women's liberation movement are all evident. They are as much a part of the context of televisual explora-tions as are the flight to suburbia, the expansion of the automobile industry or the habit of tourism.

TV in the US and the UK

Though television broadcasting began in Britain in 1936, the effective and systematic development of the institutions of television proceeded far more quickly in the USA. In Britain the particular economic circumstances of the immediate post-war period and the dominance of a Public Service Broadcast-ing (PSB) model resulted in a greater awareness of the differences between the two systems than of their similarities. The commercially led US system was regarded with deep suspicion in the UK, only just beginning to come to terms with its loss of world power status. But looking back at the 1950s from the vantage point of the twenty-first century the structural similarities – that is the relations between different elements of the institution – between emergent television in the USA and the UK seem more significant than perhaps could be acknowledged at the time. Thus, allowing for some very interesting national differences, it is true to say that while television's characteristic genres, per-formance styles and modes of address were evident in American television rather earlier than in the UK, there is much more commonality between the two countries than conventional histories have allowed. Though national contexts did of course impact on the ways in which the technology was de-ployed, nevertheless many aspects of the medium and its typical forms tran-scend national boundaries. All other national broadcasting systems were developed in the light of the British and American experiences – not only that, but also US and British programmes were systematically exported thus providing models for local production in other parts of the world. This means that study of television in the USA in the 1950s (and to a lesser extent in the UK) allows insight into the invention and development of fiscal and institutional structures in parallel, as it were, with the emergent and rapidly developing technology on which these structures depended. With the benefit of hindsight it is now possible to discern, for example, how the small size of the domestic screen or the economic imperative to define and attract particular audience segments seem to have impacted on the content and form of early programming and, conversely, what kinds of knowledge such programming proposed to its audiences. William Boddy (1990) and Lynn Spigel (1992), respectively, have addressed the formation of the institution and the formation of the characteristic audience, offering, between them, a broad sense of the contexts of Fifties production and reception in the USA. The essays in this volume, informed by and building on the work of Boddy, Spigel and others, plunge into the textual and discursive detail of programmes, genres and stars in the USA and the UK. In their totality these essays allow valuable insights into the relation between broadcast television and broader social developments – particularly those resting on questions of identity – at the personal, communal and national levels. Here, then, in the 'dynamics of the particular' the underlying structural forces guiding social relations may be discovered – if perhaps not always fully understood, as Silverstone cautions.

It is an inevitable consequence of the earlier development of television technologies in the USA that more material remains extant and accessible in that country than in the UK. The existence of a larger home market, and of a huge and established film industry,[5] for example, ensured earlier access to tape recording and the wider use of film: both made it possible to preserve programmes for future resale (and for future scholarship). The promise of instantaneity – the 'liveness' of television – by which the early institution set such great store also meant that much programming was ephemeral (in 1950s UK the majority of it) and hence only available today as a trace in printed schedules, production notes and other contemporary discursive materials. The latter are far more widely available in the US than they are in Britain where, though the archives of the BBC and of the British Press Library contain much valuable material, it is less easy for researchers to gain access to the documentation of those commercial production and broadcasting companies active in the 1950s.

The experience of television in the USA and the UK is widely, and rightly, perceived as different, largely as a consequence of the funding arrangements on which the national institutions were (and are) based. While in the USA the profit motive for programme production and dissemination was enshrined in an unashamedly market-based system from the start, in Britain PSB was dominant as the BBC drew on its celebrated wartime radio experience in modelling its initially minor 'television department'. Commercial broadcasting was not permitted in Britain until 1955, and multi-channel viewing not available nationwide until the early 1960s. The 1954 Television Act, which enabled the start of commercial broadcasting in September 1955, also provided for a regulatory body (the Independent Broadcasting Authority) intended to exercise control over the activities of the companies, as did the FCC (Federal Communications Commission) in the USA. Despite their crucial differences, therefore, both countries acknowledged the need for state controls at some level. Just as the market-place produces profit as a primary motive, so state controls imply at the least some ideological assumptions about the nature of the 'public' and 'private' spheres and what the relation between these should be. This is, of course, a key issue and one explored implicitly or explicitly in much television scholarship – not least in this volume. It raises complex questions turning largely on understandings of what audiences *do* with the texts they 'consume'.[6] Here the argument approaches the very stuff of everyday life – the material from which experience is drawn and from which both aspiration and recollection are constituted. In the late twentieth century, industrialized world television – unequivocally first among all media – is deeply implicated in this material. Even in an entirely commercial system questions concerning who may broadcast, what may be broadcast, when it may be broadcast, how and where it may be viewed are considered to be the business of the state, that is to say the use of the airwaves is regulated and the content of broadcast material subject to the same constraints of decency, copyright and so forth as other forms of publication. In both the USA and the UK the post-war economic boom allowed and, in a sense, also *required* the very facilities offered by mass broadcasting in order to stimulate consumer demand. The power of broadcasting to suggest, mould and define social behaviour had been tested and refined during the recent wartime experience of both countries.[7] The patriarchal state's post-war requirement to reinstate a paternalist hegemony coincided with the emergence of mass broadcasting and, as many of the subsequent essays will demonstrate, this was a struggle in which broadcast television played a significant role.

In both countries, too, public recognition of the central importance broadcast television was to play in informing and moulding national consciousness was noted, in 1953, apropos two major broadcasting events in which television's potential as the site of spectacular demonstrations of national identity was unequivocally demonstrated. These were President Eisenhower's inauguration, in the USA, and in the UK the coronation of Queen Elizabeth II. While for audiences this recognition signalled their delight in the novel access television appeared to allow to public events, for contemporary academics television's apparent power to 'speak' from what they saw as a dangerously unified position – simultaneously to 'show and tell', as it were – signified an unacceptably monolithic control over the interpretation of public events. Hence for political theorists, social psychologists and cultural critics the emergence of television as the crucial national arena represented a serious threat to a democracy still conceived on the model of the Greek *polis*, despite the anomaly of such a model in a mid-twentieth-century, industrialized and capitalist society. The 'effects' debate, informed by a crude and behaviourist concept of the audience as passive recipients of broadcast diktats, raged from the mid-Fifties, giving rise to the bulk of early sociological work on television and reinforcing suspicion of the medium's consequences for national cultures.

Be that as it may, President Eisenhower's inauguration was nevertheless hailed as 'one of the first big TV events of the decade' (Marling 1994:8) and in Britain the coronation of Queen Elizabeth II was also viewed by an unprecedentedly large national audience and accompanied by a boom in the sale of television receivers. There were those, too, whose prescience about the wider fiscal implications of large viewing figures informed their speculative experiments with televisual form. In April 1954 it was announced that a theme park, Disneyland, would be built at Anaheim in Southern California. In a deal with the so-called 'third' (and struggling) network, ABC, a weekly television show also called *Disneyland* premiered in October. Walt Disney recognized the symbiosis: 'I saw that if I was ever going to have my park, here was a way to tell millions of people about it – with TV' (Marling 1994:122). *Variety*'s television reporter Bob Chandler observed that the systematic integration of the two arms of Disney's business went further than the simple use of the television programme as publicity for the park. *Tomorrowland* and *Frontierland* were both physically available at the park and virtually available (as we would put it now) to millions of domestic viewers at 7.30 pm each Wednesday evening – the success of this intervention into televisual form being evident in the fact that within three months the programme had reached the top ten in the ratings. *Tomorrowland*'s futuristic hardware, Marling notes

> was not dissimilar in appearance ... to the products of American industry on display during frequent commercial breaks: a Ford Fairlane with options and a push-button kitchen range heralded a future of magical ease as surely as any lunar vehicle did. Television suburbanized a future ... a technological wonderland available for purchase with no money down and twenty-four months to pay (1994:123)

and Frontierland 'validated suburban mobility' while also contributing to the mythologizing of America's 'western' history – in the process generating a further appetite for TV westerns. *Davy Crockett* in the 1954–55 season was the first one-hour prime-time western series and gained the highest ratings of the decade as well as producing 'a bonanza of product spin-offs' (1994:124). Marling suggests further that not only did the theme park TV show tie-in stimulate consumer demand in general terms but also that the 'spatial sensibility' of the theme park derived from the specific form of television's address to its viewers. In Disneyland at Anaheim the scenes and rides enjoyed by tourists were discontinuous and episodic – like the TV series – and like the TV series too each 'ride' was punctuated with visits to the rest room, the snack bar or the souvenir shop – the equivalent in the Anaheim experience to the commercial break at home (1994:125).

The Essays in this Collection

The essays which follow are distinguished by their attention to detail, to specifics of genre, programme or star, but in the contextualizing of their varied subject matter their broader concerns naturally overlap. Collectively they allow insights into the complex and fluid interactions of developing television technology, performance styles, and thus, not least, to the emergence of the television institution itself – in both the USA and the UK – with its own intricate relation to governmental policies, the exigencies of the market place and the imperative to find, build and maintain audiences. In the consequently multiple connections between all of these concerns the scholars contributing to this volume tease out the part played by television in the 1950s and early 1960s in emergent discourses of post-war society. Of principal interest amongst these are the tensions between personal and national identities, hence many essays focus on definitions of women, the family and ethnicity as these were articulated in televisual representations.

Given the complexity of these concerns it was difficult to arrive at a logical sequencing of the essays: some readers will begin at the beginning, as if following a narrative, while others will go directly to particular essays, constructing their own route through the volume. I've aimed to take account of both reading strategies. The collection thus opens with Derek Kompare's discussion of late twentieth-century rerun cable channels' recycling of the texts of Fifties television, 'I've Seen This One Before: The construction of "classic" TV on cable television', in which he invites consideration of how it is that we make sense, as viewers, of this 'historical' material, and it closes with Lisa Parks' exploration of the context in which viewers of the 1950s had access to this same material, 'Cracking Open the Set: Television repair and tinkering with gender'. Looking at such perennial favourites as *I Love Lucy*, or *The Burns and Allen Show*[8] through the technologically sophisticated viewing apparatus available to us now, it is easy to forget that for audiences in the 1950s – in the USA as well as the UK – the television receiver itself was a mysterious device, frequently prone to failures of one kind or another. The development of 'habits of viewing', then, was accompanied by the delivery of receivers to homes, the installation of aerials, the necessity for tuning, re-tuning and so forth, assisted by what were then vital elements in the television 'landscape': the TV repair shop and the TV repairman.

Following Kompare's opening are six essays about aspects of television in the USA, then five dealing with the UK experience. The American topics are on the whole located *within* the 1950s, while some of the British ones deal also with UK television in the 1960s, thus there is a certain chronological logic to the sequence, acknowledging implicitly the fact that development of television technologies and audiences proceeded somewhat more slowly in the UK than it did in the USA – principally because of the complete cessation of television broadcasting in the UK during the Second World War. The whole collection is framed, as it were, by Kompare's and Parks' attention to the contexts of current and historical viewing practices.

Television is a 'young' cultural form with a short history. It is only recently, indeed, that scholarship has begun to acknowledge the need for separate critical and historical discussion of the medium – as Corner has remarked 'It [television scholarship] has sometimes worked with a frantically contemporary agenda' (1999:126). It is appropriate, therefore, that this collection should open with an essay in which the very formation of television's history is the focus. Kompare's discussion of the cable channel Nick at Nite which began broadcasting in 1985, and in which early programming is systematically 'recycled', speculates on the implications of this and similar channels' success for notions of what history is, on how the cultural worth of television – initially, and famously, regarded as ephemeral and therefore of low cultural status – is inevitably subjected to reassessment by virtue of its re-viewing out of its temporal context. Kompare demonstrates the shift in emphasis from the 'camp' or 'retro' address of the mid-80s programme to the weightier 'heritage' frame typical of the early 90s, suggesting that a reconstruction of history – not merely the history of television but also that of American society – is in itself a consequence of the contemporary circulation of programming from earlier periods.

Kristen Hatch in 'Selling Soap: Post-war television soap opera and the American housewife' takes the Fifties as a whole, exploring the ways in which US daytime soap operas contributed to television's agency in proposing and ordering hegemonic definitions of appropriate female behaviour – thus she initiates discussion taken up in subsequent essays, particularly those by McCracken, Bratten and Desjardins. Hatch's essay not only offers a sustained and detailed analysis of the visual form typical of soaps but also, taking her cue from Raymond Williams' pioneering study[9], considers television's *flow*. She does this by including analytic discussion of the advertisements typically appearing within and between daytime soaps, noting how powerful suggestions to the female audience were mutually reinforced by the twin address of soaps and ads. Referencing Friedan[10] and Foucault[11] she suggests in conclusion that soaps and ads developed their address through the Fifties from the didactic to the empowering (for the female audience),[12] but notes that this supposed empowerment is paradoxical since it rests on constructing value in the nurturing/supportive and patriarchally preferred female role. This close attention to the 50s articulation of the 'housewife' is continued in Allison McCracken's study of Gracie Allen, 'Study of a Mad Housewife: Psychiatric discourse, the suburban home and the case of Gracie Allen'. McCracken uses the Gracie Allen figure and sitcom to reveal the problematics of the housewife role and the ways in which this was ordered, controlled and contained through discourses of psychiatry, advertising and, crucially, television. She notes too the alienation of the newly dispersed suburban families separated from their previous urban and ethnic backgrounds and networks, linking this to observations about the gradual shift from a vaudevillian to a realist aesthetic – evident in this case in *The Burns and Allen Show* as it developed on US television between 1950 and 1958.

In their articulation of the public/private tensions implicit in televisual representations these essays begin to show how the new mass form of popular culture came to operate as a form of social control – not only of gender definition but also of ethnicity. Sue Murray's essay, 'Lessons From Uncle Miltie: Ethnic masculinity and early television's vaudeo star', focuses on the television star Milton Berle, popularly known in his small-screen persona of Uncle Miltie. Emphasizing the *work* entailed in early television production she offers a view of the tentative, pragmatic development of television genres with reference to the earliest audiences who, she observes, were predominantly urban, immigrant and ethnic groups. She notes, as does Clare Bratten apropos Dinah Shore, how early broadcasting technology privileged some modes of performance over others. Through a close interrogation of the vaudevillian sources of the earliest televisual performance style and content, and of closely associated issues such as the representations of masculinity and of ethnicity, Murray suggests that the demise of the vaudeville-based format was related to mid-Fifties suburbanization and the consequent rise of the sitcom as the paradigmatic television genre. Bratten, in 'Nothin' Could be Finah: The Dinah Shore Chevy Show', develops this theme of television's crucial contribution to the suppression of ethnic diversity in mid-century America. In her study of Dinah Shore's felicitous relationship not only with contemporary broadcasting technology but also with institutional structures in the shape of her sponsorship by Chevrolet, Bratten demonstrates that the formation of a unified white, middle-class and consumerist national identity entailed both the marginalization of ethnic difference and attempts to control the definition of women. Like Sue Murray, Bratten references the pre-television professional experience of her subject, showing how characteristic elements of performance style and modes of address were adapted to the exigencies of the close-up camera and the small domestic screen.

The star persona is an accumulation of various knowledges derived from both the star's performances and the discourses circulating around these.[13] Central to the persona's development, therefore, are the conditions of reception within which the star's image is consumed by audiences. Small wonder, then, that the very different reception contexts of cinema and television produced difficulties for performers in the 1950s aiming to make the transition. Amongst these were many celebrated screen actresses whose advancing age appeared to preclude future success in the contracting film industry. This is the subject of Diane Negra's contribution, 'Re-Made for Television: Hedy Lamarr's post-war star textuality'. Tracing Hedy Lamarr's television career over a ten-year period she shows how Lamarr's previous (film) star persona and her ethnicity both produced disruptions in television's momentum towards post-war homo-geneity. These disruptions are evidenced in her 'troubling' of television texts of which three (1956, 1967, 1964) are discussed in detail. But Negra suggests, further, that Lamarr's transition from cinematic to televisual stardom also disrupted her star persona. This was a disruption related not only to the different relations of the cinema and television institutions to their audiences, but also to television's attempts, in the USA of the 1950s, to 'normalise . . . the repression of ethnic heritage'. Each of the three texts discussed tried to resolve Lamarr's 'excessiveness' in differing ways. Mary Desjardins, in Maureen O'Hara's '"Confidential" Life: Recycling stars through gossip and moral bi-ography', continues the discussion of star persona as this developed in the context of television, focusing not only on questions of European ethnicity but also on the exploration of discursive constructions of femininity circulating in the mid-Fifties. She does this by means of a fascinating account of a particu-lar and contradictory moment (1957) in the television career of Maureen O'Hara, primarily known then, and certainly better remembered now, as a Hollywood star of the large screen. In the course of this discussion Desjardins adds to the insights of Murray, Bratten and Negra into television's paradoxi-cal articulations of the tensions between the public and private spheres, show-ing how such tensions contribute both to socially situated knowledge and to techniques of social control. Here is evidence for Silverstone's assertion that television programme content (and we might add, here, the surrounding criti-cal discourses) has a dialectical relation with the moral economy of the fam-ily (1994:50).

The essays introduced so far have situated their interrogations of television's cultural and social 'work' in terms depending on the benefits of hindsight. But it is also true that in some programming areas network managers, schedulers and production teams were quite clearly aware of the potential influence – for good or ill – of programme content. The 'moral panic' informed by behaviourist assumptions about the audience was a common feature of much contempo-rary journalism (then as now), and network planners took seriously the re-sponsibilities accorded to them in such commentaries. Matthew Murray, in '*Matinee Theater*: Difference, compromise and the 1950s daytime audience', focuses on broadcasters' consciousness of their audiences, noting the power struggles within and between broadcasting institutions as they attempted to negotiate the fierce competition characteristic of this period in which both programme content and technological change impacted directly on profit-ability. He does this by means of a careful study of NBC's Matinee Theatre (1955–58), attending in particular to attempts to define an audience segment and to mobilize that definition in the interests of NBC's competitive struggle. The essay locates and identifies points of fracture and ambiguity which dogged this attempt, noting in the process how these turned mainly on conflicting definitions of women – the preferred 50s homemaker, the deviant female viewer – and also, significantly, *acknowledged* the need to control female desire.

Madeleine MacMurraugh-Kavanagh's essay 'The BBC and the Birth of The Wednesday Play, 1962–66: Institutional containment versus "agitational contemporaneity"' references, as does Murray, the dramas' form and subject matter, privileging the politics surrounding their commissioning and produc-tion. Thus both essays deal explicitly with what was, effectively, the attempts at censorship of morally or politically provocative material by the broadcast-ers themselves. This was a censorship couched in terms of the battle for rat-ings rather than one which acknowledged a political agenda. However its consequence was, not surprisingly, to privilege drama that was uncontentious and therefore politically and morally conservative in both its form and its content. The juxtaposition of these two essays offers a useful opportunity to compare the very different commissioning imperatives in the US and British contexts. Whereas Murray focuses on the networks' struggle to claim quality while also securing the female daytime audience, MacMurraugh-Kavanagh attends directly to the power struggles between the BBC and ITV and within British society in the early 1960s, which, she suggests, are reflected in the BBC's internal battles over its drama output in general and *The Wednesday Play* in particular. Here again the question of 'quality' is at issue, as is also the struggle for dominance in the ratings but, provocatively, MacMurraugh-Kavanagh also proposes that 'contrary to popular, critical and Corporation mythology, this play strand survived the 1960s *in spite of* the BBC and not because of it' (my italics).

Helen Wheatley's '"Mystery and Imagination": Anatomy of a Gothic an-thology series' and Cathy Johnson's 'Exploring the Intimate Screen: *The Quatermass Experiment*, fantasy and the aesthetic potential of early televi-sion drama' focus on British drama production in the 1960s and 1950s respec-tively. While acknowledging the social and institutional context explored in depth by MacMurraugh-Kavanagh, both concentrate on the formal and aes-thetic detail of the drama series they discuss. Wheatley's essay takes two 1966 episodes of ABC's strand *Tales of Mystery and Imagination*, considering in detail its debt to pre-televisual forms of Gothic fantasy, and particularly the ways in which these were deliberately exploited with the small-screen, do-mestic site of reception in mind. Johnson, in an absorbing account of the BBC's 1953 science fiction series *The Quatermass Experiment*, concentrates on the debates in early 1950s UK about what kind of drama was appropriate to television. Her discussion engages directly with visual and narrative detail of the drama in order to demonstrate writer Nigel Kneale's and producer Rudolph Cartier's overtly innovative intention that *Quatermass* should 'exemplify the possibilities, rather than the limitations, of the medium' for the production of quality drama. Thus both essays focus on the ways in which some British writers and producers attempted to exploit the prevailing technological constraints in order to extend the aesthetic possibilities of the small screen and its domestic reception.

Victoria Wegg-Prosser, in '*This Week* in 1956: The introduction of current affairs on ITV' offers a detailed snapshot of a particularly important moment in British broadcasting history with reference to the emergence of 'current affairs'. This was a controversial matter in the 1950s, following the introduction of commercial broadcasting to what had hitherto been an exclusively public service broadcasting environment. Picking up the significance of the emergent current affairs genre for the British broadcasting environment as a whole, Janet Thumim then explores popular drama, the sitcoms, series and soaps (some home-produced, some imported from the USA) which filled the newly expanded broadcasting hours with relatively cheap programming thus allowing both the BBC and the companies to maximise their investment in 'quality' programming which they intended to maintain their position in what was, for the UK, the new experience of competition for audiences. Wegg-Prosser and Thumim both pay specific attention to the question of women at work: in the case of *This Week*, Wegg-Prosser notes the presence and absence of female production personnel, while Thumim explores representations of working women in popular drama. Both essays make a tentative observation about the increasing masculinization of the television institution – a feature also noted in the US context by both Hatch and McCracken.

Finally Parks' essay returns us to mid-Fifties USA though, as I have suggested, her account of the gendered discourse emerging around the technicalities of the TV set itself is equally applicable to the British experience. In Britain it was not until the early 1960s that the transmitter networks of both the BBC and ITV allowed reception in all parts of the country. We should not underestimate, from our twenty-first century vantage point, the effect of technological uncertainty – that is to say the tricky business of getting a clear picture, being able to receive *all* available channels, tuning and re-tuning and so on – on viewing practices of the mid-century, when *all* transmissions were terrestrial, in analogue form. In this context the very presence of the broadcast moving image was in itself as novel and exciting to audiences as the earliest cinematic projections were for audiences of the late nineteenth century. Television's now ubiquitous and universally assumed place in the maintenance of – or in challenges to – hegemonic definitions of national identity and its components was, like the transmission network, the receivers and the programme forms of the mid-Fifties, *in itself* under construction.

Notes

1. Abercrombie and Longhurst, in their 1998 study *Audiences*, suggest that three successive paradigms have informed audience research over the last 50 years. They argue, uncontentiously, for the discrediting of the *behavioural* model and chart its replacement by the *incorporation/ resistance* model. They go on to suggest, however, that this model in turn has 'manifested a series of stresses and strains which threaten the coherence of the paradigm itself. There have been three main sources of difficulty – the active audience, the gap between empirical studies and the theory of hegemony, and the nature of power and its relationship to commodification' (p 28). They propose the emergence of a new paradigm which they term *spectacle/performance*, suggesting that this can account for the problems they have noted with earlier models.

2. Referencing Debord, *The Society of the Spectacle* (1994), they write: 'While in earlier capitalist societies there was a transformation in human experience from "being" to "having", in late capitalist societies "having" has become "appearing". The transformation of the world into an array of images is intimately related to the development of the commodity form . . .' (1998 p84).

3. For a fictional, but nevertheless thoroughly researched account of ethnic diversity in twentieth-century America see E. Annie Proulx, *Accordion Crimes* (Fourth Estate, 1996).

4. I borrow this useful concept from John Ellis, *Seeing Things: Television in the Age of Uncertainty* (I.B.Tauris, 2000).

5. Christopher Anderson's 1994 study *Hollywood TV* demonstrates the systematic efforts of some Hollywood 'majors' to divert their production to television, thus securing their investment in plant threatened, as they saw it, by the imminent collapse of the vertically integrated and hitherto profitable studio system.

6. The activity of women romance readers in respect of the texts they 'consume' are explored in Janice Radway's *Reading the Romance: Women, Patriarchy and Popular Fiction* (1984), in which she offers an in-depth account of the reading practices of a sample group. This account has been influential in suggesting analogous ways in which television viewers 'use' the texts they 'consume'.

7. Connie Fields' film *Rosie the Riveter* (1980) documents the effectiveness of this power apropos of women in the US. Gledhill and Swanson's (eds) 1996 study of Britain in wartime, *Nationalising Femininity: Culture, Sexuality and Cinema in Britain in the Second World War*, offers similar insights into the British experience.

8. Both of these were produced in the USA and also exported to the UK, where they were just as popular with audiences in the 1950s.

9. Raymond Williams, *Television, Technology and Cultural Form* (1974).

10. Betty Friedan, *The Feminine Mystique* (Victor Gollancz, 1963).

11. Michel Foucault, *Discipline and Punish: The Birth of the Prison* (1979).

12. This shift is also to be noted apropos of the typical address of afternoon programming for women in Britain during the 1950s and 1960s.

13. See Richard Dyer, *Stars* (1979), and *Heavenly Bodies: Film Stars and Society* (1987).

CHAPTER 1

I'VE SEEN THIS ONE BEFORE

THE CONSTRUCTION OF 'CLASSIC TV' ON CABLE TELEVISION

Derek Kompare

Time in the everyday lifeworld is not undifferentiated and unhierarchical – it is textual, lending itself to the formation of boundaries and to a process of interpretation delimited by our experience with those boundaries.

(Susan Stewart 1984:13)

As our consumption-centred, media-drenched and ostensibly 'fast forward' societies career into an arbitrary new millennium, the passage of time has become one of the central concerns – and commodities – of the age. Walter Benjamin's oft-cited angel of history is blown backwards into the future not only by the usual horrors and 'wreckage' of the past century – wars, alienation, mass destruction – but also by the sheer volume and longevity of something altogether more mundane: the raw stuff of industrialized culture (1968:257–58). Despite most traditional historians' insistence that capital-H History is composed of Wars, Social Struggles and Technological Advances, the cultural torrent of films, hit singles, supermarket packaging, capricious celebrity, high fashion, low fashion, sports cars, pornography, fast food, coffee-table books and, most of all, television, certainly offers a compelling, alternative perspective on the twentieth century. Moreover, this is largely a legacy that not only survives, but thrives, piling up at the angel's feet and refusing to fade away. While the veterans of past struggles will all eventually die, as long as the engines and microprocessors of capitalism (including eBay) keep humming along, 'we'll always have Paris,' or at least Bogart's and Bergman's version of it.

Not only will we still have Paris 1940 (by way of Hollywood), we'll also have Memphis 1956, Liverpool 1962, Carnaby Street 1966, Manhattan 1977 and Seattle 1992: times and places – 'moments' – etched into popular memory through the dense signification of retro, one of the dominant cultural forms and sensibilities of the past thirty years. Retro recirculates the past as an array of mediated sounds and images, consumer artefacts that now bear the full weight of their original eras: saddle shoes, Elvis' gyrating hips, lava lamps, bean bags, Boy George's wink, James Cameron's digitized *Titanic*. Accordingly, the forward-looking narratives of constant progress, which held sway over most of the past several decades, have been largely replaced by heavily stylized, retro citations of romanticized pasts, where all is well, or at least safely 'predictable.'[1] As gaps between times and places are virtually wiped out via technology and postmodernity, *la mode retro* becomes one of the dominant modes of contemporary cultural production, and memories become exotic, attractive bundles of sights and sounds repackaged for reconsumption (Herron 1993).

Perhaps no pasts are as ubiquitous – or as predictable – as those found on television. Thanks to the regime of repetition, which essentially mandates that TV worth showing is TV worth rerunning, we'll also 'always have' Mayberry 1963, Walmington-on-Sea 1941, Springfield 1993, the Ponderosa 1888 and the Starship Enterprise 2270: televisual images and sounds of our cultural and individual pasts, constantly recirculated in the present. These are near-inescapable pasts, as much a part of our everyday experience of television as any other form of programming.

My concern here is with the most ubiquitous, and arguably most permanent, manifestation of this trend: rerun programming on cable and satellite television. Previously regarded (if at all) by critics as the detritus of bygone television eras, or (at best) the necessary attraction which fuelled local stations' revenues, reruns have become one of the most culturally significant, and financially lucrative, forms of television over the past quarter century. Reruns represent not so much a dormant past as a dynamic *television heritage*: an ever-changing body of series, genres, stars, sights and sounds, which culturally anchor the past few decades in the contemporary public memory. Since television has developed along predominantly nationalist lines, each 'TV nation' has its own system of reruns, and hence its own television heritage. Due primarily to its unique combination of local and national modes of address, the United States has far and away the most active television heritage, though over the past decade or so other countries – particularly the United Kingdom – have developed similar forms and practices.

The blossoming of cable and satellite systems (again, particularly in North America), has extended the range and reach of television, as hundreds of new, narrowcast channels have been created in several countries. While the dominant rhetoric of these systems still promotes an alternative to broadcast television, in actuality they have mostly provided extra outlets for already-produced material, whether on premium channels, where feature films dominate, or on 'basic' tiers, where channels like USA or TBS have relied in large part on reruns. Among these channels, the use of reruns has, until recently, largely been matter-of-fact; reruns were so much 'regular programming' rather than 'relics from the past.' However, since its premiere in August 1985 as a prime-time expansion of Nickelodeon, Nick At Nite/TV Land has been far and away the most visible source of rerun programming on US television, brashly offering up a half-century worth of the US television heritage. Loudly proclaiming itself to be 'the home of classic television,' Nick At Nite/TV Land does not merely run reruns; it ritually *activates* the television heritage, as a knowing play of the medium's own entextuating devices and narrative forms. During the 1990s, these channels' approaches to and reconstructions of past television have inspired similar strategies and aesthetics in other outlets, including the Cartoon Network/Boomerang, the Encore Multiplex, the Sci-Fi Channel in North America and UK Gold in Great Britain.

This essay explores how the television heritage is activated via cable and satellite channels, thus creating particular kinds of mediated pasts for contemporary consumption. Through the creative use of thematic programming and promotional material, these outlets have reinvented the televisual past as a series of disinterred sights and sounds. This results not only in nostalgia – eg, 'wish I was *there*' – but also in an archetypically postmodern sense of permanent déjà vu: the continuous commodification of televisual history via the dynamic flow of familiar texts, figures, narratives and genres. These histories have profound implications for television culture in general, and television studies in particular, setting parameters for the ways in which the past is discursively activated. After first considering how television studies has constructed its own narratives of television culture, I will focus primarily on the major outlet for this incarnation of the television heritage: Viacom's Nick At Nite/TV Land, a multimedia retro brand which functions through cable and satellite television, websites and merchandising.

Creating Television History

With few prominent exceptions, academic television studies has had little to say about the 'historicizing' mode of television programming. In many of the key works of the field, particularly those concentrating on the audience, television has been rendered as an homogenous, relatively static source of more-or-less discrete 'texts' for viewers to interpret. The medium itself is taken-for-granted, treated largely as a mere delivery system for its signs; the 'place' (on our screens, in our homes) where such signs are found.[2] While much of this work revolutionized the field of television studies, it has also had relatively little to offer about the institution of television itself, about how its

discursive modes, material conditions and aesthetic conventions are structured, deployed, reconfigured and even subverted on the 'front end' by the
medium's own technology, producers and products, well before the ostensible
television 'audience' is reached. Moreover, most critics have only focused on
television's more 'traditional' textual forms: series and programmes. TV's
other forms, including commercials, promos, programming 'events,' and 'black
box' technologies such as cable, the VCR, video game consoles and digital
media players, have been ritually ignored, aside from a handful of important
theoretical and historical studies.[3]

However, another significant, more historically-inclined branch of television studies has analyzed the medium as not as much an instantaneous text
machine, but instead as a complex, culturally-produced and situated technology of mass communication, in all the glory that the term can still convey.[4]
Particularly important among these works have been feminist historical analyses of the domestic nature of television. Like much of the previous 'audience-
centred' work, these historical studies trace the place of television in the lives
of women. But they also connect those uses to a larger sense of the institution
of television: the rhetoric and practices deployed to produce our 'television
culture.' Most importantly, these analyses locate television in relevant historical contexts. Their conceptions of technologies, networks, programmes
and audiences exist in relation to each other and particular historical narratives. That is, these studies are adamant that television is produced and received differently in different historical and sociocultural circumstances.

Significantly, more of these studies have concerned themselves with the 1950s
than with any other period in broadcasting history. While this focus has undoubtedly added to the critical understanding of the formative years of television, it has also given additional discursive weight to the dominant historical
construction of 'The Fifties.' Given a swagger and scope currently rivalled
only by its immediate successor, 'The Sixties,' the Fifties have historically
served as the effective social, economic and cultural nexus of the twentieth
century. Conventional wisdom – and conventional historiography – approaches
the decade as the high-water mark of strict bourgeois norms in modes of sexuality, work, childhood, fashion and leisure. This image is indelible: recent
revisionist accounts of the time have had to work hard to offer a different
interpretation of the era.[5] Moreover, since about 1963 (the approximate advent
of 'The Sixties') the Fifties have been uncannily persistent in our cultural histories, constantly surfacing as a spectral reminder of who we once were (and who
we still may be) at the dawn of an old new age. It is no exaggeration to say that
television has played the dominant role in endlessly circulating these particular memories of the decade. As Stephanie Coontz wrote in her revisionist account of American family life, *The Way We Never Were*, 'our most powerful
visions of traditional families derive from images that are still delivered to our
homes in countless reruns of 1950s television sitcoms'(1992:23). According to
Coontz, these *television images* of the domestic Fifties – smiling, white, profoundly heterosexual, middle-class nuclear units – have had a much greater

effect on contemporary debates about the 'proper' make-up and social role of families than the historical reality of the actual era would indicate.

Accordingly, the prevalence of 1950s television in the cultural memories – and authorized cultural histories – of the decade raises questions about the role of television as a medium of *historical* communication. Why do the Fifties loom so large in our televisual memories? Were the Fifties *really* like the Anderson household (of *Father Knows Best*), or, like the deluded David Parker in the 1998 film *Pleasantville*, have our subsequent experiences of rerun television fatally coloured our perceptions of this monochrome world? And if this reality gap exists, how are we to circulate it? How can we, literally, *tell the difference*? It is difficult to answer these questions with any certainty, for *television's* memories of 'the Fifties' – or of any other time since – have clearly become the culture's dominant images of the past, particularly for those too young to have experienced these times themselves.[6] The reasons for this are multiple, but centre on television's insatiable appetite for repetition: that is to say its unparalleled penchant for plundering the past.

Reruns as Television Heritage

The dominant sources of television's memories are reruns: old series recirculated long after their original airings. Economically, they have served as a lucrative 'aftermarket' for programme producers and syndicators, where series no longer in production are licensed to various television outlets after their initial run. If a series has produced enough episodes, it may even find success run 'stripped': airing five or more times a week in the same time-slot on local or cable stations. This market was initially developed in the 1950s as a practical way for stations to fill low-rated fringe-time hours and for producers to amortize the costs of programme production and distribution. However, since then it has become one of the dominant means of experiencing television in the United States.[7] The market for past programmes has grown steadily since the early 1970s and is now a substantial aspect of the entire media industry,[8] with rerun and licensing rights to the most popular series going to the highest bidders, across a range of video and merchandising outlets. Far from being relegated only to fringe time, reruns are now a central component of American television.

Aside from their economic importance to the television industry, reruns have also become an essential resource in our cultural vernacular. Viewing practices around reruns have long been ritual, times when we can sit down with the adventures of Lucy and Ricky, Kirk and Spock, Mary and Rhoda or

Homer and Bart at the same time every day. A generation ago, Raymond Williams famously observed that television had fostered an explosive growth in the experience of narrative (1974:59–60). Reruns offer a radical extension to this premise, channelling those narrative experiences into all-too-familiar territory, *literally* telling the same old stories again and again.

This sense of repetition is even greater when the overwhelming prevalence of rerun situation comedies (sitcoms) is considered. The sitcom – long one of television's most popular programme forms – is also particularly well suited to rerun programming. From a programming standpoint, its compact episode length and flexible scheduling order is certainly a major factor in its dominance.[9] More significant, however, to the television heritage, is the sitcom's formulaic narrative form. All sitcoms provide a regular set of characters interacting in a stable setting within a relatively narrow range of comedic plots. As analyzed by many television scholars, this 'TV family' form usually utilizes normative familial categories of bourgeois domestic hegemony.[10] Accordingly, the domestic or quasi-domestic settings of sitcoms ostensibly function as an analogue to the viewing home. As described by Gerard Jones, 'the sitcom is . . . a friendly thing to invite into the home and a comforting thing to watch with the family. It benefits from regular viewing because even its repetition is much of its charm . . . It is commercial broadcasting's perfect product' (1992:5–6). Filled with enjoyable, 'friendly' characters in an attractive, 'comforting' setting, sitcoms offer the most familiar form of television, if only because it has been so stable and dominant over the decades.

Within this stable form there are, of course, significant variations. The bland suburbia of the Stone family on *The Donna Reed Show* is not the wacky farmland of *Green Acres* or the urban angst of the Sunshine Cab Company garage on *Taxi*, after all. This interplay of similarity and variation is repeated across all television forms and outlets, but is particularly salient to the function of Nick At Nite/TV Land, by far the most significant site of rerun culture on American television. Through its selection of programmes (mostly sitcoms) and rhetorical framing, Nick At Nite/TV Land foregrounds the historical construction of what we know of as 'television,' producing a compelling blend of decades, televisual styles and memories: its own, branded television heritage.

The Television Heritage on Nick At Nite/TV Land

Originally intended as an experimental foray into prime-time programming by the Nickelodeon cable channel in 1985, Nick At Nite soon developed into a space all its own, quite distinct from the channel's ostensible purpose of quasi-educational children's programming. A decade later, it had become not only the primary outlet for rerun programming on American television, but also the most profitable partner of the MTV Networks group, due in large part to the low programming costs incurred by decades-old series. Seeking to continue their dominance of the television heritage, Nick At Nite's corporate parent Viacom created TV Land, a 24-hour rerun channel, in 1996.[11] Today both channels are staples of most basic cable packages in the United States. They have billed themselves variously as 'the home of TV Hits,' claiming to 'preserve our precious television heritage.' More directly, TV Land beckons its viewers right into its version of the television heritage: a specific, geographic *place* in our psyches ('Take me to TV Land!'). Nick At Nite/TV Land has largely lived up to these promises, shrewdly acquiring rebroadcast rights through purchases and mergers and running several dozen different series throughout its history. All of this makes obvious business sense, but what makes Nick At Nite/TV Land particularly significant for television studies is its active, exhibitionist construction of 'classic TV.' That is, the outlets' explicit 'TV-ness' serves as a unique case study within which issues of television historicity – and the construction of the television heritage – can be examined.

Nick At Nite/TV Land is no mere collection of reruns; it is a carefully mapped, constantly shifting *empire* of past television. Reruns are immersed in a heavily-stylized array of bumps, promos and events, with the effect that television's history – its 'classics' and 'heritage,' to use the channel's own vernacular – is constantly cited. This reflexive mode has taken on several guises since Nick At Nite's inception in 1985. Early on, the predominant aesthetic was high camp: a playful, and predictable, send-up of an earlier generation's styles and forms.[12] Unlike other cable channels, where reruns were aired with little fanfare or distinction from other programming, Nick At Nite utilized a stridently aestheticized mode of address, harking back to the cradle of all American TV imagery: the neverland of 'the Fifties.' This retro feel has been consistent throughout both channels, from the colourful space-age shapes used in the logos and bumps, which clearly evoke Raymond Loewy's designs, to the slogans ('Hello out there from TV land!', 'Your home for classic TV,' 'Take me to TV Land!'), announcers' voices, myriad mascots and music reminiscent of 1950s commercials. This particular iconography seemed most appropriate during the first few years of Nick At Nite in the late 1980s, when virtually its entire schedule consisted of programmes that originally aired circa 1958–63. However, it became conspicuous as more recent programmes, such as *Fernwood 2Night* and *Mork and Mindy* were taken on in the late 1980s. The camp sensibility suggested by the channel's promotions worked best with some sense of historical distance, but there was little of that when the programmes in question were barely a decade old.

However, the television heritage is a dynamic commodity; camp is not the end of the aesthetic line. As the programming shifted, the packaging shifted accordingly. As John Thornton Caldwell writes, this constant 'upgrading' of a programme or channel's onscreen identity is part of a general concern with audiovisual style which has marked most television since the early 1980s (1995:4–11). Increased competition from cable, VCRs and other outlets prompted a search for what Caldwell refers to as 'televisuality': 'In several important programming and institutional areas, television moved from a framework that approached broadcasting primarily as a form of word-based rhetoric and transmission, with all the issues that such terms suggest, to a visually based mythology, framework and aesthetic based on an extreme self-consciousness of style' (1995:4). According to Caldwell, such stylistic devices include slick, ever-changing typefaces, graphic effects and clever promotional materials. I would add to that list a more recent staple form: recombinant programming, which takes the sounds and images of the past and repackages it in contemporary combinations and embellishments. MTV Networks, the Viacom subsidiary that controls MTV, VH-1, Nickelodeon, Nick At Nite/TV Land and, since 2000, the National Network (formerly the Nashville Network), has pioneered these forms on all of its channels. For example, 1980s MTV videos were repackaged for 1990s VH-1 series *Pop-Up Videos*, which added sarcastic and/or informative commentary to the videos in the form of video 'bubbles,' which 'popped up' on the screen. Nick At Nite/TV Land is entirely premised on such repackaging, as its series are mined for audiovisual nuggets for use in promos and event programming. Accordingly, since the beginning of the 1990s, the channel and its larger offshoot, TV Land, have constantly updated their looks and repertoires, while maintaining strong ties to their initial retro-Fifties identity as a playful kind of TV museum where past programmes are lionized and attentive viewing rewarded.

Nick At Nite accelerated its programme turnover in the early 1990s, phasing out most of its 1950s programmes in favour of the 1960s and 1970s. Early staples like *My Three Sons, Make Room For Daddy* and *The Donna Reed Show* disappeared in favour of more recent series, including two of the most highly-regarded sitcoms in television history, *The Dick Van Dyke Show* and *The Mary Tyler Moore Show*. For a brief period at this time, Nick At Nite even slightly toned down the retro trappings in favour of a more austere mode of address. Programmes were now highlighted as 'classics,' with Nick At Nite acting as guardians of history by 'preserving our television heritage.'[13] Throughout the rest of the decade, series ranging from *I Dream of Jeannie* and *The Munsters* to *The Odd Couple* and *Welcome Back, Kotter* to *Newhart* and *WKRP In Cincinnati* were aired, extending the historical dimensions throughout the entire television era. By 1999, the 1950s, which had been the initial focus of the whole endeavour, had vanished almost completely from both Nick At Nite and TV Land, with the notable exceptions of perennial favourites *I Love Lucy* and *The Honeymooners*.

Even without 'Fifties' programming, however, the shadow of the decade (or at least, its 1980s-retro version) remains across the channels' sensibility.

Though the explicit invocation of 'our precious television heritage' was short-lived, the overall tone of the promotions and packaging of the series incorporated *both* a retro sensibility (with occasional camp overtones) *and* a sense of heritage, which simultaneously honoured the television past while mocking our interest in it. Thus, 1960s, 1970s and even 1980s series can be simultaneously celebrated *and* ridiculed as intriguing, 'typical' cultural relics from distant times. No matter which era of television its programmes refer to, however, Nick At Nite/TV Land continues to be a resolutely postmodern space of history, where television's past is a parade of sounds and images which foster a 'general sense' of the television heritage, in much the same way channel surfing produces a 'general sense' of television, rather than an engagement with specific programmes. Not to fully reincarnate Raymond Williams' bemused original encounter with American television – which now seems quaint in our 150-channel universes – but on Nick at Nite/TV Land, decades, representations, characters and situations blur right into each other; 'pastness' is the result, rather than a discrete sense of 'the past.' On either channel, viewers can experience television from 1977, 1953, 1969, 1974 and 1985 in one sitting.[14] Our interest in past TV (as viewers, rather than scholars) is thus coded as both 'excessive' and 'civic.' That is, by managing the extent to which it takes itself seriously, television heritage outlets like Nick At Nite/TV Land promote the interpretation of the cultural past as both crucial *and* outmoded, intriguing *and* 'fun.' This condensation and rearrangement of time is one of the things television does best, sidestepping the rules of history to reveal – and revel in – the interplay of time as manifest in the changing styles of its programmes.[15] Television marks the passage of time more attentively than any other medium, yet, ironically, thrives on the reconsumption of memories. Individual television moments are thus constantly repeated, as if we must keep track of media past and media present in order to function in society. Nick At Nite/TV Land functions as the most prolific reminder of that principle.

Repackaging the Television Heritage

Nick At Nite/TV Land's genius lies 'in between' its programmes, in promos and events that draw from and expand viewers' television memories. These devices range from thirty-second 'video bites,' to use Megan Mullen's terminology, to large-scale, months-long programming events (Mullen 1995). Regardless of the device, the goal is the same: to reward regular viewers and foster active participation in the channels' particular brand of the television heritage.

The 'heavy artillery' in their promotional arsenal is the marathon block. First utilized in May 1988 with eight consecutive episodes of *The Donna Reed Show* (a 'Donna-Thon'), the marathon block enhances the already-heightened sense of repetition, providing space to indulge in one particular programme or theme for a concentrated period. The marathon block has had many different variations, ranging from several hours on one night, to, in the ultimate test of television endurance, running an *entire series* consecutively across several days. Whether the marathon is a 'three-hour tour' of *Gilligan's Island* (get it?), '*Odd Couple* Odd Nights,' or a forty-eight hour 'fandemonium' weekend of *Charlie's Angels*, the general intent is the same: to crystallize and promote interest in *particular* aspects of the television heritage, whether they be series, stars or situations. It is important to note here that narrowcast cable and satellite channels such as Nick At Nite and TV Land have the luxury to do this: hours and even days of schedule can be shoved aside for these events without much trouble. By contrast, national, and even local, over-the-air broadcasters must continually offer a varied schedule to maintain their high general audience levels.

Other Nick At Nite/TV Land marathons have been tied to the seasons. For several years in the 1990s, Nick At Nite ran a New Year's Eve Rerun Countdown, hosted by longtime 'Top 40' radio DJ Casey Kasem, in which viewers selected the most popular 25 episodes from a variety of the channel's programmes. This event promoted both audience participation and a sense of an annual ritual (like so much 'classic' TV around the holidays). The ritual was even more pronounced in practice, as several particularly popular episodes would consistently make the list each year.[16] Similarly, several recent summers have featured an eight-week 'summer block party' event on Nick At Nite, in which each weeknight is given over to a single programme. For example, in the summer of 1997, the days of the week were redesignated *Monkee* Mondays, *Lucy* Tuesdays, *Bewitched* Bewednesdays, *Happy Days* Thursdays and *Jeannie* Fridays. By airing one series on each weeknight, these nights became special, veritable 'festivals' of whichever programme was featured.

Because of the 24-hour schedule, TV Land has more access to the marathon event and made it a weekly event in 2000, as each weekend was given over in its entirety to a different series. These so-called 'fandemonium' weekends aired dozens of episodes of series including *Adam 12, China Beach, The Bob Newhart Show* and *Sanford and Son*. Making the marathon a regular event serves several purposes for TV Land. Each weekend is 'special', which can theoretically boost interest during otherwise low viewing periods. Series can be gauged for audience interest and added to – or deleted from – the regular schedule. For viewers, the weekends can be rare opportunities to indulge in old favourites, or seldom-seen programmes, working out their eyeballs and/or VCR for two days.[17]

Occasionally, both channels have tried variations on the marathon block that consist of not one series but several, all linked by a theme. Nick At Nite featured a Sunday night block of 'The Women of TV Land' (*The Mary Tyler Moore Show, Rhoda, Phyliss* and *That Girl*) in 1996–97. This block was significant in that it doubly focused attention on historical constructions of femininity: the programmes themselves were widely cited during their initial run for their lead characters' particular updates of the 'television woman,' and their retrospective runs on Nick At Nite situated those roles within the channel's construction of the television heritage, in which the 'single sitcom woman,' as variously portrayed in each of these series, is constructed as a 'typical' representative of historical periods (ie 'the Sixties,' 'the Seventies,' etc). In other words, 'The Women of TV Land' reproduced 'history' within the distinctive parameters of Nick At Nite's 'television heritage.' However, the clearest manifestations of Nick At Nite's particular attention to the sitcom form were the 'Very Very' programming blocks. Utilized from 1993 to 1995, these two-hour blocks featured four episodes from different comedies, all centred on a weekly theme (eg, Very Very Psychological, Very Very Paul Lynde, Very Very Vacation, etc.). These segments indulged in the clichéd plots and familiar faces of television, soliciting viewers' memories in the construction of the television heritage.

While the programming events mark large-scale constructions of the television heritage, the past is continuously reinterpreted via the channels' promos and bumps: short ten to 60-second pieces run between programmes. As Caldwell argued, this particular form of television became key in the changing television environment of the 1980s and 1990s, crystallizing a channel's corporate identity in brief, intense bursts.[18] These devices must never stagnate; innovation and a constantly 'upgraded' audiovisual style are seen as competitive necessities on television. Accordingly, specific promotional campaigns and on-screen graphics (aside from logos) are fairly short-lived on both Nick At Nite and TV Land. However, all of the spots function to recreate the channels' particular construction of the television heritage, emphasizing comedy, repetition and historical distance.

One series of spots from the early 1990s, called 'Classic TV Moments,' featured brief excerpts from particularly memorable episodes of their programmes: Lucy and Ethel in the candy factory, Rob under hypnosis, Mary getting her job at WJM. These spots showcased particularly canonized moments within 'classic TV,' presenting iconic images and sounds and reminding the viewer that Nick At Nite was *the* place to see them. Another series of spots from the same period, called 'Our Television Heritage', illustrated various minutiae from particular programmes. They served to celebrate 'conspicuous' inconsistencies or (more often) consistencies across a programme's run. Their subject matter ran from iconic elements of series (eg the 'Major Nelson Howl' from *I Dream of Jeannie*, the 'Reuben Hair Shift' from *The Partridge Family* or the 'Unger Leap' from *The Odd Couple*), while other times they revealed production histories (eg the recurrent appearance of Dick Van Dyke's personal assistant Frank Adamo in episodes of *The Dick Van Dyke Show* or the controversy concerning Barbara Eden's navel in *I Dream of Jeannie*). The 'television heritage' in this case could only be attained with close, attentive and (ostensibly) repeated viewing of each of these series: the citation of actor Tony Randall's 'Unger Leap' as an artefact from the annals of cultural history is *only* conceivable within a television environment which consistently shows reruns; the 'heritage' is not natural, but the result of repeated, contextual viewing.

A more recent campaign on TV Land, titled 'Times Change, Great TV Doesn't,' perfectly crystallizes the production of the television heritage, or at least Nick At Nite/TV Land's version of it. In these spots, scenes from old sitcoms are (mis)matched with stereotypical 'contemporary' dialogue. For example, in one spot, the demure sisters of *Petticoat Junction* are seen warbling a hillbilly version of the Spice Girls' 1996 global pop hit, 'Wannabe'. In another, *Family Affair*'s gruff Uncle Bill tells an excited Buffy and Jody that he's going to get a nose ring. In each spot, the dissonance of past and present is marked not only by the content of the dialogue, which highlights anachronisms, but also by the aural quality of the dubbing itself, which wilfully avoids any trace of verisimilitude (eg, the voices of the *Family Affair* children are obviously an adult male speaking in falsetto). The sensibility encouraged by these spots is somewhat ambiguous. It wants old, familiar, 'great TV' kept intact, as a 'safe haven' against the more complicated present. But it also wants to maintain a mocking sense of superiority, keeping these series' original discourses firmly in the past.

TV Land also features a more direct link to the televisual past in its 'retromercial' segments. 'Retromercials' are real television advertisements from years ago, run verbatim, except for a small logo in the corner. They extend the discourse of the television heritage outside specific programme texts and into the generally all-but-forgotten commercials. The temporal dissonance of past and present on TV Land is promoted – and potentially blurred – even more by these spots, which are run in the midst of contemporary ads, without any intros or outros. Accordingly, these spots, and their presentation, are perhaps the most interesting television heritage devices in the channels' arsenal, for they highlight (and in uncharacteristically unobtrusive ways, at that) the gaps in our acknowledgement of the television heritage. Significantly, this was a gap that was not *supposed* to be breached. Advertisers – who have always had, to say the least, an ambivalent relationship with the past – are somewhat wary of these spots, for they fear viewers will confuse them with their contemporary campaigns. TV Land even suggested that advertisers substitute their current ads with the oldies, a plan that, of course, has never materialized.

All in all, these programming devices reinforce Nick At Nite/TV Land's particular vision of the television heritage. Since they promote the channels in general – that is, the whole environment of Nick At Nite and TV Land – they are arguably more important than the rerun series themselves, providing the stylistic glue binding all the programmes. Without them, the reruns would run, but without being interpolated into the channels' distinctive reconstruction of the televisual past. The package has superseded the programme.

Conclusion: Beyond TV Land

The ambiguity of TV Land's 'Times Change' campaign is emblematic of our relationship with past television. To what extent has time, indeed, changed? Or is the continuous fascination with and programming of reruns indicative of a desire to see time arrested via television, to be able to encapsulate and endlessly replay history? How we – as viewers or scholars – 'remember' the television of a particular time is inescapably bound to how television remembers itself for us. Accordingly, by encapsulating the 'Fifties', 'Sixties', 'Seventies' and 'Eighties' as retro-packaged bundles of televisual style, Nick At Nite/TV Land produces a particularly effective television heritage, one that integrates itself seamlessly into the general stylistic flow of television.

However, Viacom is far from alone in this endeavour in the current television environment. Virtually every cable network that features reruns has adopted similar framing devices and programming strategies, including TNT, TBS, the Encore Multiplex, USA and the Sci-Fi Channel. Old programmes are attractive to new channels seeking a mixture of stable familiarity, retro or camp identities and, in the particular case of the Sci-Fi Channel, potentially loyal and lucrative cult audiences.[19] In addition, the development of the Internet has allowed programmers to solicit viewer/fan participation in their television heritage. Nick At Nite/TV Land, and each of the networks mentioned above, maintains informative web sites on their schedules, including detailed episode guides to their rerun series. Some of them host message boards and gauge viewers' demands for particular episodes, fostering a sense of community in their particular television heritage; ie, a place where regular viewers can have a say. Even old-fashioned, over-the-air broadcasting is taking up the lessons of Nick At Nite/TV Land. Citing the cable successes of 'classic branded programming,' Columbia Tri-Star television revived their old Screen Gems moniker in 1998 for a daily one-hour package of reruns drawn from their programming library, including *Bewitched, I Dream of Jeannie, The Partridge Family* and *Starsky and Hutch*. Episodes are run not in order, but thematically, in a manner similar to Nick At Nite's Very Very blocks. Trivia questions and TV-Land-like promos are interspersed within the hour each day, soliciting audience participation in recreating the television heritage. Furthermore, the television heritage is a mobile, if not entirely global, concept; despite the longstanding programme trade, TV cultures remain decidedly nationalist. Rerun cultures were slower to develop outside the US, in large part due to the limitations of state-sanctioned broadcast monopolies. However, some cable, satellite and even terrestrial channels in the UK, Japan and Australia have adopted a rerun ethos, running programmes from their respective television heritages.[20] As a corollary to this, television heritage can apparently be imported and exported: BBC America, the US cable outlet for the BBC, has introduced a whole new television heritage to its American audience, one which includes old British series such as *Dad's Army, The Young Ones* and *Some Mothers Do 'Ave 'Em*.

The television heritage is historical knowledge. The recent cultural past is continuously recirculated horizontally and vertically in TV schedule grids, web sites and home video collections. In an era of ongoing investment in past styles and popular cultures, reruns are perhaps television's ultimate form. By offering up the past in familiar, tantalizing morsels, Nick At Nite/TV Land provides a retro-stylized alternative to the present. Rerun economy and rerun culture are a permanent aspects of contemporary life, not only on television, but also off of it, where licensing has sprouted a wide variety of merchandise and media centred around programmes that are often decades old, producing the likes of *I Love Lucy* commemorative plates, *Starsky And Hutch* t-shirts and *Charlie's Angels* feature films. Still, rerun channels are only one aspect of a retro fixation that continues to pulse through popular culture. The mechanisms of history and memory are changing in the face of significant economic, technological and cultural shifts. In-depth historical studies, such as the other essays in this collection, are essential to our understanding of the media, but we need to attend to *how* history is produced through contemporary media as well, developing models to analyze more of these phenomena, as they represent the most dominant modes of contemporary cultural production.

Notes

The author wishes to acknowledge Gwen Burgess of Columbia Tri-Star television, for providing materials on Screen Gems; and the editor of this volume, for her sheer determination.

[1.] Even past *futures* have been reinvoked. In 1994, the 'imagineers' of Disney theme parks abandoned Tomorrowland's once-earnest vision of a high modernist, space age utopia and refashioned it as a retro world of *yesterday's* tomorrows, which drew on the futuristic (and vestigially fascist) visions of 1920s and 1930s architecture, design and science fiction. In the words of Paul Osterhout, the Disney designer in charge of Tomorrowland's makeover, 'It's an optimistic, romantic look at the future. It's somebody else's future.' See Christine Shenot, 'Tomorrow is a long time coming for Disney', *Wisconsin State Journal* 26 February 1995:14D. Of course, the Disney Corporation has a longstanding policy of refashioning pasts and presents into its own image, not only at its theme parks, but also at its equally produced communities, like Celebration, Florida; see Ross 1999.

2. Particularly influential among these works were Ang; Fiske; Jenkins; Morley; Penley; and Seiter et al.

3. See Browne; Dienst 3–35; Mullen; and Williams 1974:44–118.

4. See especially Caldwell; D'Acci; Mellencamp; Liebman; Spigel 1992; and Spigel and Curtin.

5. See Belfrage; Brienes; Halberstam; and Meyerowitz.

6. See Spigel 1995 for an interesting ethnographic study in this area.

7. The rest of the industrialized world, with historically more limited broadcasting systems, has only recently begun to experience 'rerun culture.' Great Britain has gone particularly nostalgia- and retro-mad over the last several years, with old BBC and ITV programming becoming popular all over again on the broadcast networks, satellite channels and home video.

8. Viacom, a company formed in 1971 ostensibly to handle CBS's syndication and cable holdings in compliance with the Federal Communication Commission's Financial Interest and Syndication (Fin-Syn) Rules, is now one of the largest media corporations in the world, particularly after its 1994 merger with Paramount Communications and its 1999 oedipal acquisition of CBS. Much of its explosive growth is due to the ever-increasing value of its programming libraries, which include series such as *Star Trek, I Love Lucy, The Honeymooners* and *Cheers*.

9. *Star Trek* has been the only 60-minute series to find long-term success in reruns.

10. For examples, see Bathrick; Hamamoto; Jones 1992; and Taylor.

11. Rich Brown, 'Nick at Nite becoming Nick at Nite-and-Day', *Broadcasting & Cable* 30 October 1995:15.

12. See Bergman; Ross 1989:139. I am using 'camp' here in the broad context of amusedly revelling in an object's aesthetic excesses, particularly when that object was taken more seriously in the past. Though long identified with homosexual cultural practices, camp has also become accessible to dominant, heterosexual society as well. Not to diminish the political significance of gay camp, but the camp sensibility also entails issues of class and cultural capital, in addition to normative sexuality. As David Bergman writes in the introductory essay of the *Camp Grounds* anthology, camp 'can be mobilized only within a very privileged setting . . . The playful excess of camp can resonate only against the already fluttering strains of extensive superfluousness' (1993:12–13).

13. In keeping with this spirit, television legend Dick Van Dyke was even appointed 'President' of Nick At Nite. This was certainly a continuation of the campy theme – a TV King for TV Land – but it was also an acknowledgement of the cultural ascendancy of television, as one of its all-time great comic actors became the de facto curator of its archives. Van Dyke appeared in ad campaigns promoting the 'new' Nick At Nite throughout 1992. During the early 1990s, he even sat on the channel's advisory board and helped pursue a variety of promotional and cultural projects centred on 'classic TV.' Allison Fahey, 'Van Dyke to lead Nick's move from "campy" to "classic" ', *Advertising Age* 4 May 1992:46; Joanne Lipman, 'Nick At Nite Uses Chairman to Make Pitch', *Wall Street Journal* 2 July 1992:B6.

14. Moreover, the presentations of already-nostalgic series like *Happy Days* and *The Wonder Years* mark a *double* retro appropriation. *Happy Days* was originally broadcast during the Fifties retro binge of the 1970s, while clearly Nick At Nite's aim in running it is to capitalize on the *Seventies* retro binge of the 1990s (a binge which included a *Happy Days*-themed

music video, 'Buddy Holly' by Weezer, which was directed by Spike Jonze). While the choice of *The Wonder Years* – produced from 1988 to 1992 but set in 1968–1972 – does not mark an Eighties retro trend, it does memorialize a programme that was all about memory to begin with.

[15.] An experiment to capitalize on this was tried in 1991, when the channel debuted its first original sitcom, *Hi Honey, I'm Home*. The premise had a 1950s TV family – replete with stereotypical 1950s gender and family roles and the ability to live in black and white – move to suburban New Jersey under the 'TV Family Relocation Program'. The interactions with their next-door neighbours – an equally stereotypical 1990s family with a harried, working-class feminist single mother, teenage son and preteen daughter – provided most of the comedy. Besides the interactions of 1950s and 1990s clichés, the programme was also heavily influenced by the wacky anarchic tone of *1960s* sitcoms such as *Bewitched*, *I Dream of Jeannie* and *My Favorite Martian*. See Bill Carter, 'ABC agrees to broadcast cable show', *New York Times* 30 May 1991:D1+.

[16.] These include familiar, well-cited segments like 'Job Switching' (*I Love Lucy*), 'Coast-To-Coast Big Mouth' (*The Dick Van Dyke Show*), 'The LSD Story' (*Dragnet*) and 'Chuckles Bites the Dust' (*The Mary Tyler Moore Show*).

[17.] It should be noted that these weekends have also provided TV scholars similar opportunities for 'indulging' in their (research) passions.

[18.] See also Mullen, for some thoughts on the significance of the short duration of these so-called 'interstitials.'

[19.] The Sci-Fi Channel has also featured event blocks called 'chain reactions,' which feature several hours of the same series.

[20.] It is significant, but not terribly surprising, that part of that heritage is derived from imported American programmes like *I Love Lucy* and *Star Trek*. In addition, it must be noted that the functional heritage of British or Australian television is much more limited in terms of history because relatively little television of the 1950s or even 1960s remains. Instead, in Great Britain at least, the 'golden age' of television centres largely around the 1970s and series such as *Dad's Army*, *Man About The House*, *Fawlty Towers* and *Doctor Who*.

CHAPTER 2

SELLING SOAP

POST-WAR TELEVISION SOAP OPERA AND THE AMERICAN HOUSEWIFE

Kristen Hatch

The housewife persists in the popular imagination as an icon of 1950s America. For some she represents a halcyon era when gender roles were sharply defined. For others she is a symbol of the decade's oppressive drive toward conformity, a prisoner in her 'comfortable concentration camp', as Betty Friedan described the middle-class home. In fact, neither interpretation accurately captures the contradictory meanings attached to female domesticity during the post-war era. Contrary to contemporary images of 1950s America, the period saw a rise in the employment of women, particularly white, middle-class married women. Further, the women who did devote themselves to the full-time care of the home and family were characterized in contradictory ways by their contemporaries. While cold-war rhetoric invoked the housewife and her domestic domain as symbols of national superiority, post-war Freudians blamed a myriad of social ills on the housewife, who was variously depicted as neurotic and over-doting or lazy and slothful. Joanne Meyerowitz attributes our misperception of the unanimity of popular opinion on the subject of female domesticity to the influence of Betty Friedan's *The Feminine Mystique*, the 1963 treatise that helped to launch second-wave feminism in the United States. In fact, examining popular magazines of the decade preceding the publication of Friedan's bestseller, Meyerowitz argues that the popular press was full of articles that explored 'the same central contradiction – between domestic ideals and individual achievement – that Betty Friedan addressed' (Meyerowitz 1994:232).

However, if the housewife was anything but a stable and uniformly conceived category, as a category she did play a crucial role in the development of network broadcasting, a fact that created its own set of contradictions. Michelle Hilmes argues that the bifurcation of the radio schedule – with prestige shows reserved for prime time and the daytime schedule inhabited by

shows derided for their crass appeal to housewives – was not the result of
economics alone. Rather, it was in the networks' interest to displace criticism
of commercialism in broadcasting onto daytime programming:

> Broadcasters during this period of contested credibility had two formidable projects
> to undertake. One was exploiting an economic base that clearly rested on the
> female purchaser of household products . . . The other . . . [was to] convince regu-
> lators that their mission consisted as much of public service programming as of
> sheer commercialism . . . in order to rebuff educational broadcasters' claims on the
> spectrum . . . [A] way of achieving this end was to create a differentiation between
> daytime and nighttime programming, by which daytime became the venue for a
> debased kind of commercialized, feminized mass culture – heavily dominated by
> advertising agencies – in contrast to the more sophisticated, respectable, and mas-
> culine-characterized arena of prime time, also dominated by agencies but subject to
> stricter network controls. (Hilmes 1997:153–154)

By the same reasoning, with the establishment of regular television schedules
in the 1950s, the networks depended upon the fiction of a clearly differentiated audience, with daytime programming suited to the putative interests of
housewives, to absorb much of the criticism of the new medium.

Likewise, sponsors and advertising agencies found the prospect of a segment of the programming schedule reserved for a homogeneous audience of
homemakers appealing. Market research indicated that women made most of
the nation's household purchases. By defining daytime programs as appealing to housewives, sponsors like Proctor & Gamble and General Mills could
fine-tune their appeals to women without alienating a 'general' (implicitly
male) audience that might balk at being identified with this disparaged category of viewer. Further, because daytime was devalued, networks charged
advertisers less for shows aired during the day and the FCC permitted more
advertisements to be aired per program than during prime time, making daytime highly profitable for sponsors.

Clearly, the fantasy of a female audience of middle-class housewives at
home during the day was appealing to networks and sponsors alike. However, the very stereotypes that contributed to the denigration of the housewife
(and hence the profitability of daytime) posed a problem when daytime television was introduced. If the housewife was meant to be labouring in the
home during the day, how was she to find the time to watch television? This
conundrum influenced the early development of television soap opera, as did
the persistent question of how housewives were to develop a fulfilling public
identity while confined to the domestic sphere. The result was a genre riddled
with its own contradictions, which were gradually resolved in such a way as
to permit the housewife to develop a rewarding sense of self through her
activities in the home. While the radio and television serial dramas of the
post-war period drew upon women's sense of patriotic duty, suggesting that
women could best *serve the nation* through their work in the home, by the

1960s the manner in which the shows appealed to women had undergone a significant transformation. Now white, middle-class women were offered the promise of a satisfying *identity* through their work in the home.

Serial drama was already a well-established staple of network radio by the time the television networks began airing programs during the day. However, with the move from radio to television, the narrative elements of daytime serial drama changed dramatically. The most popular of the radio soaps featured women in a variety of roles and locales, providing listeners with a means to escape the drudgery of their lives within the home. The soaps that succeeded on television, on the other hand, focused squarely on domesticity, imagining the home as a site of drama and intrigue.

On radio, many of the most long-running soap operas focused on the adventures of working women. Ma Perkins, in a show bearing the same name (1933–1960), operated a lumberyard and performed a motherly role for the members of her community. *Myrt and Marge* (1931–46) were a mother-and-daughter vaudeville team. *Woman in White* (1938–48) focused on a hospital nurse. *Joyce Jordan, Girl Intern* (later *MD*, 1938–55) was a young medic. Portia, in *Portia Faces Life* (1940–51), was a lawyer. And in *This Is Nora Drake* (1947–51), Nora was the assistant to the head of a mental clinic. Alternatively, daytime dramas described the lives of young women from humble backgrounds who married wealthy men, thus circumventing the quotidian problems most women faced in the home. *Betty and Bob* (1932–40) was about a secretary who married her wealthy boss. The announcer on *Our Gal Sunday* (1937–55) daily wondered if 'this girl from a mining town in the West [could] find happiness as the wife of a wealthy and titled Englishman.' And *Backstage Wife* (1935–59) told the story of 'a little Iowa girl who married Larry Noble, handsome matinee idol, dream sweetheart of a million other women, and her struggle to keep his love in the complicated atmosphere of backstage life.' Finally, *Stella Dallas* (1937–55) was 'a continuation on the air of the true-to-life story of mother love and sacrifice in which Stella Dallas saw her beloved daughter, Laurel, marry into wealth and society, and, realizing the differences in their tastes and worlds, went out of Laurel's life' – only to be drawn back into it by such tragedies as Laurel's abduction by wealthy Arabs and such. (Schemering 1985)

Television serial dramas did not immediately take on the contours that now define the genre. Rather, those developed during the medium's nascence continued the trend toward stories focused on working women. *A Time to Live* (1954) was about a proofreader who became an investigative reporter. *The Seeking Heart* (1954) had a young doctor become romantically involved with her married boss. Decades before Mary Richards arrived in Minneapolis, *Golden Windows* (1954) featured a young heroine who left her fiancé to pursue a career in New York City. *The Greatest Gift* (1954–55) explored the difficulties faced by a woman doctor returning home after serving in the Army Medical Corps in Korea. *Portia Faces Life* (1954–55) brought the radio story of a lawyer to television. *Woman with a Past* (1954) focused on a New York dress designer. And *Today Is Ours* (1958) was about a divorcee who became an assistant principal at a high school.

Other programmes experimented with the narrative conventions of the daytime serial. *A Date with Life* (1955–56) was an anthology serial, with different stories stretching over periods ranging from four to six weeks, tied together by the direct-address commentary of two brothers. *Modern Romances* (1954–58) was a more successful attempt at daytime anthology, based on stories from the magazine of the same name; likewise, *Way of the World* (1955) was an anthology serial with stories drawn from women's magazines. *One Man's Experience* and *One Woman's Experience* (1952–53) were back-to-back anthology dramas that extended over the course of a week and focused on the story of an extraordinary man and woman respectively. Both *The First Hundred Years* (1950–52) and *The Egg and I* (1951–52) experimented with serialized comedy. *Follow Your Heart* (1953–54) was a serial adventure drama featuring spies and mobsters. And *The Verdict is Yours* (1957–62) was a courtroom drama in which cases extended over the course of a week or two and were argued by attorneys, not actors, with the outcome determined by a twelve-member jury drawn from the audience.

However, while the decade saw a great deal of experimentation with regard to plot elements and narrative techniques, the highest audience ratings consistently went to home-centred dramas. In 1951, two of the top-rated shows focused on single-parent households in which young widows struggled against poverty and malicious family members in their efforts to bring up their children alone. *Search for Tomorrow* (1951–86) centred on the trials and tribulations of a woman bringing up a young daughter and fighting against the interference of her domineering in-laws. *Love of Life* (1951–80) was also about a woman raising a child on her own, this time struggling against the machinations of her selfish sister. They were soon imitated by *Valiant Lady* (1953–57), which focused on another single mother, and *The Secret Storm* (1954–74), which offered a twist on the formula, focusing on a widower raising his three children with a scheming sister-in-law standing in the way of his happiness.

The Guiding Light (1937-present), the longest-running soap opera in the history of the genre, was the only radio soap opera successfully to make the transition to television, and its creator, Irna Phillips, the only prominent writer of serial drama to remain a formidable force in television. Thus the show and its creator bear close study in a consideration of the adaptation of serial drama for television. *The Guiding Light* differed from its competitors in that, rather than focusing on one central character, it had an extended family at the core of its narrative. With its focus on an entire family and its place in the community, rather than on an individual, *The Guiding Light* bore a closer resemblance to the shows that have come to define the genre than did its competitors. This may be because its creator, Irna Phillips, and her protégés,

Agnes Nixon and William Bell, went on to create many of the most popular representatives of the genre, among them *As the World Turns* (1956-present), *Another World* (1964–1999), *One Life to Live* (1968-present), *All My Children* (1970-present) and *The Young and the Restless* (1973-present). However, even within Phillips' oeuvre, the daytime drama underwent a number of important transformations during its first decade on television.

Phillips was already well established as a radio serial writer by the time *The Guiding Light* appeared on television. She is credited with having invented serial drama when she wrote and acted in *Painted Dreams* in 1930, which was soon followed by *Today's Children* (1933–37; 1943–50), *Woman in White* (1938–48), *A Brighter Day* (1948–56), *The Right to Happiness* (1939–56) and *The Road of Life* (1937–59). Her first attempt at television drama, *These Are My Children* (1949) failed miserably. However, Phillips remained undeterred and produced two kinescopes of *The Guiding Light* at her own expense in order to prove to Proctor & Gamble that the show could work on television. Her ploy was a success, and the show aired on both radio and television from 1952. In 1954, *The Brighter Day* then premiered on television, followed by *As the World Turns* in 1956 and *Young Doctor Malone* in 1958. The first half-hour soap opera, *As the World Turns* immediately became the most popular daytime serial on television, and Phillips was to remain a dominant force in daytime programming until shortly before her death in 1973.

Phillips' television plots were centred squarely on the home, demonstrating that the stuff of women's lives – marriage, parenting, and the complications that arise from extended families – are worthy of drama. A character's marriage did not signal the end of her story, but the beginning, since Phillips' plots explored familial relationships as much as they did romantic ones. However, far from representing the family as a stable structure upon which to build one's life, Phillips' narratives create families that must repeatedly face the threat of self-destruction. Marriage is no guarantor of stability. Husbands stray and wives run away, couples bicker, misunderstandings lead to annulment or divorce, and disagreements lead to murder. Nor are the ties between parent and child absolute. Paternity is often in doubt, children are given up for adoption, adopted children are reclaimed by their birth parents, children die, run away, or simply reject their families. In other words, the family is a source of endless anxiety, but, even as individual family ties prove to be impermanent, the ideal of the family remains unshakeable.

During soap opera's tenure on radio and into its early television years, Phillips' shows were characterized by a didactic presentational style that constructed the audience as requiring moral guidance and education. Robert Allen traces the origins of the serial drama's moral didacticism to domestic novel of the nineteenth-century (Allen 1985:148). During World War II soap opera had been the target of much criticism, accused of heightening the neurotic tendencies of their listeners. Ellen Seiter reports that Irna Phillips spent as much as $45,000 defending the genre during the war years (Seiter 1989:31). Further, Phillips deliberately incorporated public service messages into her plots, earning praise from various social agencies ranging from the War Department to the Food and Drug Administration.[1] The development of the genre for television raised additional concerns about women's work within the home. Lynn Spigel has shown that, when television was introduced into the domestic sphere of the middle-class home, one widespread concern was that it would distract the housewife from her chores. Writing to Proctor & Gamble in 1948, Irna Phillips articulates these fears:

> As you know, I have had very little interest in television from a daytime standpoint and unless a technique could be evolved whereby the auditory could be followed without the constant attention given to the visual as far as the home maker is concerned, I see no future, for a number of years, in televising the serial story. In other words . . . if once a week a woman could take a few minutes off to look and when she's not able to look but only listen she will not feel a sense of being cheated, then I believe something could be done with the daytime serial if the cost is not too great.[2]

Thus, the television soap opera represented a double threat – to women's productivity within the home and, with the widespread perception of the genre as maudlin and inane, her mental well-being.

It is not surprising, then, that within the context of dramas that highlighted the problems associated with women whose lives were devoted to home and family, a patriarchal voice of authority governed the interpretation of events. *The Guiding Light* was originally conceived as a story about a minister and his congregation. Stories would centre on the problems faced by the community served by Dr Ruthledge, the 'guiding light' of his community, who would offer helpful words of advice in times of crisis. Indeed, some episodes were devoted entirely to Ruthledge's sermons, which were eventually collected and published as a book that sold over 300,000 copies. After the actor who played Ruthledge joined the army in 1944, a succession of ministers assumed the role of moral beacon within the show's narrative. When *The Guiding Light* was introduced on television in 1952, the characters consulted another minister, Dr Keeler, for advice about their complicated lives. However, the sponsors were concerned that the character amounted to dead weight, since no story lines revolved around him specifically. After pursuing a story line in which Dr Keeler's sister is murdered, Phillips dropped the character, and other male characters within the drama assumed the eponymous role of 'guiding light'.

Reinforcing the moral advice offered by these fatherly ministers were the practical words of wisdom provided by the family patriarchs in Phillips' narratives. As *The Guiding Light* evolved, the Bauer family gradually became the show's centre. Papa Bauer was a German immigrant, a carpenter with three grown children, Bill, Meta, and Trudy. While the action tended to focus on the younger Bauers, Papa Bauer was always present to offer kindly advice, intervening when his son and daughters seemed to go astray. In a 1952 plot line, Bill's work takes him out of town, often in the company of another woman, which makes Bertha jealous. Papa advises, 'When you're in the house, she's patient. When you're out of the house, the patience goes too. I think Bertha she ain't all wrong. The place for a husband and papa is at home.'[3] Likewise, when Meta and her husband, Joe, quarrel Papa helps to negotiate a resolution to their differences: 'Willie, you go right to the telephone and tell Joe that Meta comes home tomorrow and that he should be at the airport to meet her. The foot I am putting down.'[4] By contrast, Bertha's mother contributes to her daughter's marital difficulties through her meddling. (Indeed, mothers-in-law tend to contribute inordinately to the show's plot complications.)[5]

In the radio shows, these male voices of authority were reinforced by the presence of an announcer who set the stage in the strictly aural medium and welded the soap opera narrative to the commercial messages. Robert Allen suggests that in this way the radio announcer positioned himself (announcers were invariably male) as a mediator between the audience and the characters. Further, the announcer guided the audience to the correct interpretation of plot developments. A 1945 episode of *Today's Children* illustrates the point. A nurse-in-training, whose husband is fighting overseas, discovers that she is pregnant. Desperate to complete her training, she tells her doctor she must have a 'profession to fall back on in case [her husband doesn't survive the war].' But her doctor warns that her first duty must be to the unborn baby: 'I know that nursing has become a means of livelihood. But your first job is to see that new life gets here.' The would-be nurse insists, though, that she has no choice but to pursue her career, assuring the doctor that she will be careful. But the audience's faith in her decision is undercut by the announcer, who wonders aloud, 'How can a nurse be careful? She can't be careful and continue her training, can she?'

Although the announcer's role was greatly diminished on television, the shows continued to enunciate moral lessons by referring to the advice of off-screen experts. On *The Guiding Light*, for instance Bertha Bauer may not be the ideal housewife, but with the help of her paediatrician she does know what's best for her child. In an argument with her husband over whether or not to feed the baby before they go to bed, she tells Bill, 'My paediatrician told me to take him off his 10:00 bottle.' Bill testily replies, 'Your paediatrician doesn't happen to live here.' But Bertha's rational response echoes the advice of childhood development experts: 'Look, he'll cry for a few nights, but not because he's hungry, because he wants a little attention. We're not going to spoil him.'[6] Similarly, in a later episode of the program, a pregnant Kathy prepares for her role as a mother by reading up on child psychology, explaining, 'I want to know all there is to know about children, the phases they go through, the understanding and guidance they need.'[7]

The message, that mothers should bolster their instinctive maternal knowledge with advice from medical experts, reinforces the authority of commercials in which doctors and scientists offer housewives advice on how to maintain healthy children and germ-free homes. Likewise, the masculine voice of authority created within the show's narratives and by the announcers is duplicated in the advertisements, in which men extol the qualities of the products being advertised. Only on rare occasions do women exhort viewers to buy the sponsors' products. Rather, male spokespeople are associated with particular brands ('Dick Stark for Crisco'). Further, the ads repeatedly cite doctors and scientists as experts to authenticate their claims for the beneficial properties of their soaps, foods, and cleaning products. Doctors recommend Crisco because 'it's digestible' and Duz cleans better than the competing detergent 'when tested under ordinary home conditions.'

Oddly enough, early advertisements show little appreciation of women's labour in the home. Commercials aired during television soap operas in the early 1950s elide any reference to the marital discord so central to the dramas themselves, and it is the housewife herself who is perceived to derive the most pleasure from her own labour. The ads are full of images of happy housewives, made exuberant by the use of various products. Tide gets the wash so clean 'you'll really want to sing.' Wives are so pleased with Crisco, they beam as their husbands eat fried chicken. Spic and Span is so easy to use, the housewife happily hums while she scrubs her kitchen walls.

But there was a discordant note in this symphony of patriarchal voices. The narratives themselves often depict women whose feminine, usually maternal, values are at odds with a male-dominated society. This becomes particularly clear when a popular character is on trial for murder, a plot device that was used repeatedly in Phillips' shows. These trials pit an alienating world of law and science against the noble motives of the woman who has been accused of a crime. While the shows never suggest that there is anything inherently wrong with the judicial system, they do suggest that women are somewhat at the mercy of a masculine system of knowledge and understanding that is antithetical to their own. Outside the sphere of home and family, women are subject to masculine rules and values, and women's alienation from science and technology will be the source of danger.

In a plot line from the late 1940s, for instance, Meta Bauer kills her husband because he bullies their son, Chuckie. The audience is encouraged to sympathize with Meta, who has acted out of concern for the well-being of her son. When the police arrive, she is disoriented, still holding the gun, telling her dead husband, 'I told you not to force Chuckie to take boxing lessons' and assuring Chuckie, 'Your father won't hurt you any more. Don't be afraid, he can't hurt you.'[8] The legal system descends on Meta, and a trial ensues in which a cold-hearted, legalistic DA prosecutes the woman for protecting her child. Eventually, Meta is exonerated, found not guilty by reason of insanity.

Several years later, in 1952, Meta's stepdaughter, Kathy, is on trial for the murder of her husband, Bob. As with Meta, Kathy's values put her at the mercy of the judicial system. Although Kathy did not commit the crime, she feels responsible for her husband's death because she had asked that their marriage be annulled minutes before he wrecked the car. The DA interprets her guilty behaviour as evidence that she is legally responsible for Bob's death and aggressively pursues the case against the young woman. Kathy is finally released when her father, having tracked down the auto mechanic who worked on Bob's car, provides evidence that the car wreck was the result of faulty brakes. Because she is ignorant of both the law and technology, Kathy's freedom depends on the expertise and benevolence of the men around her. And while the judicial system is never challenged, women's relationship to it is demonstrated to be problematic.[9]

Women in the audience clearly responded to the dilemmas their favourite characters faced when put on trial, and tended to put more trust in their interpretation of character than in the forensic evidence brought out at trial, which suggests that these representations of conflict between masculine and feminine modes of understanding had resonance in their own lives. In a 1948 plot of *Today's Children*, Bertha Schultz is on trial for murdering Tom Lemming. In an effort to gauge the audience's response to the show, the sponsor solicited reactions from fans, promising that they would be the jury for the trial; their verdict as to Bertha's guilt or innocence would determine her fate. Listeners were unanimous in their support of Schultz, a verdict based not on the physical evidence, which clearly implicated Schultz, but on an analysis of her character and motives. Typical is the letter from a Chicago woman who explained:

> Bertha Schultz is absolutely innocent of Tom's death. Unworthy as he was, she loved him far too dearly to ever have had even a thought of such a crime . . . Her words sounded as if she had known nothing of it before, and yet there was something under the surface that seemed to indicate that she was not surprised, though at the same time she was so cool and casual about it that one was led to feel his death gave her satisfaction, not regret, though I believe she also expressed herself as still loving him . . . About the fingerprints, I do not know . . . I think [Bertha] became hysterical, immediately felt that she would be blamed, and ran down the back stairs. How her fingerprints appeared on the instrument of death, I do not know.[10]

Nearly twenty years later, in a 1966 plot line for *As the World Turns*, Ellen is on trial for killing her son's nanny. As in Meta's case years earlier, Ellen is guilty of the crime, but her act is justified because, in the words of Irna Phillips, '[t]his recent tragedy . . . was not an act of violence; it was Ellen's maternal instinct to protect her son – a sheer effort to try to stop Franny from telling Dan something she knew would cruelly injure him perhaps permanently.'[11] While the judicial system proves to be benign (Ellen is freed in the end) the narrative suggests yet again that women's needs and values contradict those of the dominant masculine culture. But other changes had taken place in Phillips' drama, eliminating the contradiction between the chorus of male voices – of priests, fathers, doctors, announcers and product spokespeople telling women within the narrative and, by extension, in the audience what to do – and the repeated narratives in which women are at odds with patriarchal authority. Within the realm of the soap opera, male authority was no longer paramount. The didacticism of the 1950s soap opera and its advertisements gradually faded, giving way to a more sympathetic tone that celebrated women's abilities in the home. The method for encouraging housewives to embrace their domestic role no longer turned on patriotic duty, but on the pleasurable sense of identity she might achieve through her domestic role.

The conditions that had helped to create didacticism in the post-war soap opera had changed. In the wake of game show scandals, the networks turned their attention to prime time schedules, wresting programming control away from sponsors. However, daytime continued to be the sponsor's domain, owned by their sponsors rather than the networks. At the same time, Newt Minow's famous description of television as a 'vast wasteland' had shifted attention from the vilification of women's programming to that of television in general, leaving daytime programmes relatively free of public scrutiny. In this context, sponsors and writers spent less time justifying the genre. Finally, the rhetoric surrounding female domesticity had radically shifted. Whereas during the late 1940s and throughout much of the 1950s, women were exhorted to leave the work force so that returning service men might have their jobs, in the 1960s women's domesticity began to be framed in relation to the budding women's movement.

Within this context, the patriarchal, didactic tone of the narratives gradually faded as women's voices and opinions began to dominate. This can be seen in the development of the character Bertha Bauer on *The Guiding Light*. When the show was introduced to television in 1952, Bert was a shrewish housewife, a negative example to viewers at home. Her criticism drove her husband, Bill, out of their house and into the bars, where he inevitably met another woman. Only through the intervention of Papa Bauer and Dr Keeler were Bert and Bill able to survive the crisis in their marriage. Fourteen years later, in a 1966 episode of the same show, Bert is a model wife and mother, while Bill is a drunk and a philanderer. Far from the shrewish demeanour she exhibited in earlier episodes, Bert now reprimands her son for criticizing Bill rather than showing sympathy for the man who is 'like a wounded thing, suffering.'[12] Empathetic to the point of relinquishing her own claims to emotion, she has come to represent the ideal homemaker.[13]

Likewise, the virtual elimination of an announcer contributed to this shift in the manner in which the audience was addressed. The other top-rated television soap operas of the 1950s – *Love of Life* and *Search for Tomorrow, The Secret Storm* and *Valiant Lady* – had retained the practice of having an announcer recap episodes by interpreting the characters' actions. However, when *The Guiding Light* went on the air in 1952, the announcer's role was limited to the repetition of the bland phrase, 'We'll learn more about this in a

moment,' before the commercial break. And within the decade, other shows
were following suit. As a result, right and wrong were no longer determined
by an announcer, but interpreted by the audience, largely through visual
cues.

Whereas earlier television soaps employed the visual register of the medium for little more than establishing the space in which a scene was played,
by the end of the 1950s, viewers who took the time to look at the screen were
provided with privileged information. Early kinescopes of *The Guiding Light*
display minimal visual effect, due in no small part to the technological limitations of the new medium. More often than not, a static camera captures the
characters in medium two-shots, widening occasionally to accommodate character movement. A 1963 episode of the same show provides striking testimony to the visual transformation of the genre during its first decade on
television. It opens with an extreme close-up of the face of Bertha Bauer. The
camera moves awkwardly to the equally emotive face of Papa Bauer, slipping in and out of focus as it pans in tight close-up from one character to the
next, finally resting on Meta Bauer while she calls the hospital to inquire into
the condition of Julie Bauer, Bert's daughter-in-law, who is pregnant and in a
coma. In the following scene, Bert's son waits anxiously at the hospital, ex-
pressionistically lit through the slats of Venetian blinds as he voices his concern that his wife might not survive the birth of their child. And in the delivery
room, viewers are introduced to the obstetrician through a particularly striking point-of-view shot; from the vantage point of the birth canal we see the
doctor's face peering between the pregnant mother's legs, forceps moving
toward the camera lens. Clearly, the show was pushing the limits of the medium, exploring new ways to convey emotional meaning in the absence of the
explanatory voice of the announcer. As a result, the viewer assumed the
announcer's mantle of expertise, interpreting characters' actions and emotions for him or herself.

A similar transformation took place within the shows' advertisements as
the sponsors began to address women as experts within the home, acknowledging the difficulty of their labour while also offering a solution to their
problems. A comparison of two Ivory soap commercials bears striking testimony to this shift in the manner in which housewives were addressed in soap
opera advertisements. In a 1952 Ivory commercial, the off-screen announcer
asks a doctor about the photographs of babies that decorate his walls. The
doctor replies that he 'brought all of these little girls into the world,' managing to overlook their mothers' role in the process, and explains that one 'poses
for magazines now' and another 'was voted prettiest girl at her university,'
implying that he is also responsible for their beauty because he sent them
home with Ivory soap. With his words, the camera zooms into the individual
baby pictures, which dissolve into moving images of young women going
about their daily routines, unaware that they are being observed.[14] Thus both
the doctor and the announcer are in a privileged position, mastering the new

television technology that permits them to observe women in their homes without themselves being perceived. And women's value, it is suggested, lies in their beauty; the women are not observed working, but reading and admiring themselves before the mirror. Given that the girls being observed are models and college students, and that they have been introduced first as babies, one would imagine that the viewer is meant to identify as a mother to these girls, rather than as one of them. Thus the housewife, the implicit viewer for the shows and their advertisements, remains off screen and is never directly addressed within the advertisement.

Ten years later, in a 1962 advertisement for the same product, the sponsor's strategy has shifted radically. The announcer (still off screen) directly addresses the housewife in her home. Not just any housewife, she is an expert mother; 'You have 14 children Mrs Cruxton . . . What a handsome family.' Mrs Cruxton chats amiably with the announcer, explaining that she has managed to keep her hands looking as young as her teenage daughter's, 'even though [she washes] mounds of dishes,' by using Ivory soap. The commercial ends with an image of Mrs Cruxton and her oldest daughter washing dishes together. No longer positioned off screen, the housewife has become the expert in the home, one who is passing on her secrets for success to her daughter as well as to the audience.

Gone are the singing housewives and didactic announcers of the previous decade. In their place are women who have successfully overcome the difficulties of managing a busy household through their use of the sponsors' product. While earlier advertisements had represented the housewife's work in the home as a pleasurable pastime, later ones suggest that her labour is equivalent in both value and difficulty to that performed by her husband in the office. One remarkable ad suggests the equivalence visually, through the use of a split screen, suggesting that both husband and wife use sedatives in order to preserve a marriage frayed by the daily stress of their jobs. It begins with a couple kissing each other goodbye before the husband leaves for work. In voiceover, we are informed, 'Most days start pleasurably. Both you and your husband feel fresh, rested, ready to face the world.' The image shifts to a split screen, on the left of which is the husband at the office, while on the right the wife is in the kitchen. 'But when the tensions of a busy day boil up within you, by late afternoon your nerves are upset.' The ad ends with the suggestion that the couple stop and take Miles Nirvene to soothe their nerves, rather than bickering over dinner.

More common are the advertisements in which the housewife's skill in running the home is acknowledged when her work is temporarily performed by others. Husbands are particularly popular in this regard. An ad for Comet has a new father cleaning the house while his wife recovers from the birth of their first baby. When he's stumped as to how to clean the dirty sink, the off-screen announcer suggests he try Comet. Successful at last, the father brags to the announcer, 'Give me a can opener for food (holding up a wrench) and

Comet for cleaning up and housework's a cinch!' While reinforcing the ideal of separate spheres for men and women, the advertisement suggests that, far from being a 'cinch', housework is best left to the experts in the home. Other advertisements use paid labourers to get a similar message across by equating the housewife with professionals who work outside the home. The skipper of a boat, the woman who runs a boarding house, the superintendent of an apartment building and Josephine the plumber all share with housewives their secrets for getting the job done.[15] No longer are the male announcers the primary means of conveying household advice. Rather, this advice is provided by housewives and others whose work involves cooking and cleaning within the domestic sphere.

The net result of the changes undergone by the soap opera in its first decade on television was to help the housewife to articulate a sense of identity and self worth through her domestic role. While earlier shows and advertisements had adopted a didactic tone in addressing the implied audience of housewives, by the 1960s, soap operas and their advertisements had adapted to address women's need for a fulfilling sense of identity. And, whereas the earlier shows had inadvertently produced a tension between the distrust of patriarchal authority within the narratives and the patriarchal mode in which they addressed the audience, by the 1960s television serial drama had resolved this contradiction by creating narratives and advertisements that worked to affirm women's authority within the home.

However, while it is tempting to read this shift simply as a sign of the growing recognition of women's labour, it must also be understood as a method for reinforcing women's position as care-givers within the home and family. By giving women this feeling of power within their own lives, serial dramas encouraged women to participate actively in the regulation of gender roles. The shift from a didactic tone to one that encouraged women to interpret the dramas for themselves, and from narratives that positioned father figures as the central voice of authority to ones that centred on empathetic mothers, helped women to associate emotional care-giving with pleasure and a sense of mastery. Sandra Lee Bartky argues that unreciprocated care-giving may provide a sense of power and control to women who are otherwise disempowered within our culture. By subsuming their own feelings into those of the other, women may achieve an otherwise unattainable sense of agency and personal efficacy. However, as Bartky reminds us, the feeling of power is not equivalent to the having of power. In fact, the provision of emotional sustenance involves great peril to the care-giver, who risks disaffection and loss of her own sense of reality. By empathizing with the other, the care-giver adopts the other's perspective on the world, losing sight of her own moral guideposts.[16]

Likewise, while the advertisements aired during the daytime dramas began to address women as experts in their own right, they did so in a manner that encouraged women to define themselves in relation to their ability to perform well their work within the home. Bartky argues that, in a culture in which women are consistently devalued, keeping up appearances becomes a means of achieving a sense of control. The housewife's husband and children, as well as her own body, are symbols of her abilities within the home. By presenting herself to the world well-groomed and well-dressed, looking young and attractive, she conveys the sense that she does her work thoroughly, with style and ease. As a consequence, through the use of the sponsors' products, she is offered the promise of mastery over herself and her environment. Advertisements from the 1960s offer their products as a secret weapon in the battle to keep up appearances. (The catch line for one detergent is 'Ready, Aim, Salvo!') Viewers are reminded that their children's appearance will make public the extent of their mothering abilities, making the decision as to which detergent to buy all the more important. Similarly, in commercial after commercial, housewives are shown to engage in friendly competition with their neighbours. Duncan Hines has a savvy housewife reluctantly give away her 'secret recipe' for the cake she has prepared from a mix, while Pillsbury has a housewife serving cookies she made from frozen dough to an admiring neighbour.

In this manner, the soap opera offered women a means of resolving the tension between their domestic role and the need for a sense of individual achievement that Betty Friedan had articulated. Indeed, Irna Phillips saw her characters as spokespeople for women whose identity remained linked to the home. In an interview, she explains, 'Nancy [Hughes, a central character on *As the World Turns*] is my answer to the "feminine mystique". She is doing exactly what she needs to make her happy. "Why," she once asked, "do I have to go out and prove myself at a political rally?" '[17] Thus both the narratives and the advertisements aired during soap operas encouraged their imagined audience of white, middle-class women to cling to the identities they developed through their work in the home rather than hoping to find that identity through paid labour or participation in the public sphere.

Notes

[1.] Interestingly, while Phillips had once proposed that television soap operas incorporate the sponsors' messages in a similar way – having two women engaged in conversation as they did their wash, for example – the sponsors rejected this method of product endorsement.

[2.] Letter to William Ramsey, 7 September 1948 (Irna Phillips Collection).

[3.] *The Guiding Light*, 10 July 1952 (UCLA Film and Television Archive).

[4.] *Ibid*.

[5.] Unlike *The Guiding Light* and the shows she was to create thereafter, Phillips' earlier shows had revolved around mothers (*Today's Children*) or working women struggling to decide between marriage and career (*Women in White*). However, even within these narratives, mothers, though full of advice, are often the cause of grief, prompting one viewer to accuse Phillips of 'mother phobia' (Museum of Television and Radio Seminar, Agnes Nixon).

6. *The Guiding Light*, 30 October 1952 (UCLA Film and Television Archive).

7. *The Guiding Light*, 30 December 1952 (UCLA Film and Television Archive).

8. Undated plot outline for *The Guiding Light* (Irna Phillips Collection, University of Wisconsin).

9. Interestingly, Phillips had included a similar plot line in another of her serial dramas and was cautioned by the ad agency not to include too pointed a critique of the judicial system within the show's narrative: 'I think, Irna, that it would be well to consider changing this speech so that Helen could make her bitterness apply to men only, and not to the injustice of our present judicial system.' (Letter from Gilbert Ralston, Compton Advertising Agency, 3 June 1942, Irna Phillips Collection) As a result, a reasoned complaint about the treatment of women prisoners was transformed into a generalized rant about men.

10. Letter from Catherine H. Apgar, Chicago, IL, 5 June 1944 (Irna Phillips Collection).

11. Open letter from Proctor & Gamble, *Daytime Doings*, June 1966, n. 10 (Irna Phillips Collection).

12. *The Guiding Light*, 7 June 1966 (UCLA Film and Television Archive).

13. The dramatic change in Bert Bauer's character may be partially attributed to the change in the show's head writer, which occurred in 1958 when Agnes Nixon took over for Phillips so that Phillips could devote herself to *As the World Turns*. However, similar changes were to be seen on *As the World Turns* as well, where Nancy Hughes became a more likeable character as the show developed and the patriarchs of both of the shows' central families, the Hughes and the Lowells, faded in importance.

14. *The Guiding Light*, February 1952 (UCLA Film and Television Archive).

15. The advertisements also provide an interesting class commentary. The housewives in the ads are implicitly middle class, looking attractive and well groomed as they face problems with their plumbing or a broken washing machine. The labourers who come to do the minor repairs in their home wear stained overalls and often speak in accents associated with New York neighbourhoods. So, while there are similarities between the housewife and the worker that make it possible for them to trade tips on household chores, their differences suggest that the housewife is in a position of enviable privilege.

16. Perhaps the loss of personal moral perspective helps to explain why soap operas have been able to introduce controversial subject matter to a degree that is somewhat surprising given the presumed conservatism of the shows' audiences. Adultery, illegitimacy and divorce were staples of the genre long before they became commonplace on prime-time network television.

17. Date and publication unknown. Irna Phillips Collection.

CHAPTER 3

'STUDY OF A MAD HOUSEWIFE'

PSYCHIATRIC DISCOURSE, THE SUBURBAN HOME AND THE CASE OF GRACIE ALLEN

Allison McCracken

The rebellious and dizzy housewife was a common and popular character in early US television comedy. Lucy Ricardo of *I Love Lucy*, Joan Davis of *I Married Joan* and Gracie Allen of *The Burns and Allen Show* are frequently cited as the most famous representatives of this type; Lucy physically and aggressively rebels against her role as housewife, while Gracie Allen verbally confounds those around her. These characters have long been of interest to feminist critics, who have focused on how their comedy and pathos derives in part from their seeming lack of fit in the domestic world and their frequent subversions of domestic order, qualities which set them apart from later naturalized 1950s housewives like June Cleaver of *Leave it to Beaver* and Margaret Anderson of *Father Knows Best*.[1] One reason for their uniqueness, according to critics, was that they reflected a vaudeville aesthetic, based in familiar comic stereotypes (including the unruly wife), rather than an aesthetic of theatrical realism.[2]

Because of its roots in urban, working-class culture, vaudeville-influenced programming suggested class, gender and ethnic tensions that were at odds with the new middle-class suburban homogeneity of the post-war era. The character of the disruptive housewife, especially, suggested the disjunction between the societal definition of the housewife role in the 1950s as natural and passive and the conventions of vaudeville. Post-war domestic containment policies ruthlessly pathologized women who rebelled against their sex role, allowing them no role model but that of housewife as dependent, passive nurturer; the vaudeville aesthetic, however, continually foregrounded the artifice and absurdity of this role, denaturalizing it. Gradually, as television aesthetics changed, the disruptive housewife largely disappeared and was replaced by the contented suburban good wife.

One of the few unruly housewives to survive into the late 1950s and retain immense popularity was Gracie Allen. In *Burns and Allen*, however, vaudeville conventions were adapted to serve cold war gender ideology rather than challenge it. The programme used vaudeville techniques like direct address and artificial staging to graft popular psychiatric ideas of the irrational, dependent female and the psychiatrist/patient relationship onto the wife and husband, and thus turned their suburban home into an asylum. Because of its unique staging, I would argue that Gracie's dysfunction does not indicate merely dissatisfaction with the housewife role (on the part of the character or the larger public), but rather reveals the *underlying pathology of the role itself* as it was constructed by contemporary psychiatric discourse. By examining *Burns and Allen* in terms of its relationship to this discourse, we can better understand how cold war ideology worked to police and contain the housewife and the complex role television played in this process.

The War at Home: The Rise of the Mental Health Industry

Women needed to be trained how to live in suburbia, how to consume, how to spend their leisure time and how to raise their children in this new environment. In the absence of old friends and urban/ethnic traditions, women turned to new sources: the mass media, especially television and magazines, and the 'expert' advice of (invariably male) doctors, especially psychologists and psychiatrists. For suburban women, this reliance on experts, over 90 per cent of whom were men, was very damaging. Women were assigned responsibility for the well-being of the nuclear family; consequently, they were blamed for every perceived failing within it, particularly any 'deviant' behaviour by children. The influence of Freudian psychology was beginning to be felt in mainstream post-war society, and experts used Freud generally to berate suburban moms: if a child misbehaved, the mother was too dominant and castrating; if the child was withdrawn, the mother did not love him enough. Any expression of desire on the woman's part was interpreted as aggressive, and was severely discouraged and pathologized by 'experts' in the popular press as well as by the psychiatric establishment.[3] Psychoanalytic theories of the time repeatedly 'insisted upon the female need for self-denial' and passivity, according to historians Barbara Ehrenreich and Deidre English. The contradictory nature of expert advice put women in a double bind. Ehrenreich and English differentiate the specific problems of women's post-war position by contrasting it with early twentieth-century ideas of domesticity:

> Energy, intelligence and ambition were precisely the characteristics the scientific mother needed to run her household and raise her children in the 1920s. To say now that it was not energy but passivity, that held a woman at home, not ambition but resignation, not enjoyment but pain – was to say from a masculinist point of view that the female role was unthinkable, and those who fit it were in some sense insane. (Ehrenreich and English 1978:273)

It's not surprising, then, to discover that women who could not walk the fine line between, in sociologist Stephanie Coontz's words, 'nurturing motherhood and castrating momism' were 'labeled neurotic, perverted, or schizophrenic' and consequently often institutionalised (Coontz 1992:32). The cold war abroad may have been run by the military and the government but cold war ideology at home was most effectively disseminated by psychiatrists and advertisers, groups that depended for their livelihood on their ability to predict and control the actions and desires of their biggest market: housewives. Mary Beth Haralovich has insightfully traced the way advertisers trained and exploited middle-class women consumers, but less attention has been paid to the extraordinary growth and influence of the psychiatric industry during this period. In 1954 and 1955, the number one identified health problem in the United States was 'emotional disease.' In 1954, 150,000 adults entered mental hospitals and 700,000 mental patients received hospital care (in comparison, physical disorders accounted for only 600,000 patients). That same year, over a billion dollars was spent for the care of people diagnosed as mentally ill. In 1955, the year minor tranquillizers first became available outside of hospitals, 75 per cent of patients were being treated in hospital settings, over half a million people, compared to 150,000 in 1980. And although the wide availability of tranquillizers meant that hospital stays decreased by the late 1950s, there were still over a quarter of a million people employed in the industry, and hospitals continued into the late 1950s to report staff shortages.[4]

Over half of the patients in these hospitals were women, the majority married (Warren 1987:25).[5] Like the advertising industry, the mental health industry depended on its ability to convince people that their happiness and well-being required the consumption of the industry's products. But in terms of even the most basic use-value, the mental health industry was in a more difficult position than other advertisers because its products were not as tangible and their effectiveness not as measurable. People had to be convinced of the doctor's authority and of the soundness of his prescriptions; they also had to have nowhere else to turn. Again, it's not surprising that women, particularly newly isolated and therefore probably depressed suburban housewives, should become the chief sources of revenue for the new industry. In her groundbreaking 1972 study *Women and Madness*, Phyllis Chesler reported that housewives represented 'the largest single category of both attempted and completed suicides' during the 1950s and 1960s (Chesler 1972:48). This 'problem that has no name', as Betty Friedan later called it, provided an ideal source of funds for the industry because it was both inexhaustible and self-perpetuating; the industry which helped cause the disease perpetuated it through treatments that reinforced the importance of continued passivity and domesticity.

In addition, sociologist Carol Warren has pointed out that housewives were particularly vulnerable to institutionalization because state mental health laws often allowed married people to commit their spouses to psychiatric hospitals on the advice of a single licensed physician who did not need to be a psychiatrist (Warren 1987:15). Because housewives were economically dependent on their husbands and more socially isolated, they were committed in this way much more often than their husbands. For such women, Warren argues, 'the effect of mental health legislation in the 1950s was to reinforce the patriarchal authority of the husband with the medical authority of the (usually male) psychiatrist.' (Warren 1987:24–5) As a result, Warren argues, housewives were often institutionalized for their inability or unwillingness to perform domestic chores. Her study of 17 hospitalized schizophrenic women in 1950s San Francisco documents how institutionalization and electric shock treatments 'were used to force women to accept domestic roles and their husband's dictates.' (Coontz 1992:32)[6]

Warren's work supports Chesler's contention throughout *Women and Madness* that women were often diagnosed as mentally ill because of their perceived 'sex role alienation.' Chesler cites a related study of 1950s housewife patients conducted in 1968 in which psychiatrist Shirley Angrist tried to ascertain the effectiveness of psychiatric treatment in the lives of three hundred women. By comparing the overall functioning and attitudes of former patients to those of the housewife 'controls' who had never been patients, she found there were almost no differences in behaviour and attitude between the two groups (both were 'grouchy', 'edgy' and 'restless'). Several of these ex-patients were rehospitalized by their husbands primarily because they had refused to function properly 'domestically', although Angrist found that they were actually no different from the housewife controls in 'terms of their willingness to participate in leisure activities such as traveling, socializing or enjoying themselves.' (Chesler 1972:50)[7] Indeed, the husbands who readmitted their wives 'expressed significantly lower expectations for the total human functioning of their wives. They were willing to tolerate extremely childlike and dependent behaviour in them as long as the dishes were washed.' (Chesler 1972: 51)[8]

These studies suggest specific ways in which post-war women's anxieties were socially constructed as 'mental illnesses' in a manner that served both corporate America and the cold war nuclear family ideal. Whereas in the 1920s home economics was a science, by the 1950s, the housewife herself had become an object of study, her home an asylum. It is this positioning of the housewife that *The Burns and Allen Show* both exploited and negotiated so successfully.[9]

The Burns and Allen Show: Domestic Containment Comedy

George Burns and Gracie Allen began working together as a vaudeville team in 1925 and were very successful, but it was radio that made them household names. Although their 'Burns and Allen' routines were featured in a number of films during the 1930s, on radio the wittiness of their dialogues was foregrounded, and radio sustained their stardom from their 1932 debut until their move to television in 1950.[10] George Burns and Gracie Allen were married for 35 years; in both their radio and television programmes they played themselves, and plots revolved around their dating and subsequent domestic life (they married on radio in the early 1940s) and the production of their weekly show. Their television show was set almost exclusively on the 'homefront': their front porch, living room, kitchen and back porch and those of their neighbours, the Mortons, provided the main sets for the first few years.

It made sense for Burns and Allen to transfer their programme to television. Many industry people and critics perceived television in the late 1940s and early 1950s as a revival of vaudeville, or at least of the 'vaudeville aesthetic' of comedy (Spigel 1992:144). Cultural critic Henry Jenkins defines a vaudeville aesthetic in opposition to an aesthetic of theatrical realism. According to Jenkins, early twentieth-century vaudeville was characterized by liveness, direct address, spontaneity, excess, atomistic spectacle and star performance, as opposed to the narrative coherence, character consistency and causal logic expected of theatrical plays during the same period. (Jenkins 1992:42–43) Although both Jenkins and Spigel make clear that the audience for vaudeville was historically both middle and working class, Jenkins associates a vaudeville aesthetic with working-class Americans and theatrical realism with the middle class by tracing the development of vaudeville entertainment at the turn of the century and showing how it clashed with established middle-class ideas of comedy that had developed during the Victorian era.

The 'New Humor' that emerged at the turn of the century offered a different aesthetic to the public, one that privileged visceral and emotional effect over intellectual appreciation. Jenkins argues that this New Humor, which had previously been associated chiefly with male working-class amusements and oral street culture (particularly ethnic culture), became more broadly available during this period through mass market publications, increased immigration, and the rise of commercial entertainments including vaudeville, which were aimed at both sexes and all classes. Not only did vaudeville players and audiences consider pleasure a desirable goal in its own right, they also recognized that time was at a premium for working people, and thus the use-value of cultural experience was very important. (Jenkins 1992:45) Immediate response determined the success of a vaudeville performer, and vaudeville bookers paid for the number of jokes per minute. (Jenkins 1992:32) In contrast to theatrical realism, vaudeville's emphasis on immediate gratification, novelty, performer excess and spontaneity provided an aesthetic of disruption and disorder.

In *What Made Pistachio Nuts*, Jenkins traces one form of the vaudeville aesthetic, the anarchistic comedy, through its translation from vaudeville to film in the 1930s. Jenkins characterizes Burns and Allen as an anarchistic comedy team, and cites several of their films, including the *Big Broadcast* series (1932, 1936, 1937), *International House* (1933) and *Here Comes Cookie* (1935) as belonging to this particular genre, one in which 'narrative structure and character development are subordinated to foreground comic performance; they are marked by a general questioning of social norms. They celebrate the collapse of social order and the liberation of the creativity and impulsiveness of their protagonist.' (Jenkins 1992:22–23)[11] While the 'disorderly wife' character was a staple of vaudeville and films, Jenkins sees Gracie as more of a gender-neutral clown character, an individual who is socially disruptive because she is ignorant of social norms, rather than a wife who is consciously angry with her husband and whose antics must therefore be punished. This distinction became an important factor in Gracie's successful transition to television in the 1950s.

Burns and Allen's move to television led observers to expect that their programme would continue to foreground the anarchistic antics of Gracie, just as other performers like Jack Benny and Milton Berle had retained their programmes' vaudeville characteristics in the move to television. Their shows were performed live and employed variety acts, direct address, and privileged cultural 'types' over character development, all trademarks of a vaudeville aesthetic. What separates *Burns and Allen* from other vaudeville-inspired programmes, however, is its domestic setting. The conflation of the vaudeville clown with the suburban housewife redefined the disorderly wife character for the cold war era of the 1950s and suggested new reasons for the clown's disruptiveness.[12]

In his discussion of disruptive clown characters in 1930s films, including those featuring Gracie, Henry Jenkins cites two primary characteristics of the role: 'poor assimilation into the social order' and 'contradictions, irreconcilable impulses'. (Jenkins 1992:223–4) Jenkins emphasizes that these characteristics must be historicized, and I would argue that the contradictions of the housewife role of the early 1950s made it ripe for clowning:

> the clown is thrown out of his familiar environment into another whose rules and conventions have only been imperfectly mastered . . . The clowns' displacement . . . provides the preconditions for their play with cultural categories and their unrestrained disturbance of the peace. The clown's performance becomes a play with identity, a merging together of often contradictory categories within a single figure. (Jenkins 1992:224–5)

The distinctive and disruptive element of Burns and Allen's comedy had always been Gracie, whose irrational rationality kept the plot spinning and the other characters (often including George) bewildered. Patricia Mellencamp describes Gracie's verbal technique in her television comedy as 'a derailing of laws and logic' that refers to 'either the nearest or most unexpected referent as a comic turn on the arbitrary and conventional authority of speech.' (Mellencamp 1986) Gracie's literalness and mixed metaphors were staples of their vaudeville and radio routines and became central to their television programme as well. When asked if her parents 'enjoyed good health', for example, Gracie replied 'Oh yes, they loved it.' When George protested that he could 'straighten out a problem in no time' Gracie replied, 'It's too late – you've buttered your bread, now sleep on it.' Gracie felt 'taller in winter' because 'the days are shorter.' Gracie mailed her mother an empty envelope because 'no news is good news.' (Blythe and Sackett 1986:32 & 117)[13]

When narrativized, Gracie's lack of regard for conventions of speech and custom enabled her to disregard social boundaries. 'Gracie,' writes Henry Jenkins, 'inhabits a world where social relationships are reciprocal and reversible rather than hierarchical and structured.' (Jenkins 1992:230) Within the television narrative, Gracie is able to subvert patriarchal authority and foreground the silliness and arbitrariness of the roles that people play, particularly gender roles. In one example, the 'Swami' episode from 1952, Gracie continually humiliates and bewilders a divorce lawyer she has invited over to handle her divorce from George. She both persistently destroys a key emblem of the lawyer's masculinity (she keeps sitting on his hat) and openly interrogates the gendered nature of everyday domestic chores by asking him to 'salt some meat' and then mocking him: 'What's the matter? Don't you know how?'

Gracie's ability to expose and undermine, however, is complicated because this ability is the direct result of her ostensible insanity. Her insanity, as Mellencamp notes, protects her from hurt because she is oblivious to the insults of others, but it also denies her the power to change the rules governing her situation. (Mellencamp 1986:97) As a result, Gracie exemplifies the position of the insane housewife, who can never give the right answer to questions and ultimately has no significant power within the household. Yet we know the instability she produces is threatening because of the lengths the programme goes to in order to contain her – just as an asylum resident must be contained.

The conflation of the figure of the asylum resident with that of the house-wife is reflected in the set design of the show and the roles Gracie and George play in relation to it. During the show's first two years, which were shot live, the set was behind a curtain. Only George could escape the diegesis, going beyond that curtain directly to address the audience. Gracie was thus con-fined within the boundaries of the stage set, like a madwoman in a cage. As audience members, we are invited by her husband George to observe her through the windows he provides for us. He both protects her and exhibits her, thus demonstrating traditional middle-class gender roles (wives are to be protected and displayed), but also directly linking this kind of marriage dis-play with the freak show. Gracie is the idiot savant and the promise of her idiot-savant freakiness is what draws audiences to the show. The Burns' middle-class suburban home is thus analogous to an asylum: Gracie is the insane patient/housewife and George is her psychiatrist/husband. As in the psychia-trist/patient relationship, George narrates Gracie for us; he directly addresses the audience, predicts her moves and interprets her for us. He is the subject, she is his object of study. Gracie is always under surveillance by George, who, as the all-seeing father/husband/psychiatrist, has constant access to her. And, like the psychiatrists of the 1950s who depended upon housewives for their livelihoods, George Burns is profiting from his exhibition of his wife. He is the executive producer of the show, as well as its star. In the press of the period, George admits his financial dependence on Gracie's 'insanity': his management and exhibition of her, he says, have always been the key to his success. In his introductory monologue to the first show, George claims 'I discovered my talent and married her' and, throughout the programme, he continues to acknowledge his debt to Gracie's 'madness': 'I guess if she made sense I'd still be selling ties.'[14]

By exhibiting Gracie in ways that mirrored how psychiatric discourse had framed the housewife, George made the disruption caused by the vaudeville conventions of the show more amenable to cold war ideology than other vaudeville-influenced programmes, especially those that relied on ethnic com-edy and cross-dressing in their routines (such as Milton Berle's programmes). I would argue that *Burns and Allen* is able to negotiate this compromise between vaudevillian and realist conventions more successfully than other programmes only because of the way it uses its vaudeville conventions in the service of a larger, overarching narrative structure: George's display and narration of Gracie as 'insane' housewife.

The historical context is important because this structure marked a depar-ture from Burns and Allen's previous work in which George did not have a narrator role, nor was he always the standard of common sense and modera-tion. In their radio shows and films, for example, George rarely knows about

Gracie's schemes, allowing him to be the butt of the joke. Because of his narrator role on the television show, however, George often introduces the storyline, so he is much more rarely caught unawares, especially as the show progresses. (Blythe and Sackett 1986:111) In addition, on radio George has his idiosyncrasies, including egoism and the delusion that he has particular talents, such as singing, which proves to be unfounded. His anger at Gracie in these radio programmes is not so much that of an irritated parent toward an errant child, as in the television show, but rather that of a jealous or frustrated spouse whose ego has been bruised. In previous media, Burns and Allen's relationship to the audience was similar: both used direct address in their vaudeville routines, and neither used it on film or radio (except at the very end of radio programmes and film shorts). On television, however, George cut Gracie off from her audience; he mediated her appearances, keeping the audience distanced from her madness and preventing her direct contact with them. This diminished relationship between performer and audience meant that George became the bigger star, a reversal of Gracie's historic position as the star attraction of the team. The one time she does face the audience in the television programme – during the couple's final exit – George directs her speech with the command that, significantly, became their trademark: 'Say Goodnight, Gracie.' This final exchange reassured viewers that the insane housewife was safely contained until the next week. (Clements and Weber 1996:21 & 26)[15]

While containment was the usual end for vaudeville's anarchic characters as well, particularly for disruptive women, such containment resonated in the 1950s differently from the 1920s and 1930s. As I have shown, middle-class women's containment within the suburban home was an essential part of cold war policy in the 1950s. For this reason, *Burns and Allen*'s use of vaudeville conventions was not disturbing for 1950s audiences because they served to underline Gracie's 'insanity' and the need to contain her. The self-reflexivity of *Burns and Allen* thus exposes the conflation of the suburban home and the asylum, and the programme's success indicates the cultural acceptability of that conflation. There was historical precedent for such a reading however; in *Madness and Civilization*, Michel Foucault notes that the designers of the first asylums at the end of the eighteenth century meant them to be symbolic reconstitutions of the social structure of the patriarchal bourgeois family, in which reason was seen as the province of the Father or warden, while inmates were to be viewed as unreasonable children in rebellion against the Father. In accordance with bourgeois family values, asylums also upheld the virtues of work and moral purity, using these as transcendent standards with which to judge an inmate's 'sanity'. As Foucault points out, these values 'protected the asylum from history and social evolution'; it did not have to adapt to changes within society. (Foucault 1967:254–5) In many ways, the suburban home of the 1950s is the descendant of these original asylums, similarly organized around the middle-class family unit and also 'set adrift in history'. (Foucault

1967:255) As in Foucault's asylum, suburban dwellers mimicked the family roles constructed for them by their immediate environment, especially by television, because they no longer had access to identities rooted in history.[16]

Like the asylum, the suburban home functioned as a site of display and surveillance. The housewife, though isolated, was at the same time under continual scrutiny, not only from her neighbours but also within her family. Carol Warren notes that once a housewife was labelled 'sick', she was 'continually monitored by her closest relative or spouse for signs of trouble recurrence and was liable to have her actions interpreted as symptoms of mental illness.' (Warren 1987:34) Spigel remarks that television, too, was seen as instrumental in this surveillance. She noted how magazine articles and ads suggested that the public viewed television as a possible Big Brother, both potentially spying on its domestic viewers and constantly reflecting back to them its vision of how they should be. (Spigel 1992:199)

The Burns and Allen Show foregrounded these elements, even to the extent that in the fourth season George began observing Gracie and the other cast members through the TV set in his den (by this point the programme was no longer broadcast live). As the show evolved, the proscenium set became less prominent, although George still spoke directly to the studio audience. In the fifth season, Gracie's character was further naturalized as a 'proper' 1950s housewife through the regular appearance of Ronnie Burns, the couple's grown son. Ronnie's acting career and personal life became the central focus of his mother's energy, largely replacing her previous more 'selfish' desires such as buying a mink coat or going out to dinner. George, consequently, appeared less often on the show, and became even more of a father/surveyor as he watched his wife and son through his television screen.

Gracie's basic characterization, however, remained unchanged throughout the run of the series. To my mind, what is remarkable and disruptive about Gracie's character is not how badly she fits the description of the good, docile housewife, but *how well* she fits it. In Phyllis Chesler's discussion of insane 1950s housewives, the most threatening type was the aggressive housewife (labelled schizophrenic), who, although not as emotionally distressed as the depressed housewives, was considered more threatening because she rejected her wifely passive role and exhibited 'masculine' traits such as physical aggressiveness and controlling behaviour. (Chesler 1972:52–3) Lucy Ricardo clearly fits this notion of a strong-willed housewife who consistently shirks her domestic responsibilities. But if Lucy is 'insane' because she rebels against the housewife role, Gracie is 'insane' because she performs it all too well. She exposes its irrationality because although she is incoherent and nonsensical, she is performing her wifely role perfectly according to contemporary marriage 'experts'. She is gracious and ornamental, devoted to her husband, and most importantly, never without a domestic task.[17] In almost every scene, she is sewing, cooking, arranging flowers or doing some kind of domestic chore.[18] In fact, Gracie's character suggested that the housewife role as constructed by the experts did not require or value mental competence. As the husbands who institutionalized their wives attested, the incoherence and dependence of their wives were not a problem and could actually serve to make them more endearing. One bit of dialogue from the show illustrates this point. Gracie is fearful of facing George after denting the car fender (a recurring joke):

> Harry Von Zell: Gracie, why are you washing the dishes?
> Gracie: I haven't any dirty ones. I've been too upset to eat.
> Von Zell (with genuine concern): You are upset.
> Gracie: Yes, but upset or not, a woman has to do her housework.

Gracie's embodiment of the irrationality of the housewife role made her character important for viewers in this period, particularly housewives who saw themselves being asked to perform roles that would seem to make them as 'insane' as Gracie. By continually performing housewife norms, Gracie points to that which is not normative about the 1950s housewife: although she has no power to change her position, she denaturalizes it, and in this lies her importance and what separates her from the more successfully 'naturalized' television housewives who followed her.

The new middle-class aesthetic that achieved dominance in post-war America reasserted turn of the century conventions of theatrical realism but added a new component, psychiatric discourse, which became thoroughly naturalized in suburban settings no longer disrupted by vaudeville conventions or characters. By the late 1950s, television domestic sitcoms had lost their connection with the vaudeville aesthetic. Stage sets had been replaced by realistic suburban interiors; direct address, self-reflexivity and variety acts no longer interrupted narrative flow; 'magazine' format commercials divorced salesmanship from performers (thus naturalizing character still further); and the narrative focus became the children's lives rather than the married couple's presumably untroubled relationship. These changes clearly marked the transition from a heterogeneous working-class, vaudeville aesthetic to an homogenous middle-class one that naturalized the non-ethnically marked white suburban family and emphasized moral instruction, conformity, and likeable characters over sensual pleasure and star performance.

Most significantly, the housewife as clown disappeared. The housewife was no longer a transitional figure, caught between working-class and middle-class identities, but a permanent fixture of the suburban world, a woman without a history. Housewives like June Cleaver, Donna Reed and Margaret Anderson did not exhibit any of the irrational, idiosyncratic traits of a Lucy or a Gracie.[19] In their way, however, the contented housewives of the later sitcoms are just as significant if we examine changes in housewife characterizations on television in relation to changes in the psychiatric industry. The development of tranquillizers in 1955 (the use of which doubled in one year, from 1957 to 1958) meant that most middle-class housewives could be 'treated' at home for emotional pain instead of going to clinics.[20] If the incoherence of

Gracie Allen could seem the result of extensive shock treatment, the relaxed, contented nature of Margaret Anderson or Donna Reed and the bewildered geniality of June Cleaver better reflect the effects of tranquillizing drugs.

As Jason Mittell has shown in his study of gender and tranquillizers in the 1950s, both medical and public advertisements for tranquillizers targeted housewives as the main recipients of these drugs and encouraged doctors and the public to think of the drugged housewife as the ideal: 'housewives are represented . . . [either] as dysfunctional and in need of drugs or as drugged and well-adjusted to their situation'. (Mittell: 10) The drugged housewife was not concerned with her own pleasure: she was passive, obedient and content. Mittell argues that the emphasis given to such terms as 'calm and relaxed' and 'tranquil' in industry ads reveals the importance of making docile the out-of-control body of the female patient. (Mittell: 13)

Like the patients in Carol Warren's study, these ads indicate that what was most important to mental health professionals was not women's actual mental health, but their ability to perform their allotted roles effectively. And yet how convincing was June Cleaver? Certainly her camp legacy as the perfect-housewife-as-cultural-icon indicates that the idealization and artificiality of her role have become public knowledge, but the ads in Mittell's study suggest that June's seeming contentedness was anathema even in the 1950s. In *The History of Sexuality*, Foucault argues that the historical repression of sexuality in bourgeois society did not produce silence on the subject but instead 'a veritable discursive explosion'; knowledge of sex became a form of power, and institutions exercised power through the creation and regulation of sexual discourses. (Foucault 1978:17) For the middle-class of the 1950s, mental illness emerged as perhaps the single most important of such discourses, and housewives became the primary targets of those who controlled it: 'the problem that had no name' (Friedan 1963) was thus continually discussed and represented in the discourses surrounding housewives in the 1950s. They were unhappy women, and their discontent was visibly monitored, and controlled through legal, medical, and social means: via psychiatric discourse, advertising and decreased employment opportunities; through laws that prevented women from controlling their mental health; through institutionalization and shock therapy; and, ultimately, through physical drugging. Before Friedan, television characters were an important means for representing and negotiating the housewife's precarious situation. Even as housewife characters became more middle-class and more peripheral in the mid-to-late-1950s, housewife characters like June Cleaver continued to expose the consequences of cold war hegemonic practices, which offered housewives the compensation of consumer goods and tranquillizers in exchange for their adherence to roles that erased their individuality and prevented any form of autonomy.

While television retained the trope of home as asylum throughout the late 1950s and 1960s, the focus changed to the psychological and social development of adolescents instead of the housewife herself. Psychiatric discourse was thus deployed around the children, who grew up to become the psychologically self-conscious and sophisticated characters of 1970s sitcoms. Programmes like *Mary Tyler Moore* show the degree to which the middle-class aesthetic of the 1950s had been completely naturalized by the 1970s. Female characters in 1970s sitcoms, in particular, perceive themselves as psychological subjects with particular insecurities, complexes and fixations that inevitably reference the psychiatric discourse of their parents' era. What television critic Jane Feuer has described in her study of MTM programming as depth and complexity of character could instead be viewed as a result of these characters' and their audience's common history. The rootless suburban asylum of the 1950s has provided a shared history for the new middle class. (Feuer 1984:33–40) The psychological depth of *Mary Tyler Moore*'s Mary Richards is based on her internalization and naturalization of this psychiatric discourse and the aesthetic of theatrical realism. The solidity of this foundation permits the programme to shift its nuclear family unit from the domestic asylum to the workplace. A domestic setting is no longer necessary because the middle-class aesthetic is so firmly naturalized that alternatives to it, like the characters of Norman Lear's 1970s sitcoms, are perceived as cultural 'stereotypes' or 'caricatures'. (Feuer 1984:46) While Feuer suggests that characters like Mary Richards 'caught the cultural moment for the emerging new woman in a way that provided a point of identification for the mass audience as well' (Feuer 1984:37), I would argue that the level of identification Feuer perceives was made possible only through a sense of shared history between television characters and audience that did not begin with women's liberation, but rather with their containment.

By examining Gracie's world, we can trace the way in which the ideologies of patriarchy and consumerism came together in the psychiatric discourse of the post-war period to ensure women's continued social isolation by transforming their homes into asylums where they could be both observed and confined. By performing her role not wisely but too well, however, Gracie herself suggests the slippage within hegemony and the important role television played – and continues to play – in building, maintaining, and exposing the workings of hegemony and the boundaries of women's domestic asylums.

Notes

This essay originally began as a short paper for Lauren Rabinovitz's 'Women and Television' class at the University of Iowa; her early support of my ideas and our class discussions of the material were essential to its development. I wish to also express my deepest thanks to Janet Thumim, Taylor Harrison, Jason Mittell and Joe Wlodarz for their help in editing and revision. This essay is dedicated to Joe, for reasons which are well known to him.

1. *Burns and Allen*, CBS, 1950–1958; *I Love Lucy*, CBS, 1951–1957; *Father Knows Best*, CBS/NBC, 1954–1962; *Leave it to Beaver*, CBS/ABC, 1957–1963.

2. For a thorough discussion of the changes in housewife characters and television aesthetics throughout the 1950s, see Lynn Spigel, *Make Room for TV: Television and the Family Ideal in Postwar America* (1992). For a discussion of the gender politics of Gracie and Lucy in particular, see Patricia Mellencamp, 'Situation Comedy, Feminism and Freud: Discourses of Gracie and Lucy,' in *Studies in Entertainment: Critical Approaches to Mass Culture* (1986).

3. I examined advice columns from *Women's Home Companion, Ladies Home Journal* and *McCall's Magazine* from 1953 to 1956. The advice of the male medical experts in these magazines is stern and paternalistic; their advice to women in troubled marriages encourages them to blame themselves for their troubles and shames them into suppressing their own desires and needs (what the counsellors term women's evil 'pride') in order to preserve the happiness of their homes. The security and happiness of the home can only be achieved, according to these experts, through the wife's total self-effacement.

4. 'Mental Illness', *The Encyclopedia Americana* (1993); 'Psychiatry' and 'Psychology' listings, *The Americana Annual* for the years 1953–1957. See also Jason Mittell, ' "Her Life is Less Frenzied . . ." Gendered Discourse and the Introduction of Tranquillizers in the late 1950s' (manuscript, 1996) and Shirley Angrist et al, *Women After Treatment: A Study of Former Mental Patients and Their Normal Neighbors* (1968).

5. According to sociologist Carol Warren, married women were the 'typical majority' in state hospitals in the 1950s. In a survey of all schizophrenic patients admitted to state hospitals in California in 1953 and 1954, the majority of total patients admitted were women and 55 per cent of women patients were married compared to 29 per cent of men. Carol Warren, *Madwives: Schizophrenic Women in the 1950s* p.25 (1987).

6. Carol Warren, quoted by Stephanie Coontz. Warren's findings are shared by Phyllis Chesler: in *Women and Madness*, Chesler cites several studies, including Shirley Angrist's, which attribute women's mental illnesses to their inability to perform their sex roles. Warren's study is especially useful, however, because she charts the relative nature of women's insanity over a historical period. When the 1950s patients files were re-examined in 1972, only five of the seventeen originally diagnosed as schizophrenic were again given that diagnosis. Most were instead characterized as depressed, suffering from 'character disorders' or ' delusional'. (Warren 1987:26–28)

7. Shirley Angrist, quoted in Chesler. For a full account of Angrist's study, see Angrist, *Women After Treatment* (1968).

8. Significantly, Angrist notes that the women who were re-admitted as patients were of a higher class status than those who were not, suggesting that the standards for domestic functioning (as opposed to human functioning) were higher in middle-class households and that the pathologizing rhetoric had perhaps taken stronger hold in the upper classes. This finding supports Foucault's assertion, in *The History of Sexuality, Vol. 1*, that it was the upper and middle classes who first submitted themselves to narrow definitions of sexual behaviour before imposing such definitions on the lower classes. If sexuality is 'originally, historically bourgeois', so too can mental illness be considered one of the chief concerns and characteristics of the new middle class during the post-war period, serving the double purpose of keeping middle-class women domestically contained and feeding the coffers of a new industry. See Michel Foucault, *The History of Sexuality, Vol. 1* p.127 (1978).

9. In a recent essay in Spigel and Curtin (eds), *The Revolution Wasn't Televised: Sixties Television and Social Conflict* (1997), Jeffrey Sconce also employs Carol Warren's work to suggest how the suburban home can be looked at as a 'domestic asylum'. He argues that before the 1960s science fiction programme *The Outer Limits* (1963–1965, ABC) 'television had no language with which to engage the potential mental disintegration of Mayfield,

Springfield, and the other well scrubbed communities of televisionland' (Spigel and Curtin 1997:21–45). My contention, however, is that 1950s television did indeed expose and negotiate the domestic asylum through the confused, frustrated, bewildered language of its housewife characters: Gracie Allen, Lucy Ricardo and June Cleaver, respectively.

10. For a detailed account of Burns and Allen's radio career, see Cynthia Clements and Sandra Weber, *George Burns and Gracie Allen: A Bio-Bibliography* (1996).

11. George Burns and Gracie Allen appeared in 14 films together between 1932 and 1939. Gracie was the star of the duo and appeared in three additional films minus George: *The Gracie Allen Murder Case* (1939), *Mr and Mrs North* (1942) and *Two Girls and a Sailor* (1944).

12. For a thorough discussion of Gracie Allen's character in a 1930s social context, see Margaret T. McFadden's Chapter 6, 'Dizzy Dames and Gendered Knowledge', in her dissertation *Anything Goes: Gender and Knowledge in the Comic Popular Culture of the 1930s* (UMI, 1997): 9713695 (Yale University). McFadden sees Burns and Allen's relationship in the 1930s as mirroring class differences and the breakdown of knowledge created by the Great Depression: 'The working class dizzy dame exemplified by Gracie Allen could use her "alternative" knowledge of the world and her "illogical logic" to thwart the attempts of her male counterpart George Burns to impose patriarchal control over her sexual and economic circulation. Her resistance to him simultaneously figured workers' resistance to employers' attempts to control them, as she was often cast as a worker to his boss.' McFadden sees Allen's character as one of exceptional subversive power, a power I would argue is greatly compromised by the couple's move to television in the 1950s. McFadden's discussion helps explain why Burns and Allen remained popular as a comedy team for over three decades: they adapted their act to suit different social contexts, particularly major shifts in heterosexual relationships. In the 1930s, Gracie was a working-class girl, in the 1940s she and Burns got married (on radio) and, by the 1950s, she was a middle-class suburban housewife.

13. All examples cited in Cheryl Blythe and Susan Sackett, *Say Goodnight, Gracie: The Story of Burns and Allen* pp 117 & 38 (1986).

14. Variants on these quotations can be found in the popular press, George's various memoirs and Blythe and Sackett. George always credited Gracie with having all the talent of the pair and being responsible for their success. For example, George confesses in his memoirs that he married Gracie in part because he could be a success with her: 'I fell in love with Gracie because she was pretty, smart, nice and talented. But I'll tell you the truth. I also fell in love with Gracie because I fell in love with making a good living.' See George Burns, *Gracie: A Love Story* p 59 (1988). Also, see George Burns with Cynthia Hobart Lindsay, *I Love Her, That's Why* (1955).

15. This exchange, one of a number of the team's stock phrases, began in vaudeville but was used only intermittently in vaudeville and on radio; most radio programmes did not end with the exchange. On television, however, the exchange ended the programme every week and became their primary trademark, significantly foregrounding the parent-child relationship as the team's comedic legacy.

16. For a thorough and complex discussion of television's historical role in erasing class and ethnic identities, see George Lipsitz, 'The Meaning of Memory: Family, Class and Ethnicity in Early Network Television' in his *Time Passages: Collective Memory and American Popular Culture* (1990).

17. These qualities are the ones most emphasized by women's magazines of the period (cited above) as being essential to the good housewife.

18. In *Say Goodnight, Gracie*, Blythe and Sackett note how Gracie Allen as an actress was similarly compulsive about these tasks and would complete them even after the cameras had stopped running. (Blythe and Sackett 1986:47)

19. June Cleaver of *Leave it to Beaver*, CBS/ABC, 1957–1963; Margaret Anderson of *Father Knows Best*, CBS/NBC 1954–1962; and Donna Reed of *The Donna Reed Show*, ABC, 1958–1966.

20. 'Psychiatry', *The Americana Annual* for 1957.

CHAPTER 4

LESSONS FROM UNCLE MILTIE

ETHNIC MASCULINITY AND EARLY TELEVISION'S VAUDEO STAR

Susan Murray

In the late 1940s and early 1950s, as television was gradually becoming the dominant form of domestic entertainment in the USA, broadcast networks, sponsors, advertising agencies, talent unions, talent agencies and the audience actively renegotiated the meaning and functions of broadcast stardom. Working from the premise that 'TV can be as good as the talent it presents', the trade press debated what qualities and experience a television star should possess.[1] Although a brief flurry of discussion on the potential advantages of the legitimate stage actor's crossover to the nascent medium occurred in 1947–48, eventually, commentators assumed that the stage comic (trained in vaudeville, burlesque and night clubs) would be best suited to television work. This was primarily due to the trained comedian's ability to maintain the intensive schedule of television, their penchant for improvization in live work and, of course, the broadcast experience which many of them had acquired on radio. Most importantly, however, stage comics could maximize the visual immediacy of television. The National Director of TV Programming at NBC, Norman Blackburn, was quoted in *Variety* in early 1949: 'performers with stage and vaudeville background have taken to TV like a duck to water; they usually have a quick study, know what to do with their hands, and realize that a bit of sight business conveys much more meaning than the spoken word.'[2] Talent agencies were also cognizant of the importance of the vaudeville comic and by 1948 were 'shifting vaude specialists into the radio departments on the theory that it was more important to know the visual angle than to know broadcasting.' (Rose 1995:124)

After the proven commercial success of early variety programmes such as *Texaco Star Theatre, Your Show of Shows* (1950–1954, NBC) and *Toast of the Town* (also known as *The Ed Sullivan Show*, 1948–1971, CBS), the vaudeo star became the most sought-after performer in broadcasting. Jack Benny signed an unprecedented ten-year contract with CBS worth almost $1 million in 1950. And, during the following year, Milton Berle penned a deal with NBC that would cost the network up to $200,000 a year for 30 years. Clearly, networks and advertisers were quite confident about the long-term earning potential of such stars – in fact, it would seem that they assumed television's vaudeo trend would continue in perpetuity.

In actuality, vaudeo would be absorbed into the sitcom format by the end of the decade and many of the genre's top stars would watch their careers fizzle out by the early 1960s. But during the late 1940s and very early 1950s, Berle's brash, stagy, New York vaudeville style was the prototype of the television star. The broadcasting industry was initially interested in exploiting ex-vaudeville stars for the way in which their performance style emphasized the visuality, spontaneity, immediacy and intimacy of the television medium; moreover, they seemed to exude an authenticity that captured people's appreciation. Ex-vaudevillians were also a convenient pool of talent from which to draw as many of them were New York regional performers and the television networks were all broadcasting from flagship stations in Manhattan. However in poaching vaudeville performance styles the television industry was forced to confront the more indelicate aspects of variety format humour which threatened to erupt unexpectedly on live television. Ex-vaudevillians had a tendency to ad lib sly sight gags, asides and subtle gestures to connote sexual references or situations. So, in this perilous terrain of a live *visual* domestic entertainment medium, the bawdy antics of stage comedy had not only to be eliminated from the script in pre-production, but their spontaneous appearance in the programme also had to be anticipated. One way to ease the reception of such content was to contain or construct rhetorically a personality for the comedian that would befit the values of the television audience.

In relying on the proven variety format, using older vaudevillians and radio performers, the television industry was referencing a traditional form of entertainment (hoping in this way to secure its audience) while simultaneously urging the novelty, the 'newness,' of the medium itself. It is in this context that the analysis of the appeal and cultural resonance of these early television comics becomes so significant. In considering the morally tenuous state of the variety format and the ageing, ethnic and somewhat flexible masculinity of the top comedy stars, alongside the industry's desire to be perceived as a natural extension of the American family's interaction, the television industry might appear to have been working at cross purposes. Yet, these apparent contradictions in the construction of early comedy stars bespeak rather coherent symbolic constructions of ethnicity, masculinity and anxieties over the changing demographics of the American cultural landscape.

In this article, I will argue that although a performer's particular ethnic identity was rarely addressed outright in television, traces of many vaudeo stars' Jewishness were embedded in their personas and performance styles. In particular, the cultural and religious heritage of individuals such as Berle,

Burns, Caesar and Benny were obliquely referenced through their connection to the traditions of vaudeville, their affiliations with specific geographic areas/neighbourhoods, their relationships with their extended families and their representations of a particular feminized masculinity. The subtle nature of these ethnic cues helped these comedians address the cultural experiences of the largely Northern and urban television audience of the late 1940s television audience without completely alienating viewers from other regions.

The Vaudevillian and Urban Ethnic Masculinity

The industry's presumptions about the connection between live television and stagework and the pre-sold celebrity of ex-vaudevillian headliners led to the hiring of large numbers of male vaudevillians. Many of these performers, including Berle (formerly Milton Berlinger), Sid Caesar, George Burns (Nathan Birnbaum) and Benny (Benjamin Kubelsky), had embarked (with varying degrees of success) on radio and film careers prior to their entry into television. For example, Benny was one of the most popular radio stars of the 1930s and 1940s. Although he was initially reticent to enter television production (largely because of the work involved in reconceiving and performing his programme for the new visual medium), both NBC and CBS considered him to be a guaranteed audience attraction. After accepting a capital gains deal from CBS in 1948, Benny was eventually lured into television work by the promise of a larger audience and salary. Berle, though, was a risky investment as his radio programmes (*The Philip Morris Playhouse* and the radio version of *Texaco Star Theatre*) were largely considered a disappointment. Yet, the physical comedy and sight gags he acquired during his years on the vaudeville circuit forecast a nice fit with television's aesthetic economy.

In considering the collection of performers who were television's early stars, it seems a bit curious that an industry so concerned with emphasizing the visual aspects of the new technology would choose individuals so significantly older and less *glamorous* than their counterparts in film. As post-war Hollywood promoted the virile hero and/or the psychologically tormented detective, television offered a less traditional vision of maleness. In 1948, the year in which Berle became a household name with *Texaco Star Theatre*, films were released starring Montgomery Clift (*The Search, Red River*), John Wayne (*Red River*), Humphrey Bogart (*Key Largo, The Treasure of the Sierra Madre*) and Clark Gable (*Command Decision*) in roles as war heroes, prospectors, tough guys and cowboys. Although the appearance of film noir during these years presented psychologically troubled and morally compromised protagonists, the presentation of masculinity through Hollywood product was still within the traditional white Anglo-Saxon masculine paradigm. Even Hollywood screen comedy had moved away from the anarchistic vaudeville-inflected format and toward the narratively integrated romantic comedy that highlighted stars such as Gable and Cary Grant. The vestiges of the vaudeville aesthetic in film were found in the teams of Dean Martin and Jerry Lewis and Bob Hope and Bing Crosby (with each pair containing a romantic and 'adolescent' lead – all four of whom were already popular broadcast stars).

In relation to the more hardened male types found in film, the goofy, gangly, mugging Berle would hardly appear to be anyone's ideal man, or man-to-be. Nevertheless, his awkward physicality and psychological vulnerability expressed through self-deprecating humour were integral to the currency of his urban-based character. In his study of Berle's career, Arthur Frank Wertheim (Wertheim 1983:56) found that Berle 'personified a flippant city slicker – a character most viewers could understand.' Moreover, Berle's mobilization of nostalgia for turn-of-the-century city culture and more specifically for working-class theatre (which depended on a revisionist history of its original amoral discursive construction), was a primary component of his on-stage skits. While Berle certainly was not the last word in post-war virility, he did possess a homey familiarity and nostalgic resonance that was paramount to his popularity. And, surprisingly, his gender play and brash sensibilities actually worked for an audience who were assumed by the industry to be seeking moral reassurance and middle-class values from the new domestic medium.

Masculinity, in a strategic cultural performance of signifiers, is mobilized in relation to other social constructions and positions. In reading the personae of television stars in the late 1940s and early 1950s, the functions of ethnicity and class are often difficult to disentangle from gender codes since these work to inform one another. While it's convenient for scholars to try to distinguish clearly among categories of identity, the complexity and misrepresentation of these categories must also be addressed. In discussing the process of identification Judith Butler points out that individuals may wish to see coherence and authenticity in gender identity, but words, acts, gestures and desire are 'fabrications manufactured and sustained through corporeal signs and other discursive means.' (Butler 1990:136) A consequence of understanding masculinity as performance is that its mobilization as a congruency of signs within the system of media representation produces a mirroring effect that is overwhelming in its obfuscation. In television, as in film, performers represented and reconstituted signs present in contemporary culture that were meant to signal a specific form of gender identity. Thus, the performance of gender witnessed in everyday 'reality' is replayed for viewers through these individuals' screen acts, words and gestures and contributes to a further distancing of the signs of identity from its human object. Nevertheless, by discussing the various reference points each type of performance is aiming to incorporate we can perceive an underlying structure informing individual characterizations of specific identity types. In the case of many early television stars, the 'fabrications' of gender, class and ethnicity are vital not only to their extratextual performance of functionally idealized public identities, but also to their on-screen allusions to historically and generically defined characterizations. Their on- and off-screen personas, which are most often co-determined, are constituted not only via the text of the television shows in which they perform, but also through the historical and rhetorical devices and intentions of the culture at large.

Vaudeo stars were peculiarly adept at playing with signs of gender and ethnicity as they were required by variety format simultaneously to inhabit numerous character types. For example, Caesar was known for his portrayals of a regular cast of characters. While in his role as host of *Your Show of Shows*, he would perform a rather straight version of 'himself' – or at least a consistent representation of who he was purported to be in the press. In his sketches, however, he created characters such as storyteller Somerset Winterset, the German Professor, jazz musicians Progress Hornsby and Cool Cees and, along with his partner Imogene Coca, Doris and Charlie Hickenlooper an 'average' middle-class Staten Island couple. It would seem that with Caesar's ability to take on so many characterizations it would be difficult for the audience to locate one stable identity for him. Yet as prolific as his representations of different identities were, his construction through the cultural legacies that arose out of the variety format along with the publicity materials that accompanied his rise to television stardom assembled a context for Caesar's reception as an individual and hinted at his 'authentic' gender and ethnic identity.

Most important in the creation of such a context were the origins of the vaudeo performance style. The variety format was understood as a modern extension of the turn-of-the-century vaudeville circuit, an industry largely populated by working-class performers of particular ethnic backgrounds; the most predominant being Irish and Jewish. Many vaudeo stars, including Caesar, had begun their careers in the circuit and had later performed in the 'Borsht Belt', a collection of Jewish hotels located in the Catskills, which managed further to emphasize their ethnic and religious affiliations. The publicity generated for Caesar, Berle and Burns consistently referred to their early careers in such venues as well as to their childhoods and familial connections in New York ethnic neighbourhoods such as Harlem, Yonkers and the Lower East Side. In some instances, articles would not only reveal the neighbourhood of the performer's birth, but also the exact street address.[3] These elements formed the basis for their reception as men who maintained affiliations with specific regional and cultural conceptions of men. They were clearly not raised to become traditional Anglo-Saxon heroes in the form of cowboys, drifters, or tough guys. Instead, their roles as comedic performers were constructed and received through historically and culturally specific signifiers of ethnic masculinity. In addition, the variety format in which they worked (with its emphasis on multiple characterizations, ethnic humour and drag) granted them the room in which to play with these signifiers and to further complicate assumptions about a stable, traditional American masculinity.

Traditions and Constructions of Comedic Performance

Many of the stock characters created by comedians such as Berle and Benny for their variety programmes were amalgams of American assumptions about masculinity and ethnicity. As Henry Jenkins has discussed, the implementation of easily recognizable class, ethnic, gender or regional traits into vaudeville characters allowed for the lean economy of the form's truncated narratives and 'olio' structure. Jenkins describes, for example, how the traditional male Irish stock character was created through the use of 'a collarless shirt, an oversized vest, a pair of loose workman's pants with a rope belt, a battered hat, all predominately green; a red wig and a set of red whiskers arranged as a fringe around the face; a propensity for epithets and slang, a sing-song vocal pattern, and a thick brogue.' (Jenkins 1992:70) Jewish characters, which did not become popular in vaudeville until the early 1900s, were often created through the donning of a long, pointed beard, large spectacles, long black coat and dark plug hat. (Gilbert 1940:287)

Michele Hilmes notes that this vaudevillian practice continued in golden age radio, but since it was required to reside in the purely aural, the skills of the ethnic dialectician were emphasized (Hilmes 1997:89). Race, ethnicity and class were fashioned through vocal cues and underscored by stereotyped behaviour. This practice of turning performance into an identity shorthand was picked up in vaudeo, allowing a similar economy to inform variety show production. Although dialect would continue to play a role in broadcast variety, there was also a return to an emphasis on visual display as performers could again rely on mannerisms and dress to connote identity.

Although the vaudeo star's own ethnicity did not always dovetail with the ethnicity of the characters he/she had created, the audience may have assumed a certain amount of cross-fertilization between performers' on-stage characters and their own authentic identity. Richard Dyer discusses the way in which the 'real' personality of the star is assumed to seep out of his/her on-screen characterizations (Dyer 1991). The assumption is that the media text provides clues for the audience to tease out the 'authentic' self underpinning the fictional construct. The question of the performer's 'real' identity in relation to his/her characterizations is theorized as pivotal to audience relationships with the star/performer in both cinema and vaudeville. Moreover, the vaudeville aesthetic overtly courted the conflation of on-stage/off-stage personas by breaking the boundaries of theatrical realism, allowing for a higher degree of intimacy between performer and audience. In *What Made Pistachio Nuts?* Jenkins quotes vaudeville performer Walter DeLeon: 'Actor and audience are closer together, know each other better [than in legitimate theatre] . . . therefore he aims to be as simple, as direct and as genuine as the medium of his art permits.' (Jenkins 1992:73)

Variety television programmes borrowed much of vaudeville's style and continued to emphasize the relationship between performer and audience through such devices as direct address and studio audience interaction. Television also courted audience assumptions about the authenticity of television performers through its persistent claims to intimacy. Because television was placed within the domestic and was initially live, the industry sold itself to audiences as being more intimate and real. Furthermore, because television performers were required to act sincere and trustworthy in this environment in order to sell their sponsor's wares, they often worked to come across as more genuine. For vaudeo stars the representation of what could be construed as their authentic on- and off-stage personas occurred while they were acting as their show's host – during monologues and in their (relatively) straight interactions with their guest stars. They would then go on to perform in sketches as a number of different characters but, in their self-referential asides to their audience, they would often return to what was understood to be their core personality.

Both the operations of television stardom and those of comedy performance helped determine the identity of early television comedians. Moreover, their ethnicity and sexuality are at stake both in their on-screen performance of specific character types and in the construction of their off-screen personae. As such, the disruptive nature of what Steven Seidman calls 'comedian-centred comedy' has ramifications for the audience's subsequent perceptions of the comedian's 'authentic' identity in relation to his/her characterizations. (Seidman:1981:8–11) Recent work on the comedy genre by Seidman, Jenkins and Frank Krutnik, amongst others, has revealed the ways in which comedian-centred, gag or slapstick comedy will often disrupt classical narrative continuity by allowing the audience to linger on the spectacle of performance. In discussions of film comedy, examples such as Hope's cross-dressing in *Road to Rio* are used to elucidate the way in which the comedian's over-the-top performance can intrude into an otherwise coherent, stabilized narrative.

These scholars also suggest that the comedy star's characterization/identity may be destabilized by such narrative ruptures. Speaking specifically about classical Hollywood comedy, Frank Krutnik suggests, 'the comedian figure deforms familiar conventions of film heroism, unified identity, and mature sexuality' and he goes on to conclude that, in the play of narrative disruption and containment, these films 'circulate around questions of gendered identity.' (Krutnik 1995:29 & 36) The variety format is not as coherent in its structure as is the classical Hollywood film. However, the vaudeo star's ability to cross over from one sketch to another, to embody numerous characters, to provide a base or stable personality in his role as host and spontaneously to interrupt guest performances reveals similar moments of disjuncture caused by the seemingly uncontrolled nature of the format's lead performer.[4] Vaudeo's presentational, comedian-centred, gag and slapstick style figure the vaudeo comic's persona as one that is fluid in both its relation to narrative as well as to constructions of authenticity and performance. Specifically, vaudeo appears to be fascinated with the reticulations of gender and ethnicity. The vaudeo star plays with the signs of both of these categories of identity and complicates them through his decentred position within the narrative and his intimate relationship with his audience.[5] Berle's performance style provides a good example of this process, as he was known for his constant interruptions of his show's sketches and guest stars' performances. While a sketch was in progress, Berle would make asides to his audiences out of the sketch's character, often making references or inside jokes to what the audience knew of his on-stage persona. While performing his drag bits, Berle's extreme physical plays on femininity (such as batting his false eyelashes or pursing his overly made-up lips in a faux-seductive manner) were often disrupted by moments where his voice would dip and he would speak to the audience with his normal baritone voice. For example, in one 1951 episode of *Texaco Star Theatre*, he opened the show as a bride escorted by a portly groom. The audience howled as he swished his hips and batted his eyes, singing a ditty about how he married an elephant. As the groom left the stage, however, Berle continued his monologue in his own voice and as Berle, but with the occasional feminine gesture. Still dressed as a woman Berle discussed marriage from a male point of view, commiserating with the married men in the audience. He ended by taking off his wig and introducing the evening's guest star.

Moments like this would serve to disrupt the continuity of Berle's characterizations, highlighting their artificiality and confusing the distinctions of gender codes. Berle would also 'spontaneously' break into the acts performed by his musical guests. The mini-narrative of even these smaller moments within the variety format were made discontinuous by Berle's intrusive persona.

Although Berle is a more extreme example of the vaudeo star's decentredness, Burns and Caesar would also go in and out of character in a similar manner. This process results in a destablization of all characterization, emphasizing the constructed nature of identity, but at the same time it reasserts a consistent personality that exists beneath their performances.

4.1. Milton Berle, whose drag routines were an essential part of his on-screen persona, appears here as a bride in an episode of Texaco Star Theatre.

Signs of Jewish Identity in the Vaudeo Star

The strong conflation of 'real life' and 'reel life' which occurred in the reception of the television comedian was contained within the destabilized identity that is part of the narrative play in comedian-centred comedy. Thus, the comedian's persona may have been rendered as contradictory or even incoherent. In attempting to forge a unified identity for these performers which satisfied the perceived desires of the domestic broadcast audience, the network publicity offices and talent agencies had to assemble a narrative for the stars' life that would assimilate the various, and often disjunctive, aspects of the comedians' sexuality and ethnicity. This was most often achieved through discourses on the 'real-life' ethnic and familial pasts of vaudeo performers. Many of the men who were heralded as the first names to consolidate a regular viewing audience were fashioned as ethically (and ethnically) justified recipients of television fame. This meant that discourses on domesticity were constructed around these men that spoke to pertinent social concerns and memories that were circulating in the post-war culture. In particular, discourses that served to remind viewers of the ethnic and immigrant make-up of the urban areas from which they came were important elements in positioning the domestic histories of the typical vaudeo star. However, the very ethnic identities and working-class origins of these vaudeo stars that were comforting reminders of America's immigrant past, could also be deleterious elements of their persona in the years immediately following the Second World War. Therefore, few of them would openly acknowledge their ethnicity – especially for those who were Jewish, besides the occasional note of a performer's birth name (for example, Eddie Cantor as Edward Israel Iskowitz) or, in the case of Burns and Allen, an acknowledgment of a 'mixed' marriage. Instead, there were covert signs of ethnic identity embedded in the representations of the performers' work and familial histories, their constructions of feminized masculinities and their imbrication in urban values.

Barry Rubin asserts that in the immediate post-war era relatively few Jews living in the public eye would play openly on their background since 'For most, the market's dictate did more than any prejudice to make it preferable not to seem too Jewish lest this cut one off from the best opportunities and widest audience.' (Rubin 1995:98) He remarks that although comedy was dominated by Jews and Jewish humour, 'The Jewish comedians, all products of Orthodox, Yiddish-speaking homes, retained none of these characteristics themselves.' Instead, audiences could infer their ethnic background through the stories told about their pasts as well as subtle inflections, gestures and regional references. Rubin notes that Americans in the 1950s did develop a fascination for Jewish culture since it represented difference in an era of extreme homogeneity. He quotes Robert Alter, who wrote frequently on Jewish identity, as saying that during this period it was significant that

> the Jew has a special language, a unique system of gestures, a different kind of history which goes much further back than that of other Americans, a different cuisine, a kind of humor and irony that other Americans don't have, the colorfulness and pathos which other Americans aren't supposed to possess anymore.[6]

Those differences that were found in American Jewish culture acted as nostalgic reminders of the different nationalities and cultures that were assimilated into the country's urban culture during the prior century's waves of immigration. Although an immigrant label was not synonymous with a particular type of ethnicity, the influx of immigrant groups into different poor or working-class neighbourhoods of New York at the turn-of-the-century led to a confluence of an individual's ethnic background with the urban space in which he/she was raised. For example, much of Burns' extra-textual material mentioned his years growing up as the child of immigrants in New York's Lower East Side. Although not every resident of this area was of Jewish extraction, it was historically known by East Coasters as a largely Jewish enclave: a first stop for Eastern European Jews in their initiation into American culture. Thus, Burns' geographic origin and the performance and speaking style he acquired from the neighbourhood were clues to his ethnic and religious background. This was also true for Caesar. Karen Adair suggests that, 'Though Caesar never made a point of his Jewishness while performing, nevertheless it did emerge in some of his inflections and phrasing . . . such as "Darts, they're playing." The almost talmudic lament of "It'll be a miracle!" is the sort of thing Jewish mothers wail when their kids are growing up.' (Adair 1988:77)

Jenkins' study of Cantor's film persona reveals the ways in which the comedian's Jewishness was assimilated into general connotations of urbanity in the late 1920s and early 1930s in order to appeal to film audiences in regions outside of East Coast urban centres. Jenkins notes that

> while the question of ethnic identity was a key concern within urban areas where the immigrant masses struggled to define their place in American society and therefore a prime field for the construction of jokes, it did not prove as amusing in the hinterlands, which either found the question irrelevant or too threatening to provide much humour. (Jenkins 1990:43)

As a result, Cantor (who had made much of his Jewishness in publicity materials early in his career) was forced to avoid direct references to his ethnicity and instead to allow his persona to retain only 'subtle textual traces of his Jewishness, all but invisible to regional viewers, yet potentially meaningful to minority audiences.' (Jenkins 1990:46) What occurred to Cantor during the late 1920s and early 1930s is similar to the management of the vaudeo persona that occurred twenty years later. Although early vaudeo stars were playing to largely urban audiences who would recognize ethnic tropes and allusions, performers such as Burns, Berle, Benny and Caesar allowed tales of their origins and urban sensibilities to speak softly for their Jewish heritage, so as to not offend rural and suburban viewers.[7]

The portrayal of stars' domestic lives was an essential extratextual element of the production of star personas during this period. It was particularly important for television stars as the industry was trying to construct television as a family-friendly entity that rightfully belonged in the centre of American home-life. Although the popular press often initially portrayed the married vaudeo male as the head of his own happy family in the popular press, this narrative would often have to be rewritten in light of domestic discontent. Benny and Burns, both well known in the broadcasting industry from their success on radio, were easy to portray as family men since both of them worked closely with their wives and adopted children during their broadcasting careers. Berle had also adopted a daughter during his tenure as 'Uncle Miltie' but his role as 1950s patriarch would also be tainted by marital problems. In early 1950 *Redbook* reported that 'The domestication of Milton Berle has proved a challenge even to the persuasive resources of his wife, a former showgirl billed as "Joyce Matthews, the prettiest girl in America." There have been troubled moments in the union, including a divorce.'[8] Matthews, after divorcing Berle for the second time around, in 1952 attempted suicide in the apartment of her married lover, theatrical producer Billy Rose.

In light of the threat such scandals posed to the stars' credibility as 'happy family men', it was far more advantageous for publicity agents to emphasize the performers' extended family over their nuclear one. Vaudeville was a handy tool in this process because it provided the appropriate backdrop for the typical American success story. Moreover, cultural memories of the massive influx of immigrants arriving in the USA in the early 1900s were potentially stimulated by the move of more than one million Americans from cities to suburbs during the post-war era. Douglas Gomery elucidates the connection that exists between these two significant demographic shifts:

> To appreciate the scope of this internal migration, compare it to the more famous transatlantic movement from Europe to the United States around the turn of the century. In 1907, when migration was at its peak, more than one million Europeans landed in the United States. This was precisely the magnitude of the suburban migration of the late 1940s and early 1950s. (Gomery 1992:85)

The press often described vaudeo performers as having successfully re-negotiated their working-class positions through hard work, humour and a kind of ethnic pluck. They were providers who enabled their often large families to escape the poverty of urban immigrant neighbourhoods. Berle, Burns and Caesar, all child vaudeville stars raised in poor, Jewish neighbourhoods, were quick to describe how their families had been integral to their success in the theatre. They variously worked with their siblings, were pushed by their strong-willed mothers or were inspired by the wish to provide for their large working-class clans. Many told stories of how they resisted the Old World traditions of their immigrant parents in order better to succeed in American culture. Burns related his ambivalence towards the religious voracity of his cantor father and Benny repeatedly told the story of how his father hit him on the head with a prayer book as punishment for arriving late to Yom Kippur service. Rubin argues that

> The contrast between unpleasant Jewish childhoods and high American aspirations characterized the life of most Jews growing up between the 1890s and 1930s . . . A powerful emotional force pushed them toward success in American society and away from Jewish identity. But equally ashamed of abandoning it, they often retained a strong sentimental attachment for that background. (Rubin 1995:68–9)

Berle, whose mother Sandra regularly appeared in his television act, had been discovered at the age of five when he won five dollars in a Bronx talent contest for mimicking Charlie Chaplin. His early years as a child actor in vaudeville and in silent film were often portrayed in the popular press as a struggle to keep his Harlem-based family together. Describing his father as ineffectual in supporting his family, Berle often told stories of his mother's undying support for his career and in his ability to provide for his financially strapped family. Sandra was a constant presence in Berle's life and performances and acted as a continuing reminder to the public of his troubled beginnings and of his unending mother-love. When on television, 'Uncle Miltie' was also cleverly crafted as a family entertainer, not only through his relationship with his mother (who was often in the studio audience) but also through his implied relationship with viewing families. He always had special goodnight greetings for the children in the audience and did television specials and benefits for children. In one such special, *Uncle Miltie's Christmas Party* (NBC, 1950), Berle was subjected to water, powder and pies in the face. Although this was a rather common vaudeville joke, it also allowed Berle's masculinity to be subjugated, helping to make him everybody's favourite uncle; a non-sexual, non-threatening member of the family.

References to vaudeo performers' extended families and their ethnic working-class upbringings resonated with the pasts of many urban television viewers. But they also may have stimulated sentimental memories of extended familial structures (which were now threatened by encroaching suburbanization) as well as earlier ethnic politics and processes of assimilation occurring during the 1920s and 1930s. In the years immediately following the Second World War, the vaudeville aesthetic reminded white Americans of a time when ethnic politics *appeared* to be comparatively uncomplicated. Revelations of the Holocaust and fears associated with the Cold War came to weigh heavily on the minds of many Americans over subsequent years. And the turn-of-the-century immigration waves that had brought significant numbers of European Jews to the USA would seem in retrospect to be a time of relatively smooth assimilation. Additionally, the State of Israel was proclaimed in May of 1948 as a safe haven for Jews. In light of the discourses on the Holocaust, the television vaudevillian, largely understood as 'ethnic' and most often Jewish, would be a comforting sight to many Americans who had only recently learned of Nazi Germany's attempted extermination of the Jews. Henry Popkin, who complained bitterly about the lack of Jewish characters or performers in film during the immediate post-war period wrote in a 1952 edition of the conservative magazine *Commentary* that:

> Whatever may happen in the future, one fact is encouraging; in television, as in radio during its heyday, there prevails what might be called the New York idea, that Jewishness is not freakish or embarrassing and there might as well be Jewish comedians as any other kind. Hence one finds the sort of Jewish reference, whether comic or not, that stands in refreshing contrast to the rest of our antiseptically 'Aryanized' popular culture: a Yiddish phrase spoken, a Jewish dialect or intonation, an identifiably Jewish ironic quality ... All of this expresses no attitude, breaks no lances against anti-Semitism; it only recognizes one fact of experience: that Jews do exist.[9]

Despite the fact that subtle references to ethnicity may have been comforting to urban and Jewish viewers of early television, Jewish performers were in many ways suspicious figures in American culture during the late 1940s and early 1950s. This is precisely why Levenson expressed such trepidation about Jewish humour and stereotypes. The implementation of the broadcasting blacklist after the publication of *Red Channels: A Report on Communism in Broadcasting* in 1948 revealed that many Jewish performers were unfairly targeted as communists because of their ethnic heritage. For some, the Rosenberg trial in 1952 was the pinnacle of the rhetorical confluence of anti-Semitism and anti-communism.

Such events as the publication of *Red Channels* and the Rosenberg trial belie the complicated, and often treacherous, signifiers that often piggy-backed on the codes of Jewishness. So, while Jewish ethnicity may have been essential in the revitalization of the vaudeville aesthetic and, subsequently, in the naturalization of the television medium as a legitimate form of cultural production, it was difficult to acknowledge routinely and overtly. Instead, ethnicity was commonly moderated through the codes of urbanity and immigrant childhood and family. Yet, another significant way to obliquely reference Jewishness was through the performance of masculinity. The male vaudeo star's multivalent sexuality had the potential to activate long-standing assumptions about the nature of his ethnic background.

Mobilizing Ethnicity by Troubling Masculinity

Although his on-screen comedy was largely based in wordplay, insult jokes and topical gags, Berle's costume acts were the most popular segments of *Texaco Star Theatre*. The comedian was known for his female impersonations of, for example, Cleopatra, Carmen Miranda and the Opera star Dorothy Kristen (who was so insulted by his portrayal of her that she took him to court). As the *New York Times* wrote in a 1990 retrospective article, Berle 'was a man who wasn't afraid of a dress and for four years he owned Saturday night.'[10] Although his cross-dressing was a long-standing practice in vaudeville and was not often directly described in the press as being sexually transgressive, a 1951 article in *Sponsor* implied that sponsors and broadcasters were aware of such tensions:

> Some eyebrows in the trade are up more or less all the time at TV's tolerance of 'swish' routines and impersonations. They think that's going too far, projecting a special brand of big city tenderloin into the family circle. Other observers are more relaxed about the 'swish' stuff, [sic] think it will be interpreted as nothing more than a spoofing of sex characteristics.[11]

Berle's propensity for donning a dress would have been especially potent when considered in relation to his ethnicity since many theorists have argued

that femininity has long been considered a concomitant feature of male
Jewishness. Citing examples from the early Church to Nazi propaganda films,
Garber notes that 'Not only sartorially, but also scientifically and theoretically, the idea of the Jewish man as "effeminate" as well as "degenerate" has
a long and unlovely history in European culture.' (Garber 1992:224) The
characteristics that seemed to set Jewish men (particularly those of the Hasidic
sect) apart – the way they spoke, dressed, gestured – were regarded by many
gentiles as not only foreign but also 'woman-like'. Daniel Boyarin, in his
detailed analysis of Jewish masculinity, suggests that the European conception of the Jewish man as half man, half woman was asserted by the Jewish
culture itself. It is a reaction to its marginalization since 'Jewish society needed
an image against which to define itself and produced the "goy" – the hypermale
– as its countertype, as a reverse of its social norm [sic].' (Boyarin 1997:4–5)
Boyarin goes on to suggest that this alternative gender typing is a historical
strategy for cultural survival: instead of imitating their oppressors, Jewish
men embraced the antithesis of Anglo 'hyper-masculinity.'[12] Although Boyarin
never specifically mentions any of the vaudevillians who worked on television, Garber ultimately finds Berle's form of cross-dressing a strategy which
reasserts feminization of the Jewish man. She claims his drag impersonations
were a 'prerogative' of power because he chose to cross-dress and to directly
confront the stigmatization of the Jewish man as feminine. Garber writes
that, 'for a Borscht Belt comedian like Milton Berle, whose routines so often
included a drag act, to cross-dress for success, recuperating, however uncon-
sciously, this "feminization" of the Jewish man and deploying gender parody
as an empowering strategy.' (Garber 1992:233)

Beyond referencing the feminization of Jewish masculinity, another de-
terminant in Berle's 'feminization' was his relationship with his mother. His
publicity material, which focused primarily on his childhood performances
as a working-class Harlem native, repeatedly emphasized an overbearing,
yet loving Jewish mother. In an article entitled 'My Son, Uncle Miltie',
published in the LA Examiner on Mother's Day 1952, Sandra Berle writes:

> As for a good many years, wherever he went I did go, getting the bookings, fighting
> the would-be managers and agents and talent developers, cooking over a can of
> Sterno in hotel rooms for the both of us, living out of a trunk. Those were the hard
> days and then came the good ones, all these good ones. Thrills? Milton asking me
> to stand up and take a bow, in the audience, in cities coast to coast. Milton, the first
> time he played the Palace in New York as a single actor, buying me something I'd
> always wanted – a mink coat.[13]

Berle's attachment to his mother managed to domesticate him, to connect
him with family life, yet at the same time demasculinized him further, even
if his attachment was couched in the comforting discourse of immigrant
culture. The brashness and sexual innuendoes of Berle's live performance
were tamed and the longstanding stereotypes about Jewish mothers and

their sons were clearly reinforced for the television audience. Berle told Gladys Hall, a writer for *Radio/TV Mirror*, that he always included Sandra in his life and performances because of all that she did for him during his childhood:

> Some forget, when they grow up what their mothers did for them and gave to them. I don't forget. I remember . . . all the sacrifices she made for me and the things she went without so that I could succeed. I don't think there is ever enough that you can do for your mother. Ever.[14]

In a 1989 interview, Berle expressed concern over his feminized image. When asked why he had so many extramarital affairs, Berle responded by saying, 'Maybe I had to prove my manhood to the outside world that always saw me with my mother and wearing dresses in my act. Is she his "beard"? Is he gay? Maybe that's why I played around so much.'[15]

Benny, whose vanity, posture and gestures could have been construed as feminine, was a tamer version of the Jewish male comic and was much slower to enter into the arena of television. Unlike Berle, Benny often avoided the use of the puns and slapstick moves of traditional vaudeville routines, choosing instead to place his radio and television narratives within a situational context. However, the use of the cheapskate stereotype, his violin-playing and his reliance on self-disparaging humour were definite components of both his vaudeville performances and his ethnic background. According to Hilmes and Margaret McFadden, Benny's feminization originated in his radio programme. Hilmes writes that:

> Jack comically violated all the norms of American masculinity. Obviously wealthy but unable to spend money, thinking himself the pinnacle of masculine attractiveness but unable to interest women, suave and debonair but unable to handle simple situations, the authoritative host of a major radio programme but unable to command the respect of his employees (and, later, a white man totally dependent on his black servant, in a relationship with strangely homoerotic implications). (Hilmes 1997:194)

McFadden argues that the construction of Jack and Rochester as an interracial couple is undermined by both characters' pursuance of women within the programme's text. She argues, therefore, that the subversive potential of their relationship is contained, as:

> Their aggressive heterosexuality, like that of the other men in the cast, obscures their all-male family and thus makes it acceptable. Further, this ambiguity allows the construction of a family where certain non-threatening women and some feminine qualities in men are permitted, but where no culturally idealized wives and mothers intrude.' (McFadden 1993:126)

Denise Mann, however, contends that Benny's 'aggressive heterosexuality' in relation to the female film stars who appeared on his show actually feminized him further, at least momentarily, by placing him in the role of ogling fan. She notes that:

> Benny's power and autonomy vanish once he adopts the 'feminized' position of the adoring fan in the narrative skit. It returns once he reappears on stage as the star of his own show and speaks to the audience in 'direct address.' These changing power dynamics are the result of shifting rhetorical positionings rather than some essentially female characteristics of desire. (Mann 1992:53)

Still, Benny had little trouble fitting within mainstream America's conception of a domestic entertainer. This was, in part, the result of a consistent publicity campaign that depicted him as a benevolent family man. Benny's stage persona as a curmudgeonly, vain, penny pincher was disavowed as who he was in real life in numerous press releases and publications during the late 1940s and early 1950s. Unlike the publicity surrounding other vaudeo stars of the period, which worked to conflate performers' on-screen personalities with those of their off-screen identities, articles and press releases about Benny denied any direct connection between the two identities. This may be attributed to the fact that the situational narrative of *The Jack Benny Program* required Benny, unlike Berle and Caesar, to remain in one character during its entire broadcast. And, although this character could be endearing at times, he could also be quite despicable. In order to prevent broadcast audiences from believing that Benny was really as vain and cheap as his on-screen character, Benny and his publicists carefully managed to retain the most positive aspects of Benny's broadcast persona, while denying the 'reality' of the most offensive aspects of that image. The story of his rise to fame as a child violinist as well as that of his generosity and his role as a dedicated family man and loyal friend were circulated as means to this end. In a 1944 article in *American Magazine*, Benny's radio personality was suggested to be a great psychic burden to the 'real' Benny. Jerome Beatty writes:

> If you or I made $10,000 every Sunday we wouldn't care if the world thought we were Jo-Jo, the dog-faced boy. But Jack Benny, at 50, takes life and public-opinion as seriously as a candidate for the US Senate and spends most of his spare time chasing his shadow, trying to stamp it out.[16]

In a 1949 CBS press release, Livingston claimed, 'Jack has his own hair and teeth, is not anemic, is in perfect physical condition, can play a pretty good violin and in my opinion and in the opinion of almost everyone who really knows him, is the greatest guy in the world.'[17] In addition, Benny often played with the constructed nature of his broadcast character and public image. For example, a 1951 layout of Benny and his family in *Look* parodied the supposed 'real-life' publicity photos that Hollywood stars typically had taken of them in staged domestic settings. Stanley Gordon writes facetiously in the introduction that 'From now on, Benny intends to be photographed like the Hollywood stars in movie magazines – in cozy family scenes to warm the hearts of his many fans, pictures to show that the Benny's are, after all, "just plain folks." '[18] Jack, Joan and Mary participated in the accompanying photos that have them doing the dishes, working on Joan's homework, cleaning the car, singing at the piano. A caption to a shot of Jack hanging laundry on the line read, 'The domestic type: Jack hangs out a few things in the laundry yard (A full-time laundress is really the one who does the family wash daily.)' Accompanying the image of Jack, Mary and Joan sitting around the piano singing and playing the violin, a caption read 'After dinner, the Benny's always gather round the piano for a musicale. (In fact, Jack keeps violin in bathroom, plays only on his CBS program.)' By pointing out the media fabrication of stars and their home lives through these joking asides, Benny destabilizes the authenticity of his fictional persona. In doing so, he was able to pick and choose which characteristics he wished to emphasize and which he would de-emphasize. He could remain the vain fall guy on-screen or in radio, but was also able to claim that he was still 'authentic' in the way that the public would value (ie he was trustworthy, caring and generous), thereby making him an acceptable role model and product pitchman.

Although the assumptions of Jewishness and a peculiarly feminized masculinity mobilized around Benny continued to make him popular throughout his career, they were also denied in an effort perhaps to bolster his fiscal and social standing in the 1950s. By recreating an image of the hardworking, generous and often guilt-ridden Benny, the home viewing audience could be more comfortable with his extraordinarily glamorous lifestyle – and, specifically, his much publicized post-talent raid salary. But even the revised Benny, although now in recoil from some of the more long-standing Jewish stereotypes of his earlier persona, was still entrenched in the mythic struggle of a working-class boy made good. This struggle, as I have shown, was firmly imbricated with nostalgia for the immigrant and extended family and domestication of the vaudeville aesthetic.

Conclusion

The form of ethnic (read Jewish) masculinity that helped shape the careers and personas of early television comedians had a limited utility in the subsequent development of television's industrial and cultural operations. For a brief period, coinciding with the years of the FCC's freeze on licenses, performances of men who cultivated a flexible, yet historically defined and culturally determined, gendered identity dominated television. The industry was able both to exploit and to counter the signs of an alternative form of masculinity during its campaign to enter the American home by mobilizing the cultural memory of an audience unsettled by recent social upheavals and the break-up of the extended family.

By the mid-1950s the variety show was clearly in decline. As noted by many television historians, this was due, at least in part, to the lifting of the freeze and the changing demographics of the television audience. No longer primarily urban, nor as ethnically mixed, the audience was now largely middle-class and increasingly living in rural and suburban areas: the cultural references made by Jewish vaudeville comedians ceased to be familiar to a large part of the audience's cultural experience.

Furthermore, as Lynn Spigel argues, during the early 1950s when government officials were focusing much of their attention on television content, vaudeo bore the brunt of the censorship debates.[19] Concerned about the bawdy antics, ethnic jokes and sexual asides of vaudeo comedians, these politicians pointed to the format's New York sensibility as the root source of its offensiveness.[20] In *Television Program Production*, Carroll O'Meara contended that:

> What many entertainers fail to realize, actually, is that the areas containing the bistros, night spots, and bright lights are only a segment of America. And yet, somehow, they insist on broadcasting to the entire nation comic and other material which is definitely not acceptable in the average American home . . . Our nation consists of 160 million citizens, most of whom live in small towns, go to church on Sunday, attempt to bring up their children decently, and do not regard burlesque as the ultimate in theatre.

The public calls for censorship by public officials and cultural critics made sponsors nervous. Out of fear of losing their consumer base, they were forced to reconsider many of the basic tenets of vaudeo humour. A 1951 article in *Sponsor* claimed that television carried with it a greater risk of offending viewers than radio or film and recommended that sponsors censor problematic programme content:

> Advertisers are by now pretty well briefed, or they ought to be, as to the everyday hazards lurking in racial jokes, dialects, characterizations, and superiority-inferiority situations. The pictorial factor in TV increases the danger . . . So long as the sponsor's goal is universal good will for his products and services he cannot indulge in heavy-handed kidding and race-trait burlesque and then be surprised if Italians or Mexicans, or Irish, or Jews pass him by at the retail firing line.[21]

The ethnic and brash urban personalities that made vaudeo such a success in the late 1940s were now considered inappropriate for the increasingly national, middle-class audience. As a result, critics and politicians singled out the vaudeo star as an example of the tastelessness of network broadcasting. Many vaudeo producers responded by altering the structure and sensibility of their programmes by introducing sitcom plots, erasing ethnic references and making their programmes more family-friendly overall. However, these changes would not ultimately save the vaudeo comedians who built early television. By 1953, Dick Powell, president of the Television Writers of America, was claiming that the 'death of video comedy stars is being caused by censorship . . . If Will Rogers were alive today, he would probably go back to rope-twirling.'[22]

In the early 1950s the television industry was also forced to appease audiences and critics who were becoming bored with vaudeo performers and sponsors who tired of paying their exorbitant salaries. Consequently, sponsors and trade critics' frequent and forceful cries for new faces and formats had a significant impact on the industry's eventual embrace of the sitcom. More concerned with the repetitious nature of vaudeo than with its inability to resonate culturally outside of the East Coast, some sponsors and critics expressed concern over the long-term viability of the vaudeville performance style and the age of its television headliners as early as 1950. Sponsors were also deeply worried about the financial implications of what *Variety* dubbed the 'New Talent Crisis', a period in the early 1950s when the industry, feeling the strain of its prior disregard for talent development, enabled vaudeo stars' salaries to skyrocket and dramatically increase the variety format's overall production costs. As a result, the sitcom format, with its emphasis on narrative and reliance on a regular cast (rather than expensive, high-profile guest stars), looked like an economically viable venture for sponsors and independent producers alike especially with successful examples already on-air.

Although traces of the vaudeville aesthetic tradition were still present in television comedy, plot-driven, 'realistic', suburban sitcoms dominated network programme schedules by the late 1950s and early 1960s. This format offered viewers a new vision of domesticity, identity and consumer culture that differed dramatically from that of early variety shows and ethnic sitcoms. George Lipsitz suggests that 'For Americans to accept the new world of fifties consumerism, they had to make a break with the past.'(Lipsitz 1992:75)[23] In the case of television, the industry and its audience were ready to break with vaudeo, as the format's references to prior traditions of ethnic masculinity and immigrant life were no longer culturally relevant to viewers now eager to embrace the 'good life' promised in suburbia.

Notes

I would like to thank Janet Staiger and Janet Thumim for their suggestions and support for this article.
1. *Variety*, 23 June 1948:24.
2. Norman Blackburn, 'But Names Will Never Hurt Me', *Variety*, 5 January 1949:195.
3. The *Saturday Evening Post* reported in 1949 that Berle was born at W. 118th Street. Robert Sylvester, 'The Strange Career of Milton Berle', *Saturday Evening Post*, 19 March 1949:38.

4. In 'How Milton Berle Got Into Television', *LA Examiner*, 29 April 1951:21, Berle was quoted as saying, 'Some people say I'm in the show too much and some people say I'm not in it enough. They accuse me of interrupting the acts but there's a difference between interruption and integration . . . To come from left field and interrupt an act without any thought given to how it will look would be dangerous. If there isn't any actual reason to come into the act, I assure you I will never do it.'

5. Although borrowing from film theory in order to elucidate television can be a questionable endeavour, the interpenetration of performance styles and narrative strategies in and amongst television, radio, film and vaudeville during this period warrants close comparison. Part of the difficulty in studying early television comedy is the lack of research on the genre with regards to the specific characteristics of the medium. In future work, I plan to explore this area further.

6. Rubin 1998. Rubin quotes Robert Alter, *America and Israel* (New York 1970) 10.

7. Yet, even the relatively innocuous signs of urbanity also caused problems for the entertainers as critics complained that their 'big city values' were offensive to small-town middle-class viewers. References to performers' urban sensibilities in this context were used to negatively connect their geographic orgins with the use of blue and ethnic humour and sexual innuendo. Consequently, the same signs used to place a performer within a particular cultural mileu were also seemingly suspect, and potentially offensive, to many television critics during this period. An argument could be made that there existed anti-Semitic undertones to this conflation. Leslie Fiedler argues that 'the discovery in the Jews of a people essentially urban, essentially Europe-oriented, a ready-made image for what the American longs to or fears he is being forced to become.' Leslie Fiedler, 'Saul Bellows', in *Saul Bellow and the Critics*, ed. Irving Maline (New York 1967) 2–3.

8. Edwin H. James, 'Anything for a Laugh!', *Redbook*, January 1950:51;94–96;100.

9. Henry Popkin, 'The Vanishing Jew of Our Popular Culture: The Little Man Who is No Longer There', *Commentary*, vol. 14, no. 4 (October 1952) 50.

10. Jeremy Gerard, 'Milton Berle Browses at Home and the TV Audience Gets a Treat,' *New York Times*, 11 December 1990:C15.

11. 'Be Careful on the Air: On TV, the Risk of Offending is Even Greater Than on Radio or in the Movies,' *Sponsor*, 24 September 1951:36–7; 6–80.

12. Robert Meeropol, the son of Ethel and Julis Rosenberg, contends that the government and the press feminized his father during the years of his incarceration, trial and execution. He writes, 'The fonts of conventional wisdom also helped popularize the characterization of my mother as dominant and my father as submissive. Such a relationship was widely viewed as "unnatural" in the 1950s. Morris Ernst, co-counsel for the ACLU, first offered to represent my parents if they would confess and then offered the FBI his analysis of the dynamics of my parent's relationship. Ernst, the amateur psychologist who had never met my parents, concluded that "Julis is the slave and his wife Ethel is the master." ' From Robert Meeropol, 'Rosenberg Realities', in *Secret Agents: The Rosenberg Case, McCarthyism and Fifties America*, ed. Marjorie Garber and Rebecca L. Walkowitz. (New York 1995) 241–2.

13. Sandra Berle, 'My Son, Uncle Miltie', *LA Examiner*, 19 May 1952.

14. Glayds Hall, 'Everybody's Uncle Miltie', *Radio/TV Mirror*, June 1951:80.

15. Dorothy Rader, 'The Hard Life, the Strong Loves of a Very Funny Man', *Parade Magazine* in *The Boston Globe*, 19 March 1989:6. Besides gossip on his extramarital affairs, there were many rumours about the immense size of Berle's penis. Perhaps this discourse can be also be interpreted as an attempt to assert a more conventional masculinity for Berle in order to thwart questions of his sexual preference.

16. Jerome Beatty, 'Unhappy Fiddler', *American Magazine*, December 1944:28–9;142–3.

[17.] Mary Livingston, 'By His Own Doing, He's the "Most Maligned Man in the World," Says Mary Livingston of Husband Jack Benny', *CBS Press Release*, 7 February 1949.

[18.] Stanley Gordon, 'The Rebellion of Jack Benny', *Look*, 8 May 1951.

[19.] In 1952, indecent content on television was just one concern of government officials. 'At the moment five main areas offer continuing problems: 1) plugs that fail; 2) beer and wine commercials; 3) indecency; 4) racial stereotypes; 5) violence.' See Bert Briller, 'TV Code has upped Necklines, but Long Plugs, Beer Blurbs, Violence, Race Carbons Still Pose Problems', *Variety*, 31 December 1952:20;27. Also see Spigel 147–149.

[20.] New York-produced live anthology dramas were also considered to appeal to only 'urban tastes'. For more on this, see William Boddy, *Fifties Television: The Industry and Its Critics* (1993) 93–107.

[21.] 'Be Careful on the Air: On TV, the Risk of Offending is Even Greater Than on Radio or in the Movies', *Sponsor*, 24 September 1951:36–7; 76–80.

[22.] 'Low State of Comedy Blamed on Censorship, Pressure Groups,' *Variety*, 25 February 1953:1.

[23.] George Lipsitz, 'The Meaning of Memory: Family, Class and Ethnicity in Early Network Television Programs', in Spigel Mann (eds) (1992) 75.

CHAPTER 5

NOTHIN' COULD BE FINAH

THE DINAH SHORE CHEVY SHOW

Lola Clare Bratten

Among the flickering images that Americans consumed in their night-time television during the 1950s was a blonde singer with a big smile whose variety show offered an idealized vision of the new American woman. Constructed as the incarnation of a wholesome blonde with a sunny personality and a happy family life, Dinah Shore, a singer and television personality, also became virtually synonymous with her sponsor, Chevrolet. This construction was predicated on two processes: the diminishment of Dinah Shore's Jewish heritage; and the trend of 1950s television advertisers to identify their products with television stars and personalities who seemingly embodied the all-American ideal man and woman – middle-class, white and Anglo. For that reason, Dinah Shore is a particularly interesting study since she simultaneously embodied both the erasure of ethnicity in American television stars and the consumerism naturalized by the 1950s.

Chevrolet had sponsored Shore in a 15-minute radio show that migrated to television, airing before the evening news, once a week.[1] In 1956, NBC approached Chevrolet with a proposal to build an hour-long show in the time slot considered best on the schedule – Sunday 9pm Eastern time. NBC and Chevrolet agreed to an expanded one-hour musical variety show to be called *The Dinah Shore Chevy Show*. With the central role of the automobile in newly emerging suburbs and the growing presence of televisions in American homes, Chevrolet banked upon television sponsorships as one way to reach a sizeable and prosperous market of middle-class families. Gasoline was cheap, the US economy was strong and 'the world was America's oyster', according to Richard D. O'Connor, former Chairman of the Board for Campbell-Ewald, Chevrolet's advertising agency since the 1950s. Dinah Shore's weekly rendition of the show's opening and closing jingle, 'See the USA in your Chevrolet!'

SUNDAY TV NEWS
Week

DECEMBER 29
to
JANUARY 4

DINAH SHORE

5.1. A 1957 photo of Dinah Shore on the cover of a TV Week *insert for a Philadelphia newspaper, promoting her NBC show and her title 'Mother of the Year' for 1957.*

ended with her trademark 'Mmmmwhaaa' – as she expansively blew a kiss at the television audience.

The upbeat song was perhaps one of the most memorable openings and closings in 1950s television variety shows. According to one fan of vintage Chevrolet, 'in our family we often sang "See the USA in your Chevrolet!" with great gusto, right along with Dinah.'[2] Shore's personality and enthusiasm were contagious and she delivered that weekly jingle with verve and her trademark smile. O'Connor of Campbell-Ewald remembered that 'Chevrolet provided the platform and Dinah Shore provided the image – an all American, fun, up-beat image that we were looking for.'[3]

In crafting a sponsored musical variety show, Chevrolet and Dinah Shore joined a sizeable group of variety shows that crowded the 1950s TV schedule with singers as hosts. Liberace, Perry Como and Eddie Fisher were amongst these, though in fact the programme form rather frequently headlined women such as Rosemary Clooney, Kate Smith, Patti Page and June Allyson. Most lasted little longer than a season. Dinah Shore, however, was a perennial, returning season after season from 1956 to 1961. A part of this may have been Shore's image of the well-scrubbed, likeable suburban woman that had a semiotic resonance with the all-American image Chevrolet had historically sought to portray.[4]

Chevrolet also had a pressing concern. Consumer spending on private automobiles had grown by a factor of four between 1950 and 1956 – from $22 billion to $65 billion, or 20 per cent of the Gross National Product – and Chevrolet wanted to maintain that volume of production. (Marling 1994:145)[5] However, some of the spending on new cars had been induced by the concept of 'dynamic obsolescence' whereby manufacturers changed automobile styling to lure more frequent trade-ins for new cars. As Karal Marling notes, the desire for newer car models was enacted through 'a whole panoply of expressive shapes. Fins spawned finlets, Dagmars[6] multiplied . . . the car of the 1950s – "a chorus girl coming, a fighter plane going" – was a semiotic anagram' with interesting contradictions for a family car.[7] (Marling 1994:140–141) Therefore, the ability of automobile manufacturers to sustain their post-war prosperity depended on their ability to convince the American public to trade in their old cars for newer models. Just as importantly, the car manufacturer launched marketing to persuade families to buy second cars. Reaching the suburban household and encouraging a second car for the suburban wife was therefore a key marketing goal for Chevrolet.

Two years before *The Dinah Shore Chevy Show*, Chevrolet launched a campaign of ads aimed at women and placed them in a number of women's magazines as part of its strategy. With headlines such as 'Do You Take This Car for Your Very Own?' or 'Here Are Some Things You'll Want to Show Your Husband about the 1955 Chevrolet', these 2/3 page ads marked out the home-maker in the role of what the advertising industry calls an 'influencer'. By 1956, the ads had assumed a tutorial mode of address, schooling the female consumer on how to coax her husband into the expense of that second car. Ad headlines suggesting 'Fetch his Pipe and Slippers . . . Then show him this!'[8] or 'Something to Show your Husband . . . after his favorite dinner!'[9] indicate that the automobile industry was struggling to find an effective way to address women who could influence, but not control, the decision to buy a car.

Dinah Shore shared the role of celebrity spokesperson for Chevrolet with Pat Boone, a young smooth-faced singer with a squeaky-clean image who sang 'April Love' and 'Love Letters in the Sand' and sported white buckskin shoes. Boone provided Chevrolet with a teen heart-throb who was wholesome, middle-class and white Anglo-Saxon – a bland alternative to Elvis Presley. Boone's image was paired mostly with the sporty new Corvette model. A 1958 advertisement for *Automotive News* pitched Dinah Shore and Pat Boone to automobile dealers as the 'Two Top TV Stars . . . on the Top Automotive Selling Team!' extolling them as 'known – and loved – just about as far and wide as TV reaches.'[10]

Dinah Shore was constructed in the media as a natural and unaffected personality in public relations and through her on-air personality. She was feminine while at the same time not too alluring; her persona had none of the overtones of a sultry chanteuse or sexual adventurer. The *Detroit Free Press* reported that even though she would 'love to wear a slinky sheath style to show off her svelte figure and 23-inch waistline . . . her fans insist on the bouffant-skirted, southern-belle style that fits her husky Tennessee accent' – meaning fully skirted and tight-waisted.[11] The bodices of her dresses were frequently adorned with large bows, ostrich feathers or detailing, but never had plunging necklines or revealing décolletage. Dinah Shore's profile was that of the 'good girl' in a full prom dress. Similarly her hair was a sensible medium length, neither a boyish bob nor a vamp's long tresses. She was usually framed from bust up, with the cameras occasionally pulling out to waist-level framing: neither framing was likely to emphasize womanly curves. Shore smiled while she sang, energetically snapping her fingers or using enthusiastic punching gestures to punctuate a song; not for her the slouchy, languid movement of a Marlene Dietrich. Tan, fit and good-natured she was the image of the ideal girl next door, the 'Miss Cheerleader' from her own cheerleading past. Shore's personality was constructed on television as the peppy girl-next-door at a particular moment in American society when the proper role of women in the post-Second World War consumer culture was constructed by the media to be that of the happy home-maker.

The Dinah Shore Chevy Show was scheduled on a Sunday night when family viewing was optimal and targeted a middle-class suburban audience with stay-at-home wives and mothers. Chevrolet could link its product with the constructions of femininity popularized in 1950s media through the publicity surrounding Dinah Shore. Shore was not only constructed as an upbeat, popular television star, wife and mother, but also as a fashion leader. Shore refused to wear couturier-donated clothes in exchange for a plug in the credits and instead purchased her wardrobe out of her own pocket.[12] She was named a winner of the 1957 *Harper's Bazaar* fashion citation as the 'the outstanding fashion woman in television', along with Rosalind Russell and Cyd Charisse for their style in theatre and motion pictures respectively.[13] Neiman-Marcus also announced Shore as the winner of its own fashion award and reported in a press release that half of the fan mail the singer received each week was about her wardrobe – a collection of '55 different dresses per season'.[14] In attempting to market itself to the woman as consumer, Chevrolet had earlier adopted some of the discourse of designer fashion in promoting its product to women. A 1955 print advertising campaign in women's magazines linked Chevrolet cars with fashion in a series of ads headlined 'About Clothes and Cars' that featured models in various trendy outfits with a Chevrolet to match the mood. The sales address was made directly to the female consumer, with language such as 'kitten soft foam-rubber cushion . . . lavish fabric and trim . . . exciting colors . . . rich thick pile carpets'.[15] Chevrolet capitalized on its association with Dinah Shore both as a celebrity spokesperson for the company and as a feminine fashion leader when she appeared in a series of advertisements in designer gowns alongside the new 1961 Impala and Corvair models in fashion magazines *Vogue, Harper's Bazaar, Glamour, Charm* and *Mademoiselle* magazines.[16] In this way, the sponsor used the media construction of Dinah Shore to maximum advantage to promote both its image and its product.

Shore became a workhorse for Chevrolet, performing her duties as a Chevrolet spokesperson agreeably and with apparent sincerity. 'She went everywhere Chevrolet wanted her to go and Chevrolet treated her like a queen.'[17] One member of the advertising community reminisced at the time of Dinah Shore's death that a Chevrolet zone manager had brought a group of 'dozens of dealers all under umbrellas in heavy rain'[18] simply to greet Dinah Shore when she returned from a trip. Chevrolet also controlled her appearances outside of their own show. She was restricted from appearing in events sponsored by competing automobile manufacturers. In the 1958 Emmy Awards show the singer was yanked from a production number that mocked western and 'song' shows. Chevrolet, apparently, was not comfortable with the fact that the number mocked their own variety show format and also with the fact that the Emmy Awards show was partially sponsored by another automobile manufacturer.[19] Chevrolet, like many other powerful sponsors in the 1950s, had a power of veto over Dinah Shore's performances and reviewed all her scripts.[20] Her public persona was so intertwined with Chevrolet that, according to *Advertising Age*, Shore 'made the car the No. 1 nameplate on the new interstate highway system and in suburbia'.[21] *Time* magazine reported that 'Her longtime sponsor, Chevrolet, is delighted to pay $145,000-a-show bill, considers its link with Dinah to be one of the most enduring love affairs in TV'.

Erasure of Ethnicity

Ironically, Dinah Shore's construction of the blonde girl next door belied her Jewish ethnicity and her early career as a dark-haired singer who was far more 'ethnic' in both appearance and performance. She was born in Tennessee as Frances Rose Shore, daughter of a prominent merchant, Solomon Shore. Shore's repertoire comprised many bluesy songs, including the song 'Dinah' originally recorded by the African-American singer Ethel Waters. In fact, Shore adapted her first name from the song when radio producers referred to her as 'that Dinah girl', after she had sung the number during an audition. During the 1930s and 1940s, Dinah Shore made her reputation as a blues singer. In the 1941 radio show *Chamber Music Society of Lower Basin Street*, she was introduced as 'Mlle. Dinah Diva Shore, who starts fires by rubbing two notes together.' The radio show declared itself a Chamber society whose members had dedicated and 'consecrated their lives to the preservation of the music of the three Bs – Barrelhouse, Boogie-woogie and the Blues.'[22] Shore was identified as a 'white singer of dark songs [who] is no longer of Lower Basin Street and never was in fact', a curious definition by inversion.

In the 1940s, Shore, as a 'mood singer', had become known for her rendition of 'Blues in the Night', 'It's So Nice to Have a Man Around the House' and 'Yes, My Darling Daughter'.[23] Her voice was described by Liberty magazine in 1941 as 'bluesy and moanin' low' with 'something else – personality'. Along with these descriptions of a musical form associated with African-American culture were other cultural associations. Describing Shore as a 'slip of a girl with the great big voice. Her eyes are brown, and her hair is raven black', the journalist suggested that her appearance 'like her voice, has that indefinable something called *schmaltz*', a Yiddish word pointing to more identifiably Jewish attributes.[24] Shore's association with racially specific music was a prominent part of her early success and may have explained why listeners occasionally speculated about her racial or ethnic heritage. However, Shore also traded on what the *New York Times* identified as her 'down-home image and Southern drawl', with a number of novelty hits such as 'Shoofly Pie and Apple Pandowdy' and 'Pass the Jam, Sam' and it was this construction, along with her physical metamorphosis into a blonde, ethnically neutral showbusiness personality that helped propel her to success on 1950s television.[25]

Shore's transformation to blonde and all-American icon began during the Second World War, as a result of her affiliation with the radio show, *Command Performance*. A performance was also being filmed by Warner Bros. and a screen test resulted in a recommendation by Warner's make-up department, which pronounced her nose too long with 'a noticeable hook'. As Sander Gilman has argued, the Semitic 'hooked' nose is perhaps the pre-eminent signifier of

5.2. *Known as a 'white singer of dark songs', Dinah Shore sang blues ballads and boogie-woogie in NBC's 1941 radio show* Chamber Music Society of Lower Basin Street *and performed as a regular guest on the show* A Time to Smile, *with host Eddie Cantor.*

visible Jewishness.[26] Shore's nose was shortened with cosmetic surgery. In addition, her teeth were filed down and capped to eliminate a gap between the front two teeth. Her complexion was 'naturally quite dark, almost swarthy', which, in combination with her jet-black hair, 'made her photograph much too dark', in the words of a pop biography of the star. (Cassiday 1979:52) This 'problem' was solved by new lighter, golden foundation make-up and by bleaching Shore's dark hair into a honey blonde shade. Shore was thus made whiter, hence more racially 'neutral' by her acquired blondeness.[27] In his study on Marilyn Monroe, Richard Dyer notes that the 'desirable woman is a white woman' and most often blonde which is 'the most unambiguously white you can get', a guarantee of racial 'purity'. (Dyer: 1986:42–43)

After being made visibly 'whiter' and less ethnic, Shore was also marked as more American and less ethnic by her athletic outdoor pursuits[28] and her upper-middle-class California lifestyle. The discourse of publicity surrounding Shore emphasized her all-American girl persona and rendered her Jewishness virtually invisible. This appearance of neutral 'Americanness' offered by the new Dinah Shore was reminiscent of the characteristics of many of the film stars of classical Hollywood. As Ian Jarvie notes, the ethnic profile of top movie stars tended to be 'bland, lighter-skinned, light-entertainment, ethnically-hard-to-differentiate'. (Jarvie 1991:102) The effect of this effacement, or minimization, of ethnicity was that 'when seen through its top stars, America did not seem to be an ethnic mosaic. On the contrary, the stars represented a non- or anti-ethnic image of "all-Americanism"'. (Jarvie 1991:108) Unlike her contemporary, Marilyn Monroe, however, Dinah Shore's sexuality was contained by her costumes, her mannerisms and her construction as 'the sweetheart of song, the girl of your dreams, the doll next door and the honey bun wives never get jealous of all wrapped up in one zestful, bouncy, pink-ribboned package.'[29]

All-American Icon

The transformation to American television star with a generic American identity was ably assisted by publicity agents as Dinah Shore's 'personal life' was routinely brought out for public examination and articles about her appeared regularly in the pages of general circulation and women's magazines. A 1951 interview for the *Saturday Evening Post* represented her as a busy young wife and mother, only coincidentally pursuing a career as a television singer. *Good Housekeeping* ran an article by-lined by Dinah's six-year old daughter, Missy, in May 1954, emphasizing her role as a celebrity mother. Dinah Shore's marriage to American film actor George Montgomery also became a source of publicity.

Such discourse, however, proposed that Dinah Shore valued her family life over her career. 'I'm much more interested in the success and durability of my life as Mrs. George Montgomery than my career as Dinah Shore' quoted one article headlined 'Husband, Kids Most Important to Dinah' or, similarly, ' "Without George, I'd be a Flop," says Dinah.'[30] These representations produced the paradigmatic American success: an attractive, morally upright woman with a handsome film star husband and two children thriving in the entertainment world by dint of her charm, energy and devotion. This construction of Dinah Shore in the pages of American magazines and newspapers as an unpretentious, supportive woman who would prefer to concentrate on her identity as 'Mrs. George Montgomery' had its corollaries in the way other women stars in film and television were treated in the popular media in the 1950s.

The tropes of femininity in the discourse of 1950s popular culture required women in heterosexual marriages functioning in the role of the supportive 'helpmeet' to their husbands and as devoted mothers. Even the far more sexually adventurous film star Elizabeth Taylor was promoted as the loving and dutiful wife and mother by the 1950s press. Stories of Taylor's marriage and children by Michael Wilding simultaneously domesticated Taylor within the confines of marriage while romanticizing her relationship with Wilding with stories about numerous 'honeymoon' getaways the couple took in the first year of their marriage, as reflected by headlines such as 'Diamonds and Diapers' and 'Honeymoon With Baby'.[31] Of course, these constructions worked to contain the realities that television and film stars such as Shore and Taylor often worked gruelling schedules that required them to leave children at home with nannies and husbands, unattended for long hours. These realities of working women in the 1950s have been amply documented by recent scholarship;[32] however, the construction of the American woman in the popular discourse of general-circulation and women's magazines represented the nuclear family with its sole wage earner as the norm. These media representations appealed to what Eileen Meehan calls a 'commodity audience' – the ideal audience as perceived by the advertiser. (Meehan 1990) The commodity audience of the mid 1950s, from the point of view of advertisers, was the middle-class family, able to purchase automobiles, major appliances, furniture and renovations for the home, along with an assortment of packaged foods, cigarettes and liquor.[33]

It was only after her transformation into a neutral ethnically unmarked image of American femininity that Shore became attractive to a car manufacturer hoping to align itself with American singers and television personalities who embodied the American 'can-do' attitude and the norms of white middle-class America. But Dinah Shore's suitability as a Chevrolet celebrity was also a result of her apparent 'naturalness' and lack of pretension in her role as host for the show. A *New York Times* review of Shore's previous 15-minute musical variety show for Chevrolet approvingly noted that she was a perfect 'fit' for the more intimate technology of television:

5.3. Cover photo by Pete Vose for Look *magazine, 6 December 1960. Dinah Shore was featured in a story that covered her personal life as Mrs George Montgomery, her life as a mother to her children and a behind-the-scenes look at her professional work as a television star.*

Miss Shore is blessed as not every young lady in video is: she looks lovely before the electronic cameras. Last week, on her initial appearances, she was the picture of

poise and naturalness and conducted the show with a disarming combination of
authority and humility. Hollywood had better have a second look at Miss Shore.[34]

But this review did not account for the different talents demanded by the
technologies of film and television. Although Dinah Shore had attempted
some Hollywood films, her natural girl-next-door looks could not withstand
the competition from more beautiful stars as the film screen's room-sized
close-ups showed.[35] For example, she competed for the part of Julie in the
film *Show Boat*[36] but it went to Ava Gardner, even though Gardner could
not sing. This incident is telling because it demonstrates how the technology
of the medium influenced the perceived suitability of stars. In *Show Boat*,
because the medium allowed separate manipulation of sound and image
tracks, Shore was dispensable and MGM could cast instead a beautiful
starlet, overdubbing the vocals.

The new medium of television with its emphasis on live performance,
however, suited Dinah Shore. She was a low-key singer whose appearances
on both the music hall stage and the radio developed a range of skills uniquely
suited to television. Through her stage appearances, she learned to be comfortable with live performance without the protection, enjoyed by film stars,
of another take. In one of her 15-minute radio shows during wartime for the
Armed Forces Radio Network, she and her co-stars sang a mock opera reminiscent of the kind familiar from the *Chamber Music Society of Basin Street*
radio show, in which she broke up laughing at one point, unable to continue
singing for a few bars.[37] Such informality was part, together with her breezy
ad libbing, of the bonhomie of her show and helped to impart a sense of their
'liveness'. The audio technology of radio and television delivered a pleasing
reproduction of her mellow contralto voice. Furthermore her strong but attractive visual features and her oversized smile gave her face a distinctive
and friendly appearance in the medium or medium-long shots which were
generally used for television variety shows of the era.

Like her father, a merchant who helped to establish consumerist desires for
'store bought' items in a small town market, (Ewen and Ewen 1982:59) Dinah
Shore would become closely linked with both the institutions through which
the transformation and assimilation of the 'ethnic other' was accomplished –
the manufacturers promoting consumerist desires and the mass media which
disseminated desirable images.

It is curious that Dinah Shore appealed so effectively to audiences of middle-
class white suburban America. She was, after all, a woman who had boldly
made a living as a jazz singer, touring with bands in a Gypsy life, appearing
on radio shows, marrying a film actor and dyeing her dark hair blonde.
Nevertheless, Dinah Shore's image emerged as a reassuring picture of domesticated and easygoing femininity, American to the core. Though she was
Jewish, her image was a 'Southern belle'. She was a successful star, yet she
was billed as a woman more interested in her family than in her own success.

However, like much 'official knowledge' or discourse, there also existed a counter-knowledge to the dominant construction of Dinah Shore. A persistent rumour indicated that not all Americans accepted the constructed persona they were fed in the mainstream media. The rumour (Turner 1993:5)[38] was that Dinah Shore was part black and 'passing' and that her secret became known when she bore a child who clearly looked black. Examination of the public 'facts' of the performer's life reveals the inaccuracy of these rumours: Dinah Shore and George Montgomery had a white-skinned daughter named Missy, who strongly resembled her mother, and the couple also adopted a son whom they named Jody. As Patricia Turner has noted, the presence of a rumour is interesting not for the status of the rumour as the bearer of some objective 'truth', but rather in its illustration of counter-knowledge used to express anxieties or to fill the gap between the 'seamless' representations which support the hegemony of those in power and those realities which threaten to subvert it. The rumour appears to have circulated as early as 1954 and at least as late as 1963.[39] These dates are particularly interesting in that they also mark the time between the establishment of Shore's television stardom until a year or two after the end of her association with Chevrolet and the demise of her marriage.

1954 was a particularly fraught time in the South;[40] other factors which possibly may have spurred the circulation of this 'counter-knowledge' might be public recall of her transformation from blues-singing brunette (Rose 1974:82 & 115) to bleached blonde American icon. In addition, her past association with jazz and blues[41] may have provided additional 'evidence' of blackness.[42]

The rumours of 1960 through to 1962 coincide with Shore's divorce from husband George Montgomery and may have been used to 'explain' the divorce. An article in *Good Housekeeping* offered other reasons for the divorce, framing the break-up in terms familiar to the ideology of its middle-class readers: 'Dinah Shore: How a "Good Wife" Failed'. According to the article, George Montgomery's affair with 24-year-old Israeli co-star Ziva Rodann was not the 'real' reason for the break-up. Rather the article implies that the *real* problem with the marriage was Dinah Shore's success, describing George's attempts as a film writer-director-actor, which had resulted in lacklustre films and that, after a preview of one of his films, everyone clustered around Dinah. In the article, an anonymous friend of the couple described the 'sight of George, standing apart, almost alone, while Dinah tried to manoeuvre her way to him through a mob of chattering sycophants' as evidence of the stress in their relationship.[43]

While exposing some of the tensions in the persona of Dinah Shore, the article on her marital break-up blamed both her success and even her efforts to help George Montgomery's career ('too much help from a wife can generate a lot of unspoken bitterness in a man'). In a sense, the carefully constructed public persona of Shore as a devoted wife and mother whose career was secondary to her marriage fell apart. Shore was narratively castigated for having violated one of the premises of 1950s femininity – a successful marriage predicated on the willingness of the wife to please her man. Yet for other members of the public, a counter-narrative already existed – one which highlighted the struggle of groups such as blacks and Jews to succeed in a society which privileged the white and middle-class.

Chevrolet cancelled its sponsorship of the Dinah Shore show in 1961 before the break-up of her marriage in order to underwrite the western *Bonanza* in the coveted Sunday night slot instead.[44] Bordens Milk briefly sponsored her but, within a year of her divorce in 1962, Dinah Shore no longer appeared as a regular host of any television show. Instead, she worked mostly club dates and concentrated on raising her children.[45] It would be eight years before Dinah Shore hosted her own show again.[46]

The intersection of discourses surrounding Dinah Shore in the 1950s demonstrates how the power of the socially dominant ideology represented by the mass media worked to construct images of Dinah Shore as a white, middle-class, happily married woman at a time when social hierarchies of gender and ethnicity were being reinscribed. Only the presence of a rumoured 'counter-narrative' pointed to the artificiality of this construction and exhibited the tensions surrounding both the grinding sense of political and social conformity of the 1950s and anxieties over the nation's ability to assimilate citizens of varying ethnicity and race.

Her suitability as a television star was not only the result of her talent but, just as importantly, her ability to appear natural and relaxed on the small screen of 1950s television while working within the confines of its cumbersome technology. Dinah Shore's persona represented both what her sponsor and her public *wanted* to believe about her. Her personality for a time appeared to embody the optimism and conformity of the era along with the preferred belief in husband, family and the good life provided by consumer goods such as Chevrolet. As the details of her personal life became public and the demands of the commercial base of television changed, Shore's suitability as an image for a particular era, a particular television genre and a particular product sponsorship faded away. While it lasted, however, Dinah Shore reigned as the upbeat spirit of America embodying an idealized 1950s lifestyle and attitude. Dinah Shore's emergence as a figure of all-American femininity, coded as middle class, white and non-ethnic, and as a spokesperson for Chevrolet was therefore the result of a complex synergy. Indeed, it is hard to determine whether it was Dinah Shore who helped to construct Chevrolet as all-American in the popular imagination or visa versa – as Eric Barnouw notes, in his work on *The Sponsor*, 'Commercials not only exploit, but seem to confer status.' (Barnouw 1978:80) Shore was connected with Chevrolet in the public mind and her persona helped to construct the car as the vehicle with an almost anthropomorphic all-American quality or persona of its own.[47] Fifty years later, *Advertising Age* would cite her alliance with Chevrolet as one of the most potent partnerships in advertising history.[48]

Notes

1. Telephone interview with James L. Steffensen, 15 May 1996. Steffensen, a professor of theatre at Dartmouth College, served as a page at NBC and for *The Dinah Shore Chevy Show* in 1956.

2. 'The Heasley File: "See the USA in your Chevrolet!" ' http://www.speedvision.com/pub/articles/classics/04muscle/200603a.html accessed 9 September 2000.

3. Author interview with Richard D. O'Connor, Chairman of the Board, Campbell-Ewald Advertising, 9 July 1996.

4. In a later decade, Chevrolet used a jingle which self-consciously identified itself as an American icon in the lyrics 'Baseball, hot dogs, apple pie, and Chevrolet'.

5. Marling quotes *Fortune* magazine in August of 1953 that car manufacturers were secretly shipping unsold new stock to used car lots to maintain the perception of banner sales years. *Time* magazine also reported at the time that Chrysler sales had dropped 42 per cent and that Packard had taken a loss and Studebaker was asking its employees to take a 15 per cent pay cut. 'Automakers' troubles', *Time* 16 August 1954 Vol. 64:84.

6. Breast-shaped protrusions named after a busty actress popular in the 1950s.

7. Marling uses this catchphrase quoted from Christopher Finch, *Highways to Heaven: The AUTObiography of America* (New York: Columbia University Press, 1992) 36.

8. *Ladies Home Journal*, March 1956.

9. *Ladies Home Journal*, April 1956.

10. 'These Two Top TV Stars Are On The Top Automotive Selling Team!' Advertisement, *Automotive News*, 17 March 1958. Campbell-Ewald Co. advertising archive.

11. 'Dinah Hoards Those Clothes', *Detroit Free Press,* 18 August 1957. 12-TV.

12. Dinah Shore had a public fight with the IRS over whether gowns were a legitimate business expense. She was only allowed to deduct those that the IRS agreed could only be used for her work as a television variety star – those in which she could not sit down. This distinction was determined by an IRS agent who visited her home and assessed her ability to sit in each gown as she modelled them.

13. Joan Dean, 'Three Actresses Win Fashion Citations', *Detroit Times,* 21 March 1957, Part 2, 1.

14. Neiman-Marcus press release. Dated for release on Sunday 11 September 1960. Campbell-Ewald Co. archives.

15. *Ladies Home Journal*, April 1955.

16. Chevrolet 1961 print campaign. Advertising proof sheets. Campbell-Ewald Co. advertising archive.

17. Author interview with Richard D. O'Connor. O'Connor is also quoted 'There wasn't anything [Shore] would not do that Chevrolet asked her. She was part of Chevrolet and Chevrolet was part of her' in 'Nancy's Next Challenge', *Advertising Age*, Spring 1993: 23. The Detroit papers routinely reported Dinah Shore's presence at charitable functions, such as benefits for kidney research or a Detroit City Club holiday show, industry trade shows or dealer promotions. See Bete Gillespie, 'They've Been Invited to "Dine with Dinah" ', *Detroit Free Press*, 13 April 1960. See also 'Happy Holidays Program Committee', Detroit City Club program/newsletter. Campbell-Ewald Co. advertising archive.

18. Joe R. Eisaman, 'Letters to the Editor: Dinah Shore and Chevrolet', *Advertising Age*, 21 March 1994.

19. Hal Humphrey, 'Stars Can't Go Near Competitors', *Detroit Free Press*, 13 April 1958, 4-TV.

20. Author interview with Richard D. O'Connor, Chairman of the Board, Campbell-Ewald Advertising, 9 July 1996.

21. Adrienne Ward Fawcett, 'The 50 Best', *Advertising Age* special edition: '50 Years of TV Advertising', Spring 1995:36.

22. Frederick Lewis, 'The Private Life of Dinah Shore', *Liberty* magazine, 14 June 1941:20.

23. Myrna Oliver, 'TV Pioneer, Entertainer Dinah Shores Dies at 76', *Los Angeles Times*, 25 February 1994, Part A, 1.

24. Frederick Lewis, 'The Private Life of Dinah Shore', *Liberty*, 14 June 1941:20.

25. Although early television had more representations of ethnic characters than were found in the cinema, the presence of visibly ethnic characters and personalities on television disappeared gradually throughout the 1950s in favour of representations of a cultural white, middle-class homogeneity. Noting that the working class is marginalized in discourses and 'social economy of consumption' and that minorities are simply absent, Mary Beth Haralovich describes how an ideal white and middle-class home life was 'a primary means of reconstituting and resocializing the American family after World War II.' (Haralovich in Spigel and Mann (eds.) 1992:112)

26. Sander Gilman, *The Jew's Body* (1991).

27. Cassiday quotes Shore from an interview with a columnist: 'They like to killed me *(sic)*. They filed my teeth and put on caps, they angled my eyebrows, they dyed my hair.' (1979:54).

28. Shore was an avid tennis player and golfer.

29. Herbert Kamm, 'A Test on Gridiron: The Story Behind Dinah Shore', *Detroit Free Press*, 15 October 1957, 1.

30. Charles Denton, ' "Without George, I'd be a Flop" Says Dinah', *Detroit Free Press*, 6 September 1959. TV Prevue Section. Campbell-Ewald advertising archive.

31. 'Honeymoon With Baby', *Photoplay*, February 1954. 'Diamonds and Diapers', *Photoplay*, April 1954:80. 'Liz Takes French Leave', *Photoplay*, June 1954:44.

32. Scholars who have capably revised the Fifties 'myth' of suburban domesticity for women include Joanne Meyerowitz in Meyerowitz (ed.), *Not June Cleaver: Women and Gender in Postwar America, 1945–1960* (1994); Elaine Tyler May, *Homeward Bound: American Families in the Cold War Era* (1988); Stephanie Coontz, *The Way We Never Were: American Families and the Nostalgia Trap* (1992); and Mary Beth Haralovich in Spigel and Mann (eds), *Private Screenings: Television and the Female Consumer* (1992).

33. Author survey of advertisements in general-circulation *Life* magazine issues in 1955 and 1956.

34. 'Dinah Shore Scores in her New NBC Video Series – Ethel Barrymore Stars With Jimmy Durante', *New York Times*, 3 December 1951, 28:2.

35. One film was entitled 'Belle of the Yukon'. Pete Martin, 'I Call on Dinah Shore', *Saturday Evening Post*, 19 October 1957, Vol. 230:52.

36. Ibid. It is also ironic that the mixed race character of Julie who 'passes' for white was the part for which Shore was being considered since Shore was Jewish and also, in a sense, 'passing' for a non-ethnic American.

37. *The Dinah Shore Show*, 25 December 1942, NBC Blue, Armed Forces Radio Service. University of Memphis radio archives.

38. Patricia A. Turner distinguishes between rumour and contemporary legend or myth by their narrative construction. A *rumour* is simply a 'short, nonnarrative expression of belief' [such as 'Dinah Shore is part black'], where *legend* refers to 'more traditionally grounded narratives of belief', and *contemporary legend* refers to grounded narratives 'containing particularly modern motifs'. Therefore the extended form of the rumour approaches Turner's designation as legend: 'Dinah Shore is passing for white, but when her child was born, this fact was discovered by her husband and this precipitated the divorce.'

39. Letter to the Editor of *Parade Magazine* from Virginia Beres of Detroit, Michigan, *Detroit Free Press Parade Magazine*, 13 June 1965. Campbell-Ewald advertising archive.

This asked: 'Dinah Shore's parents – was one a Negro or had Negro blood?' The rumours have also been confirmed in author interviews with Hugh D. Merrill, Atlanta-based author of *Esky: The History of Esquire Magazine* and *The Red Hot Typewriter*, 14 May 1996. Merrill heard the rumour in Anniston, Alabama. Also an interview with Mary Desjardins, Assistant Professor, Radio Television and Film, University of Texas at Austin, 15 May 1996, confirmed that Desjardins heard the rumour in 1962 in California. Darrell Newton, in an interview on 16 May 1996, confirmed he heard in 1960 from his grandmother that Dinah Shore was 'passing' and related the experience of a black 'passing' as natural, since so many blacks had white blood. According to Newton's grandmother, Shore had simply lightened herself some more and dyed her hair. This rumour was 'confirmed' by Newton's mother two years later in 1962 in California and again by an aunt in Tallahassee, Florida, in 1963. Newton's Florida aunt used Shore's alleged mixed-race heritage as the reason not many of her commercials and programmes were seen in Florida (Shore's variety show had been cancelled by this time). Newton's uncle surmised that the lack of screenings may also have had something to do with her being a Jew, indicating that the African-American community was aware of her Jewish background and handled it as a separate, additional factor to the complex of Shore's identity as part black.

40. It was the year in which Brown vs. the Board of Education resulted in a ruling to desegregate schools and the conservative and racist 'Dixiecrats' (who had bolted the Democratic party in 1948) still represented a vocal and action-oriented presence in the political discourse of the South. Sensitivity to racial issues was therefore acute and such a rumour may have reflected the cultural anxieties of the time.

41. Basin Street was a well-known red-light district in Storyville near New Orleans where jazz, blues and boogie-woogie musicians and prostitutes flourished from 1898 to November in 1917. Storyville was particularly famous for 'sporting houses' (such as Mahogany Hall, run by Lulu White, 'The Octoroon Queen,' and one run by Countess Willie Piazza) which featured octoroons. Shore's association with a show called *Chamber Music Society of Basin Street* therefore conjured up connotations of light-skinned blacks and the kind of music sung by Shore.

42. Other stars such as Joseph Cotten and Elizabeth Taylor were rumoured to have Negro blood at the time. Charlene Regester reports on rumours about Elizabeth Taylor in her paper 'Unveiling Whiteness and Negotiating Blackness', Consoleing Passions 1997 paper presentation. For rumours on Joseph Cotton see Michael Sheridan, 'They Say . . .', *Motion Picture Magazine*, November 1951, Vol. 42, no. 4.

43. Carl Schroeder, 'Dinah Shore: How a Good Wife Failed', *Good Housekeeping*, April 1962, Vol. 89:182. The article also described differences between the couple, which points to how thoroughly Dinah Shore's image was constructed as a home-loving suburbanite when the reality was quite different. 'Strangely, however, although Dinah admired and constantly boasted about George's home-building talent . . . she never cared particularly for suburban living, while he relished everything "ranchy" . . . one of Dinah's writers . . . says, 'Dinah, contrary to her public "gingham girl" image is really a gay sophisticate. Comparing husband and wife, I'd say that George is "Day People" while Dinah is "Night People".'

44. Although officially the reason for the sponsorship cancellation was that the ratings were not high enough for the expense of the show, a cryptic note appears in the Campbell-Ewald Co. advertising archive files in early 1961 asking a research company executive to 'keep an eye on the publicity Chevrolet is getting about Dinah'. This may have been a reassessment of the show's effectiveness, particularly in light of ratings for *The Rebel*, a cowboy styled show, which consistently beat *The Dinah Shore Chevy Show* and was said to be one reason why Dinah's sponsor decided to switch to a western, *Bonanza*, for the next season. However, Shore's husband, George Montgomery, was having a public affair with his co-star and the

race rumours about Shore had been circulating for some time. Letter to Dr. Burleigh Gardner, Social Research, Inc. from Arthur Boyd, Vice President Marketing & Research Dept. Campbell-Ewald, 21 February 1961. See also Frank Judge 'Success is No Payoff for 3 Television Stars', *Detroit News*, 26 March 1961.

[45.] 'Dinah Shore', *The Times*, 26 February 1994, Features Section. In 1963, she married Maurice Smith, a professional tennis player, but the marriage lasted less than a year.

[46.] Shore did host specials such as a salute to the Peace Corps in the early 1960s with Harry Belafonte.

[47.] On one show, for example, Dinah Shore worries aloud whether guest actor Boris Karloff will 'fit' the image of the show, asking her sidekick Art Carney 'Is he [Karloff] Chevy?' *The Dinah Shore Chevy Show*, 1957. Videotape from Shokus Video, Van Nuys, California.

[48.] 'Nancy's Next Challenge', *Advertising* Age, Spring 1993:23.

CHAPTER 6

RE-MADE FOR TELEVISION

HEDY LAMARR'S POST-WAR STAR TEXTUALITY

Diane Negra

In the context of shifting 1950s-era discourses on ethnicity, this essay provides a reading of the celebrity of a female film star who embodied a link to an ethnic past which significantly determined her meanings in television. As one of the most significant star 'imports' of the studio era, Austrian-born Hedy Lamarr was consistently deployed through the 1930s and 1940s as a sign of American mastery over ethnic femininity. Throughout the 1940s, publicity about Lamarr's private life attended closely to her escape from her first husband, an Austrian munitions manufacturer who was likened to a Nazi, her activities with the Hollywood Canteen, her wartime frugality and adherence to rationing programmes and, remarkably, her invention of an anti-jamming device for radio-controlled torpedoes to be used in US defence. Such accounts cumulatively combined to sketch a public portrait of the actress as a sign of incorporable white ethnicity. She was ethnically Austrian, but ideologically American. Thus, while Lamarr's pre-war and wartime celebrity is significantly illustrative of the cultural parameters of white ethnicity and gender in the studio era, this article is designed to inquire into Lamarr's post-war persona, particularly the way in which her stardom was recycled for television in the 1950s.

In the apparent consensus culture of post-war America, suburbanization, the Cold War and an onslaught of commodifying, homogenizing initiatives in popular culture cumulatively reinforced the eminence of white, middle-class American dogma. Despite the sunny superficiality with which America represented itself to itself during the 1950s, and still imagines life in that period today, scholars such as Sheri Chinen-Biesen see the 1950s as a decade which 'witnessed many failures of the American Dream. The establishment of the North Atlantic Treaty Organization (NATO) in 1949 signaled the loss of the myth of an isolationist America. The resurgence in immigration to the USA in the late fifties and early sixties reinforced this cultural demythology.'[1] Such an atmosphere called for new ways of formulating national consensus around white, suburban and consumer identities. Even for those Americans who lived in urban or rural areas in the 1950s, the logic of suburbia infiltrated the broader culture. Linked and reinforced to consumerism and an emergent set of commodities deemed necessary for middle-class status, a suburban perspective became the normative way of looking out at the world. In an essay entitled 'The Lure of the Suburbs', Margaret S. Marsh and Samuel Kaplan observe that:

> While our national image is one of ethnic and cultural diversity, on a community level we have tended to prefer homogeneity. However, there never have been any general rules on which groups were to be excluded. That depended on the times and the particular suburb under consideration. These attitudes, working in concert, have encouraged Americans to seek communities of like-minded residents within which to raise their families, and an environment as far removed from congested urban centers as their jobs and finances would carry them. The lure of the suburbs, therefore, is an expression of an antiurban bias in one of the most highly urbanized nations of the world and it is an affirmation of the American commitment to homogeneity in the midst of ethnic and cultural diversity. (Marsh and Kaplan 1976:38)

The post-war American family's attempts to secure and stabilize itself thus frequently entailed an accompanying rejection of the urban culture that had sustained immigrant ethnicities. In the 1950s, as Tyler-May points out:

> Much of what had provided family security in the past became unhinged. For many Americans, the postwar years brought rootlessness. Those who moved from farms to cities lost a familiar way of life that was rooted in the land. Children of immigrants moved from ethnic neighborhoods with extended kin and community ties to homogeneous suburbs, where they formed nuclear families and invested them with high hopes. (Tyler-May 1988:24)

While post-war mobility acted to disconnect white Americans from their urban, ethnic pasts, public policy decisions and government allocations supported mortgage plans, affordable suburban housing and highway initiatives which helped to set in place a physical/ideological geography that associated 'colour' with an urban milieu and suburbia with an untroubled whiteness. As Lipsitz notes:

> The suburbs helped turn European Americans into 'whites' who could live near each other and intermarry with relatively little difficulty. But this 'white' unity rested on residential segregation and on shared access to housing and life chances largely unavailable to communities of color. (Lipsitz 1995:374)

The term most frequently employed to describe the outcome of all these developments is, of course, 'White Flight'. Lynn Spigel has shown how 1960s television employed this widely shared experience at the level of everyday life as a discursive context for making intelligible and pleasurable 'the cultural colonialism at the heart of the space race'. (Spigel 1997:49) I want to propose that the concept of 'White Flight' had a somewhat similar function in 1950s television, but one which entails a kind of inverse reading of the term. In other words, 'White Flight' has most often been associated with racial separation, but it also had much to do with leaving behind white ethnic identities in the city. In this respect, we can say that the term 'White Flight' connotes a flight toward homogeneous whiteness as much as a flight from colour and that particularly for working-class families of recent immigrant origin the ability to leave the urban milieu was a confirmation of the secure white status conferred on them by post-war prosperity.

This is not to suggest that white ethnicity disappeared from the horizon of popular culture in the 1950s, rather, it was channelled primarily into a nostalgic register that helped post-war Americans negotiate their own transformations by fashioning fictions based on 'ethnic memory'. The early 1950s saw a number of television programmes (some adapted from radio) that fictionalized white ethnic immigrant experience. Yet, as Donald Weber has observed, both programmes set around ethnic families such as *Life with Luigi, Bonnino* and *Mama* and ethnically-inflected variety shows such as *Texaco Star Theatre* and *Your Show of Shows* had disappeared from television by the mid-1950s. (Weber 1997:145) When television did depict ethnicity it was generally in an urban setting and some genres such as the anthology drama clearly linked ethnicity to the past or to a set of problems that suburban relocation would help to solve. Yet, as I will show, consideration of genres and even programmes may not enable us fully to document the ethnic character of early television. If we are to do so, we must also attend to television's more diffuse, less programmatic features. In this way, we can track a pattern in which 1950s television generated contradictory, conflicted versions of ethnicity that sometimes seemed to 'bubble up' from beneath the surface of dominant representational paradigms.

In the context of the idealized common culture of the 1950s, it seems clear that the definition of American consensus was linked to the renunciation of fractured, partial or marginal whiteness. Hyphenated Euro-American identities were increasingly left behind as Americans were called upon to profess themselves fully American, fully white. In exploring this issue, I want to point out that even the availability of such an option indicates something of the privileges which accrue to European ethnicities in American culture, for white and non-white ethnicities are not comparable in their degree of alterity. Race is never an issue for whites (even ethnic whites) to the degree that it is for persons of colour. Lower status whites are susceptible of assimilation through channels generally unavailable to African-Americans, Asian-Americans and Latinos. Yet in referring to whiteness in this fashion, I am locating my argument within the body of work in recent critical studies of race and ethnicity which problematized the 'invisible' or 'unremarkable' status of whiteness.[2] As Richard Dyer has noted, 'The point of looking at whiteness is to dislodge it from its centrality and authority'. (Dyer 1997:10) By focusing my attention on white ethnicity, I am seeking to theorize and historicize the internal hierarchies of whiteness. It seems clear that 'all whites do not benefit from the possessive investment in whiteness in precisely the same way', (Lipsitz 1995:383) nor, I would add, to the same degree. This was especially true for ethnic whites in the 1950s.

Clearly, Lamarr's Americanization did not challenge her image of erotic inaccessibility. Indeed, newsreel footage included in NBC's *Life Goes To War* (broadcast in September 1977) provides at least one image that demonstrates the compatibility of these two facets of her persona. Here, a GI contest winner at the Hollywood Canteen is shown being invited to kiss Lamarr and he emerges from a wolf-whistling crowd to tentatively approach the actress who has closed her eyes in expectation of a passionate embrace. Instead, the GI kisses Lamarr on the forehead, accepts an autograph and quickly retreats. At this moment, and throughout her film career, Lamarr's desirability was connected in large part to her unavailability, her distance, her glamorous implausibility. In a recent reminiscence of the actress, columnist Russell Baker notes that 'You never saw women who looked like Hedy Lamarr. Anna Magnani was a plausible woman; Hedy Lamarr was hot. One could imagine an evening with Anna Magnani. An evening with Hedy Lamarr was inconceivable.'[3]

As television struggled to recycle and rewrite Lamarr's exotic glamour, the dynamics of proximity and distance related to cinematic and televisual stardom were tellingly revealed, for that recycling process asked Americans to take exactly the position of access and intimacy that Baker describes as 'inconceivable' – to undertake an evening with Hedy Lamarr.

Lamarr appeared widely on American television throughout the 1950s and 1960s, most often as a talk show guest, as a celebrity panellist on a quiz show or as a variety show participant. These appearances problematized Lamarr's Hollywood star persona in ways that are in keeping with Denise Mann's argument in her analysis of the television celebrity of stars such as Martha Raye and Charlton Heston. Mann has drawn attention to the destabilizing effects of television on Hollywood stardom, the most acute effects perhaps felt by so-called 'auratic stars', those whose image of glamorous distance from spectators worked well in the context of cinematic stardom but appeared strikingly out of place in the domestic context of television. Mann observes that 'The transfer of Hollywood stars to the home via television during the transitional period from 1946 to 1956 shifts the viewing context not just from a public, community event to a private, isolated experience, but also restructures the spectators' fantasy engagement with the movies'. (Mann 1992:41) I want to argue that Lamarr's television stardom produced a pattern that is largely in keeping with Mann's argument, yet is also distinctive for the way it activated Lamarr's ethnic persona and its capacity both to define and disrupt post-war American culture. Less compatible with Americanization than it had been in the 1940s, Lamarr's European ethnicity proved problematic for television, for it distinctively reinforced her ties to the 'Old Worlds' of Europe and classical Hollywood and challenged her suitability for the new broadcast medium.

Lamarr's appearances on television coincided with the overall depreciation of her Hollywood celebrity. There was the publication of a titillating autobiography, the circulation of a previously banned film from early in Lamarr's career, *Ecstasy* (1933), which featured a notorious nude scene, publicity for several divorces and re-marriages and unfavourable commentary on her auction sales (and later her shoplifting activities). As a result of all of these, Lamarr's persona was undergoing revision in ways that seemed to dispossess her of the image of glamorous distance and unattainable beauty that had sustained her Hollywood career. She was ageing (in her early 40s at the time of her first TV appearances) and her distinctive association with classical Hollywood was a clear liability at a time when films such as *Sunset Boulevard* (1950) and *Whatever Happened to Baby Jane?* (1962) were writing the epitaph for old Hollywood and focusing their concerns around the 'grotesque' figure of the ageing female film star.[4] In addition, Lamarr's role as one of the paradigmatic exemplars of ethnic femininity was eroding, as ethnic female sexuality was being redefined by younger stars such as Sophia Loren and Brigitte Bardot, who epitomized a more bluntly sexual allure out of keeping with the norms of classical Hollywood stardom. At the same time, the 1950s saw the arrival of new prototypes for the desirable all-American woman in stars such as Jayne Mansfield and Marilyn Monroe.

Lamarr's sole dramatic appearance on television featured her in the role of Consuela in the telefilm series *Zane Grey Theatre*'s broadcast of 'Proud Woman' on CBS in 1957. Only a few years after the end of her American film career, Lamarr's celebrity is activated as a key selling point for the show and she is prominently credited above the title. *Zane Gray Theatre*, a western anthology series hosted by former musical star Dick Powell, was broadcast on CBS from 1956 to 1962. The show was part of the barrage of telefilm series in the late 1950s whose staple generic concerns centred around crime/ mystery, international intrigue and the western, all of which, as Erik Barnouw has observed, depended upon the discovery and defeat of the criminal. These genres proliferated in early television, Barnouw suggests, because they celebrated the forces of law and order and featured the unproblematic identification and eradication of the evildoer. As he notes 'Telefilms rarely invited the viewer to look for problems within himself. Problems came from the evil of other people and were solved – the telefilm seemed to imply – by confining or killing them.' (Barnouw 1990:214) In 'Proud Woman', Lamarr is linked through ethnicity with the forces of disruption, but demonstrates a crucial transferability.

Lamarr's all-purpose ethnicity serves as the rationale for her casting here as a Mexican-American woman. To set the tone for the piece, host Dick Powell opens the show with a discussion that provocatively complicates distinctions between American and foreign cultures, suggesting that our understanding of the cultural purity of artefacts of the American West may need to be challenged. In a direct address to camera, Powell observes that:

> The Pony Express was strictly American, but the mail was delivered in Spanish. And these genuine American chaps? Spanish chaperos! Doesn't that chap you? Of course, it always works both ways. For instance, this is tequila, Spanish firewater. Really Spanish. Mmm. Hmm. Strictly 100% American. The Indians made it first.

Powell's introduction posits a logic of cultural appropriation that will reveal itself to be central to the narrative of 'Proud Woman'. As Consuela, Hedy Lamarr is seen as the inheritor of a sterile and dysfunctional Latino culture whose traditional patriarch (Consuela's father Don Miguel) is confined to a wheelchair and unable to defend his interests. This crisis of culture becomes a crisis in Consuela's femininity, as she makes rough gestures, wears masculine attire and exhibits a disturbing tendency to sling around a riding crop. Consuela's aunt bemoans the fact that her niece 'rides the rancho like a man trying to take [her father's] place'. The discipline of ethnic femininity becomes a task for the American male, who enters the story in the form of Frame, a cowboy who tells Don Miguel, 'Well, I've tried a little of everything. Railroading, stagecoach guard, mining,' to which Don Miguel admiringly replies, 'Well, it sounds like you've covered a lot of territory.' At the arrival of Frame, Consuela's 'dysfunctional' femininity undergoes immediate correction and she substitutes frilly dresses for jeans. While it is clear that Frame's presence/desire for Consuela civilizes her, it is equally evident that the attraction of Consuela for Frame lies in her ability to broaden his range of experience. As the couple kiss for the first time, he tells her 'All the places I've been, all the woman I've known – you never happened to me before'. However, romance is not the only stake in the narrative: Frame and Consuela meet through his involvement in a plan to steal her father's prize stallion, a symbol of Latino heritage. As a stablehand observes, 'He is more than a horse. He is a way of life.' In the end, Frame helps to thwart the horse thieves and learns to channel his energies into more sanctioned forms of cultural appropriation by obtaining Consuela as a trophy for rescuing her family (and symbolically their way of life). The ethnic feminine thus rehabilitates the criminal American, while he restores her to an appropriate femininity.

An especially resonant narrative paradigm in American film and television of the 1950s and 1960s, the western, as Richard Slotkin has noted, puts into play a number of political, economic and ethnic categories highly relevant to America's post-war predicaments at home and abroad. In discussing the ideological utility of the western narrative in US culture in the late 1950s, Slotkin writes that:

The language and conceptual categories of the Frontier Myth were particularly important during the formative period of counterinsurgency doctrine. That myth taught us that historical progress is achieved only by the advance of White European races/cultures into and against the terrain of 'primitive', non-White 'natives'. The native races are inherently lacking in the capacity to generate 'progress'. The best of them are seen as passively willing to subordinate themselves to the progressive Whites. The worst are seen as savagely opposed to progress, preferring extermination to either civilization or subjugation. (Slotkin 1992:446)

'Proud Woman' complicates the operative distinctions between those who possess the privileges of whiteness and those who do not. Through the casting of Lamarr, whose whiteness is more secure than that of the Latino character she portrays, the telefilm suggests a post-war awareness of the hierarchies of whiteness. Similar to the casting of Natalie Wood a year earlier in *The Searchers* (1956), Lamarr becomes more a sign of whiteness gone native than a symbol of true racial difference and she therefore personifies fears of the decline of whiteness, rather than non-whiteness altogether. As an example of the genre, 'Proud Woman' seems to recycle Hedy Lamarr's Hollywood persona to re-tell the story of successful American white patriarchal appropriation of ethnic femininity. In this respect, it draws not only from the narrative of Hedy Lamarr's own Americanization, but also from film roles in the late 1940s and early 1950s in which she consistently served as an ethnic trophy for the white American male. For instance, in the 1950 Bob Hope comedy *My Favorite Spy* Lamarr had played Lily Dalbray, a member of an international spy ring who transfers her allegiance to the Americans, facilitating the fantasy that even the average American male can glorify himself through the international defence of American interests. There are, however, some crucial differences between such films, in which Lamarr was always unproblematically trans-ferred to the heroic white male, and 'Proud Woman', which emphasizes Frame's incorporation into Consuela's universe. This conclusion suggests that he is being assimilated into her culture and will now play the role of son and new patriarch in which Consuela had been forced to masquerade. In this respect, recuperative closure hinges on the restoration of appropriate gender roles and the preservation of ethnicity in a separate sphere, as 'Proud Woman' empha-sizes the geographic and cultural isolation of the ranch, rendering the issue of integration a moot point. In part a fable of the assimilation process, the telefilm concludes by evading the more complex dynamics of ethnic intermarriage. Instead, it highlights the revival of an economically moribund ethnic way of life through the agency of a white male in a fiction that was ideologically compatible with US foreign policy initiatives in the post-war era.

Hedy Lamarr's guest appearance on NBC's *Perry Como Show*, on 30 March 1956, constitutes one of the most striking instances of her deployment as a sign of unruly ethnicity. Popping up unexpectedly throughout the telecast in ways that seem to acknowledge both her marginalization as an ethnic figure and the hesitation of television to acknowledge classical Hollywood celebrity, Lamarr consistently 'troubles' this text. Although the show uses Lamarr as a guest star in its musical/variety format, it does so in such a way that her poor fit with the new medium of television is insistently referenced. In a remarkable opening sequence that introduces Lamarr as literally alien to the show's universe, Como and the Louis da Pron dancers begin a jaunty performance of 'Hi Neighbour', which segues into a fanciful sketch featuring aliens on the moon. Very much a product of Cold War culture, the sketch light-heartedly explores (though not without a certain nervousness) the question of US relations with other global powers, imagining such intercultural relationships as amicable and incorporative. Indeed, the sketch goes on to perform a fantasy of Americanization and co-optation as the dancing aliens are displaced by Como's staid group of male and female performers (conservatively dressed in dark pant and skirt suits), who then welcome Como to the moon. To close the number, the aliens reappear and a mixed group of Americans and aliens surrounds Como as he sings the last chorus of 'Hi Neighbour'. As he does so, he takes a closer look at the female alien to his left, removes her helmet and exclaims, 'Hedy Lamarr!' to the audience's applause. Having established Lamarr's placement as a disruptive element classed with the aliens rather than the natives, the ensuing conversation between Como and Lamarr goes on to set the tone for Lamarr's appearances throughout the telecast:

> Como: I thought it was you, Hedy. What are you doing sneaking around dancing? You're a wonderful actress. Why are you dancing with the chorus?

> Lamarr: Well, it's my idea. You see, I might be Hedy Lamarr on the outside, but inside I'm Piper Laurie. TV producers think of me as Peter Lorre.

Shortly following, Como dismisses Lamarr, saying, 'So now you go back to your dressing room, Hedy and I'll call you when I need you. Now go.' Lamarr retorts, 'OK, but I'll be back.' With this exchange begins a pattern of self-conscious commentary on the way in which Lamarr's appearances in this telecast are both uncontrolled and disruptive, to some extent beyond Como's authority as organizing sensibility and master of ceremonies. In comparing herself to Peter Lorre, Lamarr alludes both to the fact that her residual film stardom is unproductive in the context of television and that in the public imagination female films stars in some sense become 'monstrous' as they age. As Lamarr exits, she brushes past Como's next guests, the comedians Rowan and Martin, who lecherously chime in unison, 'Hi honey'. Lamarr gives them a withering look and says nothing and Rowan turns to Martin and says 'Who do you figure she thinks she is, Hedy Lamarr?' To which Martin replies 'No, that's Peter Lorre.' The exchange is remarkable not only in continuing the comparison between Lamarr (an actress renowned for her beauty) with Lorre (an actor whose fame was tied to his depictions of monsters) but because it suggests a certain level of resentment against Lamarr for her unavailability and unreceptivity to the sexual advances of the two comedians. To assuage the effect of this rebuff, the two comically remind one another that they have not been rejected by a beautiful actress but by someone whose erotic power and authority have been diminished (implicitly as a function of age, gender and re-contextualization within a new system of stardom). The incident, however, resonates for its striking difference from the numerous other contexts in which Lamarr's availability is highlighted.

As the broadcast progresses, Lamarr becomes increasingly the catalyst for the Italian-American Como to call upon his own ethnicity.[5] As Lamarr appears for the second time in a group of dancers performing in support of a Polish-American singer, Como concludes the performance by thanking them in a mock Italian accent, saying 'You sing-a real good.' As the show accumulates references to 'the foreign', it becomes evident that this edition of *The Perry Como Show* consistently employs discourses on ethnicity. Rowan and Martin's comedy works in this register, as they make jokes about samurai warriors and a police officer who must get on his knees to give a ticket to the driver of a foreign car and Como's musical performance does as well, as he sings a medley of songs about romance in Europe against the backdrop of a faux-Parisien street scene. Lamarr infiltrates this sketch as well and as the scene clears, she is left sitting at a cafe table. Como spots her, saying 'I was wondering how you were going to creep into this song' and Lamarr replies 'Oh, Perry, I just had to be in this number'. In unison the two begin to sing 'A Little Paris Song', then trade verses in their 'native' languages, after Como sings, 'Would you sing a chorus in your native Viennese?' and Lamarr responds 'Oh, if you promise you'll do an Ita-li-an reprise'. The two are subsequently joined by the Polish-American singer who adds verses in Polish until the song breaks down and becomes parodic, a culmination of words and phrases such as 'veal parmigiana' and 'egg foo young'. The number makes clear the way in which Como counters or matches Lamarr's ethnicity by recalling his own Italian ethnic background and the scene becomes (at least briefly) an eruption of ethnic memory and a celebration of identities largely repressed in post-war American culture.

Lamarr's attempts to keep herself visible in a medium generally unreceptive to ageing female film stars are once again satirized as Como moves on to a sketch based on viewers' letters. An elderly woman is invited to appear on the show as a result of her fan letter to Como but, once again, Lamarr appears, transparently made up and costumed, cueing Como to exclaim, 'Hedy Lamarr! This is too much! Now, you're never gonna be an old lady'. (Como's comment is trenchant in the sense that he inadvertently speaks to the disturbing qualities attached to the ageing female film star's body and to our wish that they might not go through the ageing process at all).

At the episode's conclusion, Lamarr reappears in her Hollywood incarnation – for the first time she is costumed according to the conventions of cinematic glamour, in a sequined gown, jewels and a chiffon wrap. Como looks starstruck and tells her, 'This is one goodbye I don't like saying.' Lamarr replies, 'Oh Perry, don't say it. It sounds so final. Why don't you say like we do in Austria, "Auf wiedersehn"?' Como repeats the phrase breathlessly and Lamarr adds, 'Or like you would say, "Arriverderci," Como.' In briefly restoring Lamarr to Hollywood glamour here, the scene clearly references ethnic nostalgia, while displaying an awareness of the way that, as a function of her age, gender, ethnicity and ties to classical Hollywood, on television Lamarr lost agency and was forced to operate in a more comedic register, despite moments of self-reflexive commentary such as her appearance here.

It is important to observe that while Lamarr's 1950s TV appearances strongly suggest the anxiety and/or nostalgia provoked by European ethnicities, by the 1960s, Lamarr's ethnicity could be deployed implicitly to critique the concerns of American women. Appearing amongst a diverse pool of stars in the telecast of *Celebrity Game* broadcast on 6 September 1964, (including Joseph Cotten, Della Reese, Ray Walston, Betty Hutton and Paul Lynde among others), Lamarr is referenced as positively 'non-American' and a fitting object of erotic interest for the male contestant.

Celebrity Game offers a particularly rich text in terms of star/audience relations for it features a rotating panel of nine celebrities and three weekly contestants who won cash prizes for correctly guessing star responses to selected questions. Host Carl Reiner explains the premise of the show at the start of the broadcast: 'We ask our celebrity panel a question on some particular topic and ask contestants to read the minds of the stars!' In mediating the star/contestant relationship, Reiner asks the stars probing personal questions by way of bantering with them and he also provides cues to the desirability of each celebrity.

Particularly illuminating in reference to popular understandings of star psychology (since winning is based on second-guessing the way the celebrity will respond), *Celebrity Game* is indeed only nominally a quiz show; its real base is tied to the epistemological pleasures of stardom.[6] Contestants explain why they thought a particular celebrity would answer a question in the way they did and stars justify their responses, in the process giving us better understanding of the way they see the world. Contestants are rewarded for their knowledge of star psychology and their ability to put it to use in matching answers with the stars, but the show also blurs the boundaries of star-based knowledge and erotic desire. In this broadcast, when called upon to make a selection, the first contestant (a middle-aged man) responds emphatically 'I'll pick Hedy Lamarr!' to which Reiner replies 'I don't blame you.' As Reiner authorizes the desire of the male contestant for Hedy Lamarr, he also regulates a female contestant's interest in Joseph Cotten. In response to her statement 'I'll take Joseph Cotten', Reiner replies 'You can't have him – he's married.' Thus, the desire to know (in the form of the star's response to a mundane question) is understood by the host to camouflage erotic interest. In this respect *Celebrity Game* quite directly plays out Richard DeCordova's Foucauldian model of star/fan relations which posits that stardom is often designed to inspire the contemplation of sexual behaviour constituted as se-cret. These kinds of secrets are probed here in the form of quiz questions that implicitly engage norms of gender and coupling.[7] Central to Lamarr's star persona is the implicit assumption of her availability in contrast to that of Cotten.

In the second question put to the panel in this telecast, 'Have American women become too diet conscious?', a contestant correctly guesses that Hedy Lamarr's answer is 'Yes'. In a response that tellingly differentiates her from 'American women', Lamarr comments 'I don't understand where they find time [to diet]. Taking care of my house, the kids and my husband keeps me thin'. In this instance, Lamarr's ethnicity becomes a vehicle for a critique of American women, disguising the fact that women diet largely to re-shape their bodies in the interests of patriarchal consumerism and blaming them for a narcissism, self-interest and abandonment of family obligation coded as 'American'.

Through the chronology of these three television appearances by Hedy Lamarr, we may track the evolution of her star persona in relation to shifting ideological norms of white European ethnicity. Through her film career in the 1940s, Lamarr incarnated a wartime ideal of national and ethnic unity, while by the 1950s, her ethnicity was strikingly problematic in the context of television's attempt to normalize and commodify the repression of ethnic heri-tage. By the 1960s, ideological norms were again in flux and *Celebrity Game* offers us hints of a reversion to ethnic femininity as fantasy. Hedy Lamarr's appearance on *The Perry Como Show* offers important evidence of the way that mainstream television was surprisingly susceptible to ethnic infiltration in the 1950s and 1960s. While media historians have tended to assess the nature of ethnicity in television by cataloguing the number and assessing the functions of programs explicitly oriented around ethnic content, this analysis has suggested that ethnicity could be a small but crucial element in texts not explicitly designed to investigate an ethnic universe. American post-war cul-ture consistently defined itself in relation to 'the foreign' and the content of these telecasts suggests that white ethnicity was a more prevalent element in American television than we have acknowledged. Whether she was featured as an ethnic reward to a white hero in a western like 'Proud Woman', posi-tioned as a marker of traditional gender roles in her appearance as a guest star in *Celebrity Game* or used as a catalyst to elicit Perry Como's Italian ethnicity in *The Perry Como Show*, Lamarr's ethnicity did not disappear in her television roles, indeed it was centralized. Yet it is also clear that Lamarr's ethnicity was 'troublesome' to television in ways that were largely without precedent in her film career. Lamarr made the transition to television at a time when a wartime culture that could acknowledge white ethnic differences as positive gave way to a post-war culture that sought to suppress the signs of ethnicity. As the cultural determinants for the depiction of ethnicity altered, Lamarr was framed in a discourse of disruption rather than one of inclusivity.

Taken as a whole, these three appearances also tell us something about the apprehensions attached to the transitions of female film stars into television in the post-war period. Clearly, appearance on television shifted the terms of reception in favour of more accessible, less arcane definitions of stardom. For Hedy Lamarr, whose Hollywood celebrity had been predicated on her aloof exoticism, this transition represented a profound rupture in her persona. We may well speculate that the domestic context and the more disruptive flow of the television text acted against the mystery and glamour which were the necessary preconditions for Lamarr's exotic allure. Although they take place in a range of different programme contexts, all three of Lamarr's guest appearances discussed here centralize her new-found availability and accessibility in the new medium. Whether she is presented as a reward to Frame for his help in defending the ranch in 'Proud Woman', subject to the accessing claims of male contestants in *Celebrity Game* or anxiously represented as too available (too present) in *The Perry Como Show*, the televised Hedy Lamarr seems to have been consistently linked to a process of coming to terms with her no longer remote stardom.

In principle, Lamarr's appearance in 'Proud Woman' in 1957 extended the stardom of her late film career by repeating the kind of role she had already played in early 1950s dramas such as *Lady Without a Passport* (1951) and comedies such as *My Favorite Spy* (1950). As Consuela, Lamarr plays the familiar role of token of achievement for a deserving American hero, yet it is the hero who appears to be integrated into Latino culture at the conclusion. *Celebrity Game* takes the notion of Lamarr as reward out of the realm of fiction, re-directing it into the quiz show as her beauty and traditionalism make her the fantasy object ambiguously available to male contestants. In this respect access to ethnic femininity as a form of cultural capital is being vied for more than the actual economic capital presented as the ostensible reward. *The Perry Como Show*'s production of a knowledgeable discourse on Hedy Lamarr's 'alien' status in the world of early television is certainly the most complex of the texts considered here. The comedy grounded in the recognition of her hypervisibility seems rooted in a fundamental anxiousness in relation to this new accessibility. It seems likely that just as Perry Como was more comfortable with the cinematic, glamorous Hedy Lamarr, so too was the American public.

As post-war culture came to define American centrality and superiority as ideologically normative, the repression of European ethnicity became an increasingly necessary part of the process of building post-war consensus. Hedy Lamarr's circulation in a fairly wide variety of television genres seems to confirm that her age, gender and ethnic status necessitated that she be 'remade' for television in ways that expressed latent conflicts over European heritage and American culture. Further study might confirm the hypothesis that lies at the heart of this paper, namely that post-war American culture was heavily invested in repressing white ethnicity and for that very reason ethnicity tends to operate as a crucial structuring absence or as an element of disruption in the texts of early television.

Notes

1. Sheri Chinen-Biesen, 'West Side Story, Kennedy's Camelot and American National Identity in 1961', paper presented at 1996 Film/Culture/History Conference, Aberdeen, Scotland, p. 5.

2. This work has been done by scholars working in a wide variety of fields, from labour history to sociology, to literary, film and ethnic studies. For some of the most important work in this area, see Toni Morrison, *Playing in the Dark: Whiteness and the Literary Imagination* (1992); Ruth Frankenberg, *White Women, Race Matters: The Social Construction of Whiteness* (1993); David Roediger, *The Wages of Whiteness: Race and the Making of the American Working Class* (1991) and *Towards the Abolition of Whiteness: Essays on Race, Politics and Working Class History* (1994); Matt Wray & Annalee Newitz, *White Trash: Race and Class in America* (1997); Daniel Bernardi, *The Birth of Whiteness: Race and the Emergence of US Cinema* (1996), Richard Dyer, *White* (1997); and Mike Hill, *Whiteness: A Critical Reader* (1997).

3. Russell Baker, 'Movie Fan Tells All', *New York Times*, 10 February 1996:A15.

4. Perceptions of Lamarr as an ageing star clearly exacerbated her problematic status for television and its audiences. In *Aging and Its Discontents: Freud and Other Fictions*, Kathleen Woodward has shrewdly analyzed the relationship between psychoanalytic theory and 'the social consequences of perceiving the elderly as alien to ourselves.' (69) It seems likely that Lamarr became 'alien' to the world of 1950s television for this reason as well as others.

5. Born Pierino Como, the son of Italian immigrants, the pop music star and television personality's ethnicity was represented in most accounts as fully compatible with his all-American appeal. A 1953 *Newsweek* profile of Como and his music observed that 'The best description of him was given by a friend: "Did you ever live next door to a nice young Italian fellow with a wife and a few kids? That's Perry. And that's all he is." ' ('A Decade With Como', *Newsweek* 41, 29 June 1953:84). In this respect, Lamarr seems to epitomize the persistence of ethnicity, while Como represents its assimilation.

6. This assessment of *Celebrity Game* is echoed in the show's entry in *The Complete Directory of Prime Time Network TV Shows 1946–Present*. The authors note that 'At times this series seemed more like a comedy variety program than a quiz show . . . The individual panelists decided yes or no and each contestant tried to guess which way a given panelist had voted and why. The "why" gave the panelists the opportunity to make funny responses. Contestants won money for correct guessing but the money was incidental to the humor.' (173)

7. See DeCordova's *Picture Personalities: The Emergence of the Star System in America*.

CHAPTER 7

MAUREEN O'HARA'S 'CONFIDENTIAL' LIFE

RECYCLING STARS THROUGH GOSSIP AND MORAL BIOGRAPHY

Mary Desjardins

A March 1957 *Confidential Magazine* article described established Hollywood film star Maureen O'Hara as recently having 'taken the darndest position to watch a movie in the whole history of the [Grauman's Chinese] theatre', spread across three seats with her 'happy Latin American' boyfriend in the middle seat.[1] In the playful tone characteristic of its account of the alleged incident the article proclaims that as 'far as Maureen was concerned, this was double feature night and she was giving away more than dishes.'[2]

Less than a month after this issue of *Confidential* was distributed to a claimed circulation of four million readers, the US television show *This is Your Life* broadcast a live episode honouring Maureen O'Hara's life. Host Ralph Edwards – ever sentimental and obnoxiously presumptuous – lost no opportunity to present O'Hara as a stereotypical 'fighting Irish Colleen' whose life revolved around her close-knit family of parents, siblings and young daughter. A variety of father-mentor figures – including O'Hara's actual father, actor Charles Laughton, producer Erich Pommer, director John Ford and a famous Irish soccer hero – appeared on camera to wish this 'very nice girl' well (Laughton's words) and to testify to her loyalty and professionalism. Neither the annulment of her first marriage nor the messy custody battle involved in the divorce of her second husband were mentioned, as Edwards focused on O'Hara's sympathetic mothering abilities. The recent *Confidential Magazine* article, and O'Hara's anger over it, which would result in a multi-million-dollar lawsuit, were also absent from Edwards' account, despite the fact that they could be said to define O'Hara's life at that moment in March 1957 as much as anything revealed by the popular television show.

This essay examines O'Hara's 'recycling' through 'new' media in the late 1950s to explore the conditions under which two so seemingly disparate discourses about a star could circulate simultaneously. Television, one of the 'new' media of the 1950s, created knowledge about film stars at this time by producing moral biography, while the tabloid magazines circulated star narratives through scandalous gossip. Both television and scandal magazines became available for mass consumption between 1949 and 1959. In this period, the media industries' production, distribution and regulation of social knowledge were inflected by economic and legal restructuring of the film industry and its star system, by increased competition among all leisure activities and by new understandings of audience segmentation and differentiation.

By taking into account that television, scandal magazines and their promotional discourses were likely experienced at the same time by audiences (a fact often acknowledged, at least implicitly), the essay will suggest how *contradictions* in the social imaginary could be exposed when multiple players in the new media made exclusive or competing truth claims. The March 1957 recycling of Maureen O'Hara through moral biography and scandalous gossip complicated the exclusivity of the truths that television and scandal magazines promised to tell about the stars and in the process revealed the complex multiplicity of publicly available images of sexuality. This period's beliefs about sexuality are best understood in terms of a fluid discursivity, in which television and scandal magazine discourses participated through their negotiations of stardom.

This is Your Life

This is Your Life, a popular television programme of the 1950s, combined aspects of talk, game, inspirational and variety shows to present stars in settings or situations that emphasized their private lives or feelings. Positive audience feedback for a 1946 episode of his popular radio programme *Truth or Consequences* spurred producer-host Ralph Edwards to launch *This is Your Life*. Edwards presented a disabled World War II veteran having a hard time adjusting to post-war life. Edwards' spin on the veteran's situation was in line with the goals of 'inspirational' shows – the story of someone's life can be an example of hope and courage to others. *This is Your Life* first aired on radio in 1948, becoming a live television programme in 1952, running until 1960 on the networks and reappearing in a syndicated version in the early 1970s.[3]

In the opening moment of each edition of *This is Your Life*, the guest subject was surprised by Edwards with his announcement, 'this is your life!' People from the subject's past were periodically introduced during Edwards' dramatic narrative of his/her life. In the case of a star subject, the private life and career were usually intertwined. For example, the subject's second grade teacher might speak of a past event that seemed to presage the subject's achievement of stardom, while directors and co-stars recounted incidents that would reveal the ordinary human qualities of the star.

Since the 1920s, film stars had been embodiments of an 'ordinary-extraordinary' dialectic regulating the knowledge of the spectator vis-à-vis the star.[4] Critics have argued that while film stars often appear desirable precisely because of that dialectic, television constructs its stars as familiar persons with whom the viewer is more likely to feel a sense of intimacy.[5] *This is Your Life* provides an example of one way in which television in the 1950s negotiated film stardom, within its own terms of familiarity and ordinariness. Like many variety shows of the time, it did trade on the glamour of Hollywood film stardom: Edwards often surprising the programme's star subjects at award ceremonies or premieres. Maureen O'Hara was surprised in this way at the press interviews before the 1957 Academy Awards ceremony. However the primary focus was the ordinary human behind the star – the star as 'authentic' individual. Authenticity was displayed on the programme through a variety of registers specific to television's particular technological capacities and representational strategies, including episode scheduling, therapeutic confession and live transmission.

Editions of *This is Your Life* focusing on stars and other entertainment personalities during its run in the 1940s and 1950s were scheduled to alternate with those presenting the life stories of 'ordinary' people who contributed in some way to their communities. Stars were thus favourably associated with 'ordinary' people, specifically those with a philanthropist bent. 'Ordinary' people became honoured media celebrities, hence, 'extraordinary' individuals in the national context rather than unsung do-gooders only known to a local community. Both kinds of surprised guests were given mementoes of their appearance and honoured at post-show parties with the people who shared memories and stories on the programme.

Ralph Edwards' conception of the programme provided justification for constructing a schedule which alternated between 'ordinary' people and stars. In trade and fan magazines he downplayed the role that *This is Your Life* might have in promoting show business or constructing media personalities, emphasizing instead the way it revealed an exemplary biography of a moral person: ' "In whatever category we pick our principle, we always try," Ralph explains, "to make sure it is a person whose deeds and character show a sympathetic nature and whose endeavours in life have been of a constructive nature." '[6]

In another interview, Edwards explicitly states that the theme of the programme is 'Love Thy Neighbour'.[7] This Christian philosophy was supported by the melodramatic and therapeutic rhetorical strategies in his sentimental introductions and coaching of both subject and guest 'witnesses' to relate touching stories about the subject's past. Such stories usually demonstrated the subject overcoming obstacles, helping others on the way and ultimately reaching goals of happiness. In this way, stars' lives became emblematic of moral journeys, with surprise guests appearing like cheerleaders on the sidelines or the weeping women of Jerusalem on the way of the cross, depending on whether the star life depicted was a happy one (O'Hara) or unhappy (Frances Farmer or Lillian Roth).[8]

Edwards' rhetoric caused one *Time* magazine writer to dub him a 'spiritual prosecutor'.[9] Indeed, he sometimes prodded both subjects and witnesses to 'confess' by asking them leading or coercive questions, such as his quizzing of former film star Frances Farmer as to the nature of the 'problem' that landed her in a sanatorium ('Was it drugs? Was it alcohol?'). Edwards was especially pleased when a show helped its subject gain happiness or boosted a career, as he claimed it did for former singer-actress and alcoholic Lillian Roth.[10] Such a result was widely circulated and used to validate the host's 'prosecution'. This warm, sentimental quality pleased sponsor Hazel Bishop Cosmetics. Company president Raymond Spector was reportedly in favour of the 'sentimental and heavily emotional' in programmes,[11] telling Edwards that the audience would believe *This is Your Life* and 'if they believe it, then they will believe Hazel Bishop lipstick doesn't smear off'.[12]

The programme's exploitation of television's capacity for 'liveness' was also a key factor in its success in constructing stars as moral and 'authentic' private individuals. In the industry as well as in television studies, liveness is understood to refer to the technological capacity of the medium to broadcast an event simultaneously with its occurrence. Although not naturally derived from television's electronic technology, liveness has come to signify co-presence, immediacy, the capturing of the true or authentic moment as it unfolds.[13] It was the combination of this liveness and the surprising of subjects that made *This is Your Life* an especially effective and privileged site for recycling Hollywood film stars. It allowed the programme to negotiate modalities of star identity (the ordinary, private self behind the distant, glamorous public persona) with the simulation of audience co-presence. The dialectics of presence-absence and ordinary-extraordinary were simultaneously displayed and displaced in the programme's live surprising. When stars surprised by Edwards were caught off-guard, they seemed as vulnerable and ordinary as anyone discovering they are on national television (some, like Nat King Cole, looked more than momentarily horrified).

Thus the attraction of *This is Your Life* both for sponsors and for the Hollywood film community was its simultaneous association with the glamour of celebrity, the therapeutic qualities of moral biography and the 'authenticity' conveyed by television's liveness. Indeed, the celebrity's surprise, because indicative of his or her non-involvement in the planning or production of the show, 'naturalizes' the association between star aura and product. It is therefore hardly surprising that the show became popular with both audiences and sponsors.[14]

The Rise of the Scandal Magazine in the 1950s

For Robert Harrison, publisher of *Confidential*, television's appeal to the audience desire for co-presence with the televised personality was legitimated by the excited response to the live televised hearings of Senator Este Kefauver's committee on organized crime in 1950–51. Harrison claimed that those televised hearings inspired him to create the scandal magazine in 1952, though he already had vast experience in tabloid and more respectable film publications since the 1920s.[15] By the 1940s he was producing 'girlie' magazines like *Whisper* (which he later revamped into a scandal magazine). 'Girlie' or 'cheesecake' magazines did well in the 1940s, helping to create and sustain the American GIs' interest in pin-up art. Such publications flooded the market as wartime paper rationing restrictions were finally lifted in 1950. *Confidential*'s success in featuring scandal stories about stars and other famous people resulted in dozens of copycat magazines and hundreds of 'one-shots' (magazines focused on one star or personality). In the midst of fierce competition Harrison and others, such as *Suppressed* editor Edythe Farrell, gave the public (the televised Kefauver hearings notwithstanding) 'what they can't get on television'[16] – exposés of star secrets, racketeering, consumer scams and politicians' peccadilloes.

Social reformers, local and national business organizations, government institutions and, of course, the subjects of the stories themselves, immediately saw the scandal magazines as problematic, subjecting them to scrutiny and legal action.[17] However despite (or because of) such censorious outcries, the magazines had a combined circulation of 15 million by 1955, flourishing in a climate in which legal, social and commercial ideas of obscenity were in flux.

Social historians suggest that the 1946 Supreme Court decision overturning the Post Office's denial of mailing privileges to *Esquire* magazine resulted in the increased accessibility of erotically explicit material in print.[18] Within the film industry, expansion of what were considered morally appropriate representations of sexuality became possible after the 1952 'Miracle Case' which extended freedom of speech to motion pictures.[19] One of the Supreme Court's most important cases on obscenity occurred in 1957, the same year as *Confidential*'s O'Hara article. The Roth case upheld local censorship efforts, but also established that sex and obscenity were not synonymous, making it clear that 'obscenity' implied an intention to arouse prurient interests.

While the core facts of a story might have occurred or been reported elsewhere as occurring, nevertheless through omissions, combinations of different events, embellishments and illustration by photographs not taken at the scene, the 'composite fact' story implied that the celebrity had engaged in immoral or indecent sexual conduct. The 1957 *Confidential* article about Maureen O'Hara was one such 'composite fact' story. O'Hara's statement about it, in which she spoke as both actress and mother, was one of the most publicized responses to the scandal magazines.

Recycling Maureen O'Hara

Throughout the 1940s, fan magazines and other kinds of publicity represented O'Hara as the spunky but pure patriotic Irish girl defined as much by her roles as wife and mother as professional woman. Her first marriage at 17 and its subsequent annulment in 1941 are rarely mentioned. Her second marriage to dialogue director Will Price, the birth of their daughter Bronwyn and the continued closeness between O'Hara and her parents and siblings in Ireland are central to almost all the promotion and publicity about her.

Photoplay, Silver Screen and *Modern Screen* titled articles on her 'Irish Pixie', 'Home Girl at Heart', 'Letter to her Daughter', 'Star-Spangled Colleen' and 'Pride of the Irish'.[20] Newspaper publicity touted her community service awards,[21] and published articles with O'Hara's pronouncements about marriage and family. In the 1947 piece 'Motherhood is Women's Real Career', she is reported to be worried about the state of American marriage and motherhood. 'She says we're slipping', that we need to 'get back to the family – and to religion, too'.[22] That same year, she stated that she was 'careful to remove every trace of make-up, wear very simple clothes and come home to my family without a trace of the studio about me.' As a proper wife, rather than a career woman, O'Hara never discusses her part, 'the day's worries or triumphs, unless of course, my husband specifically asks, which he seldom does'.[23] A 1942 columnist claims that O'Hara 'won't pose for leg art and sexy photographs.' She won't 'take a . . . bath for the movies or wear gauzy negligees' because ' "I come from a very strict family . . . They would think I turned out bad." '[24]

In her examination of the career of the Irish-American silent star Coleen Moore, Diane Negra argues that the 1920s discourses about femininity positioned the Irish girl as a corrective to the 'vamp' and other modern women. While the vamp 'foregrounded her own self-manufacture in a way that foreclosed the shaping influence of patriarchy', the Irish girl presented herself as 'a resource to be acted upon by patriarchal and capitalistic influences'.[25] O'Hara's influence in publicity and promotion as the definitive example of 'Irish femininity' seems similarly positioned in the 1950s. In *Modern Screen*'s 1949 'Pride of the Irish', Maureen's Irish heritage is credited for her dislike of modernity and her ability to create a traditional homelife for her husband and daughter.

The 1957 episode of *This is Your Life* replays many of these themes. Edwards surprises O'Hara outside the Pantages Theatre where the 1957 Academy Awards are being held. Noticeably breathless after running from the Pantages during the commercial break, the two enter the NBC studio accompanied by traditional Irish bagpipes. The glamorous setting of the Oscars is replaced by the more 'homey' stage set approximating an Irish pastoral scene with a wrought iron garden bench and fake trees.

Edwards frequently teases O'Hara about her childhood and, although positioning her spirited responses as proof of an 'Irish temper', her Irish ethnicity is most significantly associated with her identity as daughter, sister and mother. Most of the guest 'witnesses' to her life are her blood family – parents, siblings, daughter – and consequently, most of the biographical stories told about her are of her past 'private' life as a child and young woman. With obvious affection, O'Hara's siblings describe Maureen as a tomboy, with anecdotes about pranks, songs and sports providing evidence. In a discussion with her parents, it becomes evident that any rebellion signified by her desire to become an actress was tempered by a willingness to be shaped by her father's patriarchal influences: she agreed to study stenography as a 'back-up' profession in case she failed as an actress.

Actor-producer Charles Laughton, with whom O'Hara acted in three films, appears in live broadcast relay from New York to talk about their first meeting. As the camera 'captures' O'Hara alternating between laughter and tears, Laughton recounts how she looked in her first screen test: 'On the screen was a girl – she looked at least 35, she was over done-up in some night-time evening dress, very made-up face, and her hair in an over grand style. Just for a split part of a second, in the close-up, the light was off this face and you could see, as the girl turned around, this absolutely beautiful profile of yours, which you couldn't see under all the make-up.' Laughton was able to see the less mature, child-like girl he needed for *Jamaica Inn* under the make-up O'Hara had intended to make her look more grown-up and, undoubtedly, more sexual.

This is Your Life thus recirculated discourses that had been successful in constructing a wholesome image for O'Hara for some time. But some might also have seen it as a partial or selective recycling of aspects of O'Hara's persona. Since at least 1950, O'Hara's 'pure Irish lass' persona had existed in tension with a persona more befitting a 'sand-and-bosom opera queen'. Because of her frequent casting in costume dramas emphasizing sex and adventure, columnist Erskine Johnson had declared 'Maureen . . . is a movie queen whose endowments sell tickets at the box office the way a lass busting out of her bodice on a dust jacket sells historical novels by Kathleen Windsor'. Seemingly ignoring her earlier concerns with revealing negligees, she told Johnson that she wasn't ashamed of costumes accentuating décolletage because 'I feel that if God gave you something beautiful, you should use it'.[26] However, signifiers connected to her Irish ethnicity reappear in traditional fan magazine articles, functioning as reassuring proof of her wholesomeness and decency. These depict her as 'unselfconscious, a homebody' and not 'prompted by the vogue of Marilyn Monroe' to fake glamour.[27]

The negative publicity surrounding the 1955 custody battle over her daughter was less easily recouped. Newspapers reported on her ex-husband's allegations that O'Hara was an unfit mother because she had 'lived in sin' with the married Enrique Parra, described as a 'wealthy Mexican playboy'.[28] While O'Hara and Price eventually settled out of court after he withdrew his allegations, the story was revived in the following two years by the scandal magazines. When *Confidential* published its article, it dropped the narrative about custody for one about O'Hara, Parra (not mentioned by name, he is called a 'Latin Lothario'), sex and movie theatres as sites for the illicit.

The moral biography tone adopted by *This is Your Life* could have functioned as a containment of the scandalous gossip of *Confidential*, as a counter-discourse to the attacks on Hollywood and its stars volleyed increasingly by the scandal magazines in the 1950s. Although Maureen O'Hara was probably genuinely moved by the tribute paid to her on *This is Your Life*, the show must also have been a welcome support as she tried to control the multiplying discourses about her star persona and her identity as a private citizen. Although it is beyond the scope of this essay to discuss the state investigations and eventual criminal libel and obscenity trial against *Confidential* in the summer and autumn of 1957,[29] two things should be noted. First, O'Hara's testimony before a grand jury (that would eventually indict *Confidential* employees), her willingness to talk to the press openly about her own civil libel suit and the way she positioned her outrage as a concerned mother and professional actress produced recuperative discourses about her that saw her as both victim and hero, rather than as an indecent woman.[30] Second, the state investigations and the trial were both predictable culminations of what had been an on-going discussion about privacy in the 1950s. This was a discussion that encompassed not only the scandal magazines, but also television – specifically shows like *This is Your Life*.

This is Your Life, Confidential and the Private

Richard DeCordova, following Foucault, has argued that public fascination with stars since the 1910s and 1920s is due to the fact that the typical construction of stars – the revelation of the 'private reality' behind the 'public image' – 'engages us in the very processes through which our society constitutes sexuality as an object of knowledge and fascination'.[31] DeCordova's

point affirms Foucault's argument that self-identity is enacted in modern culture through confessing the 'private', the most private being equated with the
sexual. The power and pleasure of self-knowledge/knowledge of stars, is thus
intimately related to knowledge of the sexual. DeCordova notes that for this
reason scandal always exists as the underside of star discourse.

The scandal that *Confidential* created around O'Hara traded on current
tensions surrounding the sexually experimenting woman versus the virginal
and/or non-sexually responsive woman. The former category was most prominent in the Kinsey report on female sexuality, published in 1953, while the
latter was often stereotyped in movies, television and magazine cartoons (like
those in *Playboy*) as the typical American housewife. The Kinsey report on
female sexuality drove a wedge into this stereotype. Although it might read
like a playful farce, *Confidential*'s article about Maureen O'Hara was part of
their aggressive campaign to discredit Hollywood according to the terms of
public/private knowledge about sexuality. *Confidential* suggested that Hollywood was a hypocritical organisation, perpetrating stories about stars as
domestic saints and hiding their worst (sexual) sins. For this reason, *Confidential* and similar magazines recycled old scandals (either recent allegations, as in O'Hara's case, or older stories about Fatty Arbuckle, Mary Astor,
Mae West and Charlie Chaplin). These magazines attempted to gain moral
weight by describing their work as historical investigation which would tell
the *truth*, the 'real' private, rather than the packaged narratives composed by
studios and press agents. In a 1957 editorial, *Confidential* claimed

> Hollywood is in the business of lying . . . They 'glamorise' and distribute detailed –
> and often deliberately false – information about private lives . . . The trouble with
> their 'build-ups' is that they create a phoney atmosphere which spoils some of
> those who are 'built up' . . . All we have done is 'blow the whistle' on a few of these
> spoiled ones. We have given the truth to our readers who have wanted and were
> entitled to the truth. And for this, Hollywood wants to 'get' *Confidential*.[32]

The legal attacks on *Confidential*, culminating in the 1957 trial, were made
at a time when libel laws still strongly supported the rights of individuals to
privacy. But as new media (like television) and new, sophisticated surveillance devices (like those small recorders used by *Confidential* tipsters) proliferated during the decade, increasing numbers of cases concerning privacy
came to the courts. Law review articles and journalistic editorials often
focused on the scandal magazines in discussions about rights to privacy.[33]
As one federal judge put it in 1956, the state of the privacy laws was like a
'haystack in a hurricane'.[34] Indeed, many of the civil libel cases brought
against *Confidential* before 1957 had been dropped or settled out of court.
Libel was difficult to prove and court cases always risked a further circulation of the stories. Even the criminal libel and obscenity trial against *Confidential* in 1957 ended in a deadlocked jury, despite O'Hara's proof that the
magazine had lied about her (she had been out of the country when the

alleged event happened). But discursive activity was nevertheless effective in turning public attention towards the maliciousness of the magazines, though many critical editorials couldn't decide whether the magazines were bad because they lied or because they exposed 'real' truths to satisfy the indecent urges of the public.[35]

The scandal magazines overtly exploited the discourses of the sexual, but how can *This is Your Life* be understood to construct the private and personal in similar terms? This essay has suggested that the television programme participated in discourses that positioned O'Hara's private life within the 'feminine mystique' of the 1950s, rather than within that decade's growing fascination with the sexually experimenting woman. However, Foucault argues that 'silence . . . the things one declines to say, or is forbidden to name, the discretion that is required between different speakers . . . functions alongside the things said . . . There is not one but many silences and they are an integral part of the strategies that underlie and penetrate discourses'.[36] *This is Your Life*'s construction of O'Hara as loyal daughter, sister, mother and protégé of elderly male Hollywood figures functions as a strategic silencing *of*, as well as a will *to* silence, discourses about her sexuality. Absent guests include not only the infamous Parra, but all the young male co-stars of her films – such as John Wayne, Jeff Chandler, John Payne, Anthony Quinn. Her first husband is never mentioned though assiduous readers might remember him and her second, Will Price, whose 1941 marriage was 'dissolved some years later', seems only necessary to mention as an explanation for daughter Bronwyn's existence. Although *This is Your Life* gives us no reason to disbelieve O'Hara's basic decency and her patriarchally-shaped femininity, other discourses circulating about O'Hara and female sexuality in the 1950s might, at the very least, reveal contradictions in Hollywood's discourses.

To my knowledge, no negative commentary was written about the O'Hara edition of *This is Your Life*, though the programme as a whole did generate controversy about invasion of privacy, evoking comparison with the scandal magazines. Two of the most critical articles about the programme came from prominent television critics writing for national publications in 1954 and 1958, during *Confidential*'s heyday. Jack Gould, writing for the *New York Times* (1954) excoriates *This is Your Life*, putting it in the same category as other 'misery shows' like *Strike it Rich*, which exemplify television's debasement to 'the extent of exploiting the raw and private emotions of the unfortunate or catering to the craven curiosity of the mob'.[37] In *TV Guide* (1958), Gilbert Seldes argued that *This is Your Life* forced people to be emotional – they are 'compelled to expose themselves' – comparing this to the English nobility's practice of gawking at inmates of Bedlam in the eighteenth century and describing Ralph Edwards' face as 'lit not with sympathy but with glee over the tricks he has pulled'.[38] While no such articles comment on the eroticization of the spectators' curiosity, nevertheless the vociferousness of their tone indicates the charged atmosphere of the programme's reception.[39] *TV*

Scandals, for example, seemed to have intuited the potentially sexualized nature of Edwards' 'exposures': 'Week after week, people tune in to the show hoping that one of these days his fancy "element of surprise" will blow up right in Ralph Edwards' face. What then? What if the victim simply refuses to go through with the noisome spectacle, re-living his life in the glare of the lights and before the TV camera? . . . some of the stars . . . have passed the word around that they'll walk off at the psychological moment and leave Edwards holding his impotent mike.'[40]

Such reactions suggest that, although they may differ in their moral contextualization of sexuality, the strategies of *This is Your Life* and the scandal magazines exemplify the fluid discursivity around that issue in the 1950s and both ultimately assume a similar reader/viewing subject – a confessor who is in the position to judge, condemn, or empathize with the star under scrutiny. Both also trade on candid reactions to constructed surprises through the various strategies, such as liveness and composite fact stories, available through their specific media technologies and histories. In this way, they participate in a re-animation of the star system by displaying fresh markers of star 'authenticity'.

Notes

[1] R.E. McDonald 'It Was the Hottest Show in Town when Maureen O'Hara Cuddled in Row 35', *Confidential* vol. 5:1, March 1957, 11.

[2] Ibid.

[3] A British version of *This is Your Life*, transmitted on BBC TV 1955–64 and on Thames TV from 1969. Eamonn Andrews was the initial host, followed by Michael Aspel. Like its American counterpart, the programme is infamous for its 'surprising' of guest subjects: 'Footballer Danny Blanchflower was among those who tossed the "surprise" format on its head by walking off in a mixture of embarrassment and anger at the invasion of personal privacy.' See Tise Vahimagi, *British Television* (1994) 53.

[4] Richard Dyer, *Stars* (1979) and *Heavenly Bodies: Film Stars and Society* (1986).

[5] See John Ellis, *Visible Fictions: Cinema, Television, Video* (1982); P. David Marshall, *Celebrity and Power: Fame in Contemporary Culture* (1987); for a discussion focused on these issues in relation to the 1950s, see Denise Mann 'The Spectacularization of Everyday Life: Recycling Hollywood Stars and Fans in Early Television Variety Shows' in Spigel and Mann (eds), *Private Screenings: Television and the Female Consumer* (1992) 41–62.

[6] Gladys Hall, 'Four Magic Words' in *TV-Radio Mirror*, c1954, 99.

[7] Fredda Balling, 'The World is his Neighbour' in *TV-Radio Mirror* vol. 52:1, June 1959, 30.

[8] In *I'll Cry Tomorrow* (New York: Frederick Fell), her 1954 autobiography written with Gerald Frank, former-alcoholic singer Lillian Roth describes her 1953 appearance on *This is Your Life* in terms of the fascination and shock she felt as she sat on the studio stage and heard her life 'revived and made fresh to me and to the public'. This edition supposedly helped Roth's autobiography become a bestseller when it was released the following year. Frances Farmer's 1958 appearance on the programme was also a sober experience for the guest of

honour, as friends and family testified to her difficult attempts to find work and dignity after she left a mental institution. Both Farmer and Roth were told of the programme's focus on them in advance.

9. 'Sermon on the Air', *Time*, 16 February 1953.

10. Hall 1954:100.

11. 'Why I'm Through with Big TV Shows', *Sponsor* vol. 9:1, May 1955, 95.

12. Dave Kauffman, 'Ralph Edwards May Revive "This is Your Life" Hit', *Variety*, 6 January 1978. Thanks to Barbara Hall, Margaret Herrick Library of the Academy of Motion Picture Arts and Sciences, for help in tracking down this reference.

13. See Mark Williams, 'History in a Flash: Notes on the Myth of TV Liveness' in Jane Gaines and Michael Renov (eds), *Collecting Visible Evidence* (1999); Jane Feuer, 'The Concept of Live Television: Ontology as Ideology' in E. Ann Kaplan (ed.), *Regarding Television* (1983); Klaus Dieter-Rath, 'Live Television and its Audiences: Challenges of Media Reality' in Ellen Seiter et al (eds), *Remote Control: Television, Audiences and Cultural Power* (1989); Mary Ann Doane, 'Information, Crisis, Catastrophe' in Patricia Mellencamp (ed.), *Logics of Television* (1992).

14. In fact, the alternative sponsor to Hazel and Bishop was Proctor and Gamble, a household product and cosmetic firm that found great profitability in underwriting soap opera, another genre associated with both confession and therapy. See Mimi White, *Tele-Advising: Therapeutic Discourse in American Television* (1992), for the relationship between the discursive forms of television and therapy. White focuses on contemporary television, but many of her insights could be applied to early television as well.

15. Harrison had begun working for the *Daily Graphic*, one of the most notorious tabloid newspapers of the 1920s (and gossip columnist Walter Winchell's home paper), while still in his teens. Later, he worked for the motion picture trade publications *Motion Picture Daily* and *Motion Picture Herald*. Harrison claimed that publisher Martin Quigley fired him for producing a 'girlie' magazine called *Beauty Parade*, perhaps sparking his desire to compete with the legitimate motion picture press in an aggressively hostile manner.

16. Quoted in 'The Curious Craze for "Confidential" Magazines . . .', *Newsweek*, 11 July 1955:51.

17. The US Post Office attempted to ban *Confidential* from the mails as obscene material in 1955 and in-depth articles by *Time, Newsweek* and *Commonweal* in 1955 and 1956 examined it. Film industry trade publications and Hollywood columns in newspapers throughout the country railed against all the magazines, and between 1955 and 1957 a number of the publications were named in both civil lawsuits and state grand juries as libellous and/or portraying obscene material.

18. John D'Emilio and Estelle B. Freedman, *Intimate Matters: A History of Sexuality in America* (New York: Harper & Row 1988) 280.

19. While this ruling did not result in immediate changes to the Production Code, it weakened local censorship efforts and successful challenges to the Code from within Hollywood (from, most famously, Otto Preminger) preceded Code expansions of admissible representations of sexuality by the late 1950s.

20. See F. Service, 'Her Letter to Her Daughter' in *Silver Screen*, June 1945; D. O'Leary & J. Holland, 'Home Girl at Heart' in *Silver Screen*, April 1947; Herb Owe, 'Star-Spangled Colleen' in *Photoplay*, February 1948; R. and B. Churchill, 'Irish Pixie' in *Silver Screen*, June 1949; Viola Moore, 'Pride of the Irish' in *Modern Screen*, September 1947.

21. Her awards for 'outstanding mother of the year in motion pictures' and 'outstanding Catholic girl' were widely publicized.

22. Philip K. Scheur, 'Motherhood is Women's Real Career, Star Says', *Los Angeles Times*, 8 June 1947.

23. Maureen O'Hara, 'My Most Important Role' in Ivy Crane (ed.), *The Star's Own Stories*, c1947. This is reprinted as *Hollywood in the 1940s: The Star's Own Stories* (New York: Frederick Ungar 1980).

24. Sidney Skolsky, 'Tintypes', syndicated column, 17 June 1942.

25. Diane Negra, *Hollywood and the Narrativisation of the Ethnic Feminine*, PhD dissertation, University of Texas-Austin 1996:99.

26. Erskine Johnson column in *Daily News*, 21 October 1950.

27. See Gladys Hall, 'She Knows Where She's Going!' in *Photoplay*, December 1952:76.

28. See 'Ex-Husband Says Star Lives in Sin' in *Mirror-News*, 21 June 1955; 'Ex-Mate Accuses Maureen O'Hara, Demands Custody of Daughter, 11' in *Los Angeles Times*, 24 June 1955; 'Maureen Lashes Back in Custody Fight' in *Los Angeles Times*, 24 June 1955; and 'Maureen O'Hara Heard in Custody Litigation' in *Los Angeles Herald-Examiner*, 25 June 1955.

29. I go into the 1957 trial in more detail in my 'Systematizing Scandal: *Confidential Magazine*, Stardom and the State of California' in Adrienne L. McClean and David Cook (eds), *Headline Hollywood: A Century of Film Scandal* (Rutgers University Press, forthcoming 2001).

30. O'Hara was quoted as saying in response to the *Confidential* article: '[It] damaged me personally and professionally . . . And, as the mother of a 12-year old, faced with the same fears as mothers all over the world, I find it shocking that this type of literature is available to children on the news-stands of the United States.' See 'Maureen O'Hara, Liberace Hit "Lies" ' in *Los Angeles Times*, 15 May 1957:1. This statement was reprinted in many other newspapers during the Grand Jury hearings and eventual trial in July 1957.

31. Richard DeCordova, *Picture Personalities: The Emergence of the Star System in America* (1991) 143.

32. '*Confidential* vs Hollywood' in *Confidential*, September 1957:22–23.

33. See Irwin O. Spiegel, 'Public Celebrity vs Scandal Magazine: The Celebrity's Right to Privacy' in *Southern California Law Review* vol. 30, 1957; 'Putting the Papers to Bed' in *Time*, 26 August 1957; 'The Curious Craze for "Confidential" Magazines . . .' in *Newsweek*, 11 July 1955; Ann Higginbotham, 'Scandal in Hollywood' in *Photoplay*, July 1955:29; Joe Schoenfeld, 'Time and Place' columns in *Variety*, 9 and 22 August 1955; John P. Sisk, 'The Expose Magazines' in *Commonweal*, 1 June 1956:223–5.

34. Edward J. Bloustein, 'Privacy as an Aspect of Human Dignity: An Answer to Dean Prosser' in *New York University Law Review* 39, December 1964:962.

35. Don Bailer, 'False Face Put on Community by Muckrakers' in 'Hometown Hollywood' column, *Los Angeles Herald Express*, 2 September 1957; 'Confidential Held Peril to Free Press' in *New York Times*, 16 September 1957.

36. Michel Foucault, *History of Sexuality* Volume 1 (1978) 27.

37. Jack Gould, 'TV's Misery Shows' in *New York Times*, 7 February 1954.

38. Gilbert Seldes, 'Controversy: Two Points of View on *This is Your Life*' in *TV Guide*, 11 October 1958:26–27. Actress Gale Storm wrote the other point of view.

39. Even basically positive articles tended to use phrases like 'trapped guest', 'sensational', 'spiritual prosecutor' etc. See 'How Ralph Edwards Traps the Stars' in *TV Guide*, 11 September 1953; Review of 11 September 1953; Review of *This is Your Life* in *TV Guide*, 29 May 1953; 'Sermon on the Air' in *Time*, 16 February 1953.

40. Jerry Blaine, 'When the Element of Surprise Blew Up in Edwards' Face' in *TV Scandals* vol. 1, 1 August 1957:20.

CHAPTER 8

MATINEE THEATER

DIFFERENCE, COMPROMISE AND THE 1950S DAYTIME AUDIENCE

Matthew Murray

'Sex is important to us because our audience wants it,' proclaimed Albert McCleery, Executive Producer of the National Broadcasting Company (NBC)'s daytime television series *Matinee Theater* in 1956. 'Sex is all a woman thinks about while she's sitting at home and we can give it to her.'[1] Such a direct acknowledgement of female desire dramatically conflicts with popular contemporary associations of life in America in the 1950s as a decade of comfortable nuclear families, social consensus and marital harmony. All the more startling, then, to learn that *Matinee Theater* was one of NBC's most valued television projects at the time, heralded on its 1955 debut as a major cultural advance for the medium and for all women across the nation.

To my knowledge, only a handful of its episodes have survived, rendering any methodical textual analysis of the series problematic.[2] But *Matinee Theater*'s production history is well documented through promotional materials, press reports and corporate memoranda. This essay analyses the institutional decisions underlying *Matinee Theater*'s development, considering the circulation of audience knowledge and knowledge about audiences around the programme. I will describe how NBC's understanding of female audiences was produced in relation to its larger institutional mission and the cultural context of the mid-Fifties and how existing traces of viewer engagements with the programme reveal some of the ways in which women responded to the show.

Analysing the relation of broadcast representations to the formation of identity and difference in viewers provides insight into the ways in which socially positioned audiences interact in practice with those gendered subjectivities preferred by the textual address of television programmes.[3] That is to say, this study provides insight into the question: what might the use-value of fictional representations have been to the actual viewers 'at home'? The normative, centred feminine subjectivity that NBC initially reproduced around *Matinee Theater* was, relative to prevailing conceptualizations of the rest of the female audience, a construction of difference. It was different in terms of its class associations and in terms of its circumscribed female sexuality. But in other ways it was similar to the industry's more general understanding of its female audiences – as white, heterosexual, married, middle-aged, non-professional consumers. For economic reasons, NBC reconfigured its original understanding of the programme's viewership, but did so in a way that merely modified the network's sense of gendered difference. While the mechanisms behind that construction of difference continued to go unrecognized, some of the premises underlying commercial television's operating assumptions were destabilized in the process.

Matinee Theater received the heaviest promotion to date for a regularly scheduled daytime television show on a US network. Prior to its debut, NBC executives considered *Matinee Theater* 'the most important single program series of the 1955–1956 season' and internal company memoranda reveal that the network was resting its entire daytime operation on the show's success.[4] The series was initially conceived as a serious drama for a daytime audience. Two hundred personnel worked simultaneously on a rolling schedule of eight plays, most of which were broadcast live and in colour from NBC's Burbank studios in California. The programme aired every weekday from 3 to 4pm Eastern/12 to 1pm Pacific time. Many of the productions derived from original scripts, the remainder consisting of reworked classics or rewritten dramas from prime time anthology series such as *Studio One* and *Philco Playhouse*.

Given the magnitude of this operation, expenses were originally estimated at $73,000 per week (roughly twice as much as the typical daytime drama), on top of promotional expenditures in excess of one million dollars (and which ultimately exceeded that amount by three hundred per cent). NBC undertook these outlays for a number of reasons. It was well behind its rival, CBS, in ratings and sponsorships and by the mid-Fifties its lack of daytime competitiveness was considered 'one of the network's most serious problems'.[5] Also, the networks' industrial oligopoly was under almost continual congressional scrutiny at this time. Spearheading the defence of the commercial 'American System', NBC vigorously opposed both competition from subscription television pilot schemes and the entrance of Hollywood film studios into programme supply.[6] It pronounced that the future of 'free' network television would rest upon the transmission (and anticipated popularity) of live telecasts in colour. Less altruistically, this championing of colour television – at a time when the vast majority was monochrome – was coordinated with the electronics giant Radio Corporation of America (RCA), NBC's parent company, which expected that a major demand for colour receivers could be generated given sufficient public enthusiasm.[7] *Matinee Theater* would enable television salesmen throughout the country to demonstrate the splendid resolution of RCA colour sets to afternoon shoppers.

The programme is notable for being the last of NBC President Pat Weaver's pet projects to make it onto the airwaves. To Weaver, *Matinee Theater* represented a 'crusade' to provide programming appropriate to 'what evermore sophisticated viewers want and deserve.'[8] As head of NBC television programming in the first half of the 1950s, Weaver was renowned for his highbrow aspirations for the medium and his attempt to merge public service and private market philosophies. Under policy headings such as 'Operation Frontal Lobes' and 'Enlightenment Through Exposure', Weaver navigated the network towards providing 'intellectually stimulating' material designed to 'improve both individuals and the society in which we live'.[9] His plan was to blend commerce and culture and thus to forestall congressional criticisms of network television dominance by establishing NBC's reputation as a philanthropic organization dedicated to disseminating worthy, quality programming in the public interest.

For daytime television, Weaver had introduced *Today* for the early morning and *Home* for the hour preceding midday.[10] These were big budget, 'magazine format' programmes which attempted to foster a sense of educational intimacy with the viewer through informational and 'service-oriented' items on fashion, furnishings, cooking and personalized news presented by friendly hosts. Weaver believed that a strong afternoon programme was essential to NBC's daytime success. *Matinee Theater* was intended to serve as a prestigious keystone that would magnetize viewers and maintain audience loyalty to the network throughout the day. Paramount in this strategy was the need to distinguish *Matinee Theater* as an improvement in available television fare over CBS's concentration on soap operas, participation programmes and variety shows.[11] NBC established the theme 'Weep No More My Lady' to 'indicate that "Matinee" has replaced the old-time soap opera.'[12] Press releases promised that the show would 'bring a new dignity, a new respect for the dramatic tastes of the lady at home during the day.'[13] By providing 'daytime television of the kind now limited to night-time TViewers and "Big City" Theatre-goers', NBC hoped to destigmatize the practice of watching (and advertising on) afternoon programming.[14]

By distinguishing the series from daytime serial melodramas, NBC was attempting to construct a qualitatively different, upscale audience for the show. In so doing, the network simultaneously reproduced widely-held, disparaging assumptions that soap opera viewers were infantile, over-emotional and fickle in their cultural allegiances.[15] Newspaper critics proved willing collaborators to this discursive process. The mainstay of daytime fare offered 'the same heady stimulus as buffing your nails or cutting pictures out of a magazine', according to one reviewer; another expressed hope that *Matinee Theater* might start a programming trend which would 'happily mean the ultimate demise of soap opera'.[16]

NBC's bold venture therefore rested upon the predominant conception of existing female audiences among the nation's cultural elite (to which most NBC executives, agency time-buyers and critics belonged). By employing taste-based distinctions around *Matinee Theater*, NBC exercised a set of social judgements to construct a sense of its daytime audiences, modelling and containing the range of media representations it produced accordingly. Bourdieu (1984) has described how an assertion of what constitutes good taste is an exertion of power that helps to perpetuate social hierarchies. Since 'cultural capital' is unequally distributed throughout society, those with readier access to it can more easily prioritize cultural standards which benefit and stabilize their social standing. Notions of good taste, and consequent distinctions regarding the relative cultural importance of texts, work to disguise the processes through which social differentiation and marginalization are naturalized.

President Weaver's enlightenment campaign incorporated a benevolent paternalism founded upon unacknowledged distinctions regarding what constituted quality television. 'Most people do not like the higher art forms,' declared Weaver in 1955, prefiguring Bourdieu in one breath, but failing to make the critical connection in the next, 'because they have never had the privilege and the time and the money, nor the training and the experience, to know why they are so good. We will show them why they are good, and the people will follow naturally.'[17] In line with this philosophy, *Matinee Theater* was initially developed according to classist and sexist assumptions that marginalized the interests of existing daytime viewers.

Drawing upon models suggested by media theorist Ien Ang (1991), we can see how President Weaver regarded audiences as both consumers and citizens – to be sold to and enlightened within prevailing ideological premises of cultural value. As Ang (1991:13) proposes, and as the history of *Matinee Theater* bears out, the understanding that television institutions have had of their audiences has always been unfinished, precarious and incomplete (and, consequently, both epistemologically limited and manipulative) since it refuses to address 'the infinite, contradictory, dispersed and dynamic practices and experiences of television audiencehood.' NBC's understanding of its audience involved constructing a sense of expectations regarding television programming that would satisfy the economic, cultural and ideological parameters within which the network was able and willing to operate. It was a production of knowledge that made sound financial sense to the network and was conceptually unproblematic in its definitions of the audience and hence made any consideration of the viewing/buying public easier to control discursively.

In its initial promotion for *Matinee Theater*, NBC relied heavily upon the figure of the productive homemaker – the normative feminine identity of the time: an adept organizer/cleaner of the house, graceful dresser and diligent consumer and devoted wife and mother. Surveys conducted by the network in 1955 showed that on average only an eighth of households with a television set were tuned in at any point during the daytime (a figure far below prime time levels and trailing even radio). NBC estimated that its largest gains on CBS would come from the 'virtually untapped' market of non-viewers.[18] Attempting to configure *Matinee Theater*'s audience as a 'hidden army' of efficient home-makers, NBC promoted the show as a productive viewing experience for the women of America.[19] The network constructed a set of class-based differences among television's female viewers. The ideal homemaker was coded as a white, upper-middle class suburbanite in search of the artistic stimulation left behind in the city.

Mary Beth Haralovich (1989) has shown how prime time network programming in the 1950s often incorporated narrowly-defined gender subjectivities that confined the feminine and female pleasure to the efficient, maternal management of the middle-class home. But although network programming certainly participated in the privileging of certain models of femininity and gender practices over others, the hierarchies of representation were not uniformly tilted in favor of the 'domestically contained' social order (Tyler-May 1988). Producers of daytime shows frequently considered their 'mission' to be 'to ease the loneliness of women while their husbands and children are away during the day.'[20] The range of gendered representations on daytime television in fact tended to be more diverse, the scale of its discursive limits broader, than those of prime time. While female viewers were the acknowledged majority at all hours for the medium, the industry made a clear differentiation between daytime and nighttime audiences. In scheduling terms and in cultural associations, daytime was generally denigrated as a feminized discursive space. This feminization nevertheless provided the industry with the category against which the authentication and legitimization of prime time – as a realm of rational, sensible, valid (masculine) viewing – could take place.

Having located a quality drama in the afternoon, NBC had violated the neat polarization that was common industry practice regarding the scheduling of 'masculine' programmes for prime time and 'feminine' genres in daytime. As a result, the show was only able to maintain a resolutely gendered address to women through its class distinctions. In other words, the network's discursive repertoire was limited: salvaging a workable, differentiated feminine audience for the programme was possible only by deploying class-based connotations of taste around *Matinee Theater*. In this way, other socio-cultural hierarchies upon which television institutions constructed their schedules and knowledges of the audience could remain unscathed and in line with prevailing power dynamics. In the development of *Matinee Theater*, it was gender and class mobilized together that made the difference.

As daytime television was developed in the 1950s, programmes were structured in relation to assumed domestic viewing practices. It was generally conceded within the industry that, true to the model of the good housewife, most women who worked in the home were primarily concerned with performing household chores. Unlike radio, concentration on television programmes would preclude carrying out these duties. Consequently, segmented programmes and shows that repeated narrative material in order to take account of the distracted daytime viewing were created.[21] In the hierarchy of cultural forms such texts, with their high degree of redundancy and ephemerality, were held in low esteem. With its dramaturgical aspirations, *Matinee Theater* was conceived by NBC to require the full attention of audience members. Most of its episodes followed a linear, three-act pattern and were discrete texts, rather than 'incomplete' portions of a serialized plot. While this elevated the series' cultural status, it also threatened to be antithetical to the better interests of the hard-working homemaker.

To present the show as a productive viewing experience, NBC developed the convoluted rationale that the worthy housewife deserved an hour of intellectually stimulating entertainment as a daily reward for her devoted labour. *Matinee Theater* would provide a 'much needed daytime siesta' and reinvigorate the suburban mother for the impending late afternoon reunion with husband and children.[22] The series would thus 'achiev[e] popularity without dislocating American homelife.'[23] Thanks to the 'resiliency [of] "the little woman" ' in squeezing into her schedule this 'satisfying, restful hour of good drama', it was stressed that 'bread-winners may rest assured that the washing and ironing will continue, the hearth will be swept and the kiddies will not go neglected.'[24] In her 'solitary splendor', NBC argued that 'Milady's life' would be tastefully enriched in a manner consistent with the post-war feminine ideal.[25] But by advancing this distinction around *Matinee Theater*, NBC was implicitly constructing the rest of the daytime schedule as satisfying deviant feminine pleasures that were antithetical to the productive homemaker figure.

It soon became apparent, however, that *Matinee Theater* was uneasily positioned in its cultural mission and institutional function. The series' audience had been developed in opposition to the model of a vapid, implicitly slothful soap viewer, but also in contradistinction to masculine viewers of prime time dramas – all the while drawing upon the same appeals and cultural merits of such evening shows in recoded form. NBC's inability to negotiate this complex cultural standing of the programme and its audience within the confines of commercial network economics formed the basis of *Matinee Theater*'s curious textual history. Offering a show of 'nighttime calibre in the daytime idiom,' NBC initially constructed the programme's audience within a restrictive femininity that nevertheless ascribed a degree of mental acumen to viewers (in contrast to the purportedly simple, gratuitous pleasures of the soap watcher). This permitted the network to appeal to female viewers with an address that 'doesn't insult the intelligence', and to advertisers on the basis of the rich consumption habits presumed to characterize such an audience.[26]

But even though the network posited a class-based address as the central attraction of the programme, this address remained epistemologically informed by essentialist assumptions that women were primarily capricious creatures motivated as viewers almost entirely through their identification with programme characters. Earlier in the decade, *Sponsor* magazine (a leading trade publication) had cited research findings that women's 'basic psychological' make-up was 'intuitive' and 'indulgent in fantasy.'[27] In similarly paedocratic fashion, NBC considered *Matinee Theater*'s audience to comprise 'an audience with a heart and a brain!'[28] These women were resolutely 'steady, loyal and intelligent', it was argued, but could be swayed by emotional appeals.[29] The network was unable to resolve the disjunctures between its public service claims and its patronizing formulation of female audiences as easily impressionable (an overtone essential to a rhetoric aimed to attract daytime sponsors).

The series itself hardly matched the grandeur of the prime time anthology series to which it was so frequently compared in NBC promotions. *Matinee Theater*'s avid consumption of talent and resources was equated by critics with the drama factories of daytime serials. Executive Producer Albert McCleery was the pioneer of the 'cameo' studio technique, which utilized sparse sets and emphasized close-ups of facial expressions to infer 'emotional interplay.'[30] As a result of this cost-saving visual style, critics opined that *Matinee Theater* productions often resembled 'tinseled soap operas.'[31] A reviewer of the 1955 *Make Believe Mother* complained that 'the suds, at times, were just too thick', while another considered the plot of *The Big Box* (1956) to be 'a single shade above soap opera at its worst'.[32]

Despite NBC's high hopes, *Matinee Theater*'s early ratings were dismal. Network sales representatives urged advertisers to regard the series as a long-term investment that would gradually generate viewer interest. But top executives grew increasingly alarmed that they had made serious miscalculations regarding the show's viability. Just three months into its run, RCA Chairman David Sarnoff informed relevant personnel that the programme needed to become 'better advertising value' or face immediate cancellation.[33] Broadcasting live and in colour was proving to be a drain on network resources, RCA set sales were well below anticipated levels and advertisers were reluctant to pay higher rates for the marginal benefits of reaching those viewers with access to a colour receiver. NBC secretly considered its daytime line-up to lack 'real excitement' and, following management realignments, reports began to circulate that the network was finding Weaver's programme ideas 'too rich for its blood'.[34] Newly-appointed NBC President Robert Sarnoff determined to cultivate 'bread-and-butter' programming.[35] Executive changes culminated in Weaver's forced resignation as NBC turned away from 'cultural enlightenment' and towards 'mass-appeal' telecasts[36]

During this transitional phase, *Matinee Theater*'s equivocal commercial and cultural objectives became strikingly evident. The dissonance between its taste-based pretexts and the pressing need to expand the programme's audience base was unmistakable. Uneasily juxtaposed between the conventions of prime time and the budgets and audience assumptions of daytime television, *Matinee Theater* was at once praised by critics for its proclaimed cultural intentions and chastised for failing to realize those objectives. Although NBC's promotional campaign had expressed well-defined objectives and a clear-cut identity for the programme, their practical implementation had occurred within an institutional and cultural context marked by countervailing pressures. Responses to an audience study conducted in April 1956 indicated that, despite the network's proposals that the show was productive to viewers, many women nevertheless felt guilty for neglecting household duties to watch an hour of television.[37] To accommodate these competing claims, NBC salesmen resorted to pitching the show as equally enjoyable without visual concentration, suggesting that housewives could listen to the programme (and commercials) without being distracted from their work.[38] As a cultural form, then, the series paid lip service to symbols of thespian respectability, but was obliged to mute those conventions to fit the assumed tastes of women who worked at home. Both relaxation and textual engagement were cited as viewing benefits.

NBC's attempt to garner cultural acclaim and yet still achieve popular resonance for the series surfaced in programme content decisions as well. Allegedly offering nighttime quality, *Matinee Theater* presented 'adult' issues with 'maturity'. 'Selective realism' was attempted, whereby certain social tensions were introduced in programmes but were contained within conventional representational boundaries and resolved with formulaic moral tropes.[39] However, this editorial policy appeared at times to undermine the integrity of the dramatic situations – a dilemma aggravated by the divergence of interests between the network's censors (the Department of Continuity Acceptance) and the series' Executive Producer, Albert McCleery, whose directives challenged the aura of tastefulness the broadcasting corporation wished to cultivate around the show.

NBC's investment in 'quality' programming required a corresponding attention to self-censorship and representational limits, since cultural discrimination partially relies upon recognizing and textually encoding acceptable moral and aesthetic standards. This fundamental correlation between 'good taste' and 'quality programming' illustrates the link between the construction of cultural distinctions and the extent to which cultural forms challenge or reproduce normative values. In pursuing Weaver's semi-civic 'grand design for television', NBC programming had reaffirmed conservative visions of appropriate gender identities, cultural hierarchies and social behaviour.[40] Internal censorship (or 'self-regulation') performed a vital function for NBC, ensuring that textual limits mapped onto policy objectives. Weaver's agenda had been integrated into Continuity Acceptance practices in terms which equated the preservation of good taste in programming with the elevation of cultural standards more generally.

The representation of gendered sexuality is a primary means through which taste-based distinctions are established for cultural productions. As a self-legitimizing exercise, NBC intended to position its own institutional practices as commensurate with the veneration of familial stability and a female sexuality limited to a domesticated, reproductive capacity. Its Television Code of programme standards advocated 'respect for the sanctity of marriage and for the value of the family and the home as social institutions', while industry-wide guidelines required that divorce not be 'treated casually nor justified as a solution for marital problems'.[41] According to NBC's proviso, adultery and 'other illicit sex relations' could not be 'presented as glamorous or excusable'.

In late 1949, Continuity Acceptance rejected *My Good Wife* as 'out of bounds for network television airing to a family audience of a Sunday evening'. Explaining his decision, the head censor cited the 'suggestiveness' of 'the plot exploration into [the] wife's assorted love affairs'.[42] Replying to the statement 'You should start learning some of a wife's duties', the female lead in a *Kraft Television Theatre* show was to answer, 'Teach me some of a wife's pleasures first', until the response was deleted as unacceptably provocative and adulterous in insinuation.[43] In 1953, a proposed reality-therapy show entitled *Divorce Anonymous*, while not considered in violation of industry codes, was refused after Continuity Acceptance expressed 'reservations' as to whether its producers could maintain 'good taste and freedom from cheap sensationalism'.[44] 'Sassy humor' in a 1954 episode of *I Married Joan* was eliminated prior to broadcast since it was considered to be 'close to bad taste and to reduce respect normally afforded the marriage ceremony'.[45] *Bride and Groom* was initially rejected by the network 'because there was something cheap about its stunt approach to marriage'.[46]

While publicly claiming an omnipotent semiotic policing over its textual territory, Continuity Acceptance privately admitted that, in general, daytime television constituted a cultural ghetto where boundaries of taste and decency were frequently contravened. As Michele Hilmes (1997) has shown, the low visibility of daytime broadcasting comparative to evening programming encouraged production personnel to take greater liberties in their interpretation of the radio and television self-censorship codes. In 1952, NBC's chief censor confided that 'where soap opera kind of material is concerned, Continuity Acceptance can do little in the way of wholesome censorship'.[47] Two years later, his staff was busily 'cutting overdone inferences of extra marital hanky-panky' from daytime scripts, but still failing (by its own admission) to maintain prime time standards of decency.[48] While they contained sensationalism within morality tales, soap operas of the time were widely berated for including 'sordid situations', remaining ambiguous on the value of family life and displaying 'an excess of adultery and drinking'.[49]

At first, NBC attempted to configure *Matinee Theater* as morally proper and hence distinct from the rest of the daytime schedule. Given the high degree of visibility surrounding the programme's launch and its in-house production, a show of editorial strength was essential. The cooperation of the Lutheran Television Associates was secured for several performances, to bring attention to the admirable 'anti-Sin' values of the programme.[50] Continuity Acceptance revisions of scripts from the series' first months on the air reveal a litany of amendments – ranging from the elimination of 'sexual connotations' and 'sexy display', to the deletion of material 'so graphic [as] to be in bad taste', to the downplaying of 'frustrated sex implication[s]'.[51] Participating in the network's construction of the *Matinee Theater* viewer as productive homemaker,

Continuity Acceptance attempted to screen out material that was considered incongruous to that figure – notably marital discord and any displays of aggressive female sexuality. The department warned McCleery that 'overly passionate love scenes could lead to mass disapproval'.[52] And it considered this daytime slot to require 'additional editorial actions' of material originally intended for 'adult viewing periods'.[53] Such directives clearly dovetailed with the normative view of female sexuality as procreative, passive and unmentionable in respectable company. Lurking behind these editorial practices, however, were concerns that stimulation might arouse dormant pleasures and desires antithetical to the idealized construction of the satisfied homemaker.

After twelve months of production, Burbank-based McCleery regarded the exploitation and publicity that *Matinee Theater* was receiving to be 'a complete bust'.[54] As a contracted employee, managing the production unit three thousand miles from NBC headquarters in Rockefeller Center, McCleery's attitudes towards the series increasingly diverged from the network's original plans. For this outspoken producer, the traditionally lax oversight of daytime dramas provided a positive and invigorating scheduling environment. McCleery also relished the 'sexual overtones carried through the flesh colours' of his broadcasts.[55] Pursuing aims incongruous to the network censors', his production team specified to scriptwriters that 'there are no taboos' on possible subject matter since 'our afternoon audience is made up of adults. We're not under the same stringent censorship we'd be under if we were programming during the early evening children's hours'.[56]

Despite the reservations of Continuity Acceptance, McCleery's aggressive attention-grabbing devices, proven parsimony and ability to meet deadlines appealed to the economically-conscious regime Robert Sarnoff was initiating. Because of its poor early ratings, NBC acknowledged the need to reconfigure *Matinee Theater*'s audience address and allowed McCleery to assume a greater influence over the series. In addition, a number of in-depth research surveys were conducted in order to provide clues that might suggest ways to improve its popular reception. These interviews and analyses, while recorded within institutional interests and mediated by cultural preconceptions, provide a fascinating insight into daytime viewing pleasures of the time. They produced diverse responses and an ambivalent strategy from NBC, which was ultimately unable to contain the multiple cultural interests it uncovered within its own commercial requirements.

As the network had hoped, many regular viewers cited the high quality of the programme's content and production as a viewing incentive. Nevertheless, the network believed the series needed to be presented as more accessible in order to achieve a broadly popular appeal. Rather than experiment further with formatting, scheduling or promotional strategies, NBC muted the class-based distinctions of taste underlying *Matinee Theater*'s original promotion and reinvested in the familiar gendered constructions of the daytime audience. In effect, this modification constituted a repudiation of the unitary subjectivity of the idealized Fifties homemaker originally formulated as the basis of the show's difference.

Alterations took two directions: stylistic devices and diegetic elements conventional to soap operas were incorporated into plots; and the charismatic presence of John Conte, the series' host, was foregrounded. Both strategies magnified the tension facing the network between its claims to improve taste and the need to accommodate more general audience interests. Reviewing a November 1956 production of *Matinee Theater*, critic Gilbert Seldes observed that it was 'highly immoral' and 'exploit[ed] the baser passions' in a scene that was 'as explicit physically as television dares to go'.[57] The previous summer, McCleery had designated every Friday's performance for a weekly exploration of 'adult situations'.[58] In order to compete with the 'excesses' of other daytime shows, *Matinee Theater* no longer programmed itself above them: it featured more risqué themes – such as adultery, aggressive female sexuality, marital discord – while still attempting to preserve the facade of highbrow legitimacy. In a retrospective interview, McCleery noted that he had aired plays 'no one else would do . . . on a surprisingly adult . . . level'.[59] This evaluation resonated with his earlier boast that the production was 'the most sophisticated show on the air . . . because we don't have censorship of any kind'.[60] In effect, the series' 'classiness' became a foil for artistic license that now allowed the production team to push representational boundaries, under the pretense of engaging in serious, sophisticated broadcasting.

NBC also modified *Matinee Theater* by expanding the role of host John Conte. This manoeuvre was intended to focus the series around an identifiable personality and to sexualize the show's gendered address. In June 1956, NBC contracted Motivation Analysis, Inc. to investigate viewer reactions towards Conte. The resultant survey of 187 women in fifteen cities concluded that the host 'apparently has a good deal of sex appeal since [women] refer to him as a "doll", a "dreamboat", "I love that man", etc.'[61] The survey recorded that 'some watch the show just to see him'. Partially reported verbatim transcripts reveal a range of positive responses to Conte, overspilling with erotic desire in a manner antithetical to the purported interests of any contented wife and mother: 'the emcee is Oh-oo, Ah-a-a and Oomph. A honey,' declared one interviewee; 'he puts you in the mood,' said another; 'his charm and finesse was so spellbinding I burned the beans for dinner without even caring,' confessed a third.[62]

The audience surveys produced quite unexpected results and revealed that many viewers sought an effective escape in the series rather than a highbrow cultural experience. A far more complex set of pleasures and meanings was derived from the show than anticipated by the network. These heterogeneous responses confounded NBC's original construction of the *Matinee Theater* audience. So the network resorted to its pre-existing knowledge of the gendered daytime audience – discrepant though this understanding was with the sexually and socially satisfied ideal of the productive homemaker.

Away from the surveillance of the working husband, the relationship of the female viewer to daytime television could be an intensely personal one. The technology of television itself, bridging public and private realms and courting the female consumer, was steeped in a discursive subtext as an adulterous, anthropomorphized interloper (see Tichi 1991). In popular magazines of the period, as Lynn Spigel (1992:95) has shown, 'the graphic representation of the female body viewing television had to be carefully controlled . . . [T]here was something taboo about the sight of a woman watching television. In fact, the housewife was almost never shown watching television by herself.' Daytime programmers recognized the medium's libidinal and tele-adulterous potential, deploying its taboo connotations to the extent that an undertone of clandestine liaison ran throughout much of the afternoon schedule. Conte's eroticization – loaded with Latin charm, dark mystery and performative prowess – invoked secret, intimate, forbidden rendezvous. NBC cultivated this (hetero)sexualized address while providing reassurances against its threatening implications. In its promotion of the series to advertisers, the network attempted to erase the female sexual agency suggested by the interview responses, recoding Conte's erotic objectification as a more innocuous attraction. By August 1956, publicity brochures were comparing the host to classical figures such as Casanova and Lothario under the slogan 'It takes a good man . . . to woo and win a million hearts'.[63]

By the end of 1956, both the cultural signals and the constructions of the audience upon which NBC drew in its attempts to establish a broader 'Matinee habit' were thoroughly complex.[64] Viewers were encouraged to both indulge and unwind ('Take It Easy – Relax in the Afternoon') while regarding the viewing experience as both productive and regenerative.[65] The programme's artistic allusions permitted it to accentuate the more ribald elements of its period pieces and to linger on the loaded inferences of modern realist productions. Female 'misbehaviour' and domestic conflict were explicitly narrativized. Anti-matrimonial themes were explored within the guise of a legitimate televisual space, potentially enabling many women who did not respond to the soap opera address to participate in the negotiation of discordant ideas regarding gender relations.

In letters to the network, some viewers resented what they perceived as a devaluation of *Matinee Theater*'s cultural superiority, contesting the appropriateness of the changes in content and presentational form. For undermining 'what sense of decency and respect for virginity there is left in the world', a Rochester woman protested the series' tendency to 'concentrate on the unwed mother problem'.[66] A New Yorker complained that 'Matinee performances of the last few weeks' had exhibited 'low moral standards', to the point of being 'positively disgusting' at times.[67] The Los Angeles Jewish Community Council found *The Prophet Hosea* to be a 'sexational melodrama', where 'his wife's nymphomania is exaggerated'.[68] In general, however, the more polysemic textual elements of the reformulated *Matinee Theater* did allow for less overdetermined points of potential engagement with the programme. Coded in both affective and intellectual terms, *Matinee Theater* bracketed multiple feminine interests in its audience address, even while continuing to posit these as incompatible traits for any individual subject.

Once NBC had diluted the class-based appeal and its normative, prescriptive implications, a wider range of audience positions were available to viewers – albeit still within definite limits of gendered pleasure. While ratings figures are notoriously unreliable indicators of audience behaviour and interest, the upswing that took place after *Matinee Theater* reconfigured its audience address suggests that the idealized Fifties homemaker represented a subjectivity with which only a limited number of women had identified. By mid-1957, *Matinee Theater* was leading its time slot with a 40.6% share.[69] Nevertheless, NBC cancelled the series within a year. Though this was primarily for economic reasons, it is also true to say that NBC could not accommodate the contradictory textual strategies and audience pleasures associated with the programme within the commercial logistics of network broadcasting.

NBC and RCA reconsidered their colour campaign: despite the anticipated explosion of interest in the new technology, enthusiasm had rapidly waned. By 1958, RCA was producing 95% of all colour sets and had sold only 300,000 of the expensive receivers.[70] CBS and ABC refused to invest in colour programming until sufficient audience interest had been generated and widespread adoption would not become a reality until the next decade. Ironically, *Matinee Theater*'s improved popularity also contributed to its downfall. The show was sold on a participation basis, with each day's performance divided into four quarter-hour sponsorship slots. Industry guidelines provided for three minutes of advertising time per quarter-hour of daytime, a much higher ratio than for prime time. As the series' ratings improved, *Matinee Theater* became a more viable advertising proposition. At its peak, three-quarters of all available time slots were booked (more than double the number during the series' earlier commercial history), but viewers deluged NBC's offices with criticisms about the incessant narrative interruptions. One writer suggested that the series be retitled 'NBC Matinee Commercials', while others complained of losing interest in the programme during its monotonous breaks.[71] Even the West Coast head of Continuity Acceptance admitted that the amount of advertising was intolerable and, 'as a sometimes viewer, I find myself sincerely wishing for a sledge hammer with which to smash the set.'[72]

Within the hierarchy of taste, this over-commercialization conflicted dramatically with the series' remaining cultural and intellectual pretensions and ratings declined in the fall of 1957. General attrition had set in at the production centre also; the insatiable demands of daily transmission had a detrimental effect on any attempts at originality. NBC redirected its scheduling policies away from Weaver's scattered attractions and towards 'blocking' similar programmes back-to-back, a strategy intended to maintain an even audience flow throughout the day. Human interest stories and 'happiness and fun' formats were emphasized, via participation programmes, quiz shows and soap operas.[73] In contrast to the manifesto on taste presented earlier in the decade, NBC's daytime line-up by the end of 1957 included *Bride and Groom, Queen for a Day, Modern Romances* and *True Story* – all of which drew on 'confessional' motifs accentuating women's personal pleasure, grief or emotional gratification. Having invested $12 million in *Matinee Theater* during its 30-month, 666-episode run, the network claimed to have recouped only three-quarters of that amount in revenue.[74] In June 1958, two half-hour serials were developed as replacements.

Behind the scenes, however, action was being taken to save the show. A 'Foundation for the Preservation of *Matinee Theater*' was established under the leadership of John Conte's wife, Ruth, to organize a fund-raising drive designed to keep the programme alive.[75] The Foundation, with the help of thousands of volunteers and newspaper television critics throughout the country, hoped to solicit $4 million in financial contributions from viewers in order to continue the show, commercial-free, on network television. NBC's earlier attempts to promote audience loyalty and a viewing community around the show thus backfired when the Foundation was created to oppose network policy. This was a sweet reversal in the mobilization of cultural capital, since those attributes that the network had initially heralded for *Matinee Theater* – its 'uncommercial' appeal, its selectivity and its cultural importance – were precisely the ones which motivated the campaign to reinstate the programme. And yet, by forefronting the quality and theatrical aspirations of the show, the Foundation, like NBC before it, failed to generate sufficient public enthusiasm according to the terms by which it measured that commitment. Much to the relief of NBC, which had been extremely embarrassed by the attempted audience buy-out, only $312,000 was raised and the Foundation was dissolved.[76]

The tremendous investments in *Matinee Theater* (in terms of monetary outlay from NBC and in personal terms for much of the audience) makes it a particularly useful focus for the study of 1950s daytime television. This essay has sought to unravel the complex social, cultural and institutional forces behind the programme's conception, duration and cancellation. NBC had developed the series in an attempt to profit from offering diversity in the daytime schedule, but this diversity was constructed within clearly defined parameters. Racial and ethnic differences between women were significantly absent from network discourse on daytime television, an homogenization that effectively erased all women of colour from consideration in this construction of feminine identities. Moreover, NBC's institutional motives were informed by and themselves inflected, the broader social context of the period and the tenuous cultural construction of the productive homemaker. Produced as a particular intersection of class, gender, race and sexuality, this was a feminine figure that, despite its enormous discursive power, was open to disruption along any one of these axes of identity when expected to operate as a model of viable subjectivity for the majority of the female population in their everyday contexts. Insurmountable ambiguities regarding definitions of feminine identity arose between the network's assumptions, the economic imperatives of commercial broadcasting and the heterogeneous pleasures and reading practices of the programme's viewers.

Matinee Theater's audience interviews suggest that subordinated subjects utilized marginal moments and available cultural resources to cultivate aspects of their personal and social selves that were ultimately unknowable to NBC. The differences generated by the network around the programme's audience could not accommodate the multiple engagements (and refusals to engage) with the series that actually took place. To a particular group of women, *Matinee Theater* constituted a site of investment that allowed them to mobilize their viewing agency in the pursuit of pleasure, sometimes reaffirming existing structures of taste but also activating aspects in the formation of their viewing identities that clearly did not correspond with the normative construction of gender and sexuality originally reiterated by the network. These discrepancies became apparent when NBC was forced to investigate what the programme meant to women and in what ways it was meaningful. To expand its audience base, NBC had to respond to these more immediate concerns and revise its textual and extratextual address.

The complex ways in which class, gender and sexuality informed one another around *Matinee Theater* destabilized conventional industry logic, grounded as they were upon a distinct ordering of television programmes, tastes, schedules and audiences. The objectives of the 'Foundation for the Preservation' threw into confusion assumptions that culturally validated genres held an essentially masculine appeal. Likewise, the processes through which prime time had been privileged as the cultural centre of legitimated televisual practice were themselves unsettled, casting doubt upon the gendered power relations underlying that hierarchy. In its attempt to activate limited difference, NBC unwittingly made visible the narrow limits of its own institutional knowledge.

Notes

[1.] Robert Lewis Shayon, 'Sex in the Afternoon', *Saturday Review*, 17 November 1956:32.

[2.] About 20 episodes are located at the UCLA Film and Television Archives.

[3.] Following post-structuralist theorists such as Joan Scott, Judith Butler and Mary Poovey, I understand gender to constitute a material, experienced construction of social relations (see Butler and Scott (1992); Nicholson (1990); Riley (1988); Butler (1990); Butler (1993); Poovey (1988)). Scott (1988:2) has described gender as 'the knowledge that establishes meanings for bodily differences – how the sexes are understood socially as natural, distinct, visibly-identifiable categories with mutually exclusive traits and capabilities'. Differentiated gender identities accorded men and women appear logical and valid because of their inscription upon the anatomical distinctions of sexed bodies. As Poovey and Butler have outlined, discourses on gender and sexuality are also intimately related and have historically reinforced one another in the exercise of power. Culturally privileged discourses of female sexuality in the USA in the 1950s, for example, were heteronormative and validated only marital coitus. These were not, of course, the only discourses or practices circulating (see Eisler (1986); Breines (1992); Kinsey (1953)).

[4.] Jerry Chester to Al Rylander, 19 October 1955, Folder 29, Box 137, NBC Files, State Historical Society of Wisconsin, Madison.

[5.] Clyde Clem to Messrs Adams et al, 16 November 1954, Folder 25, Box 135, NBC Files.

[6.] NBC argued that, if successful, subscription television would corner the market on quality programming, thereby limiting its enjoyment to the wealthy. See Robert Sarnoff, 'Statement at Hearings Before the Committee on Interstate and Foreign Commerce of the U.S. House of Representatives, January 21 1958, on the Subject of Subscription Television', Folder 3, Box 178, NBC Files.

[7.] For more detail on the development of colour television, see Chisholm (1990:213–214). Chisholm downplays the major differences between the networks in the technology's promotion.

[8.] Quoted in Casey Shawhan to Syd Eiges, 26 January 1956, Folder 33, Box 174, NBC Files.

[9.] Quoted in CART Report, January 1956, Box 153, NBC Files. See also Boddy (1987); Kepley (1990b); Wilson (1995).

[10.] On the growth of daytime television and the development of *Home* see McChesney (1992). See also 'Why NBC's Chips Are on "Better" TV', *Broadcasting-Telecasting*, 19 December 1955, 96–97.

[11.] ABC had little daytime programming until 1956. DuMont, which had pioneered daytime network transmission in 1948, went out of business in 1955.

[12.] Kenyon & Eckhardt, 'Promotion Plan for "Matinee" ', 15 November 1955, Folder 33, Box 174, NBC Files.

[13.] NBC Color Television News Release, 14 October 1955, Folder 59, Box 151, NBC Files.

[14.] Publicity Report: Bulletin #23, 11 November 1955, Folder 3, Box 144, NBC Files.

[15.] Historian Robert Allen (1985) has described the pervasive denigration that soap operas have suffered as a broadcast genre since their inception in the early 1930s. Until recently, their audience members have been persistently presented as 'intellectually and imaginatively impoverished' in academic studies and mainstream print media texts (27).

[16.] Harriet Van Horne, 'Better Matinees For Your Parlor', *New York World-Telegram and Sun*, 2 November 1955; John Crosby, 'Afternoon Show in Large Brackets', *New York Herald Tribune*, 20–26 November 1955, P1. A similar promotional strategy was attempted with *Home* and was likewise unsuccessful. This practice of cultural differentiation paralleled the division of the women's magazine market into 'confessionals' and 'slicks'. For an illustration of the class- and taste-based plot differentiations made by their writers and editors see Hila Coleman, 'From Confessions to Slicks', *Writer's Digest*, May 1956, 16–22.

[17.] Pat Weaver, 'TV Offers A New Renaissance', Speech given to IPA, London, 27 September 1955, reprinted in *Television Digest*, 22 October 1955, 1–6.

[18.] Richard C. Dawson circular to advertisers, 19 October 1955, Folder 25, Box 391, NBC Files.

[19.] Publicity Bulletin #23, 2 November 1955, Folder 3, Box 144, NBC Files.

[20.] 'Moore for Housewives', *Time*, 2 February 1953, 47.

[21.] The former was typified by variety and service-oriented shows, the latter by soap operas. Jane Pinkerton, 'Daytime TV's Great Dilemma', *Sponsor*, 3 November 1956, 23ff; Spigel, 1992: 73–98.

[22.] 'Matinee Theatre' Week Outline, Folder 9, Box 400, NBC Files.

[23.] Marie Torre, 'NBC Discovers a "Matinee" Audience', *New York Herald-Tribune*, 19

December 1955. Reprinted in 'All to Myself', NBC-TV Promotional Brochure, January 1956, Folder 9, Box 400, NBC Files.

24. Ibid.

25. Ibid; Harriet Van Horne, 'How Ya Gonna Get Any Cookin' Done?' *New York World-Telegram & Sun*, 28 October 1955, 16.

26. Albert McCleery press release, 1956, Folder 12, Box 179, NBC Files.

27. 'How to Make a Woman Say "Yes" ', *Sponsor*, 5 May 1952, 39ff.

28. Albert McCleery press release for *Variety*, 1956, Folder 12, Box 179, NBC Files.

29. Ibid.

30. Robert Lewis Shayon, 'Just Like Radio,' *Saturday Review*, 28 July 1956, 23; see also Thiel (1977).

31. Ben Gross, 'NBC Should Pause Before Dropping "Matinee" Show', 2 March 1956, mimeo copy, Folder 59, Box 151, NBC Files; 'Matinee Theater', *Broadcasting-Telecasting*, 7 November 1955, 14.

32. Van Horne, 'Better Matinees'; Jay Nelson Tuck, 'On the Air', *New York Post*, 24 January 1956, 28.

33. Fred Wile, Jr. to John West, 24 February 1956, Folder 33, Box 174, NBC Files.

34. William R. Goodheart, Jr. to John B. Lanigan, 21 January 1957, Folder 18, Box 140, NBC Files; 'End of the Weaver Era at NBC', *Business Week*, 15 September 1956, 26.

35. 'Wide, Wide Shake-up', *Time*, 17 September 1956, 88–89; 'Robert Sarnoff Charts the Future of NBC', *Sponsor*, 15 December 1956, 32–35.

36. 'Sarnoff Defends TV Programs', *Broadcasting*, 24 February 1958, pp. 38–39; Herman Land, 'The Advertiser Too Has a Responsibility', *Television Magazine*, April 1958. For an historical account of the shifts in NBC policy in the 1950s, see Kepley (1990a).

37. Matinee Theatre Study, 27 April 1956, Folder 33, Box 174, NBC Files.

38. Shayon, 'Just Like Radio', 23.

39. 'Drama Factory', *Time*, 20 August 1956, 72.

40. Weaver speech, 1955, Folder 18, Box 179, NBC Files.

41. NBC Code, 1951, Folder 1, Box 163, NBC Files; National Association of Radio and Television Broadcasters Television Code, 1952, Folder 21, Box 129, NBC Files.

42. Folder 76, Box 171, NBC Files.

43. CART Report, July 1954, Box 153, NBC Files.

44. Stockton Helffrich to Messrs Barry et al, 30 June 1953, Folder 9, Box 368, NBC Files.

45. CART Report, November 1954, Box 153, NBC Files.

46. Stockton Helffrich, Folder 18, Box 152, NBC Files.

47. Stockton Helffrich to Ed Madden, 25 August 1952, Folder 14, Box 170, NBC Files.

48. CART Report, December 1954, Box 153, NBC Files.

49. National Television Review Board Special News Release, not dated, Folder 14, Box 570, NBC Files. See also Gilbert Seldes, 'New Bubbles for Soap Opera', *New York Times Magazine*, 12 September 1954, 25ff; 'Soap Operas – And How They Grew', *TV Guide*, 4 August 1956, 10–11; 'Before Dark: Ha Ha, Boo Hoo!' *TV Guide*, 25 September 1954, 14–15; Marya Mannes, 'Soft Soap', *Reporter*, 23 September 1954, 48–49; Art Woodstone, 'Crime on Soap Street', *Variety*, 4 January 1956.

50. 'NBC-TV, Lutheran Churches Plan Religious Programmes', *Broadcasting-Telecasting*, 13 February 1956, 106; 'Lutherans' "Anti-Sin" Tinters', *Variety*, 8 February 1956, 22.

51. Folders 59–63, Box 151, NBC Files.

52. Bob Wood to Albert McCleery, 5 July 1956, Folder 60, Box 151, NBC Files.

53. Stockton Helffrich to Bob Wood, 21 October 1955, Folder 59, Box 151, NBC Files.

54. Albert McCleery to Richard Pinkham, 18 January 1957, Folder 70, Box 140, NBC Files.

55. Thiel, 'Albert McCleery's Transfer', 286.

56. NBC Matinee Theater Release, 20 December 1955; NBC Press Department Feature Release, 9 November 1955, Folder 59, Box 151, NBC Files.

57. Gilbert Seldes, 'How Often is a Play?' *Saturday Review*, 10 November 1956, 25.

58. Bob Wood to Stockton Helffrich, 25 October 1956, Folder 61, Box 151, NBC Files.

59. Dwight Whitney, 'TV's Most Successful "Failure" ', *TV Guide*, 21 June 1958, 24–26.

60. Shayon, 'Sex in the Afternoon', 32.

61. Thomas Coffin to Hugh Beville, Jr., 6 June 1956, Folder 9, Box 400, NBC Files; see also 'The Man With 3,000,001 Wives', *TV Guide*, 27 April 1957, 28–29.

62. Ibid.

63. Folder 9, Box 400, NBC Files.

64. 'Success Story', 25 October 1956, Folder 9, Box 400, NBC Files.

65. ' "Matinee Theater Week Contest" WRCA-TV Promotion Plans', Folder 33, Box 174, NBC Files.

66. Eva Belle Kamp to NBC, 2 April 1956, Folder 59, Box 151, NBC Files.

67. Mrs D. Rodgers to NBC, 20 October 1956, Folder 61, Box 151, NBC Files.

68. John Stone to Bob Wood, 12 February 1958, Folder 64, Box 151, NBC Files.

69. Press Release, Folder 2, Box 178, NBC Files.

70. 'Chasing the Rainbow', *Time*, 30 June 1958, 37ff; 'NBC "Mat. Theatre" Facing Cold Facts of TV Economics', *Daily Variety*, 27 February 1958, 1ff.

71. Stockton Helffrich to Carl Lindemann, 28 August 1957, Folder 63, Box 151, NBC Files.

72. Bob Wood to Stockton Helffrich, 26 August 1957, Folder 63, Box 151, NBC Files.

73. 'TV's Hottest Battleground', *Sponsor*, 4 May 1957, pp. 38ff.

74. The figures are disputable. NBC was paying itself to use its own colour studios. Many other expenses were inter-departmental.

75. News releases of the Foundation are located in Folder 2, Box 178, NBC Files. Vernon Scott, ' "Matinee" Revival Try Fails', *Citizen News*, 28 November 1958; Mina Wetzig, 'This Show Must Go On', *Sunday News*, 27 July 1958, 9.

76. NBC opposed the Foundation, claiming that its aims represented a first step towards subscription television – where 'quality' programming would be siphoned away from 'free' network television and available only to those viewers able to pay. 'NBC Refuses Ads Urging Net Keep Matinee Theatre', *Hollywood Reporter*, 23 June 1958, 1. *Matinee Theater*'s cancellation became a focus of critical discourses lamenting the decline of live television drama during these years. See Frank R. Pierson, 'The Dying TV Drama', *New Republic*, 2 February 1959, 22; Jack Gould, 'Drama in Decline', *New York Times*, 18 May 1958, Section II, 11.

CHAPTER 9

THE BBC AND THE BIRTH OF *THE WEDNESDAY PLAY*, 1962–66

INSTITUTIONAL CONTAINMENT VERSUS 'AGITATIONAL CONTEMPORANEITY'

Madeleine Macmurraugh-Kavanagh

he Wednesday Play, transmitted on BBC1 between October 1964 and October 1970 when its strand title became *Play for Today*, has been accorded a privileged and even mythologized position within the development of television drama. Famed for producing groundbreaking television 'events' such as Jeremy Sandford's *Cathy Come Home*, Nell Dunn's *Up the Junction* and David Mercer's *In Two Minds*, credited with radical experimentalism in terms of form and content, venerated for its apparent refusal of public broadcasting objectivity in its direct intervention in issues of social legislation (including the legalization of homosexuality and abortion), critics such as George Brandt conclude that 'much of the history of British television drama is tied up with this programme spot'.[1] Brandt's statement expresses the widespread recognition that in the field of television drama, *The Wednesday Play* was the genuine article, a strand arising out of a particular historical moment, emblematic of its time, its successes and excesses unique, never-to-be-repeated victories. In short, it is taken to connote both the Golden Age of British Television drama and a lost era of public service vision and integrity.

The problem with this evaluation is that it is formulated from the wrong end of time. In the post-Thatcher era, *The Wednesday Play* is mourned as being expressive of writer-led drama and of staunch public service support for it in the face of intimidating external pressures. The discussion here will question this sentimental vision (which has been encouraged by the BBC) by reversing the historical angle of vision and tracing the origins of the play strand from 1962 to 1966. Extensive research at the BBC Written Archive Centre reveals that, despite well-publicised indications issued by the Corporation that the single play was to remain the Drama Group's 'flagship' throughout the 1960s, institutional policing in fact neutered the writer while sustained moves were made to kill off this genre once and for all. An investigation of Archive material surrounding *The Wednesday Play* clearly indicates that, contrary to popular, critical and Corporation mythology, this play strand survived the 1960s in spite of the BBC and not because of it.

The information presented here largely derives from BBC internal memoranda and policy statements between the years 1960 and 1967; the gap between official BBC policy direction and its 'unofficial' equivalent is examined via this documentation, while the relationship between official policy and the public perception of it is examined via press articles and journal commentaries throughout this period. Often, significant discrepancies arise between evidence from the 'private face' of the memoranda and the 'public face' of BBC statements. In this discussion, attention is also paid to the crucial socio-political shifts and rifts evident in 1960–66 Britain since these realignments are central to the conception and evolution of *The Wednesday Play* and cannot thus be dissociated from any survey of this nature. In addition, as Robert Hewison reminds us, 'every work of literature, every piece of art, is conditioned in some way by the cultural climate in which it is produced', and to overlook this emphasis would be to mistake entirely questions relating to the aims and struggles of the single play and, crucially, to misinterpret the BBC's attitude towards its Drama 'flagship', *The Wednesday Play*.[2]

Beginning, then, with a brief outline of the socio-political context in which this influential play strand found meaning, it is clear that between 1960 and 1966 Britain had entered a disorientating period of profound change. Several commentators detect a sense of national schizophrenia during these years, potentially caused by Britain's ambiguous post-Imperial situation and exacerbated by widespread (relative) affluence pitched against anxieties focused on the direction in which society seemed to be moving. It was evident that Britain had reached a turning-point, but the question was in what (or whose) image would the new society be carved? If Britain was, as Christopher Booker insisted, in the midst of 'revolution', then what kind of revolution was it, and what role was the increasingly powerful media playing in it?[3]

Television rapidly became the battleground: nothing less than the future shape of British society was perceived to be at stake. Many of those who joined the more vocal pressure-groups, such as Mary Whitehouse's National Viewers and Listeners Association (NVLA), had made a connection between social disorientation and images flickering nightly on the public service network. As early as 1960, five years before *The Wednesday Play* became a focus for howls of outrage, the BBC was already besieged by protestors certain that the Corporation was hell-bent on systematically undermining the morals and values of mainstream society through its drama output. A split in attitude (characteristic of this period of English social history in general) became apparent, and is indicated by a number of commentators from an end-of-decade perspective. A 'Staff Reporter' on the *Birmingham Post*, for example, offers a concise summary of the position: 'The moral debate [of the

1960s] took the public form of a conflict between two views of life, two types of upbringing, two types of belief and even two classes rather than specific views on specific issues'.[4] Sir Hugh Carlton-Greene, Director-General of the BBC from 1960 to 1969, expands on this rift but finds it more complex than the journalist suggests:

> It was not a split between old and young or between Left and Right or between those who favoured delicacy and those who favoured candour. It was something much more complicated than that, and if one could stand back for a bit as the brickbats flew, it provided a fascinating glimpse of the national mood.[5]

Both are *fin de siècle* analyses, reflecting upon the mood of the country across an entire decade. But this split, increasingly evident as the decade wore on, was manifested in public reaction to television drama as early as 1960; moreover, and this is crucial to the discussion here, the tensions caused by the clash between conflicting outlooks, attitudes and visions of the future was evident within the BBC itself. It was in this context that *The Wednesday Play* was born, and in this context that its numerous battles were fought.

Anxiety became focused on television drama as it became clear that a changing society (that so many were keen to fight, evade or deny altogether) was invading the domestic sphere in this previously comfortable format. Laura Mulvey discusses the nature of this invasion and indicates that a secure demarcation zone was being eroded in the 1960s by television drama that 'challenged the previous well-established separation between public and private by turning political events into spectacular drama carried out within the confines of the home'.[6] An additional problem, as protestors saw it, was that television enjoyed such an unprecedented degree of cultural penetration; by 1966, 90 per cent of the population had access to a television set and drama, potentially that most persuasive of genres, reached across class, age, gender and educational boundaries to achieve, as its individual best, the status of 'genuine popular events'.[7] Increasingly, the perception was growing that if television as a medium was an instrument custom-made for the transmission of direct or subliminal propaganda, then television drama was its chief agent.[8]

This perception intensified as the 1960s progressed and as television drama became increasingly politicized. Spurred on by the theatrical 'revolution' of 1956 (however relative this may seem in retrospect), television drama began to reformulate its codes of dramatic representation and to broaden its subject-matter and focus. Troy Kennedy Martin's seminal article 'Nats go home: First Statement of a New Drama for Television' (*Encore*, March-April 1964), was undoubtedly central to this re-evaluation. Kennedy Martin had here attempted to outline a new grammar for television drama along Brechtian lines, this profoundly influencing a whole generation of writers and film-makers, including Ken Loach and Tony Garnett who were to make such a significant contribution to *The Wednesday Play*. Television drama suddenly appeared to have become a most urgent social tool since it had the means to saturate the nation's consciousness in a way that, with their relatively limited audiences and inhibiting conditions of 'public' reception, theatre and cinema could never achieve. Penetrating the security of the home, social television drama could reach the most complacent, reveal contemporary truths, dispel myths already accumulating around the affluent society and insist upon being seen and heard. And since for Loach, Garnett, James MacTaggart, John McGrath, John Hopkins and many others, 'society' and 'politics' were interchangeable terms, charges of propaganda became directed towards this format (as contained within the single play) above all others.

That television drama had steadily politicized itself in the early 1960s is clear from a survey of the BBC single play strands that preceded *The Wednesday Play*, and from which this series evolved. An analysis of two such strands in particular provides clues as to what *The Wednesday Play* was designed to achieve, but it should be remembered that, as implied above, 'achievement' in these terms potentially connoted purely negative value as far as certain elements within the BBC were concerned. This conclusion is inevitable given that the documentation surrounding *The Wednesday Play*, though cryptic, strongly indicates that, for these elements, the single play was, in this strand, born solely to commit suicide: the reputation for integrity and public service values that the BBC enjoyed in relation to the series retrospectively is thus brought into question. An examination of precedents will suggest the motives behind this hidden agenda.

The Wednesday Play emerged from two separate single play strands, both deemed unsatisfactory to varying degrees by BBC controllers. The first of these was *Festival*, produced by Peter Luke, a highbrow strand insisting upon a considerable degree of audience knowledge. This series of plays borrowed heavily from the theatre and regularly featured such heavyweight classics as *Oedipus Rex* and *Lysistrata*. *Fallen Angels*, by Noel Coward, was about as 'contemporary' as *Festival* was prepared to go. For obvious reasons, this play strand tended not to attract mass audiences, its role being to fulfil the public service ideals of education and information, simultaneously lending the BBC cultural prestige. But in the face of increasing competition from Independent Television, 'cultural prestige' rapidly became a costly luxury, and *Festival* was eventually axed by Kenneth Adam in July 1964.

Festival was 'balanced' in terms of audience targeting and focus by *The Wednesday Play*'s closest relation, *First Night*, produced by James MacTaggart. Both MacTaggart and Peter Luke were to become producers of *The Wednesday Play* and their differing policies in relation to that series are indicated in the conceptual gap between *First Night* and *Festival*. Their conflicting outlooks and approaches towards drama (contemporaneity versus 'culture', social use versus literary tradition, smashing of form versus adherence to theatrical precepts and so on) is indicative of the split in attitude within the BBC and, in wider social terms, in the country as a whole. Several similar clashes become apparent in BBC documentation during this period: to give one important example, Donald Baverstock (Chief of Programmes, BBC1) was engaged in a bitter war over policy direction with Sydney Newman (Head of Drama Group, Television). Given the prevailing mood at the BBC of panicked re-evaluation expressive of the dominant sense of national 'schizophrenia' (both caused by the collision between emergent and residual forces), such clashes are hardly surprising, and their effects were felt throughout the 1964–1970 period. They conditioned not only the bureaucratic manoeuvring that preceded the conception of *The Wednesday Play*, but also the conflicting representational directions that this strand later took under the respective producerships of MacTaggart and Luke.

At this stage, however, it should be noted that MacTaggart's *First Night* (also axed by Kenneth Adam in July 1964) shares an identical agenda with the series it was scrapped to make way for, aiming, in the words of Sydney Newman (Head of Drama Group), for 'popularity' and for the contemporary focus:

> First Night is intended to be a 'popular' drama spot. By 'popular' I don't mean that at the end of the play the audience should necessarily say 'wasn't that nice?'. What I mean is plays about people of today concerned in problems which may be difficult or even dangerous. Plays which seem to catch hold of the very air we breathe, but at the same time have beginnings, middles and ends . . . We want plays that are clear in their development and positive in their content.[9]

Withdrawn in July, *First Night* disappeared from the schedules in October, its formidable army of emerging writers, including Clive Exton, David Mercer, Alun Owen and Hugh Leonard, left temporarily without a television voice. However, internal and press criticism of the series was unrelenting with complaints focused on a perceived over-concentration on minority groups and issues, a fascination with seediness, a certain dull worthiness, and, paradoxically, a tendency towards sensationalism. Milton Shulman is typical in his assessment of *First Night* which, he decides, 'tended too often to mistake sleaziness for sensitivity'. He continues: 'whenever the blurb spoke of a "bitter-sweet relationship between two people", the nation heaved a convulsive yawn and switched elsewhere'.[10]

Certainly, there is an element here of a by now reflex press response to any single play strand that the BBC could offer. Less right-wing sections of the press were more reasoned in their appraisals of this strand, while journal sources suggest that its attempt to break new ground was recognized as valuable (though there could be no arguing with the shrinking audience figures). Having apparently lost so much ground in this field, and with press and public primed to expect boredom and failure, it is hardly surprising that, by the summer of 1964, the future of the BBC single play looked bleak. Competition with ITV had reached fever pitch and, in June 1964, the BBC informed the press that an 'all out battle for audiences' was being planned on both BBC channels. Douglas Marlborough of the *Daily Mail* reports on 11 June 1964 that the BBC had decided to screen 'less minority and more majority programmes' in an effort to halt the unexpected erosion of the BBC's ratings advantage; the reporter then compares a 'cockahoop' ITV with a BBC whose 'morale is at its lowest level'.[11]

The BBC had clearly decided to abandon key principles of public service philosophy in favour of the commercial broadcasting ethos, the difference between the two neatly summarized by Ien Ang as the gap between 'assumptions about "what the audience wants" in the case of commercial television, and about "what the audience needs" in the case of public service television'.[12] All the evidence suggested that what the audience wanted in this instance were serials in the mould of the hugely-popular *Z-Cars* and *Doctor Finlay's Casebook*, both of which drew a massive weekly audience outstripping any programme the rival channel could pitch against them. The BBC saw the serial as the way forward, particularly if it had a historical setting and thus evaded a turbulent present; championed by Donald Baverstock, Programme Chief of BBC1, there is no doubt that this format would have unequivocally defeated the single play had not a vital contingency come into play.

Before turning to this factor, it is worth pointing out that the attractions of the serial did not lie solely in its appeal to the mass audience. Relevant to the single play in general, and to *The Wednesday Play* in particular, is the fact that the serial format suggested certain political advantages – or, to be accurate, certain non-political advantages. George Brandt suggests that drama content is more 'controllable' in the serial so that 'at times when the "message" play can stir up hornets' nests of letter-writing pressure groups, retreating to the safety of story-edited, pre-packaged drama may seem an easier option'.[13] Julian Mitchell is more explicit, introducing the 'c' word – censorship:

> Under the circumstances, there is remarkably little censorship of actual programmes . . . the reason is, the censorship starts long before the programmes are made. It is institutional censorship, the 'realism' of institutional men. When in doubt, make another historical series [or serial] instead.[14]

At a time when the BBC was particularly concerned about its relations with the Government (by 1969, its fears would be fully justified in Harold Wilson's appointment of the Conservative peer Lord Hill as Chairman of the BBC Governors), serials offered both high audiences and, more importantly, political neutrality. Also a factor was the relative cheapness of this format with its repeated sets, costumes and technical requirements, though there is frequently a sense in BBC internal documentation that this practical reason for the serial's favoured status was advanced as a smokescreen to cover the more sensitive logic outlined above.

With the advantages of the serial obvious, the Corporation ensured that these advantages were extended through to television writers, paying handsome fees to dramatists involved in this type of format writing. Single plays offered prestige to writers, but since only a small minority could earn an adequate living from them (John Hopkins was paid only £600 for *Horror of Darkness*), many of the best concentrated on serial-writing (Hopkins writing *Z-Cars* scripts, in a famous example). The BBC had, in short, stacked all the cards in favour of the serial and against the single play.

But if the death of this format seemed inevitable, one unpredictable factor was to lend the single play a reprieve: this was the appointment of Sydney Newman as Head of Drama Group in 1962.[15] As far as recent criticism is concerned, this appointment is interpreted as being expressive of the BBC's pioneering attitude in the field of television drama during these years, as evidence of its commitment to the single play format, as a bold gamble which richly paid off. Inspection of the contemporary evidence, however, suggests that, in poaching Newman from ABC, the BBC may have had less grand motives.

According to Shaun Sutton, Newman 'burst into the BBC Television Centre like a hurricane'. Sutton's retrospective enthusiasm for Newman knows no bounds:

> Sydney galvanised television drama . . . He was passionate about writers and writing, demanding new plays by the score. He was contemporary, irreverent, and a determined enemy of cant and pomposity. He spread his enthusiasm through the group.[16]

Numerous evaluations of Newman follow a similar eulogistic path, all written in retrospect and thus all from the point of view of success. But when archive and press material emanating from the 1963–64 period is examined, an interesting gap appears between what Newman had seemed likely to accomplish and what he finally did accomplish.

Newman's background was in documentary film-making, the producer having worked with John Grierson in Canada during the 1940s. Moving later to ABC, Newman achieved critical acclaim and press hostility with his series *Armchair Theatre*, a single play strand which indulged Newman's taste for socially significant, contemporary drama. In recent years, *Armchair Theatre* has been rescrutinized in relation to Newman's later triumphs with *The Wednesday Play*, the earlier series being mythologized in a similar way to the later strand. However, this sentimental vision was certainly not prevalent at the time as James Thomas, writing in 1966, indicates. Of Newman, he states:

> The man who, in his commercial days, filled the small screens with kitchen-sink plays and became the most abused drama chief in TV history now sits plumply in respectability . . . His arrival at the BBC, fresh from a perpetual drubbing for his efforts on ABC-TV's *Armchair Theatre*, was possibly one of the most controversial appointments ever made by the Corporation.[17]

Given the fact that Thomas' comments are clearly hostile to the BBC, to Newman and to new directions in television drama (the phrase 'kitchen-sink' was a favoured term of abuse in these quarters at the time), the article nevertheless suggests that the 'success' of *Armchair Theatre* was perceived at the time to be very relative indeed. Even if the opinions of a right-wing press

hunting for controversy can be discounted, and the more comforting approbation of highbrow journals accepted, it remains true that while audiences
watched *Armchair Theatre*, their response to it was always equivocal. Since,
as mentioned above, the BBC was under huge pressure from ITV's armoury of
serials and sitcoms at this time, the appointment of a man committed to a
dramatic genre that, while fulfilling audience 'needs', hardly pandered to
mainstream audience 'wants', was 'controversial' indeed.

Also relevant to the mythology that has sprung up around Newman is the
fact that his favoured dramatic material was interpreted by some as being
rather less radical than it seemed. As Michael Wale points out in an article
written prior to Newman's move to the BBC in April 1963, 'many of his
detractors refer to Newman as an "old phoney" and say that the drama he
has been presenting is not as deep or as socially significant as he would
claim'.[18] Newman's statements concerning his approach to television drama
are undeniably conflicting, though there can be little doubt that he genuinely
felt the single play to fulfil a social function, telling Philip Purser in 1962: 'I
do like art that has something to say and art that is of use . . . I think great art
has to stem from, and its essence must come out of, the period in which it is
created'.[19] In 1966, he was to sum up his position in the phrase 'agitational
contemporaneity', a soundbite guaranteed to grab the headlines and strike
fear into the hearts of the BBC hierarchy.[20] Whether such statements are indicative of rampant showmanship or of latent 'phoniness' is difficult to judge
even with the benefit of hindsight, but either way, Newman's appointment to
the position of Head of BBC Drama Group, far from being simply 'controversial', seems in the context of the time to have been positively perverse.[21]

While it is true that the impulses of *Armchair Theatre* were hardly condu-
cive to the BBC's vision of mainstream 'success', and quite definitely not the
sort of material designed to satisfy the Charter's criteria of objectivity, it is
worth emphasizing the fact that the single play formed only 6 per cent of
Drama Group's output and Newman's often-stated desire to capture the 'mass'
audience would have appealed strongly to the BBC given its plans for future
ratings success in format series and serials. Of course, if Newman could
successfully produce an acclaimed version of *Armchair Theatre* for the BBC,
enhancing the Corporation's cultural credentials, this would be a bonus: if he
failed in this project, BBC logic calculated that Newman could be persuaded
to abandon his allegiance to the single play and redirect his energies towards
serials where his undoubted dynamism and talent for showmanship would
create ratings success (as his subsequent triumphs in this field proved). By
1964, *First Night* and *Festival* had failed to attract either 'mass' audiences,
critical acclaim, or press endorsement, so Kenneth Adam decided to test the
water using the axing of *First Night* (with which Newman was perceived to
have 'failed'), and the uncertainty it caused in relation to the status of the
BBC single play, to judge what Newman's reaction was likely to be if the
format was scrapped altogether.

Newman's response to Adam's announcement (which had made no mention of a replacement play strand) was swift and unambiguous. He correctly interpreted Adam's actions as a decisive move in the campaign to eradicate the single play from BBC schedules, and he left Adam in no doubt that he was fully aware of this agenda. In a furious memo from Newman to Adam on 26 June 1964, the Head of Drama Group writes: 'the proposal to drop *First Night* is to free money and facilities for the production of a third weekly series'. He then makes a passionate case in defence of the single play before voicing his deepest suspicions and issuing a veiled ultimatum in one concise, conclusive statement: 'I did not become Head of Drama in order to preside over its dissolution'.[22] Newman could hardly have made his position clearer. Two weeks later (a suspiciously long time which suggests a period of recalculation), Adam responded with wounded reassurances that his commitment to the single play was undiminished, while Donald Baverstock was forced to concoct a rather dubious argument to the effect that this format was vital to BBC scheduling.[23] Adam then presented his suggestion for a single play strand to be called *The Wednesday Play* in which his and the BBC's support for new writers and writing could be expressed.[24] Newman had won for Drama Group a final chance with the single play and had simultaneously communicated to Adam that, even if this format would go quietly (since the bulk of press comment would undoubtedly have supported its axing), he most certainly would not. And since Newman was potentially too valuable a man in 1964, given the new imperatives of the ratings game, the BBC had no choice but to back off from the single play at this point. It would bide its time, constrain *The Wednesday Play* in whatever way possible, and let the press and public do the rest. While Newman threw himself into planning the new strand, the Corporation hierarchy looked on with suspicion and hostility, comforted only by the prospect of the strand's inevitable failure.[25]

Newman had undoubtedly seen this storm brewing and had made certain institutional changes to the organization of BBC Drama Group in order to protect the single play from assault. His restructuring of the Department is well documented elsewhere but the detail pertinent to this discussion is that Newman had divided the sprawling Group into three separate units – serials, series and single plays. Whilst arguing that this division would create greater efficiency and higher production (music to the ears of the Corporation hierarchy), it also had the advantage of turning the single play into an official cornerstone of Drama Group, a card Newman had played when he mentioned the 'dissolution' of 'Drama' to Kenneth Adam. Now that the single play had a semi-secure 'home', the unit set about shoring it up with its new flagship, *The Wednesday Play*.

Newman's vision for this strand was hardly surprising given his work on *Armchair Theatre*. From the start, he insisted that its focus was to be contemporary, reflecting the condition of a changing society, that it should be writer-led, and that it should give voice to working-class experience: as is reported in the minutes of a meeting with the BBC Midland Regional Advisory Council on 18 October 1964, Newman had stated that 'English drama has at last discovered the working class, and this was part of the new look provided by people who were at last beginning to count'.[26] Further, Newman was adamant that the new play strand had to attract more viewers in the 30–35 age-bracket, and more women.[27] Throughout his plans runs the determination to represent the 'truth' about a reeling society and to persevere with this strategy should this prove to be incompatible with viewer taste. This, of course, involved a return to the public service philosophy ('what the audience needs' rather than 'what it wants') that the BBC had publicly jettisoned so recently. But as far as Newman was concerned, *Doctor Finlay's Casebook* and *Sherlock Holmes* could satisfy 'wants': *The Wednesday Play* would satisfy 'needs'. It would rivet audiences with disturbing truths, reflect a society in crisis, shatter form, and redefine content.

Not that this was necessarily the impression that Newman and his associates wanted to give the press, so vociferous had it been in its complaints against all previous attempts to break new ground. So Newman and James MacTaggart (having learned from their experiences on *First Night*) told the press what it wanted to hear. Douglas Marlborough of the *Daily Mail* could hardly contain his joy upon hearing the BBC's 'new plans' as announced by Newman on 11 December 1964:

> The BBC is putting 'dustbin drama' into the dustbin in an effort to win viewers from ITV in the New Year. OUT go kitchen-sink plays, obsessed with sex and domestic problems. IN come plays with strong stories, having a 'beginning, middle and ending'.[28]

MacTaggart echoed his Head's 'new policy' and is reported in the same article as stating: 'We are not interested in plays on dull, uninteresting people sitting on dull, uninteresting beds, contemplating dull, uninteresting navels'.[29] Certainly, MacTaggart's populist approach to television drama coupled with Newman's sense of showmanship and his concern for mass audiences suggested that the approach to 'social truth' would be rather more stimulating than any of the 'dustbin drama' precedents had managed, but there is no doubt that the 'new direction' outlined at this press conference was a strategic exaggeration of Drama Group's policy with *The Wednesday Play*, and was designed to calm internal fears at the BBC whilst simultaneously preconditioning reception externally. Emphasizing the values of good, old-fashioned entertainment, avoiding the use of words such as 'truth' and terms such as 'working class', Newman and MacTaggart succeeded in convincing the press that the viewer would be given what he/she wanted, while the BBC would be rewarded with what it needed – audiences.

There is a tangible air of triumph in the press reaction to this apparent u-turn in BBC drama policy, the press implying that the Corporation had at last responded to its complaints. The first pieces in *The Wednesday Play* strand, which appeared during the late autumn of 1964 (preceding the opening 'season' proper which began in January 1965) must have encouraged it considerably since the radical and the challenging were avoided at all costs. Not only were these early plays subject to intense scrutiny both within and outside of the Corporation making controversy inadvisable at this stage, but also most of the first pieces were relics of the scrapped *Festival* strand (*A Crack in the Ice*, *In Camera* and so on) and clearly betrayed their origins.

As 1965 dawned, however, Newman's claims for a new direction in drama policy began to seem dubious. As Producer of the first full run of plays (which Irene Shubik dubs 'the raw season'), James MacTaggart began to present confrontational, interventionist pieces which fulfilled Newman's later criteria of 'agitational contemporaneity'.[30] Solid thrillers and comedies also appeared (*Ashes to Ashes* by Marc Brandel and *Dan, Dan the Charity Man* by Hugh Whitemore, for example), but these were interspersed with plays dealing directly with burning contemporary issues, plays which challenged traditional precepts of 'entertainment'. The audience became increasingly riveted, and though this was less comfortable attention than uncomfortable fascination, viewing figures were rising.[31]

Most notable in this 'sub-strand' during the first season were plays such as *Fable* by John Hopkins which focused on the race issue in the context of a 'reverse-apartheid' contemporary England; *Horror of Darkness*, also by Hopkins, which confronted the topic of homosexuality and which culminated in a suicide; and *Three Clear Sundays* by James O'Connor, a convicted murderer, which constituted an emotional appeal for the abolition of capital punishment. Controversy followed each of these plays and, although with each uproar audiences increased, the BBC frantically set about instituting existing controls, and devising new ones, in an effort to contain the damage to press, public, and government relations that *The Wednesday Play* was perceived to be inflicting.

One controlling device adopted by the BBC involved 'stockpiling' whereby six or seven plays were pre-recorded and kept ready to transmit at short notice. The official logic behind this strategy was that stockpiling ensured that plays of too similar a content would never be aired consecutively, thus ensuring strand variety. However, Julian Mitchell suggests that darker motives were involved here:

> The very far-sighted policy of planning all schedules for years ahead, for stockpiling programmes, for not leaving a chink in the armour through which a nasty, directly relevant idea can slip through to the viewers, was proved triumphantly successful.[32]

Certainly, the stockpiling of *Wednesday Play*s, insisted upon by Kenneth Adam as early as 1964 when he first announced that the strand was to go ahead, proved remarkably useful to the BBC in avoiding controversy. When both Hopkins' *Fable* and Dennis Potter's *Vote, Vote, Vote for Nigel Barton* were pulled from the schedules at short notice (both on directly political grounds), a stockpiled play was easily substituted. In both cases, press speculation ensued and both plays were given later transmission dates (subject to cuts in Potter's case), but the fact remains that the BBC could exert direct control over the single play strand by falling back on a self-made safety-net. This naturally limited the writer's freedom in a fundamental way since if he refused to make cuts at short notice, the play would simply be dropped until he decided to comply. With alternative pieces always stockpiled, the BBC would never be in the position where sensitive material had to be screened because there was no alternative. In effect, it had removed the gun from its own head and pointed it at the writer's instead: the myth of 'writer-led' drama, so central to 'official' and critical evaluations of *The Wednesday Play*, becomes dubious from this point on.

A further form of control was wielded following Huw Wheldon's insistence as 1965 wore controversially on that all plays must be viewed by the Head of the Unit well before transmission. Having negotiated the hurdles of story editor, producer and director, the material had finally to survive the scrutiny of Corporation officialdom; even if it had avoided the institutional gaze whilst cornered in the studio (which it could rarely do, hence, in part, the move towards location filming), it could not avoid it indefinitely.[33] The most a sympathetic Drama Chief could do was turn a blind eye to certain controversy-bound plays, but when Michael Bakewell disobeyed Wheldon's orders and allowed Michael Hastings' play *For the West* to pass onto screens unvetted (a public outcry ensued), and when he disobeyed Wheldon's reiterated orders and managed to avoid viewing *Vote, Vote, Vote for Nigel Barton* as well, he was rewarded with a volley of abuse from the outraged Programme Controller who had succeeded in intercepting the latter play with only hours to spare.[34] There is no record of Bakewell transgressing in such a way again.

Again, the label 'writer-led' drama seems suspect in the light of this extraordinary Corporate surveillance. But by far the most powerful institutional policing was effected through the constant threat to withdraw the strand on financial grounds. It is, of course, true that the single play involves the highest expenditure for the least return since overseas sales are practically non-existent except in the rarest of cases; but this lack of cost-effectiveness was converted into a weapon by the BBC hierarchy who utilized it as a Sword of Damocles suspended over Drama Group's collective head.

Newman had always been aware that *The Wednesday Play*'s survival depended on careful budgeting, recognizing that the expense of the strand was the most convenient and least controversial excuse available for its axing. In July 1964, he provided Kenneth Adam with a detailed analysis of the budgeting for the series, reassuring the Director of Television that overspending would not be an issue.[35] By March 1966, Newman was drumming home the importance of frugality to a meeting of his Drama Producers, stating: 'my strength, the strength of your Departmental Heads in maintaining the freedom for you to work, is based on the Controllers trusting us'.[36] By 1967, however, the impossibility of working within unrealistic budgets was beginning to show and BBC internal memos become scattered with warnings issued by programme chiefs. For example, a memo dated 29 December 1967 from Paul Fox, newly-appointed Controller of BBC1, to Gerald Savory (Head of Plays, Drama, Television) betrays a menacing subtext: 'the overspending in Plays Department now stands at £16,000 – most of it attributable to *The Wednesday Play*'. It becomes more menacing still when it is realized that Newman, the guardian of the single play strand that he had forced the Corporation to retain, had left the BBC that same month. With the strand finally unprotected, Fox in the same memo targets 'low audience responses', finally deciding the whole position constitutes 'a matter of urgency'.[37] Despite its manifest triumphs, the controllers were renewing their assault on *The Wednesday Play* within days of Newman's departure.

Straitjacketed by a complex system of controls, then, *The Wednesday Play* struggled from its inception against internal scrutiny and hostility. If the country as a whole was reeling from the shock of change, then the BBC was having to come to terms with an altered perspective itself, negotiating a minefield of new currents in dramatic representation that it had itself, paradoxically, helped to foster and had itself attempted to impede. Newman's appointment in 1962 was implicated in the dilemma the BBC was facing; desperate for audiences and badly in need of 'revolution', potentially in the formulation of new serials and in the phasing out of the single play, corporate men such as Adam, Wheldon and Baverstock inadvertently created the conditions whereby the format lurched to a position of reserved respect. To Newman, writing in 1966, it was 'a miracle that so much had gone so well' and, for once, he was not overstating the position; every institutional boundary had been erected to confound the survival of the single play in general and to neuter the effectiveness of *The Wednesday Play* in particular but, against all odds, it had not only survived but had 'miraculously' acquired a sizeable following.[38] However, attempts to either eradicate or reformulate the strand along less confrontational lines never ceased for the duration of its run and, in 1969, the BBC decided to take fewer chances with Newman's successor as Head of Drama Group by appointing to the post Shaun Sutton, whose previous position had been Head of Serials and whose allegiance to that format was unquestionable. The agenda implicit in this appointment speaks for itself. Newman the maverick had led BBC Drama down a road along which the Corporation had never wanted to travel: Sutton the Corporation man, however, whilst leading the Drama Department into less contentious territory, could also be trusted to accept that he was himself to be led by BBC policy direction which he would neither challenge nor subvert. Sutton was to fulfil his potential in this regard, abandoning *The Wednesday Play* strand title at the earliest opportunity, and progressively marginalizing its successor, *Play for Today*, as the 1970s progressed.

By reversing the historical angle of vision, then, it becomes clear that whatever claims are made for the 'Golden Age' of writer-led drama and BBC innovation as emblematized in *The Wednesday Play*'s groundbreaking triumphs and controversies of the 1964–1970 period, all are based on misconceptions deriving from a failure to inspect and interpret the contemporary evidence. As this analysis has revealed, the BBC's relationship with its drama 'flagship' *The Wednesday Play* was, in fact, a great deal more complex, and its interventions more motivated, than official accounts and critical commentaries have previously led us to believe.

Notes

[1.] George W. Brandt (ed.), *British Television Drama* (1980) 17.

[2.] Robert Hewison, *Too Much: Art and Society in the Sixties, 1960–75* (1986) 300.

[3.] Christopher Booker believed that the 1960s had seen a '"revolution" in almost every conceivable field'. Booker quoted in Peter Thompson, 'Labour's "Gannex Conscience"? Politics and Popular Attitudes in the "Permissive Society" ', in R. Coopey et al (eds.), *The Wilson Governments, 1964–1970* (1993) 141.

[4.] 'Staff Reporter', 'Victory for Reformers', *Birmingham Post*, 31 December 1969.

[5.] Sir Hugh Carlton-Greene, *The Third Floor Front: A View of Broadcasting in the Sixties* (1969) 136.

[6.] Laura Mulvey, 'Melodrama In and Out of the Home', in Colin MacCabe (ed.), *High Theory/Low Culture: Analysing Popular Television and Film* (1986) 98.

[7.] John Tulloch, *Television Drama: Agency, Audience and Myth* (1990) ix.

[8.] The suitability of television as a vehicle for propaganda is indicated in numerous sources from this period. The Pilkington Committee Report of 1961, for example, had commented of television: 'the power of the medium to influence and persuade is immense'. It had added: 'unless and until there is unmistakable proof to the contrary, the working assumption must be that television will be a potent factor in influencing the values and moral standards of our society'. Quoted in Mary Whitehouse, *Cleaning Up TV: From Protest to Participation* (1967) 68–69. Peter Simple, in the *Daily Telegraph* on 28 September 1966, is more explicit in his warning: 'television is not primarily fitted to be a medium for art or even for entertainment, but for propaganda. If scientists had sat down deliberately to produce an instrument for indoctrinating the masses, moulding their tastes, opinions and attitudes . . . they could not have produced one more perfect than this'. Similar comments appear throughout this period and are too numerous to detail here.

[9.] Sydney Newman, 'Writing Plays for BBC Television' in *The Author* (1963) 31.

[10.] Milton Shulman, 'Behind the Scenes, Two Men Battle to Boss BBC Drama', *Evening Standard*, 29 July 1964.

[11.] Douglas Marlborough, 'BBC in all-out Viewer Battle', *Daily Mail*, 11 June 1964.

[12.] Ien Ang, *Desperately Seeking the Audience* (1991) 40.

[13.] George W. Brandt, *British Television Drama* (1980) 22.

[14.] Julian Mitchell, 'Television: An Outsider's View', in Frank Pike (ed.), *Ah! Mischief: The Writer and Television* (London: Faber & Faber 1982), 61.

[15.] Newman did not actually take up his post until April 1963 because a piqued ABC refused to release him from his contract until then.

16. Shaun Sutton, *The Largest Theatre in the World: Thirty Years of Television Drama* (1982) 17.

17. James Thomas, 'Truth – is it Too Hard to Take on TV?', *Daily Express*, 16 April 1966.

18. Michael Wale, 'Look and Listen', *Plays and Players*, January 1963.

19. Sydney Newman interviewed by Philip Purser in 'Head of Drama', *Contrast*, 2 (1962), 35.

20. Sydney Newman quoted in Robert MacDonald, 'BBC Viewers to get "Agitational Drama" ', *Scotsman*, 17 August, 1966.

21. BBC documentation does not reveal who exactly was responsible for Newman's appointment as Head of Drama Group, or on what grounds the decision was made to poach him from ABC. In fact, there is not a single reference to this appointment at all. Given that it must have been a matter of intense debate around 1963–64, and given also that so much insignificant detail is recorded at BBC Archives, this seems a curious gap. Whatever the reason for this strange silence in the documentation may be, the result is that the motivation behind Newman's appointment to Head of Drama Group has to be deduced from a network of hints, while the question as to who was responsible for the decision remains open.

22. BBC Written Archive Centre (hereafter 'BBC WAC'), Ref:T16/62/3.

23. In a memo to Kenneth Adam and Sydney Newman on 12 July 1964, Baverstock weakly states that 'of necessity we shall have to go on transmitting at least one and possibly two plays a week . . . There is only a limited number of types of programme suitable for transmission between 8.00p.m. and 10.15p.m. . . . Plays are one of these few types'. BBC WAC Ref:T16/62/3. This argument becomes particularly spurious when it becomes clear that, in his preceding campaign to replace single plays with serials, these points had not occurred to him before. The reason was that Baverstock was fully aware that any serial episode would fit nicely into the vacant single play slot but, forced into a corner by Newman, he had frantically to search for a convincing reason to persuade the Head of Drama Group that the eradication of the single play had never been on the agenda.

24. Memo from Kenneth Adam to Donald Baverstock and Sydney Newman, 13 July 1964, BBC WAC Ref:T16/62/3.

25. Where the Director-General, Sir Hugh Carlton-Greene, stood in relation to these manoeuvrings is a matter of some debate. Sydney Newman claimed in his response to Adam (26 June 1964) that the single play had Carlton-Greene's full support, the Director-General reportedly urging him 'to reinstate the BBC's reputation as the home of the best original playwrights in the country' (BBC WAC Ref:T16/62/3). It is odd, therefore, that nowehere in the BBC documentation of this period does a memo appear from Carlton-Greene to any of his personnel stating his conviction that the single play must be retained; rather, memos from Adam to Huw Wheldon suggest that orders issued from the Director-General's office were of a rather different nature. Given Carlton-Greene's public position as spokesman for the BBC and as the first target of Parliamentary attack, his refusal to intercede on the single play's behalf is hardly surprising, whatever his private thoughts on the matter were: after all, when trouble came, it usually came in response to material transmitted in this format. Since this debate has several ramifications deserving of detailed analysis, Carlton-Greene's position here should be borne in mind even though space limitations do not allow for expansion in this discussion.

26. Minutes of Meeting with the BBC Midland Advisory Council, 18 October 1964, BBC WAC Ref:T16/62/3.

27. There is an interesting connection here between Newman's conception of the 'new viewer' and the Labour Party's conception of the 'new voter' at this time. Both were specifically targeting a new type of support; young, affluent, socially-aware, cross-gender. Both understood that their appeal to women was weak and set about analysing and attempting to rectify this problem. However, for a discussion of the 'maleness' of *The Wednesday Play*, in terms of form, content and authorship, see M.K. MacMurraugh-Kavanagh, 'Boys on Top:

Gender and Authorship on the BBC Wednesday Play', *Media, Culture & Society* vol.21, No. 3, May 1999, 409–425.

28. Douglas Marlborough, 'BBC Put Lid on Dustbin Drama', *Daily Mail*, 11 December 1964.

29. Ibid.

30. Irene Shubik, *Play for Today: The Evolution of Television Drama* (London: Davis-Poynter, 1975), 75.

31. The improvement in viewing figures was certainly impressive. In June 1966, Newman reported to Huw Wheldon that, from an initial weekly viewing figure of 5.4 million, by 1965 it had increased to 7.3 million and was standing at 8.6 million at the time of writing. Newman adds that 'in the single play field, "The Wednesday Play" in particular, we have wrested first place in quality and excitement from Independent Television'. Memo from Sydney Newman to Huw Wheldon, 15 June 1966, BBC WAC Ref:T5/695/2 – General File, 1966.

32. Julian Mitchell, 'An Outsider's View', in Frank Pike (ed.), *Ah! Mischief: The Writer and Television* (London: Faber & Faber 1982), 81.

33. For a discussion concerning the move towards film in television drama of this period in general, and in *The Wednesday Play* in particular, see M.K. MacMurraugh-Kavanagh and S.L. Lacey, 'Who Framed Theatre? The "Moment of Change" in British TV Drama', *New Theatre Quarterly*, Vol.XV Part 1 (NTQ 57), February 1999, 58–74.

34. As reported in a memo from Huw Wheldon to Kenneth Adam, 25 June 1965, BBC WAC Ref:T16/62/4 – TV Policy, Drama, 1965–68.

35. Memo from Sydney Newman to Kenneth Adam, 28 July 1964, BBC WAC Ref:T16/62/3.

36. Sydney Newman, 'The Joys, Sorrows and Professionalism of the Television Drama Producer: A Talk Given on 21st March 1966 to Drama Producers, Associate Producers, Organisers and Departmental Heads', BBC WAC Ref:T16/62–4 – TV Policy, Drama, 1965–68.

37. Memo from Paul Fox (C.BBC-1) to Gerald Svory (H.Plays D.Tel), 29 December 1967, BBC WAC Ref:T5/695/3 – General File, 1967. Fox could not argue with the audience figures so he targeted instead 'audience responses': the Controller had obviously noted that a curious feature of the statistics surrounding *The Wednesday Play* was that while audiences increased, the Reaction Index (measuring response and approval) declined. In the memo cited above in which Newman supplies Wheldon with audience statistics, the Head of Drama Group also notes that from a peak average Audience Reaction Index of 60 per cent in 1965, the figure had fallen steadily to 53 per cent in 1966. Commenting on this anomaly, Newman had stated: 'it seems that people want the truth but find it disturbing' (memo from Sydney Newman to Huw Wheldon, 15 June 1966, BBC WAC Ref:T5/695/2 – General File 1966). Whatever the truth of this perception, Fox seized upon the declining response figures and turned them into a weapon.

38. Letter from Sydney Newman to Huw Wheldon, 15 June 1966, BBC WAC Ref:T5/695/2 – General File, 1966.

This chapter first appeared in *The Historical Journal of Film, Radio and Television*, vol. 17, No. 3, 1997, 367–381.

CHAPTER 10

MYSTERY AND IMAGINATION

ANATOMY OF A GOTHIC ANTHOLOGY SERIES

Helen Wheatley

Mystery and Imagination, an anthology series of Gothic dramas produced by ITV in the latter part of the 1960s, is a remarkable example of the innovative, experimental television drama which was being produced for British television at a time of great upheaval and expansion within the UK broadcasting industry. As the need for competition increased between the two channels, fuelled by the threat or promise of a third channel and under the watchful eye of the industry's regulators, *Mystery and Imagination* was one of the series produced by ITV in order to fulfil the dual remit for both popular, entertaining television and respectable or 'culturally valuable' television drama. The following analysis of the series seeks to explore the ways in which the series' producers negotiated this demand for 'quality entertainment', whilst also paying attention to the specific challenges of translating the Gothic narrative into television drama.

Mystery and Imagination ran in five seasons from January 1966 until February 1970 and was produced by Jonathan Alwyn for ABC Television (1966–68) and Reginald Collin for Thames Television (1968–70). Based entirely on the adaptation of classic Gothic novels, short stories and plays, it marks what S.S. Prawer, in his extensive analysis of the cinematic 'terror film', described as the 'evolution' of television's own variations of the terror film for the small screen. Prawer argues that these programmes, made under 'the restraints of money, location and shooting time', were prompted to develop 'flexible, sophisticated technical equipment, specially adapted to the lower definition of the TV screen ... to disguise this.' (Prawer 1980:20). Furthermore, he states that the medium-specific production of the Gothic anthology series on television led to 'the rediscovery of avant-garde devices – violently clashing images, unusual angles of vision, frozen frames, shooting through gauze, negative prints, etc.' (Prawer 1980:21). Whilst the teleplays of *Mystery and Imagination* did not always prove as 'avant-garde' as Prawer's description may suggest, they were produced during an interesting and innovative time in the history of television drama and saw the Gothic drama on television being used to 'showcase' both new production technologies and the talents of the ABC personnel. This is not to say, however, that television drama prior to the production of *Mystery and Imagination* was primitive and uninteresting: as Jason Jacobs has pointed out, 'Innovation and modernisation in television drama is not located somewhere in the mid-1960s, but is also a characteristic of early drama production.' (Jacobs 2000:1). However, this analysis will illustrate the aesthetic innovations made by *Mystery and Imagination*'s producers in relation to the series' generic identity, looking particularly at the ways in which they dealt with representing the Gothic and the supernatural on television in the 1960s.

Throughout its five season run, *Mystery and Imagination* shifted between two distinct modes of Gothic representation: the suggestive, restrained ambiguity of the supernatural ghost story and the excessive, spectacular Gothic drama, which has far more in common with the theatrical and cinematic presentations of the Gothic than its literary and indeed radiophonic predecessors. The ways in which *Mystery and Imagination* exploited these two different trajectories will be demonstrated through discussion of the 1966 episodes '*The Open Door*' (tx. 19/02/66) and '*The Fall of the House of Usher*' (tx. 12/02/66).

Quality Entertainment: The Impact of Competition on the Drama Anthology Series

In April 1967 a document produced to accompany ABC Television's application for appointment as a programme contractor for the ITV network stated that 'ABC Television has always seen anthology drama as an opportunity for stretching the minds and feelings of peak viewing audiences beyond the narrow confines of variety acts and storytelling.' As a company which had become synonymous with quality, experimental anthology drama, most notably through the groundbreaking *Armchair Theatre* (1956–73), latterly produced by the company's Head of Drama, Sydney Newman,[1] this 'selling point', the production of innovative and challenging television drama, was, indeed, an important one.[2]

ABC's anthology drama series had enjoyed an undeniable popularity and success in the 1950s and 1960s. In addition to the fact that the making of weekly, one-off teleplays suited the production structures of the television industry (they were relatively cheap and quick to make, using small, self-contained production teams), these weekly 60- to 120-minute plays offered the opportunity for experimentation with the possibilities and limitations of television drama. Without the pressure of producing a serial drama which needed to maintain audience interest over a number of weeks, the producers, directors, writers and designers of ABC's individual anthologized teleplays were at more liberty to innovate, both in terms of challenging the received aesthetics of television drama and indeed in the kinds of plays produced for the series. For example, on writing for ABC's *Armchair Theatre* in the 1950s, scriptwriter Ted Willis stated 'Don't write down. If anything, write up! Your audience is the finest, most critical in the world, not a mob of ad-mass morons as some people would have us believe.' (ABC Television 1959:24). This series was seen as a major challenge to the BBC's monopoly on 'quality' television drama and as Andrew Crisell argues, it forced the BBC to make its drama policy 'more sharply focused' (1997:95) in the late 1950s.[3]

Production of *Mystery and Imagination* can, in part, be understood as a reaction to the criticisms levelled at Independent Television in the early to mid-Sixties. When the Pilkington Report into television broadcasting was published in June 1962:

> [T]he BBC was vindicated and ITV blamed. Pilkington retained its pristine objections to commercial television, judging it by Reithian standards and refusing to allow it any of its own . . . Claiming that the public service aims enshrined in the 1954 Television Act had never been fulfilled, the report proposed that ITV should start all over again. (Crisell 1997:111)

ITV was thus forced to re-examine its attitude towards 'quality programming' and 'public service' in relation to the broadcasting output offered by the BBC and the contractors, particularly ABC, 'renewed their efforts at high quality drama' (ibid). *Mystery and Imagination* was part of this response as it attempted to produce a Gothic anthology series which was both 'quality' and 'popular' (in the Reithian sense of the words), using teams whose reputations had been established in other 'quality' television drama, notably *Armchair Theatre*. Prestigious television writers, such as Robert Muller and George F. Kerr, directors, such as Patrick Dromgoole and Joan Kemp-Walsh, and a host of classically trained actors (Denholm Elliott, Freddie Jones, Joss Ackland) all contributed regularly to the series, as did a variety of well-respected production personnel.

Domestic Forms of Gothic Fictions

Whilst *Mystery and Imagination* grew from the popularity and prestige of anthologized drama on ITV, it drew on the presentation and reception of the Gothic narrative within the domestic setting for its particular generic heritages. A year after the beginning of *Armchair Theatre*, ABC had also produced the thirteen-episode fantasy-suspense series *Hour of Mystery* (1957). Like *Mystery and Imagination*, this series also featured the adaptation of classic ghost stories, such as *The Woman in White* by Wilkie Collins (tx. 29/06/57) and *The Bottle Imp* by Robert Louis Stevenson (tx. 12/10/57) and led the way for Alwyn's 1966 series. *Mystery and Imagination* therefore built not only on the success of the anthology format on British television in the 1950s and 60s, but also on the perennial popularity of a particular genre on television: the Gothic or ghost play. Earlier anthology series had focused on the televising of this particular genre, such as Rediffusion's *Tales of Mystery* (1961), hosted by a grim-faced John Laurie and featuring twenty-nine adapted stories of Algernon Blackwood[4] and the BBC's *Wednesday Thriller* (1965), with original teleplays dealing with ghostly subjects such as the haunted dollhouse of *The House* (tx. 04/08/65), written by Peter Van Greenaway and directed by Naomi Capon. *Mystery and Imagination* capitalized on the success of such series in drawing in viewers, but also acknowledged an earlier history of the domestic reception of Gothic fiction which preceded the beginnings of television history.

In a *TV Times* interview given to coincide with the start of the series in 1966, *Mystery and Imagination* story editor, Terence Feely, commented on the medium's suitability for Gothic adaptations. Drawing a parallel between domestic storytelling at the end of the previous century and the activity of watching television in the 1960s, he stated:

> The Victorians were willing victims of the pleasurable shudder that makes the lamp light mellower, the fire warmer . . . It is the machine – in the shape of television – which has restored these tales their original magic and power. They were written to be read aloud in the security of the family circle. In re-establishing the family audience, television has enabled us to re-create almost exactly the conditions in which their long gone authors intended these stories to be heard and to have their effect.[5]

This clearly outlines the intention of this series: to use television to *return* to the domestic consumption of Gothic stories and tales, those narratives which sought to chill or disturb their readers (or, in this case, viewers) within the family group. Implicitly, the act of television viewing was given a sense of cultural kudos here when compared to the reading of literary fiction and in the interview with Feely, as with the framing of the series elsewhere in the *TV*

Times, the programme's 'literariness' was emphasized, as if to authenticate it and assign to *Mystery and Imagination* a degree of 'prestige'. As Feely states:

> To prepare the . . . series, the producer, Jonathan Alwyn, and I had to read through more than 400 Victorian tales of the bizarre and the supernatural looking for suitable ones to dramatise . . . We read so many stories to be sure we used the best and to soak ourselves in the Victorian writers craftsmanship.[6]

These comparisons, between the reading and viewing of Gothic fictions in the home and the writing and televising of Gothic fictions for a domestic audience, speak much of the medium's anxiety about its own status in the mid-1960s and, in particular, about ITV's own position within television's institutional structures. By seeking to draw on these comparisons, the producers of *Mystery and Imagination* could fend off the criticisms of regulatory bodies and the press alike, by insisting on a very particular ancestry for their series. They sought to transpose the Gothic from the literary to the television text. It is also important to note that the Gothic as a literary genre has its own history of treading the fine line between popular sensationalism and the literary highbrow. It was therefore an appropriate choice of genre with which to satisfy both the viewing public and ITV's critics.

Feely's comments, that *Mystery and Imagination* marked a *return* to domestic Gothic storytelling, also reflected a certain awareness of the viewing situation featured in the particular stories chosen for adaptation, which more often than not centred around a haunted or disturbed house (as do both the episodes discussed in the latter part of this chapter). The importance of the domestic location was also reiterated by the 'taglines' accompanying particular episodes, often a piece of dialogue taken from the week's teleplay and published at the bottom of their *TV Times* listing. Playing upon the idea that houses formed the cathexis of fear and unease in *Mystery and Imagination*, typical taglines were: 'Fear haunts this house – it lurks beyond the candle flame – it whispers down the corridors. Fear of living, fear of dying – Fear, Fear, Fear.'(*The Fall of the House of Usher* (tx. 12/02/66)); 'Please hurry home father – mother and I are frightened out of our senses.' (*The Open Door* (tx. 19/02/66)); and 'I have seen things in this house with my own eyes that would make your hair stand on end.' (*The Canterville Ghost* (tx. 12/03/66). The programme's producers and those responsible for its marketing, clearly wished to draw parallels between the Gothic text on television and its space of consumption, the home, in order to increase the potential effect of their teleplays.

It is also telling that each episode of the first three seasons of *Mystery and Imagination* was framed by the presence of a story-teller, Richard Beckett (played by David Buck) in the guise of a Victorian romantic, who not only introduced the episode, but on several occasions became part of the drama itself; for example, in *The Fall of the House of Usher*, Beckett took on the role of the nameless narrator of Poe's story, an old school friend of Roderick Usher's and became very much involved in the narrative events, falling in love with Madeleine Usher and narrowly escaping death at the final spectacular collapse of the rotting house. This level of narrative interpolation by an omniscient or involved narrator is a classic device of Gothic fiction and was also deployed in the ghost story as presented on radio. Beckett/Buck acted as an intermediary between story and audience, drawing the viewer into the diegesis and therefore bridging the gap between the uncanny/*unheimlich* drama and the homely/*heimlich* setting. The presence of the storyteller was an established device in other Gothic or mystery television anthology series of the time (for example, Donald Pleasance introduced *Armchair Mystery Theatre* (ABC, 1960) and John Laurie did the same for *Tales of Mystery* (A-R, 1961)), but *Mystery and Imagination* was the only series in which the storyteller, on occasion, became fully integrated into the action of the narrative.

The series did not simply turn to the single heritage of the Gothic novel for inspiration. Gothic fiction also has a history in radiophonic, theatrical and cinematic representations, and the series very often drew on these when developing distinctive 'looks' for each episode. Jason Jacobs, in his extensive analysis of the development of the medium's presentation of drama, has successfully redressed the (incorrect) assumptions that all early television drama was simply 'static, boring, theatrical' (Jacobs 2000:3). However, Jacobs also argues that 'the development of television drama is not a story of the steady emancipation from theatrical values toward the cinematic, but one where producers were able to choose from a range of stylistic features, some of them associated with theatre, some with film styles, and some with the narrative forms of literature' (Jacobs 2000:117). It is this notion of choice, this sense of 'borrowing' from other media, which is most interesting in relation to *Mystery and Imagination* and the origins of its particular representation of the Gothic on television. In order to explore this the latter part of this chapter will consider two different trajectories of Gothic television drama. In its representational allusions to the Gothic radio play the episode *The Open Door* draws on a pre-televisual form of the Gothic as a domestic narrative. Conversely, David Campton's 'free' adaptation of *The Fall of the House of Usher* illustrates the series' debt to cinematic and theatrical precedents.

'A Radio Play with Pictures': *The Open Door*

As we have seen *Mystery and Imagination* was deeply indebted to the heritage of Gothic literature. The list given below of the episodes and their original authors shows a wide variety of sources for adaptation as alluded to by story editor Terence Feely, from the grand guignol horror of Bram Stoker's *Dracula* to the psychological terror of Edgar Allen Poe's tales of the uncanny and the restrained, suggestive ghost stories of M.R. James.

Season One
(1966)

The Lost Stradivarius (J. Meade Faulkner)
The Body Snatcher (Robert Louis Stevenson)
The Fall of the House of Usher (Edgar Allen Poe)
The Open Door (Margaret Oliphant)
The Traccate Middoth (M. R. James)
The Lost Hearts (M.R. James)
The Canterville Ghost (Oscar Wilde)

Season Two
(1966)

Room 13 (M.R. James)
The Beckoning Shadow (J. H. Riddell)
The Flying Dragon (Joseph Sheridan Le Fanu)
Carmilla (Joseph Sheridan Le Fanu)
The Phantom Lover (Vernon Lee)

Season Three
(1968)

Casting the Runes (M.R. James)
The Listener (Algernon Blackwood)

A Place of One's Own (Osbert Sitwell)
Tell-Tale Heart (Edgar Allen Poe)
Feet Foremost (L.P. Hartley)

Season Four
(1968)

Uncle Silas (Joseph Sheridan Le Fanu)
Frankenstein (Mary Shelley)
Dracula (Bram Stoker)

Season Five
(1970)

The Suicide Club (Robert Louis Stevenson)
Sweeney Todd (George Dibdin Pitt)
The Curse of the Mummy (Bram Stoker)

Readings of the literary ghost story had already proved extremely successful on the radio. For nine years, between 1946 and 1955, the popular broadcaster Valentine Dyall, also known as the Man in Black,[7] hosted his show *Appointment with Fear* on BBC Radio's Light Programme, featuring the dramatized readings of the ghost stories of John Dickson Carr, Edgar Allen Poe and others. The popular ghost story author Algernon Blackwood had become a radio celebrity in Britain during the Second World War and the restrained, scholarly ghost stories of M.R. James were repeatedly transmitted as readings and dramatizations on BBC Radio's Home Service, Light Programme and even Children's Hour during the 1940s and 1950s.

Perhaps as a consequence of the literary Gothic's success on the radio during the 1940s and 1950s, there was initially some resistance to the presentation of the ghost story on television in the 1960s. A typical reaction, such as the following from television reviewer Denis Thomas in the *Daily Mail* to Rediffusion's *Tales of Mystery*, suggested that 'television being a strictly literal medium . . . can do nothing to a cosy tale of death and diabolism without overdoing it. One way to cope with this difficulty is to show less and suggest more.' (Haining

1993:189) The suggestion that television was incapable of representing the supernatural suggestively and that its inherent visuality prohibited the medium from alluding to, rather than fully visualizing, the presence of, for example, a ghost was an issue with which the makers of *Mystery and Imagination* engaged. Taking the adaptation of Margaret Oliphant's *The Open Door* as a prime example of an episode seeking to address such criticisms, the following analysis will explore the ways in which the television adaptation of the ghost story began to look and *sound* like a 'radio play with pictures'.

The Open Door, adapted by George F. Kerr and directed by Joan Kemp-Walsh, was a ghost story based in the grounds of a Scottish country house in the late nineteenth century and centred around the haunting of a ruined house in its grounds. The haunting is first noticed by Colonel Mortimer's son, Roland, and then, when the Colonel returns from a trip to London after hearing of his son's 'disturbance', he himself investigates the sound of the haunting (a child sobbing), along with an army companion, the local doctor and, finally, a priest who lays the ghost to rest. The majority of the action of this episode of *Mystery and Imagination* took place on a studio set and was essentially a series of medium-long to close-up shots of Colonel Mortimer (Jack Hawkins), Mr Moncrieff the priest (John Laurie) et al reacting to the haunting sound effects of sobbing, groaning and the amplified sound of a heart beating. This sound was intentionally 'uncanny', distorted and without a visible (diegetic) origin within an inherently visual medium. As a drama built around the actors' reactions to that which, though clearly audible, is visually 'not there', the production's emphasis on audio rather than visual 'haunting' allows a description of *The Open Door* as a 'radio play with pictures'. By emphasizing sound over image the episode appears to 'borrow' from the sound design of the radio ghost-play and indeed the *TV Times* article accompanying *The Open Door* focused on the creation of sound effects for the episode. In this article the week's interview, usually given by the actor in the episode's central role, was given by the actress Amanda Walker, who played the ghost's voice. The interview begins with description from the script: 'Loud whimpering cry ... shuddering moan ... sobbing sigh ... pitiful cry ... Just a few of the sound effect instructions on the script of *The Open Door*',[8] emphasizing the inherent 'aurality' of the episode. Indeed, sound was not simply used to denote the haunting in this episode, but was also used, for example, to signify transition from day to night, where a static 'empty' long shot of the old ruins was first shown accompanied by the sound of owls hooting, then by birds singing. In effect, by centring the action of *The Open Door* on the reactions of a diegetic audience (Colonel Mortimer et al) to an audio-ghost-story, or what Mr Moncrieff (Laurie) describes in the teleplay as a 'phonetic disturbance', the episode can be seen to be heavily dependent on precedents set in radio. This was an episode of *Mystery and Imagination* which attempted to answer the call of critics such as Denis Thomas (see above) to 'show less and suggest more' by revisiting ghost-story broadcasting on domestic radio.

Showing More, Suggesting Less: *The Fall of the House of Usher*

It was not simply the heritages of Gothic literature and the radio ghost-play which *Mystery and Imagination* drew upon when developing the 'look' of individual episodes. The restrained, suggestive ghost stories, such as *The Open Door*, were counterbalanced by other, more excessively visual Gothic narratives. In his examination of the Hammer horror film, David Pirie writes:

> In certain kinds of horror – especially the Victorian ghost story and its cinematic offshoots . . . to reveal your hand is to destroy a carefully wrought effect . . . But there is another equally respectable Gothic line . . . including M.G. Lewis, Mary Shelley, Bram Stoker and all grand guignol theatre which precisely depends upon the clear visual portrayal of every stage of action. (Pirie 1973:41)

This 'equally respectable Gothic line' which Pirie alludes to in his analysis of Hammer's horror films can also be located in *Mystery and Imagination*.

Returning to Jason Jacobs' observation that 'producers were able to choose from a range of stylistic features, some of them associated with theatre' (Jacobs 2000:117) in producing television drama, the series adopted several dramatic conceits as well as drawing on visual styles and characterizations from different forms of Gothic theatre. For example, episodes from the last two seasons of *Mystery and Imagination* used intertitles before and after advertising breaks to announce the beginning and end of 'acts' rather than 'parts'. Several episodes, such as the 1970 adaptation of the stage play *Sweeney Todd* (tx. 16/02/70), combated the restraints of studio-based television production by reproducing the two-dimensional painted sets of nineteenth-century Gothic melodrama to represent a street scene. The adaptation of Joseph Sheridan Le Fanu's *Uncle Silas* (tx. 04/11/68) reproduced the degraded settings of the Gothic theatre of the late eighteenth and early nineteenth century, complete with the traditional 'trap-door' which allowed the grisly murder to take place as well as a plethora of diegetic 'proscenium' arches framing the performances of Silas Ruthyn (Robert Eddison) as the archetypal Gothic villain, driven on to torture his young wards by his Laudanum addiction, and the evil crone-like governess, Madame de la Rougiere, the French hag played by Patience Collier as if straight from the stage of Parisian Grand Guignol theatre.

Mystery and Imagination also looked to cinematic versions of the Gothic, such as the Hammer studio's Stoker and Shelley adaptations, reflected in Charles Graham and Patrick Dromgoole's 1968 adaptation of *Dracula*. This episode, featuring a cool-looking Denholm Elliott as the eponymous anti-hero and a gaggle of highly-sexualised vampire brides, took on the visceral excess and unequivocally sexual overtones of Terence Fisher's Hammer adaptations of

Stoker's *Dracula* in a way unprecedented in television drama. However, it is the 1966 episode *The Fall of the House of Usher*, and particularly its opening sequence, which most clearly acknowledges a different kind of cinematic Gothic heritage: that of the German expressionist cinema of the nineteen-teens and 1920s.

Beginning unusually without Beckett/Buck's introduction, the episode opens, after the credits, on a three-shot sequence (described below) which is clearly derivative of the striking images of Gothic horror in German expressionist cinema, such as the two dimensional coffin of the sleepwalking Cesar in *Das Kabinett des Doktor Caligari* (Robert Weine, Germany, 1920) or the splintered coffin which reveals Max Schrek's grotesque face in *Nosferatu, eine Symphonie des Grauens* (F.W. Murnau, Germany, 1922):

10.1. *Shot One: Medium close-up of two two-dimensional candles, accompanied by a fanfare of trumpets and kettle-drums. Camera tracks from the candles to a high angle shot of the top of a coffin, surrounded by four more two-dimensional candles – slow zoom to the top of the coffin.*

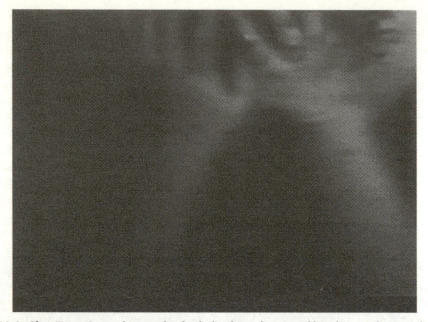

10.2. Shot Two: Cut to low angle, dimly lit shot of a pair of hands scratching at the inside of a coffin lid, frantically, as blood drips down the fingers.

10.3. Shot Three: Medium tracking shot towards the coffin, past the two-dimensional candles, onto the lid of the coffin as it is pushed through from the inside and the bloody hands break out. Camera tracks into the hands and then dissolves into the black surface of a pool.

The lack of dialogue, the dramatic extra-diegetic score, the two-dimensional properties and minimalist set and the isolated images of the scrabbling hands and the coffin all mark this as a moment of what can only be described as 'art television' in its borrowing from German expressionist film, also characterized by a preoccupation with Gothic narratives. This is a moment which exists outside of the narrative to express the more abstract concerns of episode (darkness and illumination, the insufferable claustrophobia of the domestic space and ultimately the dread and horror of being buried alive). This is achieved through a series of connected images, rather than through dialogue and exposition, just as the symbolic 'empty' shots of the night sky which punctuate this episode reflect on the fear of (super)natural power and (other)worldly forces.[9] This sequence, and the episode as a whole, are therefore in keeping with S.S. Prawer's notion that Gothic drama on television negotiated its aesthetic limitations (low budgets, studio production, etc.) and in doing so precipitated 'the rediscovery of avant-garde devices – violently clashing images, unusual angles of vision . . . etc.' (Prawer 1980:21) Working within the production constraints of television, *Mystery and Imagination*'s version of *The Fall of the House of Usher* emphasized the symbolism of Poe's story, drawing on an early art cinema tradition of Gothic visualization for its stylistic innovations.

It is also of note that the credit sequence states that Poe's story has been 'Freely Adapted by David Campton'. In his adaptation, Campton realizes what Poe leaves undescribed (he shows more and suggests less). Campton makes explicit the nature of the Ushers' hereditary madness (an uncontrollable sadism) and by adding the 'backstory' of Richard Beckett's abandonment of his fiancée in favour of his blind love for Madeleine Usher, he more fully ties the Gothic narrative to a sense of domestic trauma. One might perhaps speculate that this is important, if not essential in 're-domesticating' the Gothic narrative. The freedom of this adaptation encouraged artistic license in the television Gothic, rather than tying the medium to being an inadequate replacement for literary texts or suggestive radio plays.

In the latter two seasons of *Mystery and Imagination*, produced by the newly formed company Thames Television, the series built on this sense of artistic license and visual experimentation and with the help of new advances in video technology fully visualized both the grotesque and the uncanny. For example, in the final sequence of *Dracula* Denholm Elliott's evil Count Dracula was overcome by Van Helsing (Bernard Archard) and reduced to a pile of dust in a moment described by Peter Haining in his history of horror television as 'unlike anything ever seen before on television' (Haining 1993:292). As the videotape was dramatically switched to negative and image upon image overlaid to reveal Elliott's rapidly decomposing body in an early version of what is now termed 'morphing', the sophistication of v-t editing and prosthetics allowed the grotesque image of Gothic horror to be writ large across the small screen. Similarly, in the preceding week's adaptation of Mary

Shelley's Gothic classic, *Frankenstein*, video technology had been utilized to create the uncanny image of two Ian Holms (the actor played both Viktor Frankenstein and his abhorrent creation) confronting each other in a moment which truly visualized the horror of the doppelganger.

Conclusion

Clearly, what *Mystery and Imagination* sought to do in designing and defining the look of the Gothic television anthology was simultaneously to look back to various Gothic heritages (literary, radiophonic, theatrical, cinematic) whilst at the same time looking forward to the future of television drama production. The series was visually innovative and yet tied to earlier traditions of ghost story broadcasting. It was also 'arty' whilst at the same time commercially successful and popular. Indeed, it could be argued that it was *Mystery and Imagination*'s very popularity, not to mention ITV's identity as a populist, commercial station, which detracted from a reading of the series as 'art television' at the time of its broadcast. Discussing the comparative marketing strategies of the ABC anthology series and Jonathan Miller's adaptation of M.R. James's *Whistle and I'll Come to You* for the BBC's *Omnibus* series (tx. 07/05/68), Allan Prior bemoaned the inequities in the reviewing and marketing of the two programmes:

> Anything on ITV inevitably gets a rather popular, somewhat patronising treatment in press write-ups ... This may have something to do with the way it is presented to the press by the Press Offices of the ITV companies. Even if the piece is *art*, they would never dream of saying so in their 'handouts' because this is not the way they want it presented ... The BBC do not push or popularise. Also they do not advertise ... They are part of the literary and cultural establishment and all that. Ipso facto, they must put out the best programmes. Well they very often do. But ... if ['Whistle and I'll Come to You'] had been included in ABC's *Mystery and Imagination* series (and some very distinguished writers were) would it have got anything like the same attention? I fear not. I'm delighted for Dr. Miller's sake that his adaptation got written-up. Did it get watched much, nobody knows, probably half the audience of any *Mystery and Imagination* production.[10]

Prior's analysis of the differing status of the Gothic drama on British television according to the station that produced it therefore calls for a reconsideration of *Mystery and Imagination* as art, or at least as popular, valuable television drama, which, it is hoped, this analysis has accomplished. The anthologies produced by the independent television franchises such as ABC, at a time in which they fought to prove their 'worth' whilst their position as broadcaster was constantly brought into question,[11] are among the most exciting and innovative television dramas of the post-war period. Building upon preceding forms of the Gothic, *Mystery and Imagination* expanded the possibilities of television drama, particularly through its avant-garde camerawork and pioneering use of special effects. Indeed, later television drama, such as Phillip Saville's adaptation of Bram Stoker's *Count Dracula* (BBC2, tx. 22/12/77) and the BBC's *Supernatural* anthology series (tx. 11/06–06/08/77)[12] undoubtedly acknowledged a debt to the stylistic innovations of *Mystery and Imagination* through their use of hallucinatory visual effects and highly stylized settings. As television production techniques developed and changed, ABC's anthology series showcased these evolutions, demonstrating the ways in which new production technology would continue to be deployed by the makers of television drama in the presentation of the Gothic and the supernatural.

Notes

My thanks to Richard Dyer, Jason Jacobs and Janet Thumim, for their comments on earlier drafts of this paper, and Kees de Groot, for his unerring support.

[1.] For a discussion of the contrasting impact made on the production of television drama by Sydney Newman and the BBC's first Director-General, John Reith, see Jacobs, *The Intimate Screen: Early British Television Drama* (2000) 1–3.

[2.] ABC's application in the 1967 franchise awards was not, however, entirely successful. A reorganization of the London contractors and the formation of a star studded consortium, London Weekend Television (LWT), meant that ABC was forced into a merger with Rediffusion, the latter being the junior partner, to form Thames Television. As Andrew Crisell has noted 'the ITA wielded the surgeon's knife, causing howls of anguish and fury, and there were many who felt that the commercial television service emerged from the operation in worse shape than it had entered it.' (Crisell 1997:125)

[3.] Indeed, the BBC 'poached' Canadian producer Sydney Newman from ABC and *Armchair Theatre* and established him as its Head of Drama in 1962, the BBC's first appointment of a senior figure from ITV and a clear indication of the extent to which the corporation saw the drama anthologies of ABC/ITV as a threat to their ratings.

[4.] Algernon Blackwood, who had died a decade earlier, was immensely popular with both radio listeners and early television viewers and, as Peter Haining notes, '[His] sombre features and deep voice coupled with his unique ability to relate supernatural stories with great authenticity had earned him the soubriquet "The Ghost Man"'. (Haining 1993:189)

[5.] Terence Feely, 'My Search for the Supernatural' in *TV Times*, 29 January 1966.

[6.] Ibid.

[7.] A role which Dyall later revised for the Hammer film of the same name in 1949.

[8.] A. Davies, 'Screams behind *The Open Door*' in *TV Times*, 19 February 1966.

9. This 'natural expressionism' can also be found in Murnau's shots of pastoral 'Transylvania' in *Nosferatu, eine Symphonie des Grauens*.

10. Allan Prior in *Stage and Television Today*, 16 May 1968, 25.

11. Due, amongst other reasons, to both the Pilkington report into television broadcasting of June 1962 and the renewal of the ITV franchise awards in 1967.

12. This anthology series was created and primarily written by Robert Muller, who had previously worked on several episodes of *Mystery and Imagination*.

CHAPTER 11

EXPLOITING THE INTIMATE SCREEN

THE QUATERMASS EXPERIMENT, FANTASY AND THE AESTHETIC POTENTIAL OF EARLY TELEVISION DRAMA

Catherine Johnson

Introduction

On Saturday 18 July 1953, over a quarter of a million British adults tuned to the television as the first manned space flight crash-landed in the outskirts of Wimbledon in Surrey with only one of its three astronauts on board. Over the following weeks viewers keenly awaited the outcome of this disastrous experiment, engineered by Professor Bernard Quatermass. Finally it is revealed that the surviving astronaut, Victor Carroon, has been infected by an alien organism that threatens to conquer the earth by dispersing spores which will destroy all of its indigenous species, and it is up to Quatermass to avert the catastrophe. Of course, this was fiction, a six part drama serial exploring the potentially horrific consequences of man's foray into space sixteen years before Neil Armstrong's first walk on the moon captivated television viewers across the globe. The serial was *The Quatermass Experiment*, and it went on to become one of the most significant BBC drama productions of the early 1950s.[1] Charles Barr describes it as 'a landmark both in BBC policy, as a commissioned original TV drama, and in intensity of audience response'. (Barr 1986a:215) The initial serial was followed by two more *Quatermass* adventures produced by the BBC in the Fifties, similarly concerned with the consequences of scientific exploration, both hugely popular.[2] All three serials were adapted into films by Hammer, and *Quatermass* was even revived in the 1970s for a drama produced simultaneously as a film and four-part television series.[3]

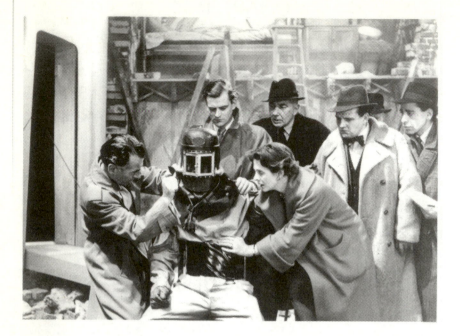

11.1. Professor Quatermass struggles to free Victor Carron from his spacesuit at the site of the crash-landed rocket. The Quatermass Experiment *episode one, BBC, 1953. (courtesy of the British Film Institute)*

The use of fantasy in the *Quatermass* serials allows the exploration of socially significant issues on a grand scale. The representations of invasion and social disintegration have been examined in relation to the anxieties of the Cold War and the changing notions of national identity in post-war British society. (see Brosnan 1978:113; and Hutchings 1999:39–41). However, *The Quatermass Experiment* and the serials that followed it, while interesting in their narrative exploration of contemporary concerns, are also significant in terms of the history of early British television drama. At a time when television was, according to Val Gielgud, 'just beginning to advance from what may be called the embryonic into the experimental and expanding stage',[4] these adult stories of space adventure, alien invasion and impending Armageddon challenged conceptions of what television as a medium was suitable for and capable of producing. Focusing on the development of the first *Quatermass* serial, *The Quatermass Experiment*, I want to consider how the use of fantasy can be understood in direct relation to the aesthetic debates around the stylistic potential of television in the early Fifties.

Written Specially for Television

The Quatermass Experiment was produced by Rudolph Cartier[5] and written specifically for television by Nigel Kneale to fill a gap in the summer schedules of 1953.[6] Kneale had worked casually reading and adapting plays for the BBC Television Department since 1951, and in 1952 was given a full-time position as an adapter for the newly formed Script Unit after Michael Barry argued that the Corporation 'cannot afford to lose his knowledge of Television built up over nine months'.[7] A year later, as the threat of competition loomed for the BBC's television service, Barry suggests that Kneale be offered a full-time contract for five years, stating that 'as a most valuable asset . . . he is worth much to the Corporation. At the same time he has a high market value outside'[8] and, in 1955, Kneale became the first staff writer at the BBC.

The question of what was possible, appropriate and valuable as *television* drama was an important point of debate in the early Fifties, a time when there was no consensus as to the criteria under which such judgements should be made. As Kneale says of his work for the Script Unit, '[I was] mostly trying to make stage plays a little more like "television", although nobody really knew what that was.' (quoted in Wells 1999:49) The desire to employ Kneale to write full-time for the BBC was therefore seen as a means of developing expertise in the specific requirements of the new medium of television, as well as ensuring that the talent nurtured at the BBC was not lost to the competition. In a memo about the future of the Script Unit written in 1954, Cecil McGivern, Controller of Television Programmes, argues for the expansion of the department in order to nurture writers experienced in the particularities of writing for television to rectify the general low quality of television scripts. McGivern makes reference to Nigel Kneale as an illustrative case in point:

> H.D.Tel. [Head of Television Drama, Michael Barry] took on a young writer [Nigel Kneale] at £5,5.0 a week . . . Soon after that he gave us the serial, *The Quatermass Experiment*. Had competitive television been in existence then, we would have killed it every Saturday night while that serial lasted. We are going to need many more 'Quatermass Experiment' programmes and series but the outlook on scripts and the script unit is still too much like it was when we could spare only £5,5.0 a week.[9]

Such documents reveal the high regard in which Nigel Kneale was held in the BBC's television service as a writer capable of exploiting the potential of television. They also demonstrate that the need to create high quality drama that would be popular was of the utmost importance as competition to the BBC's monopoly became a reality in 1955. That McGivern uses *The*

Quatermass Experiment as an ideal example of television drama is particularly significant as it suggests that this serial was considered to be exemplary of the potential for television as a popular dramatic medium.

The Intimate and Expanding Screen

The early Fifties was a period of rapid change for British television. With the increase in the sale of receivers and the extension of the range of transmission, television began to grow from a luxury medium to a household object. As it extended its reach and showed glimpses of the eventual role it would come to play in our everyday lives, the debates around its social and aesthetic function intensified. While the BBC was keen to develop quality drama that exploited the particular requirements of television, the question of what form this should take was a matter of contention.

In his analysis of 1950s television drama, Jason Jacobs suggests that 'it is possible to identify two tendencies in the production of early television drama in Britain by the 1950s: the intimate and the expansive'. (Jacobs 2000:117) Within the intimate model, a suitable television drama is defined as one which emphasizes the relay of a continuous live performance through the close-up lens of the studio camera. These intimate and penetrating images were transmitted directly into the familiar domestic location of the living room, where the small 405 line receivers, regarded as unsuitable for long shots because of the lack of definition, could reveal in close-up all the range and sensitivity of an actor's performance. Michael Barry (Head of Television Drama at the BBC) exemplifies this position in a *New Chronicle* article entitled 'TV is Creating its Own Drama'. He writes:

> There is no particular mystery in writing for television. But there are certain rules to follow. The television screen is very small, and so it is desirable to have as few characters as possible . . . The television camera is very penetrating. It shows what is going on in people's minds. Sincerity is, therefore, the most important quality required of both writers and actors . . . A great deal of television work is done in close-up. Thus, elaborate sets are often wasted.[10]

Unsuitable for crowd scenes or complex sets, television's value is located in its ability to relay the intimacy and sincerity of an actor's performance to the viewer's home. Here Barry defines the stylistic possibilities of television drama through critical assumptions about the medium's technical and aesthetic limitations, reducing its potential to the size of its screen.

Jacobs argues that it was Kneale and Cartier's arrival at the BBC 'that challenged the intimate drama directly'. (Jacobs 2000:130) Kneale characterizes early television drama as stagy and theatrical, claiming that he saw the writing of *The Quatermass Experiment* as 'an opportunity to do something different – an adventure yarn, or something that wasn't people talking in drawing rooms.' (Kneale quoted in Wells 1999:50) Similarly, when Cartier moved from directing films in Germany to working for the BBC in 1952, he felt that British television drama was 'terrible . . . the BBC needed new scripts, a new approach, a whole new spirit, rather than endlessly televising classics like Dickens or familiar London stage plays.' (Quoted in Myles and Petley 1990: 126)

Kneale and Cartier are referring here to the relative lack of material written specifically for television in the early Fifties. Adaptations of existing literature were prevalent, as was the relay of scenes from current West End plays, either recreated by the cast in the studio or broadcast live from the theatre. Gardner and Wyver have argued that this reliance on pre-existing cultural artefacts in the Fifties precluded any innovation in televisual style as 'TV drama picked up the predominant patterns, concerns and style of both repertory theatre and radio drama'. (Gardner and Wyver 1983:115) Kneale and Cartier reacted against this conception of television with its roots in radio and theatre, suitable only for the live relay of an intimate performance, by emphasizing its potential as a visual medium with a closer affinity to the cinema. Talking about the influence of the cinema on his work, Kneale states:

> In my early years I went to the cinema about twice a week and was really influenced. I wanted to make my work more visual: less making points in verbal terms and more paying off through images, which you tended not to get then. Most of the stuff was designed for actors to make big points with a big verbal display in a speech instead of what one would try to do in a decent screenplay, which was to let the camera tell the story. (Kneale, quoted in Wells 1999:49)

Kneale's rhetoric here, which opposes the visual to the verbal, relates directly to the 'intimacy' debate. Essentially, all television is visual. Kneale's desire to make his work 'more visual' needs to be understood specifically in relation to the *kind* of visuality against which he is fighting. He is arguing for a televisual style where the drama and action are to be found not only in the close-up relay of a live virtuoso performance by an actor but also in the construction of a story through images as they are framed and relayed by the camera.

Although there are no existing prints of the last four episodes of *The Quatermass Experiment*, the camera scripts give a fair indication of the shape and tone of the serial.[11] Kneale and Cartier use the fantastic premise of the story to move away from locating the action in 'a big verbal display' towards exploring the potential for spectacle in television drama. The narrative of *The Quatermass Experiment* withholds the facts of what happened to the ill-fated space-ship until the final episodes. The truth is eventually disclosed in the cliffhanger of episode five, through the depiction of Carroon, the surviv-ing astronaut who, having mutated into a huge octopus-like alien, is revealed overwhelming Poet's Corner in Westminster Abbey. Here the image plays as significant a role as the dialogue. The build-up to this visually exciting cli-max places as great an emphasis on the sheer spectacle of 'seeing' the monster as it does on resolving the narrative.

In constructing a serial which depicts a giant creature in a large historic building, Kneale and Cartier are challenging an understanding of television as an intimate medium incapable of crowd scenes or complex sets. However, the technical limitations of early television production restricted the extent to which it could be used to create visually spectacular set pieces. These scenes of the creature in Westminster Abbey were all shot live in the studio at Alexandra Palace with five bulky cameras. At a time when there was no special effects department for television production, Kneale describes the primitive techniques they used to create the model shots of the monster:

> I had a still picture of the Poets' Corner blown up to 4ft, cut a section out and put my hands through. They were covered with rubber gloves, wire, and wash leather. They looked like evil tendrils 40ft long.[12]

The climactic conclusion of the serial, in which Quatermass enters the Abbey and appeals to the remnants of humanity in the creature exemplifies the par-ticular way in which Cartier and Kneale manipulate the technical limitations of television production. This sequence is shot almost entirely in close-ups, cutting between Quatermass and model shots of the monster, overlaid by sound effects of the creature's rustling tendrils. This suggests that Quatermass and the monster inhabit the same physical location without the need to create a life-size model of the creature in the studio. Occasionally Quatermass and the monster are depicted in the same shot, but the use of close-ups allows this to be achieved through the creation of one or two tendrils which can be operated from out of shot. For example, as Quatermass plays a tape of the moment the astronauts were attacked to the creature, it becomes increasingly agitated. The camera script describes how this was achieved by remaining on a close-up of Quatermass as 'Tendrils sway into shot near Quatermass, and quickly away'. These techniques allow Cartier and Kneale to provide a visu-ally spectacular climax in which the monster is revealed while still function-ing within the limitations of live television production. Furthermore, the use of the close-up here to suggest that Quatermass and the monster are in the same place also enables the monster to suddenly invade Quatermass' space, heightening the fear and intensity of the scene.

Cartier has argued that the close-up is a particularly powerful tool in tele-vision production. He claims that within the dark and intimate environment of the living room, 'where close-ups appear life-size or even bigger', (Cartier 1958:10) the televisual close-up is capable of bringing the audience much closer to the action than they can be in the cinema. For Cartier, the intimacy afforded by the close-up in television is not restricted to an increased close-ness between viewer and character/actor, as Michael Barry suggested. It provides a specific dramatic tool which, when coupled with the domestic location of television, can be exploited to heighten tension and suspense.

Cartier's deployment of the close-up to evoke fear and horror is particularly evident in the cliffhangers at the end of each episode of *The Quatermass Experiment*. The first episode is concerned with the return of the missing rocket ship after it disappears in orbit over the earth. Eventually crash-landing on Wimbledon Common, the initial fear that it might be a bomb is dispelled. Onlookers and reporters alike have arrived to see the rocket from outer space in a scene that Kneale describes in his published script of the serial as 'something like Hampstead Heath on a Bank Holiday'. (Kneale 1959b:33) During this scene, the editing is steadily paced to heighten the sense of a gradual passage of time. The crowds are depicted, predominantly in mid-shots, waiting for the rocket to cool and the movement of characters and cameras is fluidly choreographed. This allows the atmosphere of a boisterous gathering to be created in the studio without the expense of a large number of extras, or the use of establishing shots of crowds which would appear indistinct on the small low resolution receivers.

After the rocket is opened, Quatermass realizes that Victor Carroon is the only one of the three astronauts to have returned and he marches out to confront him. Carroon, centred in the frame, with Quatermass on the left shaking him angrily, is picked out by a light directed onto his face. Instead of zooming in or cutting to a close-up of Carroon, the character falls directly towards the camera so that his face momentarily fills the screen, revealing a mere glimpse of the terror in his expression, before dissolving into a blur. The shot fades to black and the caption 'The End' is displayed. Again, Cartier uses the technical limitations of studio production to his advantage. The bulky studio cameras used to shoot *The Quatermass Experiment* lacked easy mobility and had fixed lenses making zooming or fast tracking impossible. Cartier overcomes this technical difficulty by keeping the camera still and moving the actor. The effect of this movement is heightened through the slow smooth choreography of the action leading up to this climax. After the careful build-up to the expectant return of the heroic astronauts over the episode, the sudden and rapid close-up of Carroon's terrified face is a particularly shocking and potent device. Carroon falls into the camera, literally invading and occupying the entire space of the screen in the corner of the living room.

For Cartier, television as a medium is particularly suited to such 'horrific' scenes because of its domestic reception. He argues that the viewer at home, away from the distractions and reassurances of the communal viewing experience of cinema, is more easily frightened and ready to accept the fantastic as 'real'. He uses the differing reception of the television production of *The Quatermass Experiment* against its 1955 film version to make his point:

When the viewer was watching these 'horrific' T.V. productions of mine, he was – I like to think – completely in my power, and accepted the somewhat far-fetched implications of the plot (such as the man who turned into a vegetable) without a murmur, while in the cinema, there was usually a titter or false laugh whenever one of these scenes came up. (Cartier 1958:10)

Cartier's comments about the reaction to the *Quatermass* serials presuppose a particular form of domestic television reception (the isolated viewer in a darkened living room), at a time when much television viewing was a communal activity structured around special events, and fails to take into account the differences between the television and film versions of the stories. However, they do suggest that in constructing the horrific scenes in *The Quatermass Experiment* Cartier developed a visual style that took advantage of the intimacy associated with the medium. John Caughie has argued that the large number of 'demonstration' programmes in early British television 'give a sense of the homeliness of television's early notion of the domestic and the delicacy with which the BBC intruded into the home'. (Caughie 2000:32) Cartier plays with this cosy domesticity, using the intimacy afforded by the televisual close-up, to bring the viewer literally face to face with the horrific.

By entering the home, the characters and storylines of *The Quatermass Experiment* not only invade the private space of the living room, but also intrude into the structures of daily life. As Martin McLoone suggests, 'the continuity of the television series or serial, the recurring characters, locales and situations . . . become part of the habituated viewer's domestic experience'. (McLoone 1997:89) The intimacy afforded by television's domestic location is therefore further enhanced through the integration of the serial into the routines of everyday living. For the dedicated viewer *The Quatermass Experiment* would become a regular feature of every Saturday night, its extended serial narrative offering a particular kind of intimacy between the viewer and the cast of recurring characters over the six weeks of its transmission.

Despite his desire to move away from the verbal to the visual, the theatrical to the cinematic, Kneale emphasizes the centrality of the characters to *The Quatermass Experiment*. In attempting to differentiate the serial from contemporary science fiction cinema he claims:

At that time [1953] most science fiction films were terrible, nearly always American, full of flag-waving sentiments and crude, dreadful dialogue, made with a singular lack of imagination and a total lack of interest in human characters. I wanted to get away from all that, plant it very firmly on the characters because there was no other choice, you simply couldn't launch into a load of special effects because there weren't any. (quoted in Petley 1984/5:23)

This emphasis on 'human interest' differentiates *The Quatermass Experiment* from similar generic cinema, through recourse to the potential value to be found in television's specific technical limitations. Unable to create a vast number of special effects, Kneale uses the television serial's extended narrative and immediacy (Kneale was still writing *The Quatermass Experiment* as the first episodes were being transmitted) to develop complex plots and three-dimensional characters.

This is further evident in Kneale's defence of his use of science fiction. He claims, 'The form is appropriate, if taken seriously. And that is the way I do take it. I try to give those stories some relevance to what is around us today.' (Kneale 1959a:88) For Kneale, science fiction offers opportunities to develop challenging material that tackles issues of social importance at a time when television was a relatively open arena for the exploration of new material. As he writes in 1959:

> that is the attraction of television at the present time – its readiness to tackle subjects that the film industry might balk at. Minority appeal pieces, or what later turn out to be majority-appeal pieces but which at first are new and frightening to the delicate sense of impresarios. TV is more receptive simply because its programming space has to be filled somehow, and the costs are relatively low. (Kneale 1959a:88)

Kneale here suggests that television, as a subsidized medium unhampered by the rigid film censorship in British cinema in the late Forties and early Fifties, was more readily experimenting with popular fictional forms. Although American science fiction cinema began to be critically recognized as a popular film genre after the release of *Destination Moon* in 1950 (see Sobchack 1987:12; and Biskind 1983:102), it was not until Hammer's film adaptation of *The Quatermass Experiment* in 1955 that British science fiction cinema emerged as a popular genre. The distinct blend of science fiction and horror that would go on to characterize the British cycle of the film genre over the Fifties and Sixties, has therefore been attributed to the innovations of the television version of *The Quatermass Experiment*. (see Petley 1986; and Hunter 1999a) This suggests that in this period of growth and experimentation, when as Charles Barr argues, 'TV was rapidly developing its own forms of strong popular fiction', (Barr 1986a:215) television provided Kneale with a forum to experiment with popular drama that was both stylistically innovative and thematically challenging.

Representing Cinema and Television

This move to value the specificity of television through its differentiation from the cinema, is evident in the representations of each media within the fictional diegesis of *The Quatermass Experiment*. In episode four ironic reference is made to American science fiction cinema that mirrors Kneale's critique of the genre. As Victor Carroon begins to mutate into an alien entity, he goes on the run, hiding out in a cinema screening a 3-D science fiction film, *Planet of the Dragons*. This sequence mixes pre-filmed inserts of the film, in which a Space-Girl and Space-Lieutenant find love in the face of terrible danger from space dragons, with studio shots of an audience of middle-aged women watching the matinee while eating and talking noisily.

The use here of a 3-D film is a reference to Hollywood's development of forms of cinema in the early Fifties in reaction to the perceived threat of television. According to the camera script, the 3-D effect is created by double-printing the filmed sequences from *Planet of the Dragons*. As a consequence in this scene the television image would have appeared clearer and more distinct than the filmic image. The irritated comments of one audience member, who exclaims of the 3-D spectacles, 'I dunno which is worse – with them on or with them off. Get a 'eadache or be driven loopy tryin' to watch it', denigrates the cinematic experience in favour of that of the television viewer watching comfortably at home. Furthermore, within the film, moments of action take place off-screen. The monsters are heard, but never represented. This lack of spectacle is in direct contrast to the television serial, which depicts Carroon's gradual transformation and finally reveals his monstrous alien form in the culminating episodes.

Science fiction cinema is further denigrated through the comparisons drawn between its treatment of similar thematic material to *The Quatermass Experiment*. As the Space-Lieutenant begins a characteristically corny monologue, a slide is projected onto the screen displaying a photograph of Carroon and a caption 'Have you seen this man?' followed by a police notice. The film's dialogue continues over these images as the Space-Lieutenant exclaims:

> There's a new world waiting to be built right here, Julie. Some day, maybe, on this very planet of the Dragons, kids'll be able to sit down in a corner drugstore, same as home. There'll be roads and schools and movies – same as back home. We'll build that new world, Julie . . . you and me . . . and a lot of ordinary people like us.

The juxtaposition of this monologue with the police notice to locate Carroon, makes ironic reference to the treatment of the theme of alien invasion. While in the film it is the American humans who are colonizing an alien planet through the destruction of its indigenous inhabitants, in the television series, it is earth that is threatened with colonization and humanity that stands to be destroyed. The film's cavalier treatment of this theme, in which the Space-Lieutenant's commitment to the invasion of an alien planet causes the Space-Girl to declare her love for him, is contrasted with television's more complex treatment of the consequences of alien invasion. The narrative of *The Quatermass Experiment* warns of the dangers of space exploration and complacency towards man's position in the cosmos. It depicts Carroon's suffering as he struggles to resist the invading alien entity, and the fear and bravery of ordinary people in the face of potential destruction. The insertion of this film, therefore, draws a contrast between the serious treatment of the themes of colonization, invasion and scientific experimentation within the televisual narrative and the juvenile pubescent treatment of similar generic terrain in American cinema.[13]

While cinema is represented within the fictional space of *The Quatermass Experiment* as trivial, sentimental and infantile drama, television is shown as a means of relaying reality to the public. In episode one, the scene in which crowds wait for the rocket to cool on Wimbledon Common, television interviews are conflated with the rest of the action, as the conversations between Quatermass and his fellow scientists are broken up by cuts to a reporter interviewing various eye-witnesses. This insertion into the fictional diegesis of a television broadcast presented directly to the camera, as if real, helps to blur the boundaries between fact and fiction. The plausibility of the fantastic events depicted is heightened here through the particular reference to television's acknowledged function as a realistic medium.

Throughout *The Quatermass Experiment* television is depicted as a primary means by which we gain knowledge of the real world. In the final episode a dejected Quatermass makes a broadcast across Europe and America explaining the events that have occurred and taking responsibility for the impending Armageddon. Although this monologue is transmitted on both sound and vision frequencies, it is only through the television that the public is able to witness images of the creature threatening their planet. Furthermore, it is through a television camera that knowledge is first gained of Carroon's location and mutated form. During a live outside broadcast from Westminster Abbey, a pan up Poet's Corner reveals the monster's enormous tendrils slowly descending into the building. After the programme is abandoned and the Abbey is evacuated, the deserted camera transmitting to the scanner van remains the only means by which visual information can be gained of the creature's activities.

It is particularly significant that the alien is shown in Westminster Abbey, the site of Queen Elizabeth's Coronation just a month before. The televising of this historic occasion indicated the full potential of the new medium, as outside broadcast cameras transmitted the event live to receivers across the country, watched by over half the nation.[14] Peter Hutchings sees the use of this location in the climax of *The Quatermass Experiment* as 'a kind of iconoclasm . . . a furtive pleasure in seeing the Queen supplanted by a deadly alien monster about to reproduce'. (Hutchings 1999:38) However, there is also a commentary being made here on the relative roles and pleasures of television. While the Coronation of Elizabeth II may have demonstrated the potential for television as a realistic medium capable of the live relay of significant events, the climax of *The Quatermass Experiment* suggests its capacity for a different kind of spectacle – the visual representation of fantastic events within an exciting and dramatic narrative. There is a self-consciousness apparent in this use of the Abbey, which is further reiterated in the scenes depicting the technical and organizational background of live television. At the end of episode five, a producer, his secretary and a television engineer are shown in their scanner van preparing for the live outside broadcast from the Abbey. They discuss the potential difficulties of the programme and rehearse various camera movements. Finally they go on air, and as they do so, the action moves between the producer, selecting camera shots within the van, and the actual broadcast. Thus this sequence deconstructs the production processes of live television just moments before the monster is revealed in the Abbey.

The fictional representation of television within *The Quatermass Experiment*, therefore, has a dual function. Firstly, it highlights the important role television plays in relaying significant events live to the public. Secondly, through inviting comparison with the recent televising of the Coronation, it draws attention to the new and daring nature of what is being represented within the serial, and by doing so it displays the potential for television's fictional dramatic forms to depict images of an exciting and spectacular nature.

Conclusion

The self-consciousness with which *The Quatermass Experiment* represents both cinema and television within its fiction emphasizes its production at a time when there was no consensus as to the precise nature and role of television as a medium. These aesthetic debates find particular currency in Kneale and Cartier's differentiation of television from film within *The Quatermass Experiment*, and in their discussion of the serial's production. By drawing attention to the potential inherent in its intimacy, immediacy and narrative forms, television is valued for the particular attributes that it offers: its technical constraints are exploited to become advantages. Kneale and Cartier use the fantastic premise of *The Quatermass Experiment* to explore this aesthetic potential in a particular way. In attempting to challenge a conception of television as a realist medium whose value lies in the relay of adaptations of pre-existing high cultural forms or live events of historic significance, they use the propensity for spectacle in fantasy narratives to display television's potential to deliver visually exciting forms of popular fiction.

However, in producing *The Quatermass Experiment* Kneale and Cartier were not simply attempting to create more expansive and spectacular drama. Their desire to expand television's intimate screen involved a recognition of the particular formal features of early television – live production, domestic reception, small screen, serial narrative – as exemplifying the possibilities, rather than the limitations, of the medium. What is striking about Cartier and Kneale's approach to creating *The Quatermass Experiment* is that they attempt to expand the scope of television drama into the action and spectacle afforded by science fiction narratives, while simultaneously recognizing and exploiting the familiarity and intimacy created through the transmission of an extended serial narrative into the viewer's domestic space. Cartier and Kneale's challenge to the intimate tendency in early television drama therefore entails a shift towards valuing the specific attributes of the medium as providing stylistic and narrative possibilities rather than restrictive technical limitations.

Notes

This chapter has been developed from research undertaken for my doctoral degree on telefantasy at the University of Warwick, and would not have been possible without the help of my supervisors, Jason Jacobs and Charlotte Brundson, and the financial support of the Arts and Humanities Research Board.

[1.] *The Quatermass Experiment*, Saturday 18 July 1953 to 22 August 1953, various half-hour slots between 8.15pm and 9.30pm.

[2.] *Quatermass II*, Saturday 22 October 1955 to 26 November 1955, 8–8.30pm (except episode 3, 9.15–9.45pm, due to broadcasting of the British Legion Festival of Remembrance); telerecorded repeat, Monday 24 October 1955 to 28 November 1955, 10:15–10:45pm. *Quatermass and the Pit*, Monday 22 December 1958 to 26 January 1959, 8–8.35pm.

[3.] The film rights to *The Quatermass Experiment* were bought by Exclusive Films Ltd (who owned Hammer) in 1954, and in 1955 they released a film version entitled *The Quatermass Xperiment* (a marketing strategy used to highlight its classification under the X certificate, restricting cinema entry to those over 18, which had been introduced in 1951). Further film adaptations by Hammer of *Quatermass II* and *Quatermass and the Pit* followed in 1957 and 1967 respectively. In 1979 Thames transmitted a four part television series entitled *Quatermass*, which was simultaneously produced as a film (entitled *The Quatermass Conclusion*) by Euston Films.

[4.] WAC (BBC Written Archive Centre at Caversham, UK), T16/62/1, 9 August 1951.

[5.] At the BBC in the Fifties, the title 'producer' was used for what is now generally regarded as the role of the director.

[6.] Kneale and Cartier went on to collaborate as writer and producer on a number of other productions, including the two *Quatermass* sequels produced in the Fifties, and an infamous adaptation of George Orwell's *1984* (BBC, 1954) which is discussed in depth by Jason Jacobs. (2000:139–155)

[7.] WAC, T31/141/1, 9 July 1952.

[8.] WAC, T28/124, 3 December 1953.

[9.] WAC, T31/141/1, 10 November 1954.

[10.] WAC, P655, 5 January 1953.

[11.] Telerecordings of the first two episodes of *The Quatermass Experiment* are held at the National Film and Television Archive in London.

[12.] WAC, P667, 12 November 1955.

[13.] This sequence, while denigrating science fiction cinema in favour of the televisual experience, is also offering a typically negative comment on the 'Americanization' of popular culture in the post-war era.

[14.] The BBC's research indicated that 53 per cent of the adult population of Britain watched the procession to Westminster Abbey on the television, while 56 per cent viewed the actual service. (Briggs 1979:458)

CHAPTER 12

THIS WEEK IN 1956

THE INTRODUCTION OF CURRENT AFFAIRS ON ITV

Victoria Wegg-Prosser

In the UK in 1954, when the Television Act setting up ITV (Independent Television) was passed by Parliament, it was by no means obvious that programming from the new advertising-funded broadcasters would include 'current affairs'. As a genre, it had not even been invented. News would be there, but what kind of news had still to be determined. The publicly funded channel, BBC Television, carried the news as a sound-only broadcast until as late as 1954, for fear that the audience would be unduly influenced by visual representation and interpretation. (Holland 1987:146) Within the institutional setting of the BBC, news bulletins had to compete for funding against the anachronistic 'television newsreel', and there was no systematic commitment to current affairs programmes. As noted by Grace Wyndham Goldie, the Assistant Head of the BBC's Television Talks Department, a 'topical television magazine programme' (Wyndham Goldie 1977:167) was the furthest in the direction of current affairs that television had travelled in 1953 when the BBC's *Panorama* was launched. This was to be a highly significant BBC flagship programme which became more closely linked with the notion of public service broadcasting than any other current affairs programme on British television. At the time of its launch, however, it was a fortnightly arts review programme and not a great success. (Wyndham Goldie 1977:190) When consideration was given to *Panorama*'s relaunch as a weekly programme, its new presenter, Richard Dimbleby, argued that its theme should be 'current news . . . news that didn't have to be dealt with tonight but should be covered within the next three months'.[1] ITV was launched on 22 September 1955, two days after the new look *Panorama – A Window on the World* went on air. ITV had its own news bulletins, a newsreel and also what were called 'near news programmes' (Sendall 1982:143) – 'near' as a result of both their place in the schedule and their subject matter.

The weekly series *This Week* was first broadcast on 6 January 1956, three months after the start of commercial broadcasting in Britain. It was intended to be 'a programme of stories behind the news worldwide' (Caryl Doncaster, quoted in Courtney-Browne 1975:2), and rivalled *Panorama* as a 'window on the world' for the next 37 years. The series ended in December 1992 (see Thames Television 1991). *This Week* was produced by Associated-Rediffusion, the company which had been awarded the franchise to make and televise advertising-funded programmes in the London area, on weekdays only, leaving the weekend programmes to a different contractor, Associated Television.[2] Not surprisingly, given television's appetite for programmes of similar taste, and the cross-over of staff from one broadcaster to the other, *This Week* followed very closely the format and subject matter of *Panorama*. There were usually between four and six items in each edition, with a running order that allowed for late alterations to the programme up until just before transmission. Both programmes relied on established documentary or 'short' film practice, and on the type of print journalism responsible for 'features' as opposed to 'news' pages. But whereas *Panorama* was able to adopt flexible crewing, *This Week* was hampered by an agreement. with the film workers union that insisted on the use of film crews of the same size as those for feature film productions. This anomaly was caused by a misunderstanding on the part of Associated-Rediffusion's general manager during negotiations with the union as to the nature of a feature film agreement. (Courtney-Browne 1975:5) It neatly exemplifies the many confusions surrounding the transfer of film culture and technology to television in the 1950s.

The political framework of broadcasting in Britain was set by the tone of the government-led committees of inquiry which heralded every new major broadcasting service in Britain – they worked on the basis that there was an ideal method of organizing broadcasting which a group of the 'great and good' would be able to divine. (Elstein 1999:2 and see also Glasgow University Media Group 1976) The committees' paternalistic and elitist tone was evident also in the make-up of the government-appointed Boards of the BBC and the ITA (Independent Television Authority), which were ostensibly designed to insulate the broadcasters from direct political control. Thus, although the independence of broadcasters from government was established as a principle, in practice both commercial and publicly-funded services were constrained by the threat of government interference if the 'great and good' thought that high standards of broadcasting and impartiality were not being pursued with sufficient vigour. Programmes had to be balanced in their subject matter and should not incite to crime, nor offend good taste or public feeling. For these reasons, the members of the Board of the ITA had the right to preview advance copies of the schedules, as had the Board of Governors of the BBC. Over time, the ITA's influence on commercial broadcasting was increased at the expense of the brash populism and individualism of the early ITV companies – which criticized some contractors for pandering to popular taste and initiated greater control by the ITV network over the individual contractors (Pilkington 1962:16–18).

Shortly after Associated-Rediffusion began broadcasting in the autumn of 1955, the ITA expressed concern (Sendall 1982:139; 142) over what the Board perceived as a lack of balance in the company's original programme output. Serious arts programmes were being marginalized in the schedule, they felt, and insufficient time was being devoted each day to news bulletins from ITN (Independent Television News). These complaints went to the heart of the anxieties many had expressed when ITV was first mooted, that its scheduling decisions would be governed by the 'evil' power of money (see, most notably, Lord Reith, former Director General of the BBC, quoted, for example, in *Hansard* 1962). Associated-Rediffusion wished to maximise its audience share by scheduling popular light entertainment in peak-time (6.00–11.00pm), and to minimize the costs and amount of airtime devoted to news. The company co-owned ITN with ATV, ABC and Granada and, working together, they tried to reduce the amount of news time scheduled.[3] The take-up of spot advertising on ITV had been slow to get going, and the start-up costs were substantial. The minimum working capital needed by an applicant for a franchise had been two million pounds (Thiem 1958), but by March 1956 the losses projected for Associated-Rediffusion's first year of trading were double that figure. (Sendall 1982:167) In August 1956, the majority shareholder, Associated Newspapers, pulled out of the company, leaving BET and Rediffusion Ltd to pick up the losses. (Sendall 1982:185–187) In this context, the continued commissioning of *This Week* was a brave decision.

The Audience

ITV reached a tiny audience of 200,000 homes when its transmissions first began: by the end of 1955, transmissions had broadened to cover 515,000 homes, and, after the Midlands and North franchisees started broadcasting in 1956, the figure rose to 2,725,000 homes, or around 9,500,000 potential viewers. (TAM 1965) A distinction has to be drawn between those homes which could only receive BBC signals (Band 1) and those which could receive both services, Bands 1 and 3. From a survey in November 1958 and using earlier unpublished material, the BBC acknowledged that 'as is well known, in homes with Band 1/3 receivers, there is twice as much viewing of ITV as of BBC-TV programmes'. (BBC 1959:11) Commercial television's audience measurement was undertaken by a number of outside agencies. One of them, Television Audience Measurement (TAM) reported findings even more favourable to commercial television: TAM's statistics indicated that ITV had a 65 per cent share (ie a two-to-one advantage) in 1956, but that it rose to 73 per cent in 1957, and stayed there until 1959 when ITV's share started to drop, levelling at 57 per cent in 1963, before rising again to a two to one advantage in 1965. By then, the number of ITV homes was 14 million, representing around 45 million potential viewers, or 93 per cent of TV homes. In November 1958 the BBC's survey of viewer preferences (BBC 1959:55) indicated that the ITV audience most preferred quizzes, westerns, variety, crime series and feature films, whereas the BBC audience was most inclined to watch news, travel, wildlife, current affairs, documentaries, science programmes and classical music performances.

If the audience preference amongst those who had opted for dual channel receiving equipment was two-thirds in favour of ITV, what of the division between men and women in that audience, and between their tastes and preferences? Figures giving the gender breakdown are rare in this period, but the assumption was that there were more women available to watch television than men in the daytime, and a less differentiated audience in the evening. The subject matter of advertisements on ITV reflected this assumption, although in the early days of *This Week* there were plenty of household goods advertised in the evening as well as during daytime broadcasting.[4] *This Week* occupied a thirty-minute slot on ITV in peak-time. Originally it was shown on Friday nights at 9.30pm but occasionally it appeared at the earlier time of 9.15pm or even 8.30pm. *This Week*'s running time was around 25 minutes, excluding the central commercial break and the advertisements which surrounded the programme to make up its half-hour slot – always providing the available airtime had been taken up by advertisers. The BBC's November 1958 survey (BBC 1959:53) indicated that among all viewers (ie including Band 1 homes) plays and news were the most liked programmes, with men rating their enjoyment and watching of sport, westerns and science programmes more highly than women did, while women rated plays, quizzes and religious programmes more highly than men. Given that both genders, on the basis of this evidence, liked news programmes, it seems likely that *This Week* was designed to appeal equally to both women and men. Certainly, the programme content analysis presented below bears this out.

Programme Personnel

It would be quite wrong, however, to assume that women and men played an equal part in the production of *This Week*. Leman (1987), Holland (1987)

and Thumim (1998) have shown how women were progressively and systematically excluded from most senior roles before and behind the camera, mainly
because their presence was deemed to be problematic. The first producer of
This Week was a woman, Caryl Doncaster, but when she was promoted within
Associated-Rediffusion her place was taken by a man, and thereafter no
woman attained a more senior position on *This Week* than that of occasional
reporter director. Sheila Gregg (interviewed by the author in August 1990)
was a rare female director on *This Week* in its early days (1957–9). One of
the programme's regular reporters, Bryan Magee, noted that:

> For a *This Week* interview the film unit consists of the film director and his assis-
> tant (always a girl – the only one in the group), the cameraman and his assistant,
> the sound man and his assistant; then . . . probably one or two electricians and
> another couple of men to drive the trucks. (Magee 1966:52)

The directors Sheila Gregg and Jim Pople and the then producer's assistant,
Peter Morley, interviewed in 1990, had been hired by Caryl Doncaster. Each
recalled that she could be 'abrasive' in style, but that her dedication to the
programme was absolute. She was born in about 1926 and had joined BBC
Television around 1948, some two years after its services resumed following
the end of the Second World War. She was persuaded to move as a producer
to Associated-Rediffusion Television by its programme controller, Roland
Gillett, whose previous television career had been in the USA. In January
1956, just as *This Week* was preparing to go on air, Gillett abruptly left the
company but his successor, John Macmillan, was equally supportive of the
programme. (Courtney-Browne 1975) Peter Hunt was *This Week*'s news editor and John Rhodes its first studio director. Sheila Gregg recalls that they
were very much in charge of the programme's production – Caryl Doncaster's
role was to oversee the shape of the weekly series, its finances and its internal
and external public relations profile. Doncaster was quickly designated Head
of Features and she appeared relatively happy to make programmes against
the background of A-R's escalating losses:

> The fact of having to make money to survive reduces the risk of being over-
> administered and increases the vitality of programmes . . . Round-table debates of
> pedestrian slowness can't be expected to hold an audience; they must be presented
> with on-the-spot emphasis, filmed illustration and lively, unfettered comment.
> (Doncaster, quoted in Courtney-Browne 1975:7)

Although the first edition of *This Week* was thought by staff and critics to be
too cluttered with items for its own good, praise did come quickly for the
programme, and for its producer. Herbert Kretzmer wrote in the *Daily Sketch*:
'Caryl Doncaster is responsible for three of ITV's most exciting shows, *This
Week* (. . . more fun than *Panorama*), the *Big City* series and *Look In On
London*.'[5] Bernard Levin, television critic for the *Manchester Guardian*, singled
out as one of his programmes of the year: 'Miss Doncaster's admirable news

magazine, a programme which straddles comfortably the yawning gap that separates being fundamentally serious and being delicate in style'.[6]

By the end of 1958, Peter Hunt had been made Head of Features in place of Caryl Doncaster and she went off to be what Reg Courtney-Browne carefully described as 'a' (added in ink on his manuscript) 'producer of special documentary programmes'. (Courtney-Browne 1975:12) Interviewed in 1990, he claimed that Caryl Doncaster had been 'frozen out by Mac the Knife' (a reference to John Macmillan) who was allegedly jealous of her success. Others claimed that she had allowed her personal life to intrude into her working life. Whatever the reasons for her departure, she was not alone in finding the work frantic and chaotic, exciting and demanding. The pressure to bring out a weekly programme based on stories in the news was enormous, and the danger was always that the programme would become tired and formulaic. Though this was not the case during Doncaster's two years in charge of the programme, it was a fair criticism by the time Peter Hunt left in 1961 after his six years at Associated-Rediffusion. It is not just personalities, however, that shape the future. There is also a structural tendency after the start-up phase of any undertaking to bureaucratize systems so that extravagant innovations can be limited, and organizational control imposed. No doubt it was easier to take risks with commercial television during its first year of transmission than at any time thereafter. Everything was new and happening on the equivalent of what might now be termed a 'green field' site.

The production of *This Week* in 1956 was dependent on Associated-Rediffusion's permanent staff. Their costs were fixed, and the additional variable costs which each programme incurred were charged against the programme budget. A surviving 'Estimated Programme Direct Cost Sheet' from January 1958 indicates that the budget for the programme was £1,100 and the reported costs £1,227. So long as the annual allocation was not exceeded, overspend or underspend against budget was tolerated. In this way, for example, expensive overseas trips could be offset by cheaper items from the studio, perhaps utilizing publicity material such as clips from a newly-released feature film, made available free of charge from its distributor. The direct costs included fees for scripts (used and unused), contributors (including programme personnel on contract such as guest interviewers and reporters), sets, music, stills, the hire of studio and film equipment, petty cash and expenses for the film unit and general film costs (stock, processing, dubbing, cutting rooms etc). For any one edition of *This Week*, there would be a staff producer, executive producer or news editor (with assistant), studio director, reporters/presenters, film directors with a unit of around ten people for each story, film editors and assistants, studio and transmission staff, researchers, production assistants and secretaries. The programmes were generally broadcast live from Associated-Rediffusion's London headquarters, although the first programme was devised as an outside broadcast from a restaurant in London's West End.

Programme Content

This Week was a topical television magazine programme. Its first producer, Caryl Doncaster promised: 'It won't be all political. There'll be a bit of everything in it, including humour and glamour'. (quoted in Courtney-Browne 1975:2) Apart from the humour and glamour, represented mainly by showbusiness items, *This Week*'s subject matter was not dissimilar to that in current affairs programmes of later years.[7] With its appearance on a Friday, and *Panorama*'s on a Monday, television's exploration of 'current news' became recognized as a new genre: 'current affairs'. This was reflected elsewhere in the schedules too – by March 1957, there were eleven weekly programmes on current affairs on ITV, as well as fifteen national news bulletins, ten regional bulletins and five two-minute bulletins. (Sendall 1982:254)

Most of the ground rules for current affairs programmes were laid down in the first year's production of *This Week*. No telerecording of a complete programme exists today, but the scripts and film inserts which do survive permit an understanding of the scope and style of the programme. Reliant on autocue and telecine, with reserve stories available if an item had failed to finish the editing process before transmission, and an adrenaline buzz, the approach was unashamedly populist and familiar in tone. Subjects were evenly balanced between the light and the serious. The eclectic appeal was to men and women alike, but there were few women visibly shaping the programme. Mary Hill, presenter of ITV's daytime programme for women, was the first female guest reporter to be referenced in the 1956 scripts, appearing in the 28 December edition, and her subject was, predictably, 'Fashion for Next Year'. There were plenty of candidates for the 'Man of the Week' slot, but despite the high number of women interviewees, there was never a 'Woman of the Week'. Much attention was paid to film stars Marilyn Monroe and Grace Kelly ('that wedding'[8]) but it was people like the actor Peter Ustinov or the grand old politician Sir Winston Churchill who were named 'Man of the Week'. And of course the presenter was always a man who could stamp his personality on the programme simply by smiling at one line, or frowning at another – but without telerecordings, this is only supposition.

The first three programmes in the series were anchored by Leslie Mitchell, the well-known BBC presenter and newsreader, stepping into the breach left by the journalist, Rene Cutforth, who at the last moment had pulled out of the show. The script for 20 January 1956 illustrates the start of a typical edition of *This Week*: eighteen seconds of front titles, fade up studio lights on Leslie Mitchell and twelve seconds introduction to the first filmed item, an interview with a Mrs Hinds, whose husband was on the run protesting his innocence of a thirty-eight-thousand-pounds robbery.[9] The next item was a filmed report from France on Pierre Poujade, 'The new Hitler?', followed by a link from Mitchell explaining that 'This Week's glamour also comes from France' – an interview with the skating star, Jacqueline du Bief, timed to coincide with the publication of her latest book. After the commercial break, there was a studio interview between a special contributor, the journalist Tom Hopkinson (formerly editor of the photo-journalist weekly *Picture Post*), and Barbara Castle, introduced as 'one of our all too few women MPs', on the subject of the Prime Minister's recent advice on price cutting. The final item was a filmed travelogue from Liechtenstein before Leslie Mitchell closed the programme with words which were to become the familiar sign-off : 'and from *This Week*, that's it. For us, next week's edition begins thirty seconds from now! Good night.' But for the next week, and the rest of 1956, the presenter was Michael Westmore, hired from the BBC to be Head of Children's programmes at Associated-Rediffusion, and proving that he also had a flair for anchoring *This Week*.

Understandably, the overwhelming majority of political and economic items in 1956 concerned the Suez crisis as it affected the UK and its standing as an imperial power. Reporting politics on television in the early 1950s was an uneasy business because of the 'Fourteen Day Rule' which forbade the broadcasting of talks, discussions and debates on any issues currently being debated in Parliament, or for two weeks before they were to be debated. The purpose of the rule was to ensure that Parliament remained the first forum for debate on any topic of its choosing and that its power was not usurped by unelected broadcasters. (Adamthwaite 1993:558, Sendall 1982:241–3; and Thumim 1998:95–96). There had been some doubt (Thiem 1958:35) as to whether the rule would be applicable to ITV as well as to the BBC, and it was decided that it should be, with the caveat that the Postmaster General (minister with responsibility for broadcasting) 'in practice hopes to be "hands off" in both cases'. An examination of discussion topics in *This Week*'s first year suggests that even before the Suez crisis the application of the rule was fairly lax.

Coverage of foreign affairs in general was acute and perceptive – news that Krushchev had been 'one over the eight bells at a fabulous Moscow banquet' provoked a discussion of 'how do the Russians take their drink?'; riots in Poland meant that the edition of 29 June altered its line-up of items to include at the last minute an interview by guest contributor Jeremy Thorpe with Peter Eisler 'just back from Poland'; 'a flashpoint in Cyprus is drawing near' prompted the nineteenth edition of the programme to include an item on Morocco's independence from colonial power; the US Senate House UnAmerican Activities Committee 'slapped a contempt charge on Arthur Miller, honeymooning here with Marilyn Monroe', so the programme on 27 July included a discussion of the US Communist Control Act of 1954 between its co-author, Judge Mussmanno, and Elwyn Jones MP, QC. In the previous week Judge Mussmanno had been interviewed on the programme by Maurice Edelman MP about his part in the Nuremberg Trials and whether or not

Hitler had been killed in the bunker. The scripts provide evidence of countless stories delivered in an accessible and entertaining manner which brought the world of foreign affairs into a domestic setting.

The first reference to Suez came in the edition transmitted on 27 July, one day after President Nasser of Egypt had nationalized the Suez Canal Company, outraging the British government and influential French investors, its major shareholders. In the programme, Michael Westmore briefly described 'Colonel Nasser's seizure of the Suez Canal' and then James Cameron, chief correspondent of the *News Chronicle*, conducted an interview in the studio (timed to last six minutes eighteen seconds) with Brigadier Sir John Smyth VC, MP and Julian Amery MP. Subsequent programmes in August included items on background issues to the Suez crisis such as the strategic importance of the British colony, Cyprus, and energy sources alternative to oil. On 24 August, the programme included a six minute twenty six second interview with 'Man of the Week', Colonel Nasser, in which he guaranteed the freedom of navigation of the Canal. Next day the *Star* commented: '*This Week* has been growing in stature . . . last night it leapt to manhood with its interview with Colonel Nasser, the latest bogeyman who put his case for the Suez snatch'. During September and October the crisis rumbled on until, on 29 October, Israeli forces invaded Egypt, and on 31 October, British and French forces began a limited bombing campaign against Egypt. On Friday 2 November Michael Westmore introduced *This Week* with the words: 'The foundations of our world have been rocked by the news in the Middle East' and (moving from autocue to the map at the back of the studio, according to the script) he explained where the troops had gathered, in so far as this was known at the time. Next he introduced Tom Hopkinson who conducted studio interviews with various newspaper correspondents and then with two MPs, Sir Ian Horobin and James Callaghan. They discussed the scenes in the House of Commons on the previous day as being 'unparallelled in twenty years'. As is now known (see Sendall 1982:243), the attempts by the Cabinet to curtail discussion on television of the crisis and to resist the Opposition's right of reply to the Prime Minister's broadcast on the next day, Saturday 3 November, had failed. The Fourteen Day Rule was effectively abandoned, and *This Week* continued to include debates with MPs which mirrored, without censure, those taking place in the House of Commons or House of Lords. Typically, the crisis was not just covered by contributions from experts, including some from the USA where President Eisenhower was seeking re-election on a peace ticket. *This Week* also conducted 'vox pops' – interviews on the streets of London – and provided hints on saving petrol. Editions in November 1956 were dominated by Suez and by Russian troops' invasion of Hungary. *This Week* on 23 November devoted all but its final two minutes thirty seconds to the Suez crisis. *Panorama* displayed a similar choice of subject matter, and television current affairs came of age at this time of great national uncertainty. Before November 1956, programmes like *This Week* could be characterized as topical television magazine fodder; thereafter they assumed a gravitas which made them both more sensitive to criticism and, potentially, more pompous.

This Week's coverage of home affairs, business and industry in 1956 shows the growing affluence of many British families coming out of the immediate post-war austerity years, new social phenomena, such as the teddy boy, the scooter and parking fines, and the continuing problems of low productivity in the British car industry, housing shortages and National Health Service funding which could equally well appear in current affairs programmes today, at the start of the twenty-first century. But such programmes today do not contain as a matter of course items on showbusiness or holiday features which appeared regularly on *This Week* in 1956. The trend, evidenced as early as 1956, was towards the serious and away from the lighthearted, partly as a result of the international crises which dominated the second half of the year and partly as a result of the new production paradigm which emerged from reporting those crises – more masculine in tone and more heavyweight.

Why did the programme become more serious if lighthearted items were found to be popular with audiences? Three of the interviewees from 1990 who had worked on the early editions were asked this question. Jim Pople considered the move towards the serious to be 'the trend', and for that reason he did not question it. Sheila Gregg said that originally the serious and the light were well balanced but then the programme became 'lack lustre'. She had been moved on within Associated-Rediffusion in 1959 but had returned to work on *This Week* in March 1965. By then, a young Jeremy Isaacs had been in charge of the programme for two years, and she found the atmosphere 'high-powered and stimulating, but much more controlled'. Reg Courtney-Browne thought the programme had moved towards the serious 'in order to keep up with *Panorama*'. Perhaps it became more difficult for the linkman to sustain a humorous approach when Richard Dimbleby at *Panorama* was being applauded for his heavyweight style. Perhaps the jokes fell flat. Ludovic Kennedy, a newscaster at ITN, had joined *This Week* as a reporter and presenter in 1957, but felt two years later that he had 'outgrown' the programme and decided to move to *Panorama* – Peter Black, the well-known television critic of the *Daily Mail*, commented: 'he won't be the last to switch, so long as ITV stuffs its peak hours with thrills and giggles'. (Kennedy 1982:254–5)

This Week's move towards the serious is multi-faceted. The production team sought approbation, as most people do, and they found that their serious contributions earned them praise. As the programme settled down and moved past its immediate cash crisis in 1956, the technical processes of film-making became more efficient. Standards in documentary film-making for television current affairs improved as more crews were sent out to gain experience in the field and more schedule hours were devoted to the genre. Politicians were keen to take part in studio debates, particularly after the Fourteen Day Rule was lifted, and other leading figures in public affairs were equally anxious to get their views across on peak time ITV to an audience which by 1961 had risen to around nine or ten million viewers. Pilkington (1962) showed to the world that British broadcasting would not pander to public taste in the way that US television was thought to do, and the great and good were assured of their continuing influence over what television should contain. The move was a product of push technology – the regulators and the production teams wanted to be involved with serious current affairs programmes and they were in a position to give these programmes to the consumer – they pushed them down the line even if the producing companies protested at the expense. It was a pincer movement of regulator and producer against the power of the companies to make money without regard to public service obligations. It also allowed current affairs to flourish on ITV in the 1960s and remain a genre of which British television can be proud.

Notes

1. *Broadcast*, 8 December 1975.
2. Associated-Rediffusion Ltd was owned 50 per cent by Associated Newspapers and 25 per cent each by Rediffusion, a broadcast relay company, and BET (British Electrical Traction), a road transport company. Associated Television (ATV)'s main shareholders were the three individuals who had lobbied for ITV in the first place, assisted by the showmen Lew Grade and Val Parnell. In addition to the London weekend franchise, ATV held the Midlands weekday franchise. In a similar manner, Granada Television Network (85 per cent owned by the Bernstein family) was awarded the weekday franchise in the North of England, while ABC (Associated British Pictures cinema and film company) was awarded the weekend franchise. These companies were known as 'the big four'. They supplied the bulk of their programming to each other, and to the ten new franchisees operating around the UK, starting with Scottish Television in 1957 and concluding with Channel Islands Television in 1962. (See Sendall (1982); ITA (1960); TAM (1965); and Sampson (1965:658–663) for further details concerning all these programme contractors.)
3. They failed. (see Sendall, 1982:143). The ITA insisted that at least 20 minutes each day would be scheduled as news and that the bulletins would include filmed items, as well as newsreading.
4. An analysis of advertisements in the commercial break on *This Week* in the first six months of transmission reveals that household products like Omo, Kleenex, Gleam and Vim and food products like Quaker Macaroni, Bovril, and Walls' Ice Cream were just as likely to be advertised as car products or men's clothing. Thereafter the scripts do not consistently list the particular brands advertised in the break, although the timings for the break itself are usually still included. A study of these timings shows that at first *This Week* carried very few advertisements, for example, two advertisements totalling 35 seconds only in the third edition of the programme, and one minute 35 seconds in the ninth edition, rising to two minutes 15 seconds (four advertisements) in programme 14, but dropping to 30 seconds (two advertisements) in programme 21 (transmitted on 25 May 1956). From autumn 1956, the commercial break became regularized at around two minutes five seconds (three to four advertisements per break). Thiem (1958:33) records that the ITA fixed a maximum price per

minute of advertising time at £1000 for peak-time on Saturday or Sunday, with the basic evening rate being £650 per minute. The gross income from advertising revenue for the first year of trading for the whole of ITV (Thiem 1958:31) was estimated to be in the region of eight million pounds. Appendix I of the ITA report for the Committee on Broadcasting (ITA 1960) lists Associated-Rediffusion's gross advertising revenue as being £4,179,373 for the trading year of 1956 and almost double that figure, £8,153,679, in 1957.

5. Herbert Kretzmer in the *Daily Sketch*, 12 July 1956.

6. Bernard Levin in the *Manchester Guardian*, 22 December 1956.

7. The themes which featured in *This Week* in 1956 were compared with those studied by Barnett and Seymour (1999:18 & 74–82) in current affairs programmes in each of the production years 1977/78, 1987/8 and 1997/8. The themes were similar, with the exception of three which had not emerged as subjects for inclusion in 1956: education, information technology and secular ethical issues. The number of hours devoted to politics and economics, business and industry and foreign affairs in those later years was within the parameters of hours on these subjects on *This Week* in 1956. Entertainment, consumer and leisure reports, weather and disaster stories and items on royalty featured more prominently in 1956 than in later years but items on health and medicine were less prevalent. On the basis of this evidence, current affairs in 1956 was less dependent on serious broadsheet subjects and more dependent on tabloid stories than in later years, but such generalizations ignore programme style.

8. The screen actress Grace Kelly married Prince Rainier of Monaco in 1956 and there was enormous public interest in the wedding, including a BBC outside broadcast of parts of the ceremony and associated festivities.

9. Typically, for *This Week*, the subject was returned to because it remained current news for a few more weeks, and the costs of the first report on the subject could be subsidized by a second showing. If the programme could also be mentioned in the press, this was deemed to be good publicity even if the mention were critical. When *This Week* returned to the subject of Mr Hinds two weeks later, there were complaints from politicians and newspaper columnists that commercial television had glamorized 'a man who was at present no more than an escaped prisoner' (*Cambridge Daily News*, 11 February 1956) and had twice interviewed his 'plump, loyal wife, Lile'. (*Daily Express*, 24 February 1956)

CHAPTER 13

WOMEN AT WORK

POPULAR DRAMA ON BRITISH TELEVISION
c1955–60

Janet Thumim

Introduction: Women and the Audience

In 1955 Britain was in the throes of a volatile re-alignment of its social values, what we might now characterize as a national 'identity crisis'. There were many constituents to this crisis such as the loss of colonial power; the move towards egalitarianism provoked by post-war legislation in health, education and welfare; and shifts in class, gender and race hierarchies consequent on all of these. It was into this context that ITV (Independent Television), the first commercial channel, finally came on-air in September 1955 after vociferous debate about its desirability and its probable consequences for the cultural 'health' of the nation for which the BBC (British Broadcasting Corporation), till then the *only* channel, considered itself to have a special responsibility. During the latter part of the 1950s there was thus an uneasy but nevertheless increasing acknowledgement of the central importance that television was to play in shaping British national culture. A particularly important element of this uneasy acknowledgement, I suggest, was the perception that women were crucially important in the formation of this audience.[1] Women ordered the domestic routines into which television viewing must be inserted and they were the primary purchasers of the consumer goods whose advertisers provided the funding for the second channel. Whilst there was recognition of the central importance of television to British national culture, there was at the same time a deep-seated ambivalence about the consequences of routine television viewing in itself.[2] Many commentators noted that the BBC's mission to educate while entertaining its audiences – to 'raise' the level of taste towards that of the middle-class highbrow – might be fatally diluted by its need to compete with 'commercial' programming where the raison d'être was profit likely to be had, detractors felt, at the expense of quality.[3]

In such discussions television was located at the low, or soft end of the scales by which cultural value was measured by its self-appointed arbiters.[4] This is reminiscent of the value-laden discourse of cinema critics of the late 1940s, noted by Ellis.[5] There was it seems something inherently passive, possibly even duplicitous, about the new medium. But, as Streeter and Wahl have argued, the equivalence of 'the audience' with 'the consumer' in which both are idealized in discourse, is resonant with patriarchy's mischievous idealization of the feminine.[6] All – the audience, the consumer, the feminine – are necessary to the enterprise of which they are the object, are 'served' by the enterprise but, crucially, lack any control of the enterprise. In the case of the television audience the enterprise is the market-place, in the case of patriarchy it is the maintenance of a social order in which women can be depended upon to perform certain designated tasks of which men enjoy the benefits while retaining overall social control, hence power. So while contemporary discourse proposed television as a debased and therefore by implication a feminized form, the same discourse idealized the television audience as consumer. At the same time women were addressed directly, their attention actively solicited, as well as being represented on the domestic screen. This is an unstable matrix of contradictory definitions of women and the feminine, its instability of interest precisely because of the increasing ubiquity of the medium.

How then, were women – bearers of 'the feminine', to paraphrase Mulvey[7] – represented on British television screens in the late 1950s? Leaving aside much compelling material about afternoon programming, often addressed specifically to women, and about programmes dealing with so-called women's issues aired both in the afternoon and during prime time, I shall focus in this essay on popular drama[8] because of its implicit claim to represent contemporary life. I'm referring now to series drama, some of it imported from the US, which was opposed in such criticism as exists to the prestigious *Sunday Night Theatre* (tx BBC 1955–59), *Armchair Theatre* (tx ABC 1956–69), in which both the BBC and ITV won well-deserved reputations for the production of 'quality' drama.[9] It is in the domestic and workplace series, typically broadcast in the early weekday evening 'family viewing' slot, that women viewers were most likely to find their fictional equivalents, and hence where contemporary assumptions about women's social roles are most transparent.

Before turning to consideration of the popular drama available to viewers, however, I want to signal three broadcasting issues which seem to me to encapsulate the particular volatility of the broadcasting environment of the later 1950s. These are the Fourteen Day Rule; the toddlers' truce; and shopping magazines. With hindsight these seem to contain, between them, the contradictions which characterized public discussion of the function of broadcast television in modern British society at that time. They were all concerned with the considered 'appropriateness' of broadcasting in its content or its timing, hence the relation between the domestic viewer at home and the collective – the 'body politic' – of which this viewer was necessarily a part. Here, then, are some fine details of the hegemonic struggles in which broadcasting practices in the UK were implicated at this formative stage in their development.

The Fourteen Day Rule

The Fourteen Day Rule[10] which dated from 1944 was an 'informal understanding between the BBC and the Government that "precluded the broadcasting of talks, discussions or debates on any issue being discussed in Parliament or for two weeks before such a parliamentary debate was to take place"'. (Sendall 1982:233) From 1955 this prohibition was the subject of discussion both in and outside Parliament, and parliamentary records allow delightful insights into the deep suspicion with which commercial television was viewed by the British establishment. For example Patrick Gordon-Walker (Lab), House of Commons, 30 November 55:

> This is going to be settled by the people who broadcast, and among these is commercial television. This alters the situation. If it were only the BBC I could understand some argument for a gentlemen's agreement, but with commercial television we are, by definition, not dealing with gentlemen.'[11]

There is a certain irony in this Labour opposition spokesman's haughty identification of commerce with class position. This elision of the difference between 'free speech', the democrat's grail, and 'free market', the goal of Tories who held power from 1951–64 characterized both the debates preceding the introduction of the second channel and the critiques of television per se which followed. The matter came to a head during 1956, precipitated by public discussion of the deeply divisive Suez crisis, and in December 1956 the rule was suspended.[12] At issue here was the question of whether domestic viewers ought to be privy to the views of un-elected individuals on matters of such national importance that they were to be the subject of debate between elected representatives of the people, at Westminster. Hence the real question was the scope of broadcasting's participation in informing – or forming – public opinion.

Whereas in 1955 the BBC transmitter network was almost complete, Independent Television (ITV) was operating from only one transmitter in Croydon, south of London. As the ITV network expanded, so did audiences, until by

1960 most of the country was able to receive both channels and hence a genuinely national mass audience existed and the question of television's influence on public opinion was widely debated. Proponents of the freedom of speech lobby won the argument, and this had important consequences for the standing of current affairs programming[13] but also, I would argue, for the subsequent status of all broadcast material.

Toddlers' Truce

In the earliest days of television, broadcasting hours were limited, but were gradually increased to c50 hours per week by the mid-Fifties. First the evening prime time and then afternoon periods were used, the break between them being gradually whittled down as transmission hours were extended, till eventually the 6.00–7.00pm break in transmission became known as the 'toddlers' truce'. After children's television (5.00–6.00pm) finished, it was argued, a one-hour break in transmission would allow parents (mothers) to get their children to bed before the evening's adult entertainment commenced. This arrangement suited the BBC, in continual financial difficulties as they attempted to meet the rapidly expanding demand for programmes from a licence fee income which never seemed quite enough. But when ITV began transmissions in 1955 a different set of interests came into play. ITV programming was financed by the sale of advertising space on air, so both the enlisting and the maintaining of 'channel loyalty' were crucial. Audience research studies[14] showed that viewing figures built up steadily from the mid-afternoon onwards and that therefore the 6.00–7.00pm slot was a potentially lucrative one in terms of advertising space, and if filled was likely also to secure the evening audience.

From early in 1956 discussion ensued about the domestic routines of audiences, about children's bedtimes, the preferred time of the evening meal, even the preferred place in the home for the television set. The BBC dragged its heels, in no hurry to jeopardize its investment in prime-time programming because of the necessity to fill another hour in the early evening. This was a necessity to which it felt obligated because of the other new factor – competition between channels for viewers.[15] Finally, in October 1957, the principle was accepted by the PMG[16] that broadcasters could choose their transmission times subject to a weekly maximum of 50 hours.[17]

Significant for my consideration of popular drama is the assumed relation between scheduling and domestic routines, combined with an explicit attention to the female audience, which marked discussions of viewers' domestic lives. The afternoon audience was assumed to be primarily female, while early evening and prime-time broadcasting was addressed to the 'family' in which the woman (at least for the purposes of these debates) was considered central – that is to say her approval was required in order to secure the habit of viewing as a part of national domestic routines.

Shopping Magazines, also Known as Admags

The form which commercial sponsorship for broadcast material might take was the subject of heated and anxious discussion in the years preceding 1955. Both direct sponsorship of programmes and product placement within programmes were considered unsuitable for the British audience. Instead, clearly indicated advertising was inserted between and, increasingly, within programmes segmented for that purpose. However between 1955 and 1963, when the practice was outlawed by Parliament, several advertising magazines were broadcast.[18] Here the well-tried magazine format was adopted, borrowed from print journalism via radio broadcasting, in which several separate but related short items were linked by a presenter – or 'host' – and/ or through a consistent mise-en-scene. *Jim's Inn* (AR 1957–1963), for example, had Jimmy and Maggie Hanley as a couple running a village pub in which they discussed the prices and quality of various domestic products with their customers.[19] The problem with the format seems to have been the supposed difficulty, for the audience, of distinguishing between information or opinion disseminated by partisan advertisers and that offered by the (presumed non-partisan) presenters of other magazine programmes. At issue here is the question of the perceived power of television to influence its audiences – hence fears about the gullibility of the audience – and the beloved notion of impartiality or objectivity in the face of conflicting claims.

The demise of the Fourteen Day Rule which, as I have suggested, strengthened the power of broadcasters, and the banning of advertising magazines because they might not easily be recognized as such, can be understood as two sides of the same coin. If broadcasters were to be trusted with public discussion of issues crucial enough to concern parliament, the argument ran, it follows that television broadcasting must not be debased by muddying the generic clarity of its programme boundaries. There's an uneasy paternalism at work here, in which acknowledgement of the democratic good of free speech and of open (though preferably well-informed) debate was locked in a

kind of tension with the awful possibility that viewers might not understand
the issues correctly – that is, in line with the hegemonic consensus. As Patrick
Gordon-Walker had feared, they might not all be gentlemen.

Popular Drama 1955–1960

Both the BBC and the commercial contractors supplying ITV invested as heavily
as they dared in prime-time programming, aiming to secure strong audience
figures for critically acclaimed product. But the business of filling 50 broadcast hours each week, and of building and securing audiences, also made
demands on their finite resources – that is to say on the licence fee income in
the case of the BBC, and on revenues from advertising in the case of the ITV
companies. Therefore these competitors for the British mass audience devised
relatively low-cost programming, importing some from the USA, to fill slots
adjacent to the prime-time mid-evening period. They hoped in this way to
protect their investment in the more high-profile and expensive production
destined to secure the prize of dominance in the prime-time ratings. Low-
cost programming included studio-based magazine and game shows[20] and
popular drama.

   In looking at the range of such popular drama on offer to British audiences
in 1955–60, I have tried to put on one side generic categorizations based in
hindsight and to consider from the available evidence[21] what the series' ra-
tionales were – that is to say how they were apparently intended to appeal to
their viewers. In 1955 nine popular dramas were on the air each week of
which seven were workplace or domestic series, and in 1960 there were 42
series running of which 28 were workplace or domestic dramas. The material
seems to me to fall into three groups, namely 'adventure', 'workplace' and
'domestic' drama. In the adventure series it is the spectacular action or locations, the thrill of suspense or mystery which primarily invites the viewer; in
the workplace drama the routines of a particular trade, profession or workplace and the characters inhabiting that particular world of work are the
series' raison d'être; in domestic dramas the action generally centres around
characters in a particular domestic mise-en-scene, following their experience
of life in and outside the family but always in relation to it. The western
(always a US import) has characteristics of both adventure and workplace –
sometimes even of domestic drama, for example *Bonanza* (US prod., tx ITV
1960–), and I've kept it as a separate, fourth category.

In 1955–1956 there's a fairly even spread of these 'generic' categories – five adventure series, two westerns, six workplace dramas and six domestic dramas. These include both home-produced dramas such as *The Grove Family* (tx BBC 1954–57), *The Adventures of Robin Hood* (tx ABC 1955–59), *Dixon of Dock Green* (tx BBC 1955–76) and *Life with the Lyons* (tx BBC 1955–56, A–R 1957–60) and US imports such as *I Love Lucy* (tx ITV 1955–), *The Burns and Allen Show* (tx BBC 1955–) and *Dragnet* (tx ITV 1955–). At this stage US imports were more likely to be found on ITV. In 1957 four of the existing workplace dramas were still running – these were *Dixon of Dock Green, Dragnet, Boyd QC* (tx AR 1955–1965), and *Highway Patrol* (US prod., tx ITV 1956-) and eight more began transmission. From 1958 to 1959, while most of these workplace series continued, a further spate of adventure series began, possibly in response to the ending of the toddler's truce and consequent availability of the 6.00–7.00pm slot. Few of these ran for more than two years. Similarly a new group of westerns came to British screens, most of which enjoyed longer runs and continued on-air until well into the 1960s. In 1959–1960 a further nine workplace dramas came on the air, the majority continuing into the 1960s, and five new British-made domestic dramas, one of which was *Coronation Street* (tx Granada 1960-present), began transmission.

What strikes me in looking at the length of these runs, generic categories and production sources is the comparative longevity of the workplace dramas – *Boyd QC* and *Emergency Ward 10* (tx ATV 1957–67) each ran for ten years, *The Army Game* (tx Granada 1957–61) and *No Hiding Place* (tx A–R 1959–67) for six and eight years respectively and *Dixon of Dock Green* for 21 years. The dominance of British production is also striking; though it isn't really surprising in itself the evidence seems to run counter to the hostility expressed by some contemporary critics to what they claimed to be an invasion of imported US material on British screens. In fact, apart from the westerns,[22] only the US workplace dramas *Dragnet, Highway Patrol* and *77 Sunset Strip* (US prod. tx ITV 1960–) and the domestic drama *I Love Lucy* retained a continuous presence over several years. The popularity of workplace dramas climbed swiftly and steadily, and by 1960 there were 18 such series available of which the British productions *Dixon of Dock Green, Boyd QC* and *Emergency Ward 10* were the longest running – but many held their place in the schedules for well over two years. There was a broad range of workplaces represented, too: not only medicine, the law, the police and the army but also the probation service, the newspaper business, an airport and the hotel trade – all had at least one popular drama purveying a fictional version of their routines to the domestic audience.[23]

The fascination with other peoples' 'ordinary' lives, which may also account for the late 1990s explosion of 'reality TV', might explain the popularity of these mundane dramas in the 1950s. But the dislocations of the period, noted above, produced by a distance between convention and practice in the experience of everyday life, must also be implicated. While conventional representations in popular cinema and on television upheld the ideal of the nuclear family, the stay-at-home mother and the breadwinning father, the reality for many was very different. Women had continued to enter the workforce in ever-increasing numbers following the end of the Second World War, despite the 'baby boom' of the late 1940s. Many widowed or divorced women were the breadwinners in their families. The 1944 Education Act had asserted the importance of gender equality in education and a generation of girls was growing up encouraged to look forward to the positive and self-fulfilling possibility of a career in their adult life. Despite media emphasis on stories of *exceptional* 'career women', experience showed that women's economic contribution to family income was vital in securing the newly available consumer goods, just as their labour was vital in producing them. I contend that this gap between the experience of juggling work and family responsibilities, and the conventional representations of women's lives as exclusively domestic, is likely to have have fuelled viewers'appetites for stories about contemporary workplaces. I'm tempted to invoke Ellis's useful concept of 'working through' to account for this predilection.[24] He suggests that not only does television, through its multiple frameworks, continuously offer its audience versions of the present but it also proposes contact, in the form of the shared experience of viewing, with the many and disparate others constituting the audience. Hence the notion of a collective 'working through' of versions of experience, of possibility, of propositions about how things *are*. With hindsight it is clear that the 1950s entailed much far-reaching social change which needed to be 'worked through' at the time. The destabilized relation between domesticity and the workplace, experienced daily by the majority, was explored in many of the contemporary fictions available each evening for family viewing.

I Love Lucy and *Emergency Ward 10*

I want now to offer a thumbnail sketch of two highly popular and long running series,[25] one a US-produced domestic comedy, one a British-made workplace drama, considering particularly what images and definitions of work, women and the feminine they purveyed to audiences of the later 1950s. These are *I Love Lucy* and *Emergency Ward 10*. What was it that they seemed to be 'working through'? Both series routinely offered the spectacle of women at work, albeit in markedly differing contexts. But in the later 1950s the image of the working women was, as I have suggested, a troublesome one signifying more than the simple requirements of the fiction's plot. In both series the conditions and parameters of women's work, of their participation in the public sphere, are quite clearly demarcated – indeed in *I Love Lucy* this is invariably the point of the comedy. *Emergency Ward 10*, on the other hand, though it had its moments of comedy, pathos and suspense, was essentially purveyed as the drama of a contemporary medical workplace, hence its representations were offered to viewers as fictional approximations to contemporary real world equivalents. There's a deathly earnestness about the gender hierarchy in *Emergency Ward 10*, making the fiction look like a summary of the typically regressive gender-power models sustained in the myths of Britain in the 1950s, if not in the day-to-day practice of social relations. Both series were expected to (and did) appeal particularly to the female audience whose conditions of viewing were ambiguous.[26] Women were assigned the domestic sphere as their workplace, yet frequently addressed within it 'as if' they were at leisure: hence for this section of the audience televisual representations of working women had multiple resonances.[27]

The American sitcom *I Love Lucy* appeared on commercial television in the UK in September 1955, featuring on the covers of both the first issue of the schedule magazine *TV Times* and the photo-journalist weekly *Picture Post*'s special issue to mark the advent of commercial television, subtitled 'Television's Big Week'.[28] The cover picture was of Lucille Ball in full evening dress being kissed on each cheek by two smart-suited men, members of the cast of the BBC's then well-known suburban domestic series *The Grove Family*, and was by-lined 'Lucille Ball competes with The Grove Family'. The impresario Bernard Delfont, in an April 1956 *TV Times* feature article, cited *I Love Lucy* as the epitome of 'true' television and its high audience figures and longevity in the schedules are evidence of its relevance to contemporary audiences. It was a comedy series based in, but not limited to, the domestic space of the couple Lucy (Lucille Ball) and Ricardo (Desi Arnez). Lucy is unquestionably the star, her brilliant comic performances calling on her audiences' recognition of domestic gender/power conflict. But there is a contradiction between Lucille Ball as a successful comedian, not to mention producer and entrepreneur, and her dippy on-screen performance of the proverbial 'little woman'. This construction engages with the domestic solidarity of women who, though they may acknowledge their disempowerment, also recognize and celebrate their subversive power and, importantly, *share* that recognition with other women – represented in the series by Lucy's neighbour Ethel. Frequently plot-lines dealt directly with the question of women's work outside the home as Lucy attempted to engage with various professional worlds: her attempts are however always subject to the vagaries of Ricky's views, now supportive, now obstructive, thus the underlying textual proposition unequivocally asserts the patriarch's right to control female labour. Lucy might attempt to manipulate Ricky but she never questions his ultimate authority beyond the close of each episode.

In the story concerning Lucy's attempt to get the job as showgirl/dancer in
Ricky's night club act, for example, she *does* manage to lose the requisite
12lb weight, to wear the size 12 costume and to lock up her rival in time to
make the performance of a dance routine with Ricky. It's a competent and
delightful number, but one we are invited to read as the practised routine of
an harmonious husband and wife team rather than as the rehearsed collabor-
ation of professionals, a reading endorsed by the fact that we know Lucy has
had no time to rehearse the number. Thus the audience is, at the same time,
celebrating the fictional Lucy's magical success and enjoying the professional
Lucille's performative skills. One reading subverts the other, the tension between them enhancing the audience's pleasure in the comic moment. Lucy's
triumph is, as always, short-lived. In the typical 'punch-line' of the episode,
which had begun with family discussions of Lucy's excessive weight, she is
taken off to hospital suffering from malnutrition. In another episode Ricky
has been to Hollywood and inspired a huge, star-struck following. Lucy, her
nose already out of joint, is told by an interviewer that her mission in life is to
make Ricky happy: 'Mrs Ricardo, I don't think you know what your husband
really means to everyone . . . Yours is a sacred trust'. A delightfully slapstick
set-piece follows in which Lucy simultaneously types, shines Ricky's shoes
and answers the phone, offering a comic subversion of the journalist's (and, of
course, the patriarchal) demand on Ricky's behalf. Assuming readers' familiarity with this perennially re-run comedy I don't want to do more, here, than
call attention to the series' knowing play with ideas of work and not-work,
inside and outside the domestic space, and to suggest that it is precisely this
play which constituted the comedy's striking appeal – an appeal which, we
might note, is still effective nearly 50 years later.

Emergency Ward 10, broadcast twice-weekly on ITV from 1957, was av-
idly watched, discussed and loved by audiences in the UK for ten years. It
was, as a student essay engagingly commented, 'the first medicated soap'.
But in this drama the pleasures of subversion, so central to *I Love Lucy*, are
signally lacking. Indeed the experience of viewing the two episodes still extant was a rather sobering one because of their unashamed demonstration of
male authority and privilege. All the doctors are men, all the nurses women.
The male doctors are (in these two episodes) the central characters, their
experiences on and off-duty constituting the drama's primary material and
frequently also the point of empathy for the audience. The nurses defer to and
serve the doctors, delivering care more domestic than medical to the patients,
and engage in a limited amount of 'shop floor' intrigue amongst themselves.
The more senior the nurses, the less they conform to current models of physical attractiveness.[29] Hence the programmes' strong implication that 'career'
nurses who attain seniority couldn't attract a husband, and that conversely
junior/student nurses will abandon their careers on marriage. In this fiction,
career advancement implies rejection of what was clearly suggested to be
the *alternative* role of wife and mother (despite the fact that both the series

originator, Tessa Diamond, and its writer, Hazel Adair, were professional women). The suggestion offered to audiences of this programme is that work, for women, is a temporary business, something to fill the gap between the end of childhood and education, and the start of adult life as wife and, subsequently, mother. And, perhaps just to be on the safe side, the work that these women do is remarkably close (if you ignore the uniform) to that performed in the domestic environment within which the fiction was consumed. Two other female characters – not nurses – are significant for their extremely unsympathetic representations. One is the nagging, whining wife in a middle-aged couple attending as outpatients: the husband's hand has gone numb, and he himself all but dumb until the male doctor removes him from the oppressive muttering of his wife. Here male camaraderie transcending class and professional divisions is asserted against the figure of the wife, the audience being invited to collude in what is intended as a comic moment in the drama of medical practice. Secondly the 'glamorous' girlfriend of one of the central characters, a relatively senior doctor, is suggested to be callously indifferent to his avowed desire to spend quiet lunch or dinner-dates alone with her so that he can propose marriage. She flirts with junior doctors and insists on talking about her interesting work in publishing – finally eliciting from her would-be fiancé 'Darling, you don't want to be one of those career girls, do you?' She is clearly marked as duplicitous and self-serving, and it is surely worth noting that she is the *only* character who doesn't instantly respond to male authority with a compliant subservience. The hierarchy offered is so rigid that audience attention must surely have been drawn to it – certainly that of those audience members who could engage with the subversive pleasures of *I Love Lucy* and may have viewed *Emergency Ward 10*'s definitions of women with some chagrin.

That audiences did take the material of this drama to heart is borne out by an angry reader's letter in March 1960 following an episode in which the then controversial contraceptive pill was recommended by one of the doctors to a patient:

> [I] regret that . . . you should find it necessary to refer to subjects which are undeniably outside the field of family entertainment and are certainly undesirable for the many young girls who watch *Emergency Ward 10* with the view, perhaps, of taking up nursing as a career when they are old enough.[30]

Behind this letter – and many others concerning this and other televised material of the period – is the assumption that television viewing *does* inform viewers' understanding of the world and its possibilities ('young girls watch with the view of taking up nursing') and that therefore its content ought to be subject to safeguards and/or prohibitions in the interest of maintaining a paternalist hegemony. It is this assumption, as I have suggested, which lay behind the often acrimonious discussions of the fortnight rule, the toddler's truce and the ethical problems supposedly presented by shopping magazines.

Conclusion

During the latter 1950s afternoon programmes dealing with domestic concerns – cooking, decorating, handcrafts, clothing, child-rearing – and shopping magazines purveying the multiplicity of new products then flooding the market-place were announced, presented and reviewed as being specially for women viewers. Advertisements in the two television guides and features in many women's magazines confirm the impression that women were acknowledged to be crucial to the enterprise of establishing television viewing as a routine in British households. With hindsight it is clear that, as mass television developed, much of this content was incorporated into the domestic and workplace series that came to dominate popular drama by the end of the decade. The British predilection for a quasi-documentary content to its fictions (see for example many of the Ealing comedies and the prolific low-budget output of producer-director teams Launder and Gilliatt, Relph and Dearden) may also account for the increasing dominance of work-place dramas in which conflicts between public and private, between the world of work and domestic life are played out.

In popular series drama at this time a variety of work-place settings were presented – offering to the early evening family audience insights, similar to those available in typical women's magazine features of the period, into possible career destinations for women and girls wishing to join the still-expanding work-force. But in both *I Love Lucy* and *Emergency Ward 10* the public work of women was heavily circumscribed by their subservience to, and dependence on, men. As the 1960s dawned, Britain's longest running television drama, *Coronation Street*, began transmission: here the home and the workplace are conflated, and the home itself is clearly acknowledged to be a workplace in its own right. *Coronation Street*'s narrative emphasis on the street itself, a street in which the major protagonists both live *and* work, explicitly blurs distinctions between the public and the private. The various interweaving plot-lines centre on the relations between characters, on their emotional lives and the politics of their interactions, and here too the separation between the public self of the workplace and the private self of the domestic environment is refused. And in this refusal perhaps lies the serial's appeal to female audiences in whose own experience the concepts of work and leisure are in a constant state of compromise. Further, the narrative focus on several female protagonists allows for experiential differences between women not only to be acknowledged, but also explored: I'm thinking here of differences in age, marital status, expectations. A focus on these differences counters, to a degree, the homogenizing tendency of terms like 'the feminine' as an assumed or required attribute of all women.

In the first few episodes, broadcast towards the end of 1960, all the female characters clearly destined to be central to the drama have jobs. In the very first scene the widowed Florence Linley is in the process of taking over the corner shop, having previously worked behind the bar in a nearby pub: 'I've always wanted my own little business, this'll suit me nicely'. Then we meet Elsie Tanner, separated from her husband, living with her quasi-delinquent son and her dissatisfied daughter who's just left her husband. Elsie worries about money: 'Three of us can't live on what I earn', about her son's unwillingness to look for work, about the reasons why her daughter Linda has left her Polish husband. Next door at the Barlows, a middle-aged couple with two young adult sons living at home – one 'at college', one at work – there is a family dispute referencing contemporary anxieties about class mobility. 'I bet you don't tell those high and mighty pals of yours where your mother works . . . in that hotel kitchen'. In the Street's pub, The Rover's Return, publican Annie Walker is harassing her good-natured husband, while the Street's famous harridan, the elderly Ena Sharples with her apron and her hairnet, is settling into her role as gossip and prophet of doom. Even she has a job as caretaker at the Glad Tidings Home across the street from the pub. As the characters are introduced and the narrative begins to unfold it is the differences between the many women characters that are emphasized. Though there are as many male characters in play, women predominate as the centre of interest in most scenes, while the men are – fairly or unfairly – acknowledged to be impediments, set in their ways, resistant to change, to be humoured, managed, helped. Lingering close-ups on the women's faces often open or close a scene, inviting the audience to enter the secret worlds of their thoughts and feelings.

Within these first few episodes the immediacy of these freshly delineated characters is reinforced by the range of issues and experiences concerning them – concerns undoubtedly shared by contemporary audiences. Class mobility is one such, as Frank Barlow asserts 'That lad should learn to live in his own class' and his wife responds 'I'm no martyr, Frank, I just want him to have his chance'. Employment, earnings, marriage and divorce, care of the elderly, the stigma of mental ill-health: all are woven into the dialogue and plot-lines at once. This lively referencing of contemporary concerns, this invitation to 'work through' current social problems, is a far cry from the rather heavy-handed approach of earlier serials such as *The Grove Family*, in which the whole of a 15-minute episode could be transparently didactic – dealing exclusively, as did the 21 March 1956 episode entitled *Prevention and Cure*, with an issue such as home security by means of a plot involving window and door locks, burglars and neighbourliness.

In *Coronation Street*, by contrast, the audience is invited to consider – just as in their daily experience – a multiplicity of issues which, though they might well have far-reaching national consequences, as the expansion of higher education certainly did, are nevertheless understood in terms of their effect on the here and now, within the minutiae of daily life. Frank Barlow's prohibition on his son's date at the Imperial Hotel where his wife works for a mean wage in the kitchen is one example, Ena Sharples' gloom following her employers' discovery of her expressly forbidden visit to 'licensed premises' (the pub) – 'I'll be out of a job, one of my lousy daughters'll 'ave to 'ave me' – is another, referencing the disturbing question of care for the elderly at a time when the conventional extended family seemed to be breaking down.

None of this necessarily makes a claim for *Coronation Street* as a progressive text, though there is plenty of literature which does make such a claim for soaps as a genre. The events depicted in the narrative may or may not assume the subordination or even the inferiority of women, but even when they do the opportunity is still there for female viewers to draw their own conclusions precisely because (a version of) female experience is the subject of the narrative. The absorbing feature of much late 1950s British popular television drama, from *The Grove Family* and *Life with the Lyons* to *Emergency Ward 10* and *Coronation Street*, lies precisely in its invitation to a nationwide renegotiation of the boundaries between work and home, between the public and the private. That this was a renegotiation conducted *on* the figure of the woman, around ideas of the feminine, becomes clear as we consider, once again with the benefit of hindsight, the notoriously paradoxical social attitudes to women in the 1960s. That it was an invitation taken up by many in the female audience is evidenced in the burgeoning 'women's liberation' movement of the later 1960s.

Notes

Grateful thanks to my daughter, Nancy, for her insightful and supportive comments in discussions of various drafts of this essay.

[1.] This is noted, apropos of the American audience, by Spigel, *Make Room for TV* (1992), amongst others. The early tie-ins between 'women's programmes' and women's magazines, in Britain, suggest a similar pattern.

[2.] Spigel (1992:76) notes, apropos of the US context, anxieties expressed about the possible disruption to women's domestic routines that might be caused by excessive television viewing. A similar anxiety is evident in the UK.

[3.] The anxiety is explicitly referenced in the influential 1962 Pilkington Report into broadcasting in Britain (33–35 & 64–65).

[4.] Then, as now, much television criticism in Britain was informed by the Reithian assumption that Public Service Broadcasting should 'inform and educate' while entertaining its audiences.

[5.] Ellis, 'Art, Culture, Quality: Terms for a cinema in the 40s and 70s' in *Screen* 16:1, 1975.

[6.] Streeter and Wahl, 'Audience Theory and Feminism: property, gender, and the television audience' in *Camera Obscura* 33–34 (1994), especially p 249.

[7.] Laura Mulvey, 'Visual Pleasure and Narrative Cinema' in *Screen* 1975, reprinted in *Visual and Other Pleasures* 1989.

8. The conventional opposition of the terms 'popular' and 'quality' in categorizing programming raises significant questions which have been widely addressed in television scholarship, but are outside the scope of the present discussion.

9. Free-standing series such as Kneale and Cartier's 1953 *Quatermass* for the BBC and ABC/Thames' 1966–70 *Mystery and Imagination*, in their avowed intent to broaden the boundaries of television's dramatic possibilities, also come into the 'quality' category for the purposes of this discussion. See Johnson, Wheatley, in this volume.

10. Also known as the Fortnight Rule.

11. *Hansard* for 30/11/55, col. 2362, quoted in Sendall 1982:239.

12. The suspension was agreed for an 'experimental period' of six months, and was confirmed in July 1957 – or rather it was decided to continue it indefinitely.

13. See Wegg-Prosser in this volume.

14. The ITA commissioned studies in 1956, and these showed the percentage of sets in use during one-hour periods between 3.00 and 11.00pm, in summer and winter. Between 5.00 and 6.00pm, 44%/57% sets were in use, and between 7.00 and 8.00pm, 53%/67% sets were in use. Hence the presumption that between 6.00 and 7.00pm at least 50% of the potential market was being lost to advertisers.

15. The licence fee doesn't seem to have been in jeopardy, but this wasn't so clear to the BBC's administration at the time who keenly felt the need to compete in and win the ratings war with commercial broadcasting in order to maintain their right to the license fee which all receiver owning households had to pay.

16. Post Master General: this was a government appointment with responsibility, amongst other things, for licencing the use of the airwaves.

17. The prohibition on Sunday broadcasting before 2.00pm or during the irreverently tagged 'God slot' (6.00–7.00pm) remained in force, however, for another twenty years.

18. According to a 12 June 1959 Granada memo, quoting Neilson figures, there were at that time ten companies between them producing 40 'admags' of 15–20 minutes each, attracting between 14 and 41 percent of the audience for transmissions in mid-morning, late afternoon and late evening. Granada archives box 1447.

19. Vahimagi 1994:65.

20. Some examples are: *Double Your Money* (tx A-R 1955–68); *Gardening Club* (tx BBC 1955–67); *It's Magic* (tx BBC 1955–58); *Take Your Pick* (tx A-R 1955–68); *Picture Parade* (tx BBC 1956–62). Vahimagi 1994, 46–83.

21. Such as programme titles, *Radio Times* and *TV Times* programme notes, contemporary press reviews and viewers letters available in the BBC and ITC archives, as well as Vahimagi's useful summary.

22. *Gunsmoke* (tx ITV 1956–), *The Lone Ranger* (tx BBC 1957–), *Cheyenne* (tx ITV 1958–), *Rawhide* (tx ITV 1959–) and *Bonanza* (tx ITV 1960–).

23. Medicine: *Emergency Ward 10; The Flying Doctor* (ABC 1960–1961). Law: *Boyd QC*. Police: *Dixon of Dock Green; No Hiding Place; Dragnet; Highway Patrol*. Army: *The Army Game*. Probation Service: *Probation Officer* (tx ATV 1959–62). Newspapers: *Deadline Midnight* (tx ATV 1960–61). Airport: *Skyport* (tx Granada 1959–60). Hotel: *The Royalty* (tx BBC 1957–8) starring Margaret and Julia Lockwood.

24. Ellis 2000:74–89. Though Ellis deploys this term in relation to later television than I am discussing I think it a most useful way of conceiving audience activity in relation to the ubiquitous representations available at any given historical moment.

25. *I Love Lucy*, having been shot on film, is relatively easily available – particularly to US viewers of Nick at Nite – while two 1959 episodes of *Emergency Ward 10* are available in 16mm film form at the British National Film Archive.

26. Thumim, 'A Live Commercial for Icing Sugar' in *Screen* 36:1, 1995, 48–55.

[27.] See also further discussions of this issue in Hatch, McCracken and Matthew Murray, in this volume.

[28.] 24 September 1955.

[29.] The ward-sister, for example, is excessively tall, remarkably flat-chested and never smiles.

[30.] 16/03/1960 letter from viewer Huscroft to Noel Stevenson, ITA Programme Administration Officer, in ITC library.

CHAPTER 14

CRACKING OPEN THE SET

TELEVISION REPAIR AND TINKERING WITH GENDER 1949–1955

Lisa Parks

Introduction

S earching for collectibles in a Midwestern antique mall one day I came across a 1955 TV service manual called *Basic Television*. As I flipped through the book, I discovered faint pencilled notes and diagrams scribbled across its pages – the 50-year-old traces of the man behind the manual. (See fig. 14.1) Surprised to find signs of life in this dusty book, I scrutinized the notes a little more closely, thinking I could incorporate them into my research. What became most striking about these traces, however, was the feeling of total incomprehension they evoked in me. In my mind, there was nothing 'basic' about this book's account of television and no matter how hard I tried, I couldn't understand these high-tech doodles because I lacked the technical knowledge to decode them.

I want to use this personal anecdote as a way to begin a discussion about the circulation of technical knowledge about television during the period 1949–1955. By technical knowledge, I am referring to the mechanical and electrical operation as well as the installation and maintenance of the television set. From 1949 to 1955, the consumption of television sets skyrocketed. The number of television sets in American homes grew from 910,000 in 1948 to 37,590,000 by 1955.[1] As consumer demand for television sets increased so too did demand for television repair. Knowing about the technical operation of this new 'dream machine' also meant having the power to please a vast number of people. Television repair was challenging during this early period, however, because technical standards in this rapidly growing industry went

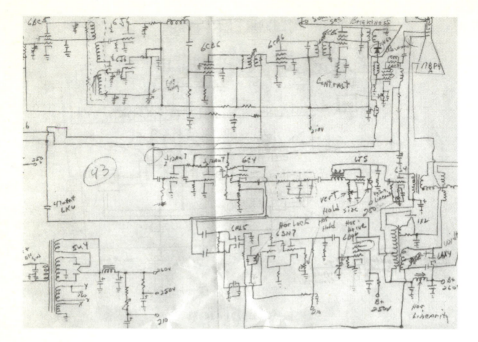

14.1. Drawing found in Basic Television *c1954.*

largely unregulated. Rampant fraud emerged in the manufacturing and service industries from 1949 to 1955 and was only compounded by the fact that other popular media characterized the television set as one of the most complicated machines ever invented. Early television repairmen thus faced many customers who had either purchased faulty sets or were simply mystified by this modern machine.

Television repairmen played a key role in the social circulation of technical knowledge about television during the early 1950s. While more than 37 million television sets were in use in the USA by 1955, there were only 100,000 TV repairmen.[2] This meant that there was a desperate need to expand the public's knowledge of television's basic technical operation. Not only did TV repairmen distribute information about new television technology in how-to books, community workshops, popular magazines and on local television programmes, they also brought their knowledge directly into the home. Often working as an independent, the TV repairman was situated between the industry and the home, relying on manufacturers for information about new television models and on consumers for a livelihood. The TV repairman's constant movement between the public space of the TV shop and the private space of the home, provided women with some, albeit limited, technical knowledge about television at a time when social and cultural discourses discouraged them from acquiring any.

As television historians have shown, popular magazines and advertisements encouraged women to interact with the television set as another piece of furniture or as part of a family circle.[3] Few such discourses ever coached women about adjusting reception, replacing tubes and pulling out the chassis.

Drawing upon television repair trade publications, popular press articles and TV parts advertisements, this article examines the practice of television repair during the early 1950s. The TV repairman's house call defined technical proficiency as something that came from outside the home rather than from within it. This brought with it a series of anxieties related to the control of new television technology. Since most consumers did not possess the knowledge necessary to repair the TV set, there was a degree of bravado surrounding those who did. Most TV servicemen had either worked in the radio field, trained as electronic engineers during the Second World War or dabbled in training and certification programmes offered by manufacturers during the late 1940s and early 1950s. Thus, it was the television repairman who ultimately had the power to make TV become a 'window on the world'. In other words, unless he grounded the electrical wiring of the TV set, installed the antenna on the roof and eliminated interference, there would never be a picture. The labour of the 1950s TV repairman (and technical knowledge of television, more generally) was integral to television's mediation of the public and private spheres, its merging of inside and outside worlds.

Television's merging of public and private spheres was especially meaningful to middle class homemakers during an era of domestic containment. The TV repairman's entrance into the home intensified the levels of desire directed toward the television set. For installing, altering, fixing the TV set carried with it the ability to please and impress those who relied upon it. Mary Beth Haralovich has shown that network television executives and the consumer products industry devised explicit strategies to target female consumers during the 1950s.[4] The TV service industry was no exception. Since TV repairmen usually interacted with homemakers, their customer service practices aimed to appease women. Homemakers' encounters with television repairmen were represented in popular culture as much more than repair sessions. They were often coded as erotic exchanges that occurred around or near the television set. Interestingly, the practice of TV repair became a site of sexual fantasy for homemakers and repairmen alike. In a climate during which television's technical standards were still developing and uncertain, the television repairman overvalued the television set as an object of sexual pleasure in order to displace his anxieties about being unable to fix it. As we shall see, TV repair led to forms of sexual fantasy that could easily be rearticulated as the homemaker's pleasure of watching television and/or the repairman's technological mastery.

TV's Technicalities

Though inventors began designing television components at the turn of the century, the American public knew little about the machine when it appeared in retail outlets in 1948. Popular science magazines characterized the TV set as one of the most elaborate gadgets ever invented, second only to radar and the computer. *Scientific Digest* emphasized the unrivalled 'complexity' of this modern, home-bound machine, announcing that:

> TV is easily the most complex gadget ever to get in the front door. It has all the workings of the radio, plus picture receiver, high-voltage amplifier, special power supply, and an intricate synchronizing hookup . . . There are 800 to 1,000 parts in one set. In the picture tube, an electron beam sweeps across the screen 15,750 times a second at 30,000 miles an hour. No wonder things get out of whack![5]

In 1951 the Franklin Institute in Philadelphia boldly displayed 'the very complex looking interior of a TV receiver' in a transparent plastic cabinet inviting its patrons to see for themselves the puzzling web inside the television set.[6]

Since television's alleged complexity could jeopardize its marketability, manufacturers quickly devised ways to assure consumers that this new machine would function once it arrived in the home. During the early 1950s television dealerships and service shops appeared in metropolitan and suburban neighbourhoods across the country. By 1955, there were 60,000 service shops employing 100,000 technicians.[7] In general, there were three types of service shops: dealerships operated by manufacturers in big cities; small businesses in suburban communities that held certifications from TV set and parts manufacturers; and neighbourhood shops that operated independently. These television service shops became the centres of authority and expertise on television technology in local communities.

TV service shop owners used modern architectural designs and captivating window displays to spotlight their presence and attract customers. During the early 1950s the storefronts of well-worn radio shops were rebuilt and made over with 'ultramodern' display windows that utilized glass and light to reflect the design of television itself. In some cities one could locate a TV shop simply by glancing at the skyline and spotting a thick line of antennas on a rooftop. Such silver sculptures not only marked the location of TV shops – they were, according to one ad executive, gimmicks designed to 'arouse interest in what has given us display material heretofore undreamed of.'[8] One article insisted that when a customer walked by, the storefront window should 'come to life' and suggested that a 'fast flashing lamp somewhere in the window dazzles and cannot be ignored; it is almost hypnotic.'[9] Marketing expert Victor Turner proclaimed 'A TV receiver is in itself an unbeatable display – let it work for you!'[10] Many TV service shop owners did just that: they set out to attract viewers just as television networks and advertisers did.

In addition to creating flashy storefronts and rooftops, TV shops showcased their service departments as well. *Radio and Television Maintenance* recommended keeping a 'brightly illuminated' and 'modern, efficient repair department' in full view of the customer at all times, for 'men working on sets with arrays of impressive test equipment give the customer confidence in the repair work.'[11] In one sense, then, TV shop design replicated the structure of television itself with its eye-catching exterior and its complex mechanisms at work inside. Once the customer entered the store, Turner continued, he should feel as if he has entered a 'television theater' with comfortable chairs and TV programmes constantly running: 'Customers can come in and sit down whenever they wish, stay as long as they desire and are not disturbed by the sales staff while watching programs.'[12]

In these showroom 'living rooms' salesmen performed set demonstrations, explaining the TV's basic operation – how to turn the machine on and off and how to tune and adjust its volume. Rather than revealing components inside the TV set, the demonstrator focused on the buttons on the front of the console making television seem non-threatening and easy to control. An article in *Radio and Television News* advised, 'In presenting the technical features of a receiver, be sure you stress what they mean in terms of enjoyment and performance . . . do not give just a technical explanation of how it works.'[13] TV dealers especially tailored their in-store demonstrations to women, focusing on the front of the console rather than the matter inside it and reproducing the comforts of the home in the show room. Knowledge about television technology was conveyed to women only when they were positioned as consumers. Even then, however, the information focused on the basic use of the set rather than its internal mechanisms. Such encounters encouraged female consumers to appreciate the ease of watching television, rather than learn about its technicalities (see fig. 14.2).[14]

While shop demonstrations helped to allay customers' anxieties about television's complexity, there were a number of opportunities for men in particular to learn about television's operation, particularly since the service industry desperately needed employees. Major manufacturers sponsored community workshops to educate set owners about minor adjustments and repairs and to interest some of them in the TV. General Electric, for example, designed a Television Dynamic Demonstrator that instantly duplicated 30 of the most common television troubles including dimmed, shrunk, rippled and compressed images and distortion common to specific localities. The company produced 30 of these 'Boxes of TV Headaches' and assigned field engineers to travel around the country and work with local TV repairmen to coordinate public workshops about common television troubles.[15] DuMont's Teleset Service Control Department organized 450 television service clinics with local service organizations across the country. The clinics included lectures

14.2. *TV salesmen were encouraged to downplay the technical aspects of the TV set during their sales pitches,* Radio and Television News, *December 1949.*

and discussions of general servicing techniques and specific maintenance programmes.[16] These workshops themselves were televised in Cleveland, where Robert Vreeland explained the operation of the Brach Manufacturing Company's two-set TV coupler on an early morning television programme. The company decided to buy the time because many of the morning viewers in Cleveland were servicemen who were adjusting and installing TV sets, or dealers demonstrating how to use them.[17]

   In addition to community workshops, repairmen published regular columns in popular science magazines with tips on TV repair. *Science Digest, Popular Mechanics, Science and Mechanics* and *Popular Electronics,* for instance, all hired TV repairmen to write articles like, 'What's Inside a TV Doghouse?', 'What You Should Know About Antennas', 'How to Hush Your TV Set' and 'Why Call a TV Serviceman?'. Many of these columns addressed the 'family man' and encouraged him to tinker with his set. For instance, one repairman wrote, 'One notion kicking around is that anyone who isn't an electronic expert should never go near the "doghouse" – that little steel box on the chassis where the high voltage lives. Don't believe it. The doghouse need not be dangerous.'[18] In his book *Handy Man's TV Repair,* Hertzberg provided general guidelines for the man bold enough to crack open the set:

Be satisfied one evening just to unscrew the back and to snoop inside as well as you can without unmounting or even touching anything. Use a table lamp or a flashlight and throw in lots of light, because there's a lot to see. Then replace the cover and wait for some evening when you're alone to make the next step of pulling the chassis. The fewer family 'helpers' around, the less nervous you'll be.[19]

Such suggestions, which acknowledged the embarrassing risk of masculine technical incompetence, authorized the family man to crack open and explore inside the TV set, extending the technical knowledge of television from manufacturers and repairmen to male consumers as well. Popular science columns rarely addressed female readers when discussing the inside of the TV set, consequently positioning it as a hidden domain unsuitable for women's eyes. Cracking open the set, then, was coded as a masculine activity.

Since manufacturing was largely unregulated during the early phases of television's dissemination, consumers purchased a number of troublesome sets. In 1951 a Better Business Bureau survey reported, 'Of the approximately 12,000,000 television sets . . . in use, at least 4,000,000 were defective when received by the dealers.'[20] Most of these sets were sold anyway. During this early period TV repairmen were extremely busy. Less than 100,000 repairmen faced the task of fixing more than 4 million defective sets. In addition, TV sets that were not defective brought their own challenges. Not only were they heavy and cumbersome, they required electrical grounding and antenna installation in order to function properly. One repairman highlighted the hazards of his trade warning, 'TV installation and repair are not jobs for the layman . . . A man and his wife were killed recently trying to install an antenna.'[21] Because of the challenges and risks associated with installation and repair, there emerged a certain heroism in being able to get a clear picture on the screen.

During the early 1950s the TV repairman became something of a public figure, appearing on magazine covers, neighbourhood billboards and television shows. This heroism only escalated as viewer interest in TV programming intensified. Images in the popular press featured TV repairmen dangling from rooftops and towers while installing antennas, working in webs of electrical wiring and safely removing television sets from flooded homes in Kansas City.[22] *Time* placed the repairman on its cover insisting he occupies a 'special niche in American folklore' somewhere between 'the river-boat card-sharp and the village idiot, part free-booting buccaneer and part plain boob.'[23] Raytheon ran a high-profile ad campaign in *Life* magazine featuring a TV repairman-cowboy riding a bucking TV set with the caption 'It takes a heap of Know-How to ride a herd of 36,000,000 TV sets.'[24] TV repairmen made cameo appearances in the Hollywood film *All that Heaven Allows* and in the TV anthology drama *The Grass is Greener*.

In some popular representations the TV repairman is figured as a gallant knight, coming to the rescue of a housewife in distress. One 1951 article, entitled 'Formula For TV Success', features a cartoon knight in shining armour, complete with repair kit and helmet-mounted aerial antenna. But as the house-wife eagerly awaits his help, he clutches his shield, protecting himself from her gaze and the equipment in her home. We learn from the TV repairman, 'Frankly, I was scared of the picture tubes!'[25] This cartoon image encapsulates the growing anxiety surrounding the practice of TV repair. The TV repairman not only had to fix faulty sets, he had to do so in the limelight of public scrutiny.

Just as public discourses began to recognize the TV repairman as a hero of the post-war era, fraud in the industry was also acknowledged. In 1951 President of the Better Business Bureau Victor Nyborg announced, 'Because of its bewildering complications, television has become one of the lushest fields for racketeers.'[26] By 1951 thousands of set owners had complained to Better Business Bureaus around the country about contractors who failed to fulfil obligations and had either gone bankrupt, given inadequate service or maliciously left town with collected fees.[27] According to *Consumer Reports*, the St. Louis Better Business Bureau 'received a steady stream of visits, telephone calls and letters from people whose experiences made them suspicious of some of the rapidly expanding television service companies in St. Louis.'[28] San Francisco's Bureau received over 100 complaints per month from consumers who complained that dealers had sold second-hand television sets as new, advertised low-priced sets which didn't exist, failed to fulfil service contracts and failed to provide contest winners with prizes.[29] Such reports threatened to undermine the credibility of the TV repairman and ruptured the public's trust in his trade, especially since this so often involved activity inside the home. *American Home* warned its readers to 'investigate your serviceman', claiming that 'hundreds of unscrupulous servicemen have set up businesses, charging exorbitant fees by exploiting the average person's ignorance about television.'[30]

During the early 1950s, then, the TV repairman was figured on the one hand as a technical expert who circulated knowledge of new television technology and on the other hand as a 'gyp' who exploited consumers' unfamiliarity with TV in order to make a quick buck. Many competent and honest repairmen were embarrassed and disgusted by the wave of service fraud. They felt trapped between irresponsible manufacturers and an uninformed public. An editorial in *Radio and Television Maintenance* complained, 'defaulting service contractors have given the service industry a black eye with its customers.'[31] To soothe this black eye, repairmen organized trade unions and filed grievances against manufacturers, charging that sets were 'poorly made, falsely advertised, carelessly shipped, remodeled too frequently, and inadequately guaranteed.' Trying to redeem the profession, one serviceman directly addressed the consumer, stating that:

Regardless of the impression you may have gained from reading the newspapers, all service men are not gyps. Admittedly, a lot of sharp and shady characters were attracted to the business . . . but they were always in the minority and are now disappearing rapidly . . . Your best bet is a neighborhood man, because he has to be fair and honest with his customers to keep the neighborhood business.[32]

Being a 'neighborhood man' involved making frequent house calls and building a reputation based on successful repairs in clients' homes.

Thus while TV repairmen were celebrated for their ability to wrestle with TV's complexity, they were also subject to increasing public scrutiny. Gravely concerned about the impact of TV service fraud upon their livelihoods, repairmen worked to cultivate stronger customer relations, particularly with homemakers. TV service trade publications, repair manuals and advertising campaigns began to focus more and more on encounters with female clients. Trade discourses coached repairmen about such issues as proper dress and behaviour, polite language and legitimate billing practices. In short, repairmen became increasingly aware of the scrutinizing and sometimes inquisitive gaze of their female clients.

Television Monitoring

Both TV repairmen and parts manufacturers had a vested interest in restoring and maintaining the integrity of the TV service profession. Television service manuals, trade publications and TV parts advertisements revealed a growing emphasis on repairmen's encounters with homemakers (see fig. 14.3). By 1953 TV repairmen established an informal code of conduct for contact with female clients. Chicago's Central Television Service published the *TV Technicians Handbook on Customer Relations* and sold 15,000 copies at $1 each. According to a *Time* review, the book 'assumes that repairmen normally meet housewives on their visits and urges them to dress neatly, be cheerful and courteous, avoid body odor, wipe their shoes, show friendly interest in the customer (e.g., "This is a beautiful rug.") and always give the appearance of knowing what you're doing'.[33] The book also provided repairmen with a number of solutions for hypothetical house call scenarios. For example, 'Problem: You call at the house and find the customer in negligee. Solution: . . . do not enter the house.' Or, 'Customer is drinking and invites you to have one with her. Solution: Under no circumstances should you accept such an invitation . . . If you are in a house where the customer has been drinking, size her up and see how much she has had. If you think she has had too much, take a quick glance at the set and then get out of there in a hurry.'[34] Such suggestions anticipated the sexual advances that might unfold around a disassembled set.

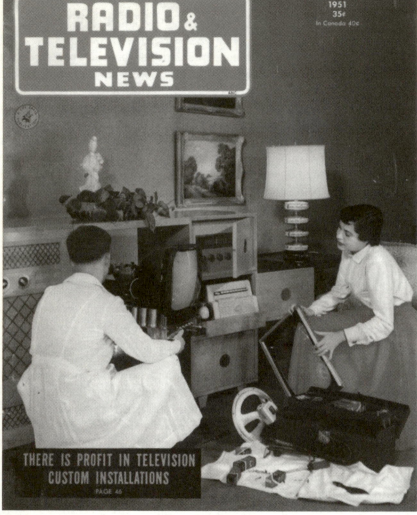

14.3. *Cover of* Radio and Television News *featuring repairman and homemaker, January 1951.*

Interestingly, they also imagine the homemaker as more interested in the repairman than in television's technicalities.

John Frye, a repairman who wrote a regular column for *Radio and Television Maintenance*, emphasized the importance of cleanliness, claiming:

> Television service requires that you meet the customer on his own stomping ground, his home; and there you will be under the critical surveillance of his Little Woman. For some reason or other, women, whose perceptive faculties and renowned

intuition give them such a disturbing penetrating insight into many matters, are absolutely no good at recognizing a diamond in the rough . . . Yes, it is almost as hard for a woman to realize that a carelessly-dressed man can be a good technician as it is for a man to grasp that a homely girl can have a charming personality.[35]

After Frye emphasized the importance of the repairman's appearance, he went on to suggest that service bills would be more legitimate in the eyes of the 'lady of the house' if the serviceman's overalls and tools were dirty at the end of the job. Frye insisted, 'The lady of the house is usually very laundry-bill conscious and when she sees how soiled your overalls become while installing her TV antenna or making adjustments on it she will receive your bill in a much more sympathetic frame of mind.'[36] Many television repairmen were self-conscious in the homemaker's presence. This obsession with her scrutiny was manifest not only in manuals and trade press, but in TV set and parts advertisements as well.

I want to describe these encounters between television repairmen and female consumers as the practice of television monitoring – an exchange of looks ricocheting around the TV set during the act of TV repair. Television monitoring is defined both by the gaze of the TV repairman who strives to produce clear reception on the screen and by the gaze of the female consumer who scrutinizes his labour in her home. These looks not only reflect a gendered division of labour, they are part of television's social and economic history. The practice of television monitoring – that is, the impulse to scrutinize the act of TV repair – is also directly related to defective TV set manufacturing and extensive service fraud during the early 1950s. The TV repairman's struggle to control TV technology went on as curious homemakers oversaw his labour on behalf of a concerned public at large. As trade and advertising discourses of the period suggest, the TV monitor was defined not as an inert box, but rather as a set of gendered, social and economic relations that unfolded around it.

Many TV parts manufacturers developed ad campaigns to assuage repairmen's concerns about the overly scrutinizing homemaker. A Raytheon ad campaign for TV replacement tubes highlights the questionable credibility of repairmen in light of television service fraud. The ad republished an editorial from the women's magazine *Pageant* entitled 'Beware the TV Gyps', which warned its readers about the antics of shady TV repairmen. In reprinting this editorial, the ad forces the repairman to recognize the powerful gaze of the female consumer, but at the same time, it represents her as an object of visual pleasure. She appears in a strapless evening gown looking in direct address at an implied TV repairman reader. Thus while the ad's print privileges the power of female consumer, its visuals position her as an object of sexual desire. The only way for the repairman to increase her confidence in his work, the ad insists, is to acquire a bond endorsement from Raytheon's electronic technician's programme.[37]

Other manufacturers also used endorsements from women's magazines to guarantee parts and service. A CBS tube ad addressed to repairmen, for

A serviceman's *"best friend"* is an RCA Tube

An RCA Tube starts working for you from the instant the customer first sees the familiar red, black, and white carton. You have her confidence from the start, because she knows and respects the RCA trademark.

But the big payoff to you begins when the tube goes to work. For, experience has proven that the superior quality of RCA Receiving Tubes and Kinescopes is your best measure of protection against premature tube failures. With RCA Tubes, you can be sure the job is well done.

Helping you to safeguard your reputation is a vital, everyday service of RCA Tubes. And that protection is yours at no extra cost.

UNLOCK THE DOOR TO BIGGER PROFITS

Here's *your* key to better business... RCA's dynamic Dealer Identification Program. Ask your **RCA Tube Distributor** for your copy of the colorful, 16-page booklet "A Magic Pass-Key to Customer Confidence." It tells you how you can become a Registered Dealer... and get *extra* sales benefits.

RADIO CORPORATION of AMERICA
ELECTRON TUBES   HARRISON, N.J.

14.4. Advertisement for RCA Picture Tube, November 1953.

instance, features a homemaker kneeling on the floor looking in awe at a bow-tied repairman handling a CBS picture tube. The copy begins with a hypothetical conversation between the two:

She: But, how do I know this is a good tube?

You: Because, this is a CBS aluminized Mirror-Back picture tube. There aren't any better.

She: And I see it has the *Good Housekeeping* Guaranty Seal, too. That's proof enough for me.

14.5. *Advertisement for Walsco antenna, May 1954.*

The copy then proclaims, '*Customer confidence* really counts when it comes to the big tube . . . For CBS tubes have the Good Housekeeping Guaranty Seal and are nationally advertised to 76.9% of your customers . . . the women of America. And 53% of these women are influenced in their purchases by that seal of approval.'[38] An ad for RCA tubes similarly capitalizes upon the

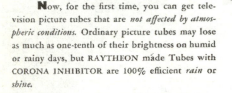

Right for Sight!°

Announcing
CORONA INHIBITOR

Now, for the first time, you can get television picture tubes that are *not affected by atmospheric conditions.* Ordinary picture tubes may lose as much as one-tenth of their brightness on humid or rainy days, but RAYTHEON máde Tubes with CORONA INHIBITOR are 100% efficient *rain* or *shine.*

This amazing new weather-proofing is so effective, that even when tested with a water spray on the high voltage contact, RAYTHEON Tubes with the CORONA INHIBITOR showed *no loss of brightness* due to arcing around the high-voltage connection.

Ask your RAYTHEON Tube Distributor for Raytheon Picture Tubes with CORONA INHIBITOR. Your customers will like them . . . and so will you.

the new RAYTHEON

development that keeps

TELEVISION

PICTURE TUBES

at peak performance

Rain or Shine

RAYTHEON
Excellence in Electronics

RAYTHEON MANUFACTURING COMPANY
Receiving Tube Division
Newton, Mass., Chicago, Ill., Atlanta, Ga., Los Angeles, Calif.
RADIO AND TELEVISION RECEIVING TUBES, PICTURE TUBES, SPECIAL PURPOSE TUBES, SUBMINIATURE TUBES, MICROWAVE TUBES

December, 1951   17

14.6. *Advertisement for Raytheon's Corona Inhibitor Picture Tube, December 1951.*

repairman's growing need for his female client's confidence. Copy, which reads, 'A serviceman's "best friend" is an RCA Tube', appears next to an apron-wearing homemaker who smiles adoringly at a serviceman as he leans into his toolbox to pull out an RCA replacement tube. The ad's fine print

14.7. *Cartoon from* Radio and Television Maintenance, *1951.*

14.8. *Cartoon from* Radio and Television Maintenance, *1951.*

"—n press this for close-ups."

14.9. Cartoon from Radio and Television Maintenance, *December 1951.*

encourages repairmen to 'unlock the door to bigger profits' by becoming registered RCA dealers (see fig. 14.4). These ads suggested it was the pleasure of the homemaker that was ultimately at stake in repairing the television set.

In the aftermath of TV service fraud, television repairmen were positioned as a class of independent labourers deemed ineffective unless they affiliated with established institutions. In these ads, the television repairman's effectiveness is contingent upon his endorsement by women's magazines and/or certified parts manufacturers. Many TV parts ads represented the TV repairman as enmeshed with the television set, fragmented and absorbed by the apparatus. In other words, the TV repairman was incomplete without the proper parts, alienated from his own labour and forced to assume a brand name in order to become a viable commodity himself. In an effort to recover control over his own labour and maintain authority over TV technology, the repairman often imagined the act of TV repair as a sexual act. This conflation of TV repair with sexual conquest allowed him to suppress the emasculating possibility that he might fail to repair the set, shifting his attention away from the TV set and toward an imagined woman for whom he was performing.

In some cases, the TV repairman's desire for his female client's stamp of approval is made sexually explicit. An ad for Walsco antennas, for instance, shows a television repairman whose face has been covered in lip prints after he has properly installed his female client's antenna. The repairman appears upside down as his sexy customer moves to plant another kiss on his cheek. The copy proclaims '. . . and all I did was install a Walsco antenna'[39] (see fig 14.5). Here, female sexual aggression is figured as the end result of successful antenna installation and the use of Walsco brand products. This ad not only reveals that manufacturers drew upon female sexuality to sell parts to repairmen, it also suggests that the work of TV repair was laced with sexual fantasy.

While the ads discussed thus far reveal the television repairman's awareness of and in some cases desire for, the monitoring female gaze, others use the feminine body to promote television parts. In doing so, they blend the practice of fixing the set with heterosexual gazing. Ads often featured television repairmen working on sets and magically generating TV pictures of attractive women. General Electric tube dealers ran full-page advertisements in *Life* and *Saturday Evening Post* presenting 'eye-opening proof' of the GE tube's function: a close-up of a pretty woman's face appears in the monitor as a repairman tunes the set in front of a young boy.[40] Raytheon's ad for the Corona inhibitor – the all-weather tube which worked in rain or shine – shows a young woman's smiling face in a television monitor with its backside cracked open. The phrase 'right for sight' implies that only the repairman's magic touch could make such a pretty face appear[41] (see fig 14.6).

Such representations linked the labour of television repair directly to the practice of heterosexual gazing. A properly installed tube, use of a certain brand name or an ambitious experiment promised to generate images of attractive women. These representations suggested that television repair was as much about sexual fantasy as it was about clear reception. This odd blending of work and desire was most clearly elaborated in a cartoon strip published in the trade magazine *Radio and Television Maintenance* entitled 'The Maintenance Mill'. These cartoons often represented the female consumer as a fetishized sex object in portrayals of her body. One cartoon featured the outline of a buxom female body emerging from a home's rooftop antenna with two repairmen gazing up at her and saying, 'It's not cut to wavelength, but it sure picks up the signals!' (see fig 14.7). Another shows a repairman in a bar, presumably after work, gazing at a portrait of a naked woman on the wall and blurting, 'Wow – whatta screen!' (see fig 14.8). Finally, another features a TV serviceman demonstrating a special function for a male viewer. As he explains, 'Press this for close-ups', a woman's face bursts through the screen and plants a kiss on the viewer's lips[42] (see fig 14.9).

In order perhaps to compensate for the repairman's potential loss of power in the feminized space of the home, where he was under the scrutiny of the female consumer on her own turf, such comedic discourses fetishized her body, overvaluing and rearticulating her power as purely sexual. This discursive transformation is a means of obviating the threatening possibility that woman in a potentially powerful position as consumer (and sexual agent) might witness a failure of masculine technical knowledge. Like the man of the house, who was warned not to attempt any repairs while under the gaze of curious feminine eyes, the repairman was faced with the emasculating possibility of technical (and, by implication, sexual) failure. These comedic representations, then, reassert the repairman's technical prowess by articulating it as transgressive sexual potency.

Tinkering and Transformation

In an era of domestic containment and in the context of highly publicized TV service fraud, the repairman's foray into the home was fraught with a series of tensions that threatened to undermine gendered power dynamics in the household.[43] First, when the repairman brought his technical expertise into the home, he challenged the authority of the family patriarch exposing his limited control over television technology. Second, the repairman often performed repairs while husbands were away, creating opportunities for unseen interactions between married women and TV repairmen. Finally, by bringing technical knowledge into the domestic sphere, the TV repairman generated the potential for female consumers to engage with the more complex aspects of television on their own terms. Whereas the circulation of technical knowledge about television in the public sphere largely excluded women, the repairman's 'house call' was one interaction that gave women at least partial access to this otherwise carefully guarded, masculinized knowledge.

Although 1950s culture discouraged women from acquiring technical knowledge of television, women did, of course, tinker with their sets. Some of this tinkering likely led to productive moments of self-discovery and empowerment for women. Consider, for instance, an episode of I Love Lucy entitled 'Lucy Does a TV Commercial'. In a scheme to convince Ricky of her dynamic TV personality, Lucy disembowels her TV set only to place her own body inside. Fred, playing along with her joke, sits on the couch with Ricky to watch a sporting event on television. When they turn on the set, Lucy pops up inside the television set, literally becoming the monitor. Notably, it is Lucy's decision to crack open the set and yank out the chassis that enables her transformation from homemaker to entertainer. During her canned performance, she bursts through the screen, reminding Fred and Ricky that not only is she the object of their gaze, she is watching them too. By 'breaking frame', Lucy moves herself beyond the domestic sphere and into the social space of television itself. But her clever manipulation of TV technology carries with it certain repercussions. Each time Lucy insists upon her place inside the set, she is jolted by its electrical current. The set finally explodes in a big blast and Lucy is forced to return to her living room where she embarrassingly displays the mangled TV parts she extracted. Ultimately, the scene suggests that women have no place inside television whether on a studio stage or inside the set.

Despite the typical closure in which Lucy is returned to her properly subservient position, the skit does suggest that the reconfiguration of the television set might lead to the reconfiguration of women's lives. Perhaps this brings me back, then, to my initial concern about my inability to discern the dusty diagram in that old TV repair manual. If women were discouraged from controlling television's technicalities we can assume that their power to transform, reconfigure, tinker, adjust or modify has been limited as well. These are powerful modes of acting in the world and they extend beyond the confines of the television set. During the early 1950s female consumers monitored repairmen working in their homes, but their gaze was carefully averted from television's electronic guts. Instead, women watched from a fringe area as men manipulated television's interior, awaiting spectacular changes on the screen. Cartoon strips went so far as to suggest that these TV adjustments could be registered on the feminine body as a set of special effects for the knowing eyes of TV practitioners. To be sure, meddling inside the television set also involved intervening in gendered power relations and generating social transformation.

Since technical knowledge about television circulated in masculinized spaces, it became the property of men. Women were discouraged from learning about the technical operation of the set, which was ironic given that women largely controlled the TV within the confines of the home. But while women's magazines told readers about where and how to place the TV within the home, rarely, if ever, did they instruct women how to unscrew the back of the set and pull out the chassis. Women were denied access to technical knowledge about television in the public sphere, in part because that masculinized knowledge was itself still frail and potentially contested.

Now, in case you're wondering about those doodles discussed in the introduction, I managed to decode them. They're Paul Reis' Electronics III final exam on which he squeaked by with an A. Paul forgot to include a key capacitor on his vertical hold circuit and reversed the polarity of a sound amplification resistor. This artefact has allowed me, like the homemakers of the 1950s who watched repairmen attempt to master the most complex machine ever to enter the front door, to peer inside the set not just to marvel at its architecture but to explore its place in social history. By cracking open the set, we see television as much more than a boxed up tube: we discover the dynamic socio-economic patterns that have always intersected with its electrical currents.

Notes

I would like to thank Michael Kackman, Michele Hilmes, Janet Thumim and Lynn Spigel for their helpful comments on earlier versions of this chapter. A slightly different version was published in the journal *Television and New Media* vol. 1, no. 3, August 2000, 257–278.

1. Harry Hansen (ed.), *The World Almanac Book of Facts for 1956* (New York: New York World Telegram Corporation, 1956) 790.
2. Ibid. 791.
3. Lynn Spigel, *Make Room For TV* (1992); also see Cecilia Tichi, *Electronic Hearth: Creating an American Television Culture* (1992).
4. Mary Beth Haralovich, 'From Sitcoms to Suburbs' in Spigel and Mann (eds), *Private Screenings* (1992).
5. 'Don't Get Gypped on TV Repairs', *Scientific Digest*, December 1952, 17–18.
6. 'TV Puzzles Children – and Experts Too Sometimes', *Radio Electronics*, October 1951, p. 20.
7. Harry Hansen (ed.), *The World Almanac Book of Facts for 1956* (New York: New York World Telegram Corporation, 1956) 791.
8. A. Edelman, 'The Electric Eye in Advertising', *Radio and Television News*, May 1949, 49.
9. Ibid.
10. Victor Turner, 'How to Display Products More Effectively', *Radio Maintenance*, July 1949, 24.
11. Ibid.
12. Ibid.
13. Carle Christensen, 'Don't Sell "Nuts and Bolts" ', *Radio and Television News*, December 1949, 40.
14. This has led to a long history of women's anxious relation to television and VCR technologies alike. For a detailed and interesting discussion of these issues see Anne Gray, *Video Playtime: The Gendering of a Leisure Technology* (1992).
15. 'G-E Starts "TV Troubles" Demonstrations Nationwide', *Radio and Television Maintenance*, December 1951, 95.
16. '450 Clinics Listed by DuMont Service', *Radio and Television Maintenance*, April 1951, 5.
17. 'TV Program Used For Technical Talk', *Radio and Television Maintenance*, November 1951, 78.
18. Robert Hertzberg, 'Why Call a TV Serviceman?', *Popular Science*, October 1951, 218.
19. Robert Hertzberg, *Handy Man's TV REPAIR and Maintenance* (New York: Fawcett Books, 1955) 17.
20. 'Dealers Hit Manufacturers at Conference', *Radio and Television Maintenance*, July 1951, 5.
21. 'The Loudspeaker Column', *Radio and Television Maintenance*, July 1950, 27.
22. 'In the Flood's Wake', *Radio and Television Maintenance*, September 1951, 74.
23. 'Modern Living: Out of Order', *Time*, October 14, 1957, 102.
24. Ad in *Life*, circa 1955.
25. John D. Burke, 'Formula for TV Success', *Radio Electronics*, December 1951, 42–3.
26. Victor H. Nyborg, 'Quacks of the Electronic Age', *American Magazine*, March 1951, 42.
27. 'TV Racket in San Francisco Hit', *Radio and Television Maintenance*, September 1951, 4.
28. 'TV Service Fraud', *Consumer Reports*, February 1952, 82.

29. 'TV Racket in San Francisco Hit', *Radio and Television Maintenance*, September 1951, 4.

30. John L. Springer, 'How to Care For Your TV Set', *American Home*, June 1953, 87–8.

31. 'Guarantee Your TV Service Contracts!', *Radio and Television Maintenance*, January 1951, 22.

32. Hertzberg, *Handy Man's TV REPAIR and Maintenance* (New York: Fawcett Books, 1955) 11.

33. Quoted in 'Honor Bright', *Time*, October 5, 1953, 85.

34. Ibid.

35. John T. Frye, 'Over the Bench', *Radio Maintenance*, June 1949, 26.

36. Ibid.

37. Raytheon Ad, *Radio Electronics*, March 1951, 6.

38. CBS advertisement, *Radio and Television News*, November 1955, 13.

39. Walsco Ad, *Radio and Television News*, June 1954, 33.

40. General Electric Ad, *Radio and Television News*, December 1951, 2–21.

41. Raytheon Corona Inhibitor Ad, *Radio and Television News*, December 1951, 17.

42. Cartoon in *Radio Electronics*, March 1949, 82.

43. For a discussion of the concept of domestic containment see Elaine Tyler-May, *Homeward Bound: American Families in the Cold War Era* (1988, reprinted 1999).

BIBLIOGRAPHY

ABC Television Ltd (1959) *The Armchair Theatre: How to Write, Design, Direct, Act and Enjoy Television Plays* (London: Weidenfield and Nicholson)

ABC Television Ltd, (unpublished document in support of its application for appointment as Programme Contractor, April 1967) *ABC Television and its Programmes 1956–1967*

Abercrombie, Nicholas, and Brian Longhurst (1998) *Audiences: A Sociological Theory of Performance and Imagination* (London: Sage Publications)

Adair, Karen (1988) *The Great Clowns of American Television* (Jefferson, NC: McFarland & Co.)

Adamthwaite, A. (1993) '"Nation shall speak peace unto nation" the BBC's response to Peace and Defence Issues, 1945–58' in *Contemporary Record: The Journal of Contemporary British History* Vol. 7, no. 3, 557–577.

Allen, Robert C. (1985) *Speaking of Soap Operas* (Chapel Hill: University of North Carolina Press)

Anderson, Christopher (1994) *Hollywood TV: The Studio System in the 1950s* (Austin, Texas: University of Texas Press)

Ang, Ien (1985) *Watching Dallas: Soap Opera and the Melodramatic Imagination*. Trans. Della Couling (London: Methuen)

Ang, Ien (1991) *Desperately Seeking the Audience* (London and New York: Routledge)

Angrist, Shirley et al. (1968) *Women After Treatment: A Study of Former Mental Patients and Their Normal Neighbors* (New York: Appleton-Century-Crofts)

Baehr, H. and A. Gray (eds) (1996) *Turning It On: A Reader in Women and Media* (London: Arnold)

Barnett, S. and Seymour, E. (1999) *A Shrinking Iceberg Travelling South . . . Changing Trends in British Television: A case study of drama and current affairs* (London: Campaign for Quality Television)

Barnouw, Erik (1978) *The Sponsor: Notes on a Modern Potentate* (New York: Oxford University Press)

Barnouw, Erik (1990) *Tube of Plenty: The Evolution of American Television*. 2nd Ed. (Oxford: Oxford University Press)

Barr, Charles (ed.) (1986) *All Our Yesterdays: 90 Years of British Cinema* (London: BFI)

Barr, Charles (1986a) 'Broadcasting and Cinema 2: Screens Within Screens', in Barr (ed.) 1986, 206–224

Bartky, Sandra (1990) *Femininity and Domination: Studies in the Phenomenology of Domination* (London and New York: Routledge)

BBC (1959) *The Public and the Programmes: A Report on an Audience Research Enquiry* (London: BBC)

Belfrage, Sally (1994) *Un-American Activities: A Memoir of the Fifties* (New York: HarperCollins)

Benjamin, Walter (1968) *Illuminations*. Trans. Harry Zohn (New York: Schocken)

Bergman, David (ed.) (1993) *Camp Grounds: Style and Homosexuality* (Amherst, MA: University of Massachussetts)

Biskind, Peter (1983) *Seeing is Believing: How Hollywood Taught Us to Stop Worrying and Love the Fifties* (New York: Pantheon Books)

Blythe, Cheryl and Susan Sackett (1986) *Say Goodnight, Gracie: The Story of Burns and Allen* (New York: E.P. Dutton)

Boddy, William (1987) 'Operation Frontal Lobes versus the Living Room Toy: The battle over programme control in early television' in *Media, Culture and Society* 9, 347–368.

Boddy, William (1990) *Fifties Television: The Industry and Its Critics* (Urbana: University of Illinois Press)

Bourdieu, Pierre (1984) *Distinction: A Social Critique of the Judgement of Taste* (Cambridge, MA: Harvard University Press)

Boyarin, Daniel (1997) *Unheroic Conduct: The Rise of Heterosexuality and the Invention of the Jewish Man* (Berkeley: University of California Press)

Brandt, George W. (ed.) (1980) *British Television Drama* (Cambridge: CUP)

Breines, Wini (1992) *Young, White, and Miserable: Growing Up Female in the Fifties* (Boston: Beacon Press)

Briggs, A. (1979) *The History of Broadcasting in the United Kingdom, Volume IV: Sound and Vision* (Oxford: Oxford University Press)

Briggs, A (1979a) 'The End of the Monopoly' in Buscombe, E. (ed.) (2000) *British Television: A Reader* (Oxford: Oxford University Press) 63–91

Briggs, A. (1995) *The History of Broadcasting in the United Kingdom, Vol V: Competition 1955–1974* (Oxford: Oxford University Press)

Broadcast (unnamed writer) (1975) '1000th edition of THIS WEEK' in *Thirty Years of Broadcast*, 8 December 1975, 16–17

Brooks, Tim & Earle Marsh (1988) *The Complete Directory of Prime Time Network TV Shows 1946–Present* (New York: Ballantine)

Brosnan, John (1978) *Future Tense: The Cinema of Science Fiction* (London: Macdonald and Jane's)

Browne, Nick (1987) 'The Political Economy of the Television Super-Text' in *Television: The Critical View*, ed. Horace Newcomb. 4th ed. (Oxford: Oxford University Press)

Burns, George (1988) *Gracie: A Love Story* (New York: G.P. Putnam's Sons)

Burns, George with Cynthia Hobart Lindsay (1955) *I Love Her, That's Why* (New York: Simon and Schuster)

Butler, Judith (1990) *Gender Trouble: Feminism and the Subversion of Identity* (New York: Routledge)

Butler, Judith (1993) *Bodies That Matter: On the Discursive Limits of 'Sex'* (New York: Routledge)

Butler, Judith and Joan Scott (eds) (1992) *Feminists Theorize the Political* (New York: Routledge)

Caldwell, John Thornton (1995) *Televisuality: Style, Crisis and Authority in American Television* (New Brunswick, NJ: Rutgers University Press)

Carlton-Greene, Hugh (1969) *The Third Floor Front: A View of Broadcasting in the Sixties* (London: Bodley Head)

Carr, E.H. (1964) *What is History* (London: Penguin Books)

Cartier, Rudolph (1958) 'A Foot in Both Camps' in *Films and Filming*, September 1958, 10, 31.

Cassiday, Bruce (1979) *Dinah! An Intimate Biography* (New York: Berkeley Books)

Caughie, John (2000) *Television Drama: Realism, Modernism, and British Culture* (Oxford: Oxford University Press)

Celebration Chronicles (1999) *Life, Liberty & the Pursuit of Property Values in Disney's New Town* (New York: Bantam)

Chafe, William (1986) *The Unfinished Journey: America Since World War II* (New York: Oxford University Press)

Chesler, Phyllis (1972) *Women and Madness* (New York: Avon Books)

Chisholm, Brad (1990) 'Red, Blue, and Lots of Green: The Impact of Color Television on Feature Film Production' in Tino Balio (ed.) *Hollywood in the Age of Television* (Boston: Unwin Hyman)

Clements, Cynthia and Sandra Weber (1996) *George Burns and Gracie Allen, a Bio-Bibliography* (Westport, CT: Greenwood Press)

Code, Lorraine (1991) *What Can She Know: Feminist Theory and the Construction of Knowledge* (Ithaca and London: Cornell University Press)

Coontz, Stephanie (1992) *The Way We Never Were: American Familes and the Nostalgia Trap* (New York: Basic Books)

Coopey, R. et al (eds) (1993) *The Wilson Governments, 1964–1970* (London: Pinter)

Corner, J. (1999) *Critical Ideas in Television Studies* (Oxford: Clarendon Press).

Courtney-Browne, R. (1975) *An Account of the History of* This Week unpublished paper prepared to commemorate the 1000th edition of *This Week*, c/o Victoria Wegg-Prosser

Cox, G. (1983) *See it happen: The making of ITN* (London: The Bodley Head)

Crisell, A.(1997) *An Introductory History of British Broadcasting* (London: Routledge)

D'Acci, Julie (1994) *Defining Women: Television and the Case of Cagney and Lacey* (Chapel Hill, NC: University of North Carolina)

DeCerteau, Michel (1988) *The Writing of History*. Trans. Tom Conley. (New York: Columbia University Press)

DeCordova, Richard (1991) *Picture Personalities: The Emergence of the Star System in America* (Urbana: University of Illinois Press)

D'Emilio, John and Freedman, Estelle (1988) *Intimate Matters: A History of Sexuality in America* (New York: Harper & Row)

Desjardins, Mary (2001 forthcoming) 'Systematizing Scandal: Confidential Magazine, Stardom, and the the State of California' in Adrienne L. McLean and David Cook (eds.) *Headline Hollywood: A Century of Film Scandal* (New Brunswick, New Jersey: Rutgers University Press)

Dienst, Richard (1994) *Still Life In Real Time: Theory After Television* (Durham, NC: Duke University Press)

Dieter-Rath, Klaus (1989) 'Live Television and its Audiences: Challenges of Media Reality' in Seiter et al (eds) (1989)

Doane, Mary Ann (1990) 'Information, Crisis, Catastrophe' in Mellencamp (ed.) (1990)

Dyer, Richard (1979) *Stars* (London: British Film Institute)

Dyer, Richard (1986) *Heavenly Bodies: Film Stars and Society* (New York: St Martin's Press)

Dyer, Richard (1991) 'A Star is Born and the Construction of Authenticity' in *Stardom: Industry of Desire*, Christine Gledhill.(ed.) (New York: Routledge) 132–140

Dyer, Richard (1997) *White* (London: Routledge)

Ehrenreich, Barbara and Deidre English (1978) *For Their Own Good: 150 Years Of Experts' Advice to Women* (New York: Anchor Books)

Eisler, Benita (1986) *Private Lives: Men and Women of the Fifties* (New York: Franklin Watts)

Ellis, John (1982) *Visible Fictions: Cinema: Television: Video* (London: Routledge & Kegan Paul)

Ellis, John (2000) *Seeing Things: Television in the Age of Uncertainty* (London: I.B.Tauris)

Elstein, D. (1999) 'The Political Structure of Broadcasting, 1949–99: Beveridge' (unpublished University of Oxford Lectures, text c/o Victoria Wegg-Prosser)

Ewen, Stuart and Elizabeth Ewen (1982) *Channels of Desire: Mass Images and the Shaping of American Consciousness* (New York: McGraw-Hill)

Fawcett, Adrienne Ward (1995) 'The 50 Best' in *Advertising Age* special edition: '50 Years of TV Advertising' Spring 1995, 36

Feuer, Jane (1983) 'The Concept of Live Television: Ontology as Ideology' in E. Ann Kaplan (ed.) *Regarding Television* (Frederick, Md: University Publications of America)

Feuer, Jane (1984) 'The MTM Style' in Feuer, Paul Kerr and Tise Vahimagi (eds) *MTM: Quality Television* (London: British Film Institute)

Fiske, John (1987) *Television Culture* (London: Methuen)

Foucault, Michel (1967) *Madness and Civilization* (New York: Vintage Books)

Foucault, Michel (1978) *The History of Sexuality: Volume One* (New York: Random House)

Foucault, Michel (1979) *Discipline and Punish: The Birth of the Prison* (New York: Vintage Books)

Frankenberg, Ruth (1993) *The Social Construction of Whiteness: White Women, Race Matters* (Minneapolis: University of Minnesota Press)

Friedan, Betty (1984, 1963) *The Feminine Mystique* (New York: Laurel)

Friedwald, Will (1990) *Jazz Singing: America's Great Voices from Bessie Smith to Bebop and Beyond* (New York: Charles Scribner's Sons)

Garber, Marjorie (1992) *Vested Interests: Cross-Dressing & Cultural Anxiety* (NewYork: Routledge)

Gardner, Carl and John Wyver (1983). 'The Single Play: From Reithian Reverence to Cost-Accounting and Censorship' in *Screen* 24:4–5, 114–129

Gilbert, Douglas (1940) *American Vaudeville: Its Life and Times* (New York: Dover Publications)

Gilman, Sander (1991) *The Jew's Body* (New York: Routledge)

Glasgow University Media Group (1976) *Bad News* (London: Routledge and Kegan Paul)

Gledhill, C. and Gillian Swanson (eds) (1995) *Nationalising Femininity: Culture, Sexuality and Cinema in Britain in the Second World War* (Manchester: Manchester University Press)

Gomery, Douglas (1992) *Shared Pleasures: A History of Movie Presentation in the United States* (Madison, WI: Univerisity of Wisconsin Press)

Gray, Anne (1992) *Video Playtime: The Gendering of a Leisure Technology* (London: Routledge)

Haining, P. (1993) *The Television Late Night Horror Omnibus: Great Tales From TV Anthology Series* (London: Orion)

Halberstam, David (1993) *The Fifties* (New York: Villard)

Hamamoto, Darrell Y. (1991) *Nervous Laughter: Television Situation Comedy and Liberal Democratic Ideology* (New York: Praeger)

Hansard (1962) 'Debate on Commercial Broadcasting' in *Hansard: House of Lords, Volume 240*, 9 May 1962, cols. 223–334

Haralovich, Mary Beth (1989) 'Sitcoms and suburbs: Positioning the 1950s home-maker' in *Quarterly Review of Film and Video* 11: 61–83; reprinted in Spigel and Mann (eds) (1992) 111–142

Herron, Jerry (1993) 'Homer Simpson's Eyes and the Culture of Late Nostalgia' in *Representations* 43, Summer 1993, 1–26

Hewison, Robert (1986) *Too Much: Art and Society in the Sixties, 1960–75* (London: Methuen)

Hill, John and Martin McLoone (eds) (1997) *Big Picture, Small Screen: The Relations between Film and Television* (Luton: John Libbey Media)

Hilmes, Michele (1997) *Radio Voices: American Broadcasting, 1922–1952* (Minneapolis: University of Minnesota Press)

Holland, P. (1987) 'When a Woman Reads the News' in H. Baehr and G. Dyer (eds) (1987) *Boxed in: Women in Television* (London: Pandora RKP) 133–150

Hunter, I.Q. (1999a) 'Introduction: The Strange World of the British Science Fiction Film', in Hunter (ed.) (1999) 1–15

Hunter, I.Q. (ed.) (1999) *British Science Fiction Cinema* (London: Routledge)

Hutchings, Peter (1999) '"We're the Martians now": British SF Invasion Fantasies of the 1950s and 1960s', in Hunter (ed.) (1999) 33–47

Hyman, Paula E. (1995) *Gender and Assimilation in Modern Jewish History: The Roles and Representation of Women* (Seattle: University of Washington Press)

ITA (1960) *Committee on Broadcasting: Review Papers by the ITA* unpublished paper held at the ITC (Independent Television Commission), London

Jacobs, J. (2000) *The Intimate Screen: Early British Television Drama* (Oxford: Oxford University Press)

Jarvie, Ian (1991) 'Stars and Ethnicity: Hollywood and the United States, 1932–51' in Lester D. Friedman (ed.) *Unspeakable Images: Ethnicity and the American Cinema* (Urbana, Illinois: University of Illinois Press)

Jenkins, Henry (1990) 'Shall We Make it for New York or for Distribution?: Eddie Cantor, *Whoopee*, and Regional Resistance to the Talkies' in *Cinema Journal* 29: 3 Spring 1990, 32–52

Jenkins, Henry (1992) *What Made Pistachio Nuts? Early Sound Comedy and the Vaudeville Aesthetic* (New York: Columbia University Press)

Jenkins, Henry (1992a) *Textual Poachers: Television Fans and Participatory Culture* (New York: Routledge)

Jones, Gerard (1992) *Honey, I'm Home! Sitcoms, Selling the American Dream* (New York: Grove Weidenfeld)

Judge, Frank (1961) 'Success is No Payoff for 3 Television Stars' in *Detroit News,* March 26, 1961

Kennedy, L. (1990) *On My Way to the Club* (London: Fontana)

Kepley, Vance (1990a) 'From "Frontal Lobes" to the "Bob-and-Bob" Show: NBC Management and Programming Strategies, 1949–1965' in Tino Balio (ed.) (1990) *Hollywood in the Age of Television* (Boston: Unwin Hyman)

Kepley, Vance (1990b) 'The Weaver years at NBC' in *Wide Angle* 12, 1990, 46–63

Kinsey, Alfred C. et al (1953) *Sexual Behavior in the Human Female* (Philadelphia: W.B. Saunders)

Kneale, Nigel (1959a) 'Not Quite So Intimate' in *Sight and Sound* 28:2, 86–88

Kneale, Nigel (1959b) *The Quatermass Experiment* (Middlesex: Penguin Books)

Krutnik, Frank (1995) 'A Spanner in the Works? Genre, Narrative, and the Hollywood Comedian' in Kristine Brunovska Karnick and Henry Jenkins (eds) (1995) *Classical Hollywood Comedy* (New York: Routledge) 17–38

Leman, J. (1987) 'Programmes for Women in 1950's British Television' in H. Baehr and G. Dyer (eds) (1987) *Boxed In: Women in Television* (London: Pandora RKP) 74–95

Liebman, Nina (1995) *Living Room Lectures: The Fifties Family in Film and Television* (Austin: University of Texas)

Lipsitz, George (1990) *Time Passages: Collective Memory and American Popular Culture* (Minneapolis: University of Minnesota Press)

Lipsitz, George (1992) 'The Meaning of Memory: Family, Class and Ethnicity in Early Network Television Programmes' in Spigel and Mann (eds) 71–208

Lipsitz, George (1994) *Rainbow at Midnight: Labor and Culture in the 1940s* (Urbana: University of Illinois Press)

Lipsitz, George (1995) 'The Possessive Investment in Whiteness: Racialized Social Democracy and the "White" Problem in American Studies' in *American Quarterly* 47:3, September 1995, 369–387

MacCabe, Colin (ed.) (1986) *High Theory/Low Culture: Analysing Popular Television and Film* (Manchester: Manchester University Press)

MacMurraugh-Kavanagh, M.K. (1999) 'Boys on Top: Gender and Authorship in the BBC *Wednesday Play*' in *Media, Culture & Society* 21:3, May 1999, 409–425

MacMurraugh-Kavanagh, M.K. and S.L. Lacey (1999) 'Who Framed Theatre? The "Moment of Change" in British TV Drama' in *New Theatre Quarterly* Vol. XV Part 1 (NTQ 57), February 1999, 58–74

Magee, B. (1966) *The Television Interviewer* (London: Macdonald)

Mann, Denise (1992) 'The Spectacularization of Everyday Life: Recycling Hollywood Stars and Fans in Early Television Variety Shows.' in Spigel and Mann (eds) 1992, 41–69

Marling, Karal Ann (1994) *As Seen on TV: The Visual Culture of Everyday Life in the 1950s* (Cambridge, Massachusetts: Harvard University Press)

Marsh, Margaret S. and Samuel Kaplan (1976) 'The Lure of the Suburbs' in Dolce (ed.) (1976) *Suburbia: The American Dream and Dilemma* (Garden City: Anchor Books) 37–58

Marshall, P. David (1997) *Celebrity and Power: Fame in Contemporary Culture* (Minneapolis: University of Minnesota Press)

McChesney, Inger L. Stole (1992) 'Capturing the "Ideal" Audience: The Emergence of

Network Daytime Television, 1948–1954' unpublished MA Thesis, University of Wisconsin-Madison

McFadden, Margaret T. (1993) 'America's Boyfriend Who Can't Get a Date": Gender, Race and the Cultural Work of the *Jack Benny Program*, 1932–1946' in *Journal of American History* June 1993, 126–139

McLoone, Martin (1997) 'Boxed In? The Aesthetics of Film and Television' in Hill and McLoone (eds) 1997, 76–106

Meehan, Eileen (1990) 'Why We Don't Count: The Commodity Audience' in Mellencamp (ed.) (1990)

Mellencamp, Patricia (1986) 'Situation Comedy, Feminism and Freud: Discourses of Gracie and Lucy' in Modleski (ed.) (1986) *Studies in Entertainment: Critical Approaches to Mass Culture* (Bloomington: Indiana University Press)

Mellancamp, Patricia (1990) 'TV Time and Catastrophe, or Beyond the Pleasure Principle of Television.' in Mellencamp (ed) (1990)

Mellencamp, Patricia (ed.) (1990) *Logics of Television: Essays in Cultural Criticism* (Bloomington, IN: Indiana University Press)

Meyerowitz, Joanne (1994) 'Beyond the Feminine Mystique: A Reassessment of Postwar Mass Culture, 1946–1958' in Meyerowitz (ed.) 1994

Meyerowitz, Joanne (ed.) (1994) *Not June Cleaver: Women and Gender in Postwar America, 1945–1960* (Philadelphia: Temple University Press)

Mittell, Jason (1996) '"Her Life is Less Frenzied . . ." Gendered Discourse and the Introduction of Tranquillizers in the late 1950s' paper presented at the American Studies Association, Washington D.C. in October 1996

Morley, David (1992) *Television, Audiences, and Cultural Studies* (New York: Routledge)

Mullen, Megan (1995) 'Surfing through "TV Land": Notes toward a Theory of "Video Bites" and Their Function on Cable TV' in *The Velvet Light Trap* 36, 60–68

Mulvey, Laura (1989) *Visual and Other Pleasures* (Basingstoke: Macmillan)

Myles, Lynda and Julian Petley (1990) 'Rudolph Cartier' in *Sight and Sound* 59:2, 126–129

Negra, Diane (1996) 'Hollywood Film and the Narrativization of the Ethnic Feminine' unpublished PhD dissertation, University of Texas at Austin

Negra, Diane (forthcoming 2001) *Off-White Hollywood: American Culture and Ethnic Female Stardom* (London: Routledge)

Nicholson, Linda J. (ed.) (1990) *Feminism/Postmodernism* (New York: Routledge)

Petley, Julian (1984/5) 'The Quatermass Conclusion' in *Primetime* 9, 22–25

Petley, Julian (1986) 'The Lost Continent' in Barr (ed.) 1986, 98–119

Pike. Frank (ed.) (1982) *Ah! Mischief: The Writer and Television* (London: Faber & Faber)

Pilkington (1962) *The Committee on Broadcasting: the Pilkington Report* Cmd. 1753, London, HMSO

Pirie, D. (1973) *A Heritage of Horror: The English Gothic Cinema 1946–1972* (London: Gordon Fraser)

Poovey, Mary (1980) 'Feminism and deconstruction' in *Feminist Studies* 14, 1988, 51–65

Prawer, S.S. (1980) *Caligari's Children: the Film as Tale of Terror* (Oxford: Oxford University Press)

Prior, A. (1968) 'Review' in *Stage and Television Today* 16 May 1968

Proulx, E. Annie (1996) *Accordion Crimes* (London: Fourth Estate)

Radway, Janice (1984) *Reading the Romance: Women, Patriarchy and Popular Fiction* (Chapel Hill: University of North Carolina Press)

Regester, Charlene (1997) 'Unveiling Whiteness and Negotiating Blackness' Consoleing Passions: Television, Video, Feminism conference paper presentation

Riley, Denise (1988) *Am I That Name? Feminism and the Category of 'Women' in History* (Minneapolis: University of Minnesota Press)

Rose, Al (1974) *Storyville, New Orleans: Being an Authentic, Illustrated Account of the Notorious Red-Light District* (Alabama: University of Alabama Press)

Rose, Frank (1995) *The Agency: William Morris and the Hidden History of Show Business* (New York: HarperCollins)

Ross, Andrew (1989) *No Respect: Intellectuals & Popular Culture* (New York: Routledge)

Rubin, Barry (1995) *Assimilation and its Discontents* (New York: Times Books)

Sampson, A. (1965) *Anatomy of Britain Today* (London: Hodder and Stoughton)

Scharff, Virginia (1991) *Taking the Wheel: Women and the Coming of the Motor Age* (New York: Free Press)

Schemering, Christopher (1985) *The Soap Opera Encyclopedia* (New York: Ballantine)

Scott, Joan (1988) *Gender and the Politics of History* (New York: Columbia University Press)

Seidman, Steven (1981) *Comedian Comedy: A Tradition in Hollywood Film* (Ann Arbor: UMI Research Press)

Seiter, Ellen C. (1989) 'To Teach and to Sell: Irna Phillips and Her Sponsors, 1930–1954' in *Journal of Film and Video* 41, Spring 1989, 21–34

Seiter, Ellen et alP (eds) (1989) *Remote Control: Television, Audiences and Cultural Power* (New York: Routledge)

Sendall, B. (1982) *Independent Television in Britain Vol.1 Origin and Foundation, 1946–62* (London: Macmillan)

Sendall, B. (1983) *Independent Television in Britain Vol. 2 Expansion and Change, 1958–68* (London: Macmillan)

Shubik, Irene (1975) *Play for Today: The Evolution of Television Drama* (London: Davis-Poynter)

Silverstone, R. and Hirsch, E. (eds) (1992) *Consuming Technologies: Media and Information in Domestic Spaces* (London: Routledge)

Silverstone, Roger (1994) *Television and Everyday Life* (London: Routledge)

Sked, A. and C. Cook (1984) *Post-War Britain – A Political History* 2nd edition (London: Penguin Books)

Slotkin, Richard (1992) *Gunfighter Nation: The Myth of the Frontier in Twentieth-Century America* (New York: Atheneum)

Sobchack, Vivian (1987) *Screening Space: The American Science Fiction Film* (New Brunswick, New Jersey: Rutgers University Press)

Sobchak, Vivian (ed.) (1996) *The Persistence of History: Cinema, Television, and the Modern Event* (New York: Routledge)

Spigel, Lynn (1992) *Make Room for TV: Television and the Family Ideal in Postwar America* (Chicago: University of Chicago Press)

Spigel, Lynn (1995) 'From the Dark Ages to the Golden Age: Women's Memories and Television Reruns' in *Screen* 36, Spring 1995, 16–33

Spigel, Lynn (1997) 'White Flight' in Spigel and Curtin (eds) (1997) 47–71

Spigel, Lynn and Denise Mann (eds) (1992) *Private Screenings: Television and the Female Consumer* (Minneapolis: University of Minnesota Press)

Spigel, Lynn and Michael Curtin (1997) *The Revolution Wasn't Televised: Sixties Television and Social Conflict* (New York: Routledge)

Stewart, Susan (1984) *On Longing* (Baltimore: Johns Hopkins University)

Streeter, Thomas and Wendy Wahl (1994) 'Audience Theory and Feminism: Property, Gender, and the Television Audience' in *Camera Obscura* 33–34, 243–261

Sutton, Shaun (1982) *The Largest Theatre in the World: Thirty Years of Television Drama* (London: BBC Publications)

TAM (Television Audience Measurement Ltd) (1965) *TAM's top Ten: 1955–1965* (London: TAM)

Taylor, Ella (1989) *Prime Time Families: Television Culture in Postwar America* (Berkeley: University of California)

Thames Television (1991) *Thirty-five Years of* This Week *from Thames Television* programme for anniversary screening, February 1991 (London: Thames TV), and related 20-part television series *This Week – Thirty-Five Years on the Frontline* produced for Thames TV by Flashback Productions Ltd

Thiel, Joan Elizabeth (1977) 'Albert McCleery's Transfer of Theatre Practice to Live Television Drama' unpublished PhD Dissertation, University of Michigan

Thiem, H. (1958) *The Re-Organisation of British Television by the Television Act of 1954* offprint from a Yearbook for International Law (undated) held at the ITC (Independent Television Commission), London

Thumim, J. (1995) 'A Live Commercial for Icing Sugar' in *Screen* 36:1, 48–55

Thumim, J. (1998) 'Mrs. Knight must be balanced – Methodological problems in researching early British television' in Carter, C., Branston, G., and Allan, S. (eds) (1998) *News, Gender and Power* (London: Routledge) 91–104

Tichi, Cecilia. (1992) *Electronic Hearth: Creating an American Television Culture* (Oxford: Oxford University Press)

Tulloch, John (1990) *Television Drama: Agency, Audience and Myth* (London: Routledge)

Turner, Patricia A. (1993) *I Heard It Through The Grapevine: Rumor in African American Culture* (Berkeley: University of California Press)

Tyler-May, Elaine (1988) *Homeward Bound: American Families in the Cold War Era* (New York: Basic Books)

Vahimagi, Tise (1994) *British Television* (London: Oxford University Press)

Warren, Carol (1987) *Madwives: Schizophrenic Women in the 1950s* (New Brunswick: Rutgers University Press)

Weber, Donald (1997) 'Memory and Repression in Early Ethnic Television' in Foreman (ed.) (1997) *The Other Fifties: Interrogating Mid-century American Icons* (Urbana: University of Illinois Press) 144–167

Wells, Paul (1999) 'Apocalypse Then! The Ultimate Monstrosity and Strange Things on the Coast . . . An Interview with Nigel Kneale' in Hunter (ed.) (1999) 48–56

Wertheim, Frank (1983) 'The Rise and Fall of Milton Berle' in John O'Connor (ed.) (1983) *American History/American Television* (New York: Frederick Ungar Publications) 55–77

White, Mimi (1992) *Tele-Advising: Therapeutic Discourse in American Television* (Chapel Hill: University of North Carolina Press)

Whitehouse, Mary (1967) *Cleaning up TV: From Protest to Participation* (London: Blandford Press)

Williams, Mark (1999) 'History in a Flash: Notes on the Myth of TV "Liveness"' in Jane Gaines and Michael Renov (eds) (1999) *Collecting Visible Evidence* (Minneapolis: University of Minnesota Press)

Williams, Raymond (1974) *Television, Technology and Cultural Form* (New York: Schocken)

Wilson, Pamela (1995) 'NBC Television's "Operation Frontal Lobes": Cultural hegemony and Fifties' program planning' in *Historical Journal of Film, Radio and Television* 15: 1, 1995, 83–104

Woodward, Kathleen M. (1991) *Aging and Its Discontents: Freud And Other Fictions* (Bloomington: Indiana University Press)

Wyndham Goldie, G. (1977) *Facing the Nation – Television and Politics, 1936–1976* (London: Bodley Head)

NOTES ON CONTRIBUTORS

Lola Clare Bratten is a doctoral candidate at the University of Wisconsin-Madison and an instructor at Middle Tennessee State University in Radio/TV Photography.

Mary Desjardins is an assistant professor at Dartmouth College, where she teaches film, television and women's studies. She has published in a variety of anthologies and media journals. Her book, *Recycled Stars: Hollywood Film Stardom in the Age of Television and Video*, is forthcoming.

Kristen Hatch is a doctoral candidate in the Department of Film and Television, UCLA. She is completing her dissertation on performances of girlhood in popular American film through the 1930s.

Catherine Johnson is researching a PhD on television fantasy at the University of Warwick, UK. She has an article on factual entertainment forthcoming in the *European Journal of Cultural Studies* (January 2001) as part of a collaborative project undertaken by the Midlands Television Research Group.

Derek Kompare is an assistant professor in the Department of Radio-Television-Film at Texas Christian University. He has presented papers on the cocktail culture revival, cable television technologies and DVD versioning and is currently preparing a book on the production of the television heritage in the USA.

Madeleine MacMurraugh-Kavanagh is a lecturer in English at the University of Reading, UK. Previously, she was Post-Doctoral Fellow on the 'BBC Wednesday Plays and Post-War British Drama' project, funded by HEFCE (Higher Education Funding Council for England) and coordinated from the University of Reading. She has published widely in the fields of Television Drama, Modern Drama and Women's Writing.

Allison McCracken recently defended her doctoral dissertation, 'Real Men Don't Sing Ballads: Crooning and American Culture, 1928–1933' in American Studies at the University of Iowa.

Diane Negra is an assistant professor in the Department of Radio, Television and Film at the University of North Texas. She is the author of *Off-White*

Hollywood: American Culture and Ethnic Female Stardom (forthcoming, Routledge, 2001).

Lisa Parks is an assistant professor in the Department of Film Studies at the University of California at Santa Barbara. She is completing a book, *Cultures in Orbit: Satellite Technologies and Visual Media* (Duke University Press), co-editing *Planet TV: A Global Television Studies Reader* (NYU Press) and has published numerous articles. Parks has produced activist videos for Paper Tiger TV and serves on the boards of CULTSTUD-L and Intensities.

Matthew Murray is Assistant Professor of Broadcast Communication at North Central College, Naperville, Illinois. He has published several articles on censorship and US radio and television history.

Susan Murray is an assistant professor of television and radio at Brooklyn College, City University of New York. She is currently completing a book on the development of broadcast stardom in early television.

Janet Thumim teaches film and television studies at the University of Bristol, UK. Her publications include *Celluloid Sisters: Women and Popular Cinema* (Macmillan, 1992) and the collections, co-edited with Pat Kirkham, *You Tarzan: Masculinity, Movies and Men* and *Me Jane: Masculinity, Movies and Women* (Lawrence and Wishart, 1993, 1995).

Victoria Wegg-Prosser has worked for some 25 years as a television producer. She recently completed an MBA and PhD in Management Studies and is currently engaged with a long-term project on the history of *This Week*, based at the University of Bournemouth, UK.

Helen Wheatley is a graduate teaching assistant at the University of Warwick where she is writing and researching her PhD thesis on Gothic Television. She is currently co-editing a book on *The Spectacular in Popular European Cinema*.

INDEX

BROADCAST PROGRAMME TITLES

Illustrations in bold

GENERAL INDEX

Film titles in italics, illustrations in bold